CW01209404

AIMING TO SAVE

AIMING TO SAVE

A Vet's Life in Conservation

LARRY PATTERSON

The Book Guild Ltd

First published in Great Britain in 2022 by
The Book Guild Ltd
Unit E2 Airfield Business Park,
Harrison Road, Market Harborough,
Leicestershire. LE16 7UL
Tel: 0116 2792299
www.bookguild.co.uk
Email: info@bookguild.co.uk
Twitter: @bookguild

Copyright © 2022 Larry Patterson

The right of Larry Patterson to be identified as the author of this
work has been asserted by them in accordance with the
Copyright, Design and Patents Act 1988.

All rights reserved. No part of this publication may be
reproduced, transmitted, or stored in a retrieval system, in any form or by any means,
without permission in writing from the publisher, nor be otherwise circulated in
any form of binding or cover other than that in which it is published and without
a similar condition being imposed on the subsequent purchaser.

Typeset in 11pt Minion Pro

Printed and bound in the UK by TJ Books LTD, Padstow, Cornwall

ISBN 978 1914471 469

British Library Cataloguing in Publication Data.
A catalogue record for this book is available from the British Library.

MIX
Paper from
responsible sources
FSC® C013056

Dedicated to the memory of Gavin and Vicky Richards

CONTENTS

PROLOGUE

BOTSWANA 2018

It was 2.00 am on a Monday morning and an elephant cow was trapped in a deep, muddy well. Her head and forefeet were protruding and her abdomen and hindquarters were firmly stuck. She resented our efforts to help and was trying to swat us with her trunk, but was getting more and more tired and her spasmodic attempts to extricate herself were getting weaker and more futile. We had been digging for hours to try to make it easier for her to clamber out, but to no avail. We needed more equipment and a new plan. No nearby village was likely to have anything as sophisticated as a JCB or other lifting equipment, but some twenty miles away, near the Namibian border, a European farmer had a large four-wheel drive tractor. He was away in South Africa on business, but his manager, after some convoluted messaging, immediately agreed to make the three-hour drive through the bush.

While we were quietly considering the next move a herd of about sixty buffalo appeared in the moonlight. They approached us warily but about fifty yards from us they turned and decided to slake their thirsts elsewhere. Other visitors during the evening had been a couple of giraffe and a number of persistent spotted hyaenas. These consummate opportunists repeatedly circled us, obviously sensing an imminent meal.

The well was one of many in the Chobe enclave, in Botswana's far north. The enclave is an area of just over 500 square miles, consisting mainly of ancient floodplains, surrounded by the Chobe National Park in Botswana and the Namibian border. The wells are dug by the local villagers to provide water for their livestock after the shallow, annual flood has receded. Constant trampling and excavating by cattle and wild animals had enlarged this particular hole and the elephants had managed to access water about six feet down. The female's hindquarters had slid into the hole and she couldn't climb back out up the steep wall of slippery black soil, but she wouldn't allow us safe access with our spades. She would have become just another statistic in what is called human–elephant conflict. Sometimes the elephants won, but the overall score was against them.

A local wildlife charity, Elephants Without Borders (EWB), had been alerted to the cow's plight on Sunday afternoon and had called me in to help. Kelly, EWB's American manageress, and I got there as soon as we could. Our Land Cruiser carried some kit, ropes and chains, but nothing capable of lifting an elephant. Another Land Cruiser belonging to the government Wildlife Department, who had reported the mishap, was already there. No matter how we approached we could not get anything below her back end to pull – the flailing trunk was too dangerous. Even if we had managed it was unlikely that we could have pulled her three-ton bulk over the steep lip.

At about 2.30 am distant headlights in the sky and then engine noise heralded a pick-up truck. A lanky Scotsman climbed out and announced that his driver was not far behind with the tractor. Since the tractor could not lift vertically we would still need to modify the earth wall. As soon as it arrived I injected the elephant with a cocktail of immobilising drugs using my dart gun. I fervently hoped that she was not too weak to take the drugs but it seemed to go well and I monitored her pulse and breathing constantly while the others got to work. By the headlights of our vehicles, the game scouts and a couple of farm labourers dug away the lip of the well under the throat of the snoring elephant. We also managed to get behind her elbows in the thick mud, waist deep on us, to fit a chain under her chest and around her shoulders and another under her tail. We needed to work quickly because I didn't want to give her more drugs if she started to come round. We had an hour at most.

After about thirty minutes we had the chains in place and the earthworks sufficiently modified. The powerful tractor was positioned about ten yards in front on one side and the two Land Cruisers were arranged in tandem on the other side. The chains were attached; all three vehicles then engaged four-wheel drive in low range and gently took up the slack, while an oblivious elephant snored on. The vehicles inched forward, skidding at first, then the three-ton animal gradually became unstuck and started to slide up and over the side of the well. The vehicles stopped only when she was about twenty yards from the hole so that she wouldn't slip back when she came round and stood up. While the chains were being removed I gave an antidote for the immobilising drugs into a giant ear vein. She should have been wide awake and getting to her feet in a couple of minutes, so we all withdrew to a safe distance and watched with mounting anticipation, but nothing happened! She lay there on her side and apart from steady, rhythmic breathing through her trunk, she didn't move a muscle. Our elation slowly dissipated and became concern. We hadn't been called until Sunday afternoon, but she'd been stuck in the well for over forty-eight hours. Maybe she was just too traumatised and weak. I thought of the circling hyaenas as I checked her vital signs by torchlight. I was aware of her eyes following me and an occasional weak twitch of her trunk – enough to make me careful, but that was all.

Our Scottish saviour and his crew left. The rest of us watched and waited, and waited. Sometimes, turning a recumbent animal over will stimulate it enough to make it get up. I had used the technique on everything from cats to cattle, usually successfully, and once years before on a bull elephant with alarming consequences. So I tied a strong rope around the lower hind leg with a very loose noose for easy removal and we tied the other end around a Land Cruiser's tow-hitch. The driver pulled in the required direction and the elephant very slowly rolled over on to her back and then flopped down on the other flank. And just lay there, motionless. We decided to leave her alone for a while, hoping she would rest, regain strength and get up on her own. The Wildlife Department left us to watch her and keep her safe from the hyaenas, lions and other prowling predators.

As daylight crept in and we were able to make out the silhouettes of nearby palm trees we began to fear the worst. I even considered a bullet in the brain as kinder than being left to the hyaenas. Maybe fifteen hours of exhausting and thirsty work had coloured my judgement, but Kelly would not hear of destroying the animal without trying everything we could. What else could we achieve with next to no equipment and many miles from help? Kelly called a co-worker in Kasane, the nearest town and the charity's base. They had recently tried rearing an abandoned elephant calf and she thought they had some leftover bags of intravenous fluids. Tempe Adams, an elephant biologist on contract from Australia, hurriedly gathered what she could find and arrived in a couple of hours with litres of fluid in plastic bags and a couple of giving sets – tubes with valves to administer the fluids.

It took us three hours to administer twenty-five litres of glucose and minerals into the elephant's ear veins. She gave every indication of being awake and watching me, but never moved. A mere flick of her trunk at any time could have been extremely dangerous, but either she accepted us or was unable to object. I was pessimistic, Kelly and Tempe remained doggedly hopeful.

About 10.00 am the Wildlife Department vehicle reappeared with a scout and a driver wanting to know the outcome. Like me, they thought there was very little chance of her survival. The temperature was climbing and there was no shade in the flat floodplain. At midday Tempe nudged me out of a doze to say the elephant was beginning to move her trunk. I walked over and yelled and slapped her and there was a very definite, but feeble response. Then she started to rock and tried to get her rear legs underneath her, just like an elephant waking from a routine drug immobilisation. She tried a couple of times but sank back, unable to muster enough strength. I let her rest for a few minutes before more yelling and slapping and she tried again. This time she almost made it into a dog-sitting position, but again lay down. She tried a few times, with more yelling and slapping, before she managed to maintain a sitting position, but there was no way she was able to stand. Her hind legs had been cramped under her in the mud for days and we weren't in any position to offer physiotherapy.

We tried to help by pulling as she tried to rise. I was able to place a rope under her tail and position it at forty-five degrees in front of her on either side and attached the ends to the two Land Cruisers. The next time she made an effort to stand we pulled equally with both vehicles and after a couple of attempts she was up on all four feet. We were ecstatic! Now she had a real chance. She stood there, immobile, her hind legs trembling. The Wildlife Department departed again, but we remained in our two vehicles, watching. I positioned my Land Cruiser between the elephant and the well – I didn't want her staggering back into it.

She didn't move for half an hour, then she took a short step with a front leg and then another, without moving her back feet. Eventually she tried moving a trembling rear leg, again just a short step. Gradually she walked a few tottering steps and stopped again with her back to us. After a while she turned unsteadily and walked very slowly towards my car. I didn't want to move because the well was right behind me. She came right up to the front of the Land Cruiser, rested her tusks gently on the bonnet and placed her trunk on the roof. A few minutes passed, she stepped back and moved down the driver's side, stopping by my window and lowered her head until her eye was level with mine. I plucked up courage and lowered the window, reached out, stroked her eyelashes and patted her, talking softly. I then put my arm around her trunk and gently squeezed for a few seconds. She remained like that for several minutes before walking away very slowly.

"She was thanking you, Larry!" Kelly cried. "That was absolutely amazing."

I wasn't so sure; I've experienced many extraordinary wildlife interactions, often with elephants, and I've heard credible accounts from other professionals whom I trust, but I still find it hard to ascribe human emotions and intelligence to these wonderful creatures. In fact, I have come to view anthropomorphism, emotionalism and sentimentality as major hindrances to wildlife conservation. Perhaps I've been desensitised by euthanasing clients' cherished pets, working in abattoirs and killing animals in the name of research or management. Maybe I've become cynical from having had to play God too often, blunting any innate sympathetic qualities I may have possessed. But as that elephant cow slowly wandered off into the vastness of the African bush I did wonder whether our paths might cross again and if there would be some sign of recognition. It was, without doubt, one of the most moving experiences of my work with African wildlife – work that began almost fifty years earlier on a dusty road in a Ugandan national park.

ONE

UGANDA 1971

The battered, pale blue Peugeot 404 pulled over in a cloud of red laterite dust. We'd left Kasese in the early morning and had been driving through undulating green hills, heading south and west towards the Congo border, with the magnificent backdrop of the massive Ruwenzori mountain range on our right. The driver cheerfully indicated the track leading into Queen Elizabeth National Park. I got out of the front passenger door, thankful to be spared more of the jarring corrugations, and retrieved my rucksack from the rear seat. The rear door had no handle on the outside, so I reached through the window. The fare, negotiated at the railway station as twelve Ugandan shillings, was immediately inflated to fifteen by the simple expedient of a lack of change. This was my first experience of an African pandemic, mostly prevalent in government offices collecting any form of revenue – from ferry fares to immigration visas, hospital fees to hunting licences – nobody, but nobody, admitted to having any change.

I was a student at University College, London (UCL), studying for a master's degree in conservation and my budget was limited. Although I had graduated the previous summer from Glasgow University as a veterinarian and had supplemented my scholarship by working as a locum during the Christmas and Easter holidays, the plane ticket had stretched my resources. Jenny and I had married shortly after my graduation and even though she had a job in the fashion business we didn't have much spare cash. In those carefree, pre-hijacking days my heavily discounted ticket had been obtained from a dubious "bucket shop" in Coventry. The outward leg, from London to

Entebbe, Uganda, appeared to be part of a round the world trip booked by a Mr Anderson from New Zealand, but, as Mr Khan in Coventry had assured me they would, East African Airways had overlooked the change in passenger name. The return leg (from Nairobi to London) was left to me to negotiate with the airline, but that was months away and far beyond the horizon of my present concerns. Anyway, having convinced the ultra-conservative Horserace Betting Levy Board (HBLB) in London to award one of their much sought-after postgraduate scholarships to a student in conservation with only a basic knowledge of equine matters, I was flush with youthful confidence in my powers of persuasion.

I had travelled overnight on a slow steam train west from the Ugandan capital, Kampala. Slow, that is, in comparison with railway travel in Europe. The locomotive was very old, probably pre-World War II, and the track gauge was narrow. These limitations certainly contributed to the slow speed of the train when it was moving, but the duration of the journey owed more to the fact that, for lengthy periods, it seldom moved at all. It had been a comfortable journey nevertheless, with Uganda Railways providing excellent food and clean sheets. The previous afternoon's ride through rolling, lush green countryside patched with innumerable banana shambas and fields bursting with tropical crops unknown to me, had been punctuated with frequent stops at small stations and sidings. Villages were not always visible, but the noisy, colourful throngs at each stop suggested that settlements were not too far away. It was usually possible to alight for a few minutes and become immersed in the social commerce, almost a mini-market, with a wide variety of cooked and raw fruit and vegetables on offer. Through the small, tight groups of traders with their hot and cold dishes and small, charcoal, cooking braziers, a few determined travellers insinuated themselves towards the carriages. Most luggage and goods were carried on heads, looking precarious to Western eyes, but never dropped. Even enamel buckets of water were carried by the women in this way, often with a small, woven grass "halo" between bucket and head. From my elevated position in the carriage I could see that many buckets had small, leafed branches or other objects floating on the surface and later learnt that these helped to prevent spillage by breaking the surface tension and reducing waves. It was all a far cry from the drab, damp Pennine valleys I was used to and very stimulating.

During the night the stops had been longer, but less frequent. The break in rhythm was enough to guarantee waking at each one. A brilliant sunny morning heralded the approach to the Ruwenzoris – the Mountains of the Moon – majestically straddling the Equator, with steep, lush green slopes giving way to wispy, white clouds and purple shadows of snow-tipped peaks. Underneath was Kasese, the end of the line, a small town with a dirt main road and a few short side streets. The scruffy, dilapidated state of most buildings and the lack of pavement or other municipal infrastructure reminded me of countless Western movies, an illusion dispelled only by the Asian names over most shop fronts and the gaudily painted, but faded, advertisements for Lifebuoy soap and various brands of tea. It had been easy to find a taxi heading towards the Congo border and therefore passing the entrance to Queen Elizabeth National Park, my destination, about twenty-five miles away to the southwest.

Leaving me by the park gate, the Peugeot pulled away, heading west towards the tiny village of Katwe on the edge of Lake Edward and then the border post with the Congo, where the driver had business connected with his brother's shop in Kasese. Being left alone by the side of the road in a remote spot in Africa was fleetingly alarming, but in a deliciously thrilling way. Everything I saw was so different; from the red laterite road and the 15,000 foot mountains (in the Lake District I had often climbed England's highest at a mere 3,000 feet), to the strange tropical vegetation spreading across the savanna, especially the cactus-like *Euphorbia candelabra* trees. More than anything though was the sense of space and freedom; everything was on such a grand scale. I had made it; from Bolton to the Big Country; from Boy Scout camping to big-time adventure!

But where were the animals? Apart from a bewildering variety of birds there had been no sign of wildlife – no teeming herds of antelope, no trains of elephant or swaying giraffe. Were my childhood dreams of African safaris about to be shattered? I had been seduced by the adventures of a young David Attenborough in *Zoo Quest.* All through veterinary school, the boring anatomy lectures and scarcely intelligible biochemistry classes, I had been sustained by the thought of working one day with African big game. I had been persuaded to go to vet school by my old careers master at Bolton School, Mr Mills. On being told that I wanted to be a game warden in Africa, his astute advice, later to prove priceless, was: "As a vet at least you'll be able to make a decent living if it doesn't work out."

I picked up my rucksack and walked towards the steel-pole boom that constituted the park gate, mounted between two low, stone walls, each about fifteen feet long. The rutted track led away south towards the Park HQ at

Mweya. On one of the walls was a metal noticeboard with peeling paint, identifying Queen Elizabeth National Park and quoting the Ugandan National Parks Act, listing the more obvious "Don'ts", such as hunting or lighting fires. Then I realised that I was not alone after all; sitting on the floor below the sign, in the shade of the wall, was a man.

"Hello" was my first, rather weak effort, then I tried *"Jambo Bwana"*, about fifty per cent of my Swahili vocabulary. He replied in English "Good morning, Bwana" and stood up. I told him I was going to Mweya, which was also his destination. Apparently he was going to visit his brother who worked as a cook at Mweya Safari Lodge. Alfred was about twenty-five, fairly tall and slim, in blue jeans, a rather scruffy, white, long-sleeved shirt and well-worn town shoes. He was carrying a small holdall. He had travelled by bus from Mbarara, a large town in southwestern Uganda, about 100 miles away, and had spent the night in Katwe village before walking up the road to the park gate. He had been waiting almost three hours for a lift, but my taxi was the first vehicle he had seen, so we decided to walk the four or five miles along the red dirt track to Mweya. I felt a little nervous, not knowing what we might encounter by way of wild animals.

We had been walking for about twenty minutes across a gently undulating plain with scattered clumps of bushes and occasional *Euphorbia* trees when we saw our first wild animals, a small group of Uganda kob about 150 yards from the road. These are medium-sized, stocky, reddish antelope. The males carry graceful, lyre-shaped horns. To my novice's eye they could have been impala, lechwe, reedbuck or any of several other vaguely similar animals – something I try to remember today when taxed by the naïve questions of new arrivals to Africa. They seemed singularly uninterested in us and, apart from the odd glance from one of the males, continued to graze. I quickly dropped my rucksack and located my borrowed binoculars. My companion took more notice of my behaviour than of the antelopes – a European was apparently far more interesting than these common animals. But this was not the case. He had never seen them before. He was merely puzzled by my overt enthusiasm – a first indication, had I been more aware, of the huge gulf between our two societies in attitudes to wildlife and the natural environment.

We continued until we caught a first view of the eastern shore of Lake Edward below us to the right. It was quite close, perhaps half a mile or so from the track. Across the flat, blue water I could see the distant hills of the Congo.

There were many animal spoors crossing the track, no doubt to and from drinking in the lake. I couldn't tell one from another, but they appeared mostly to be of cloven-hoofed animals of various sizes, except for the unmistakable, huge, round or oval footprints of elephants. Sometimes they indicated where a herd had crossed in the night, but there were occasional single tracks, usually larger, signifying a lone adult bull. What would we do if we came across the elephants themselves? I'd heard it said that you must not run if charged, but was it really possible, let alone sensible, to stand one's ground unarmed? We continued, a little more nervously on my part, but Alfred appeared indifferent.

A little further on a herd of maybe seventy buffalo spread across the track. I had read that this was the most dangerous of Africa's "Big Five"; tales of how they would backtrack and lie in wait for hunters; accounts of wood gatherers and water fetchers being gored and trampled to death. I glanced sideways at Alfred, but he showed no sign of alarm and was continuing along the track towards them. They were now about 150 yards distant and several individuals were showing a distinct interest in us. I stole another glance at Alfred, but we continued at the same pace. At seventy-five yards I was mentally estimating the distance and climbing difficulty of a selection of trees, but Alfred carried on, apparently unconcerned. At fifty yards the curiosity in our approach had diffused through most of the herd and there was an almost solid line of horns gleaming in the sunlight and what sounded to me like seriously threatening discussion in the ranks. Noses were lifted high in our direction and distinct signs of agitation, snorting and pawing the ground were spreading. I was now plain terrified, it was time to quit this insane game of chicken and get the hell out of there. As I started to speak there was a loud grunt from somewhere in the herd and the whole mob wheeled away as one organism and lumbered off to our right in a dusty clamour of belching and breaking branches. The noise receded, with the occasional distant bellow. Seconds later all that remained was a thinning cloud of red earth particles.

I managed a weak smile in Alfred's direction and we continued on through the churned-up ground and flattened grass scattered with soft pats of buffalo droppings. There was a strong, warm smell, reminiscent of British cattle yards in winter, but richer. It lodged in my memory for instant emotional recall for the rest of my life – in the same way that the smell of the upper deck of a bus had always transported me back to Saturday afternoons at Burnden Park with my grandfather, sucking Uncle Joe's Mint Balls and watching Nat Lofthouse single-handedly keeping Bolton Wanderers in the First Division.

The rest of the walk to Mweya was relatively uneventful: lots of new birds to see; a few more groups of kob; a couple of warthogs trotting away with their tails erect like radio antenna and a small herd of waterbuck – larger antelopes, greyish, fairly shaggy and donkey-like, except for the strikingly long, curved horns of the adult males.

I asked Alfred, as casually as I could, how he had known that the buffalo wouldn't charge and would run away when we got close. His reply stunned me and provided my second insight to the African psyche, so deeply distinct from the Western norm. He had known that he was safe because he was with a white man! Buffaloes, and for that matter I suppose, all other dangerous beasts, would never harm a European. I definitely couldn't confess that I had been terrified and had only kept walking towards them because he had so patently appeared to know what he was doing.

The relief I felt after the buffalo incident had made me garrulous and I pressed Alfred for more details of his family and life. He was twenty-eight and had been born in a small village close to Mbarara. His father was a small-scale subsistence farmer, growing a few bananas and vegetables. Like his father, he had been in the army, but where his father had served with the Allies in World War II, he had spent two years as a young man in the first post-independence forces of Uganda, fighting Sudanese-backed rebels in the north. For the last five years he had worked as a driver/mechanic for a garage in Kampala. He was hoping that, with his brother's sponsorship, he would be employed by Mweya Lodge, taking out tourists on game drives and able to supplement his wages with generous tips. I was curious to hear about the army officer, Idi Amin, who had seized power in a coup a few months earlier, but like almost everyone else I was to meet, Alfred was reluctant to say very much about the new president.

We walked into Mweya at about 11.00 am. It was a large, off-white complex comprising the park administrative offices, associated houses and barrack-type accommodation. Situated above the neck of a small peninsula, it enjoyed wonderful views over a bay of Lake Edward towards the Congo and, to the north, the spectacular Ruwenzori Mountains. The main building was the safari lodge, overlooking the Kazinga Channel that joined Lake Edward to the smaller Lake George to the east. The lodge catered for international tourists, providing luxurious accommodation. The lounge bar was dominated by a huge pair of elephant tusks, with immaculate green lawns surrounding a sparkling blue swimming pool. A pair of tame warthog begged for titbits from the scattered tables and were the star attraction for visitors' photographs. In the car park we met a khaki-uniformed driver cleaning out his Volkswagen minibus after the morning's game drive. I asked about the Nuffield Unit of Tropical Animal Ecology (NUTAE or "Newty" as everyone called it), which was where I was to be attached while working on my thesis on the management of African game parks. He insisted that he would take me there so, after saying goodbye to Alfred, I climbed in. It was a short ride, only a couple of hundred yards over the ridge behind the lodge to the office block and laboratories.

On the way we encountered a massive elephant bull with enormous tusks ambling towards the Park's staff housing compound. The driver explained that the bull was a frequent visitor, attracted by the kitchen waste and the gardens. Everyone knew him as John Wayne because of his enormous size, and maybe because of the obvious contempt he displayed for lesser beings as he casually toured the compound, up-ending waste bins and stealing morsels of any available vegetable matter. Most inhabitants seemed to accept his benign scavenging and went about their normal routines while giving him a wide berth. He was the first wild elephant I had ever seen, a monumental manifestation of the huge footprints and football-sized droppings I had encountered on the walk from the park gate. We waited respectfully until he had crossed our path; disputing the route would have been no-contest. At around six tons he was out of our division. I was very glad of the lift.

"G'day mate" was the greeting employed by Doug Friend, a big, genial Australian and the first NUTAE person I met. He was a research botanist and was just leaving his office, one of a row of four rooms in a single-storey building trimmed with a tin-roofed veranda. His green, short-wheel-base Land Rover was parked outside, the engine running. I introduced myself and was subjected to a vigorous handshake.

"You're the Pommie vet then," was almost a question and I was relieved that someone knew I was coming; communications between London and Mweya were hardly state of the art. "I'll take you over to Mike's place, he's been wondering when you'd arrive. He's off next week sometime."

Mike Woodford was NUTAE's research veterinarian and the man I was supposed to stand in for while he was in Zurich finishing his doctorate on tuberculosis in African buffaloes. The unit had offered me accommodation and facilities in exchange for occasional veterinary services in Mike's absence. I threw my rucksack in the back of Doug's open Land Rover and jumped in. I noticed that the top halves of the doors had been removed. We drove around the corner of the building and headed across to a group of colonial-style bungalows. Each house was surrounded by a small garden, but apart from a few purple bougainvillaea bushes and the odd frangipani there was little that seemed to have escaped John Wayne's appetite. Doug pulled up at the gate of one of the gardens. "Hey Mike, your mate's here!" he yelled. Since Mike and I had never met I thought his chosen terminology was a tiny bit presumptuous, but then I'd never met an Australian before.

Slim, tanned and good-looking, with grey hair, Mike appeared at the doorway. I guessed he was in his mid-forties. He greeted me with a broad smile. "Hello there, how was your journey?"

Doug passed me my rucksack and left for home and an early lunch. Mike, like most East Africans of English extraction, sounded more English than the BBC. "You'll be staying at the hostel. I'll take you round there after lunch. I'm afraid my wife's in Nairobi, so I'm not really organised for catering. We'll nip down to the lodge for a bite to eat later."

I sat down at a small wire-metal table outside his door while Mike made tea. He began to tell me about the Park and NUTAE's role, in particular what he was engaged in. I explained that I was very inexperienced in clinical work, having spent only a few weeks in practice since qualifying the previous July. I had been studying full time for my MSc and needed to write a dissertation on the management of African national parks to complete my degree.

"Not to worry," he said. "We don't treat many animals in the conventional sense. Most of what you'll need to do will be either immobilisations using drug darts or post-mortems on any animals found dead, if they're found before the vultures and hyaenas have got to them."

Apart from Mike's work on buffalo diseases, NUTAE managed a range of research projects: on elephant behaviour; observations on the park's unusual lions, who displayed a penchant for climbing trees; and Doug's work on vegetation. Visiting scientists were also conducting studies on marabou storks, banded mongoose, intercontinental bird migrations and, under the auspices of an American university, a long-term research project on some of the park's primates. It was a huge thrill to become a part of it – even a small, temporary one.

We drove back to the safari lodge and enjoyed a buffet lunch along with a number of tourists. I already thought of myself as different to these universally denigrated beings, whose paying presence had not yet been recognised as essential for conservation in the Third World. They seemed, for the most part, to be elderly Americans dressed in khaki safari gear, noisily exchanging game viewing experiences from their morning drives. Hippos and elephants competed with a pride of sleepy sounding lions, all eclipsed by a tale of a mother leopard and two cubs sunning themselves on some rocks. The more exciting occurrences were recorded, with their locations, on a blackboard so that other guests could try to repeat the experience. I overheard a few remarks comparing Queen Elizabeth with other parks: Serengeti, Amboseli and Murchison Falls. All familiar names, articulations of long-held dreams I fully intended to realise.

After lunch Mike took me to the small, single-storey hostel for visiting research workers and introduced me to the cook, Elisha, and his two assistants Enoch and James, who took care of every domestic chore, from washing dishes or clothes, to cleaning the rooms, ironing and waiting at table. I was allocated a small individual bedroom furnished with a bookshelf, chair, bedside table with a reading lamp, small chest of drawers for clothes and a hook on the back of the door in lieu of any coathangers. Six bedrooms shared a bathroom, shower and two toilets. Supper was scheduled for 6.30 pm in a combined dining room/lounge, or common room, where I would meet the three other current residents when they returned from their fieldwork. I dumped my rucksack and followed Mike.

Back in Mike's office I watched him prepare darts for the immobilisation of an elephant the following morning. First, he lubricated the inside of an aluminium tube with Vaseline and fitted a tiny detonator inside a rubber plunger at the tail end. A colourless drug solution was then gently squirted in from a plastic syringe. Finally, a seriously robust needle – about four inches long and almost a quarter inch in diameter – was screwed into the front of the dart and plugged with Vaseline to prevent leakage.

The drug was a narcotic known by the code name M99. Mike explained that it was roughly 10,000 times as strong as morphine – pretty potent stuff, only about one per cent of a gram, an almost invisible amount of powder, was needed to put an elephant down. This incredibly powerful drug was produced by Reckitt and Colman, who got rich by producing the yellow mustard that millions of people leave on the side of their plates every day. A whole series of these compounds had been tested, each with the prefix M (for morphine). M285, a competitive antagonist, was used as an antidote to wake the animal.

M99 is still widely used today to capture a whole variety of species, but now it is properly packaged in handy glass vials of known standard concentrations. Mike had to make up his own solution and had found it quite difficult to dissolve the white crystals in sterile, injectable water, so he lowered the pH by adding a little vinegar. The drug worked best when combined with a tranquilliser, closely related to standard travel sickness remedies, which also helped to ensure a quiet uneventful recovery period, since it was not affected by the antidote.

As Mike was showing me his dart gun, a twenty-gauge shotgun fitted with an adapter that fired .22 blanks of various strengths, a young, blond man stuck his head around the door to enquire if things were ready for tomorrow. This was John Wyatt, an English research biologist studying elephant behaviour. He wanted to paint-mark a particular elephant so that he and his assistants would be able to recognise it, follow it and record its activities. He and I walked back to the hostel, leaving Mike to finish up in his office and meet us at daybreak the next day. John had been at NUTAE for over a year and was hoping to accumulate enough data to write a PhD thesis. He shared a house in the complex with another long-term research worker, but often ate at the hostel, socialising with visiting scientists and students. He introduced me to the other hostel residents: Clive, a final-year zoology student from Bristol, who was studying pied kingfishers; and two Americans, a flamboyantly eccentric college professor called Tom Struhsaker and his young female research assistant Cathy. They were primatologists, studying colobus monkeys in the section of the park known as the Maramagambo Forest. Tom had been around for quite a while and seemed to have junior researchers scattered throughout East Africa recording the social behaviour of various groups of monkeys. He spent a good part of each year visiting these projects when he was not teaching back in the States.

Supper, served by Enoch, was my first meal with an authentic African flavour. The staple diet in most of Uganda is *matoki* – plantain or green bananas, which are used rather like potatoes are in the UK. Elisha had produced a tasty and enjoyable stew with beef, small beans, onions and pieces of *matoki,* accompanied by a vegetable dish that looked and tasted like boiled spinach. It was followed by a fresh fruit salad with pawpaw, watermelon and regular, sweet bananas. Shortly after it was time for a shower and early bed. John was driven home by Struhsaker, only a couple of hundred yards, but fraught with the possibility of unwanted fierce company. I settled in my bed and, despite a head full of exotic adventures and thrilling prospects, the noisy chorus of crickets soon lulled me to sleep.

I was awake before sunrise the next morning; the sky in the east was just beginning to lighten. I desperately wanted to impress my new colleagues and was determined they wouldn't catch me lying in. I dressed hurriedly and grabbed my binoculars and camera before wandering outside via the kitchen. James was on the early shift and already had a kettle of boiling water on the stove. With a smile, he provided a mug and spoon and indicated the jar of instant coffee. Elisha shuffled in and enquired whether or not I wanted breakfast. Although the answer was "No thanks", it was made redundant by the arrival of John's Land Rover.

We drove across to Mike's office and found him putting his metal toolbox containing his darting equipment and drugs in the back of his open Land Rover and his dart gun in the front passenger seat. He climbed in behind the steering wheel and both vehicles then drove downhill to the labour lines where the game scouts and junior staff were accommodated with their families. John had stowed tins of white and pale blue paint, brushes, buckets and other assorted hardware in the back of his vehicle. Between us on the front seat were two powerful spotlights and a box of .375 Magnum calibre bullets. The rifle was in a canvas case propped between the seats. I had absolutely no knowledge of firearms, but John stated that this was the best weapon for use on big game since it possessed the best combination of stopping power and accuracy. Solid nose bullets were essential if you wanted to stop an elephant quickly. I fervently hoped it wouldn't come to that, not least because John's youth and slight build did not instantly cast him as an experienced big-game hunter in the Clark Gable mould.

From outside a small staff house we picked up two game scouts, Jacob and Zack. Both were probably in their forties, Jacob was broad, powerful and cheerfully round-faced, Zack was taller and quite gaunt, with a much more serious countenance. John described Jacob as an ex-poacher and soldier who had probably killed more elephants than anyone in the parks' service. Now reformed and seemingly happy in his new career, his experience and intimate knowledge of elephants was indispensable to John's project. Zack was a general hand whose speciality was as a bush mechanic, but he was also an excellent tracker. Both men had only limited English and John communicated with them in Swahili.

Mike's assistant, David, was summoned from a second, identical house by a short hoot of Mike's horn and clambered in beside him. The two vehicles then bumped down the red, rain-gullied road past the entrance to the tourist lodge and out into the park. It was 6.00 am and the sun washed the broken, grey clouds in the east with pink, prior to bursting over the horizon.

We travelled towards the sunrise for a short way along a corrugated track, passing a couple of early tourist vehicles watching a herd of buffalo quietly grazing, and then around a wide shallow pool situated in bare, overgrazed ground, perhaps three or four acres in extent. The pool itself was maybe half an acre and almost filled with hippos – scores of them, packed side by side and nose to tail like great, grey seals. An occasional yawn displayed a cavernous gape, perhaps a threatening gesture, but the only other movement was the brisk to and fro beating of tails as they scattered their dung into the soupy water and over their companions. Close to the edge of the pool, on the bare ground, lay a couple of spotted hyaenas, one of which half sat up to watch us slowly skirt the pool. When we were within fifty yards they got up and loped away into the bush, glancing back over their shoulders.

About twenty minutes later the sun was well up and warm and we turned off the track and started to wander through the open scrub bush and euphorbia trees. Mike's car was in the lead and every now and then he would stop, stand on the seat and survey the gently undulating landscape through his binoculars. Jacob and Zack, standing in the back of our vehicle, scoured the area without any lenses. It was a quiet consultation between the two scouts that signalled the first elephant sighting. John attracted Mike's attention and Jacob pointed down to the right. It was a group of three animals quietly feeding about 500 yards away, a large bull, perhaps forty years old, with a couple of younger companions, known as *askaris*, Swahili for soldiers or escorts. John wanted to mark a senior bull and follow him for as long as possible, making continuous observations and recording his activities. This was a suitable trio for his purposes.

Mike suggested that I drive his Land Rover while he moved to the passenger seat, from where he could shoot comfortably right-handed. David scrambled over into the back. I was instructed to drive slowly in second gear, obliquely towards the elephants. The rest of the crew remained with John's vehicle and watched without following. The bulls were quite unconcerned – as park elephants they were quite used to vehicles and Mike expected no trouble from them. They continued to feed, aware of us but obviously regarding us as just another bunch of curious tourists. Mike told me to get within thirty yards and position the car sideways with the animals on his side. He loaded a dart into the gun and carefully pointed it outside the vehicle – an accidental discharge would have been as disastrous as with a regular firearm. I manoeuvred the Land Rover as instructed and stopped, leaving the engine running. Mike waited until he had a clear view of the large bull, nonchalantly stripping branches from a bush with its trunk and loading them into its mouth. The two *askaris* were giving their attention to a clump of bushes about twenty yards away to the left. Mike fired. The light, sharp crack of the .22 blank cartridge got their immediate attention, but they only started to move away at speed after the dart whacked into the back of the thigh of the large bull. Within seconds all three had disappeared through the bush down a slight incline. After perhaps ten seconds we heard an urgent trumpet sound from the direction they had taken, but that was all. Mike gave instructions to switch off and wait for the other car. After a short while John drove up in his Land Rover. He had followed the elephants and reported that they were calm again about half a mile away. Jacob and Zack were on foot watching them. I noticed that the .375 Magnum had gone.

Mike was driving again and we led the way, winding between bushes and carefully negotiating fallen logs and holes. We came across Zack, who clambered aboard and whispered that the elephants were still together about 200 yards in front but obscured by the vegetation. We proceeded very slowly until we could see the animals, with Jacob, downwind, rifle slung over his shoulder, about fifty yards away from them. It was now almost ten minutes since the dart had hit and the two younger animals had sensed that all was not well with their companion. They became more agitated at our approach. We stopped some fifty yards from the now stationary bull and Jacob joined us on the vehicle. The bull was swaying gently, but remained on his feet. He apparently could walk no further and his head slumped, with his trunk resting on the ground. All sorts of strange rumbling sounds were being made by the two *askaris*. The old bull staggered briefly as if dozing and fell untidily, raising a cloud of dust, with his legs folded under him. Mike called out “Let’s go!” and both vehicles advanced noisily towards the fallen giant. The two younger animals made off fast, leaving the old bull to his fate.

We pulled up next to the elephant and, at Mike’s urgent insistence, jumped off and pushed as hard as we could to topple the bull on to his side. He rolled over surprisingly easily, considering he probably weighed in excess of five tons. An elephant lying on his chest could quickly suffocate because of the pressure exerted on his diaphragm by the weight of abdominal organs and their bulky contents. We had been lucky, sometimes an elephant’s legs have to be repositioned before it can be toppled, or obstructions like tree stumps have to be dug out to enable the animal to roll over.

It had taken exactly twelve minutes from the time of darting for the bull to go down. Mike noted this down, along with details such as estimated age and weight, group composition, location, time, weather conditions, position of the dart and a host of other information. He carefully recorded the pulse from an artery behind an ear and breathing rates to ensure that nothing was seriously amiss. David pulled the upper ear forward over the eye, which remained open and could have been damaged by the strong sunlight. John scurried about measuring various elephantine statistics: tusk length and diameter; shoulder height; and total body length along the back. He also made brief notes on the elephant's individual characteristics, such as notches and holes in the ears, length and abundance of tail hairs, and anything else that might help him to recognise the elephant in future. He took a number of photographs for identification purposes – and I took some as souvenirs. Zack and Jacob brushed as much accumulated dirt and dust as possible off the upper ear, thigh and flank in preparation for painting. They then painted large figure eights in bright, white numerals, almost four feet high, on the corrugated grey skin. Mike retrieved his dart and treated the small puncture wound with long-acting antibiotic from a tube of intra-mammary preparation for dairy cows.

After about fifteen minutes of feverish activity, punctuated by deep, rolling snores that reverberated down his trunk three or four times every minute, we were ready to reverse the immobilising drug and hopefully let the elephant get up and go. We loaded everything back into the cars and drove a little way off, while Mike prepared to inject the antidote solution into an ear vein the size of a small hosepipe. After Mike rejoined us we sat and watched with the engines idling. Within two or three minutes there was a noticeable change in the recumbent elephant. The ear flapped back away from the eye and the upper hind leg swung slowly forward and then back again. He made a feeble attempt to lift his head off the ground. A stronger second attempt soon followed and the animal rocked to and fro in an attempt to gain a sitting position. After that it was a matter of seconds before he stood up. He was motionless briefly before he turned towards us, shook his huge head once with outstretched ears and ambled off into the bush. From administration of the antidote to walking away had taken about four minutes.

For the next three or four hours the elephant would be a little drowsy until the effects of the tranquilliser wore off completely. John was anxious not to lose contact with him and stayed behind with Zack while the rest of us returned to Mweya in Mike's vehicle. Jacob and I would return at 2.00 pm to take over as observers. As John's Land Rover slowly followed in the direction of the elephant's departure, we retraced our tracks and headed for home. It was 8.30

am. At the hippo pool, two minibuses full of tourists were happily clicking away through open sunroofs.

Back at the offices Mike and I chatted about his research project on buffaloes and his life as a wildlife vet in general. I had barely arrived in time. He was due to leave for Nairobi and then Zurich in a few days. For four years he had been collecting data on tuberculosis in the park's buffalo population. In a week or so he had to defend his thesis before a panel of learned academics at the Swiss university. If he were successful he would be awarded the higher degree of DrMedVet. Mike had qualified as a vet in England in 1946, before British veterinary schools awarded degrees, and he was registered as a professional through the Royal College of Veterinary Surgeons. In later years all the veterinary schools became university faculties and began to award degrees, which now qualify graduates for registration through the Royal College. British vets, like dentists, have never adopted the title of doctor, as in most other countries, preferring to retain Mister or its feminine equivalent. Surgeons in the UK also renounce the doctor title, so perhaps a little professional snobbery is involved, although I believe it actually dates back to the time when surgeons were also barbers and professionally much inferior to physicians.

I was very hungry at midday and Elisha kindly prepared an early lunch before I drove Mike's Land Rover back to the office to meet up with Jacob, who had spoken by radio to John to arrange a rendezvous. The marked elephant was apparently dozing in a thicket about a mile from where we had darted him. We collected a plastic water container and hurried out via the hippo pool again before turning off where Jacob indicated. Driving very slowly and carefully to avoid holes and tree stumps, we soon spotted John's vehicle parked in the shade of a tree.

"He's hardly moved for the last two hours," reported John. "I think he's still feeling the ACP." This was the acronym for acetyl promazine, the tranquilliser added to the dart and, not being susceptible to the M285 antidote, persisted for several hours. We could clearly see Number 8 standing quietly under some trees about 100 yards away. Through the binoculars it appeared that he was breathing slowly and regularly, with approximately a foot of his trunk resting on the ground. His great ears occasionally wafted slowly back and forth, no doubt an attempt to alleviate the midday heat.

John explained that we had to record what the elephant was doing every five minutes. He showed us his notes and handed over the book. I was to drive, keep time and record; Jacob, who had done this several times before, was responsible for the observations. Essentially, every five minutes he would describe the elephant's current activity or lack of it, and I was to write it down – pretty simple really. Jacob was also to tell me where we were and in which direction we went if the elephant moved. John and Zack left for Mweya and lunch. They would be back at 6.30 pm, just before dark, to take over for the night.

The old bull showed no inclination to move out of his shady spot and we settled down to watch. Dutifully we recorded at the required intervals everything the elephant did, which didn't amount to very much for over two hours. I spent a lot of the time peering through my binoculars, frequently distracted by colourful and exotic birds that were new to me. A group of about twenty banded mongoose scurried into view, the adults busily foraging while the smaller individuals seemed more interested in games and checking us out. After they had cleaned the area of beetles and other tasty morsels they disappeared into the undergrowth just behind the dozing elephant. A female warthog and two small piglets appeared briefly, but trotted off, tails erect, when they spotted us. It was hot, even in the shade, and we moved the vehicle with the tree's shadow.

Close to 4.00 pm our subject became slightly more animated, moving his great head from side to side and shifting his weight, occasionally crossing his hind legs, taking his weight on a single hind foot and his forelegs. Another ten minutes and he gave a mighty shake of his head, slowly left the shade and ambled downhill away from us. He looked quite comical with all the white paint on his flanks, ears and legs and I wondered what other elephants would make of him and whether or not this might affect their behaviour and thus influence the study. We let him move about 100 yards before starting the vehicle and slowly following. It was mainly easy terrain and we only had to keep him in clear sight. Jacob explained how to position the vehicle without affecting the elephant and influencing his movements.

The bull led us down a gentle slope, south towards the Kazinga Channel, a broad expanse of deep water a mile or so away. I wondered whether he might try to cross it. If he did, we would be unable to follow; the only bridge was a long way to the east on the main road. He approached a small depression with a drying pool of water surrounded by trampled mud. The water appeared fairly shallow, but contained two hippos who were managing to remain mostly submerged, while leaving enough skin exposed to play host to a couple of oxpeckers, or tick birds. The hippos did not appear to mind the elephant's approach, even when he entered the slippery surrounds of their refuge. He seemed not to notice them either and proceeded to suck up gallons of the muddy water and empty it first into his mouth, then spray and splash it over his back and belly. In a matter of minutes he had virtually obliterated the white figure eights, except from the back of his thighs. Did the elephant know the paint was there? Did it bother him, or was he just behaving normally, responding to the heat? Maybe he was feeling the after effects of the drugs and reacting abnormally? I wondered how John was going to cope with this development, which was going to make him more difficult to follow, especially at night. The old bull remained motionless at the water's edge for a while and then began to move slowly away to the west, no longer heading towards the channel.

John called on the radio shortly after 6.00 pm and Jacob described our position. I was surprised that we had returned almost to Mweya. The relief team joined us within a few minutes. John wasn't best pleased that the bull was largely back to his original appearance so soon, but shrugged and accepted it as just another irritating problem to deal with during fieldwork. John and Zack were equipped with spotlights – complete with red filters so as not to affect the elephant or other wildlife – warm clothing, sandwiches and flasks of coffee to see them through the night. Jacob and I drove back to Mweya after arranging to take over again at 6.00 am. A hot shower, supper and then early to bed after chatting with the other hostel residents over coffee concluded my first working day in Africa. I lay listening to the ever-present chirruping of crickets and other tropical sounds thinking "This beats spaying cats in rainy Lancashire!"

I was up in the dark at 5.30 am and found Enoch already in the kitchen making coffee. He had news. John and Zack had returned at 3.00 am after losing contact with the elephant, so there was no longer any 6.00 am rendezvous. John would be around at about 7.00 am and we would take it from there. They had managed to keep him in sight and to document his nocturnal activities – almost exclusively browsing – until, around midnight, he had met up with two smaller bulls, presumably his *askaris*, and then disappeared in an area of thick bush near the shore of Lake Edward. John was confident that Jacob would be able to pick up the spoor and find him quite quickly in daylight. This proved not to be the case. The bull and his companions seemed to have disappeared. Despite a prolonged search we failed to find the spoor. Some disbelieving tourists, who reported "faint but definite circular marks" on an elephant, eventually spotted the bull four days later in a spectacular area of extinct volcanic craters several miles to the north.

Anxious to give me enough experience to be able to continue during his absence, Mike and I immobilised two more elephants for John and his team to follow in the next few days. Mike also briefed me on what my other duties might involve and, just before he left, introduced me to Keith Eltringham, the Director of NUTAE, who had flown back from business in Kampala in his tiny Cessna 182 four-seater aeroplane. Keith was a prominent Cambridge academic who was under contract to run the research centre at Mweya.

Over the weeks after Mike had gone we immobilised a couple of elephants, rescued a snared lion, fed an orphaned mongoose and investigated poisoned marabou storks. But I spent more time gathering basic information on the area: its climate, vegetation, and densities of grazing and browsing animals, which were all crucially interlinked in its ecology. I was particularly interested in fire and how it affected the park. Africa's savannas burn frequently and extensively from a multitude of causes, ranging from lightning to poaching. Even now, almost fifty years on, there is still much debate about its effects, some authorities state that burning is necessary to maintain certain habitats, for instance, by preventing bushes from encroaching on grassland; others claim that too many fires are caused by man, which is resulting in undesirable habitat changes. There is no doubt that it is a complex phenomenon with an infinite variety of effects in different ecosystems and that it has been influencing how natural systems function for a very long time. Many times over the years, as I've washed sooty film from the leading edge of my aeroplane's wings after dry season game censuses, I've speculated on the waste of natural resources from an impoverished continent. My simplistic thesis of how I thought it affected one park in one small African country was hardly noticed and remains buried in obscurity, without ever being tested or implemented; its only contribution being to my benefit through the conferring of a postgraduate degree.

I had a wonderful time in and around QE Park – as it was known, and is again now, after a few years of being renamed as Ruwenzori National Park by Idi Amin. It was a dream come true and I wanted to contrive to stay on in some long-term capacity. All kinds of adventures came my way, interspersing the routine fieldwork for my degree. Peter Jewell, a visiting professor who had once taught me briefly in London, was carrying out research on topi, a colourful if ungainly looking antelope, that occurred mainly in the Ishasha area in the south of the Park, where short grass plains were punctuated by large picture-postcard umbrella acacia trees. The trees, like the more famous ones at Lake Manyara in Tanzania, were occasionally used by climbing lions as shady resting platforms away from some of the troublesome flies.

Topi occur in large groups and concentrate their calving season by synchronised breeding as an anti-predator survival mechanism. It was the height of the calving season and the plains were dotted with hundreds of topi in small groups containing lots of tiny buff-coloured calves. Peter wanted to record birth weights. This necessitated being there as the calf was dropped because in a very short time it was far too fast and agile to be caught by the likes of us.

We watched likely pregnant females very closely through our binoculars. Labour was short and relatively effortless compared with the domestic animals I had worked with on British farms. The mother stood throughout and turned to lick the membranes from the newborn calf as soon as it dropped to the ground. We drove as close as possible and one of us would pick up the newborn calf while the other prepared the small harness and spring balance to weigh the little animal. The mother would stand bleating a few yards away, looking worried, but too nervous to interfere. We carefully replaced the baby in the exact spot and retreated to the vehicle, whereupon the mother would return to complete her cleaning of the baby. Within a minute or two it would stand shakily and then wobble off with its mother to join the nearest group.

One day we had done about half a dozen weighings when I thought one mother was behaving oddly and seemed more nervous than usual. I was just replacing the calf on the ground and Peter was still entering data in his notebook when he cried, "Watch out!" A lioness streaked between us and grabbed the baby almost from my hands. It happened so quickly that neither of us had time to do more than gasp and watch as the big cat streaked away. I certainly didn't have time to be scared. We decided it was time to break for lunch, during which we recounted and discussed the incident a dozen times while eating our sandwiches.

A visiting American academic wanted to collect specimens of tampans. These are soft-bodied ticks that inhabit places where their host animals lie up. They don't cling to their hosts like normal ticks but prefer to feed and drop off again while the animal is sleeping or lying down. Warthogs sleep down burrows – usually excavated aardvark holes – that are often infested with tampans, which can be collected by stuffing a coarse blanket down the burrow and withdrawing it quickly. The process often involves crawling some way into the burrow first. As warthogs habitually reverse into their burrows, it is advisable to make sure that the tenant is absent before venturing beyond the entrance. Crawling into these dark holes to retrieve creepy-crawlies was probably the job I enjoyed least, although a slightly less claustrophobic version was just as unpleasant.

Another of these parasites fed on the blood of specific bats that spent the day in caves in the Maramagambo Forest. Collecting these meant a hike through the forest before donning plastic kagouls and trousers at the entrance to the caves and, when satisfied that ankles, wrists and necks were securely closed, proceeding by torchlight through the slippery caves to fill small sample bottles. With the bats above, the reeking guano at my feet, and thousands of scurrying tampans all over me, the experience was not among my favourites. Outside, in the sunshine, the kagouls demonstrated that they might have been waterproof but were no barrier to the tampans. Even though they obviously didn't wish to feed on me the little eight-legged beasts were everywhere. For hours afterwards my flesh literally crawled. Mostly though, the various tasks and duties were exceedingly enjoyable. For instance, observing kingfishers by lying in the sun on a riverbank and counting how many times a pair of birds made a successful dive into the water and how many times they came up empty-handed, if that's the right word?

The stunningly beautiful Lake Edward with the snow-capped Ruwenzoris as a backdrop made for an idyllic existence, but the lake did occasionally present me with a problem. I was in Professor Eltringham's open Land Rover one morning following a small group of buffalo bulls along the steeply sloping lakeshore. I drove parallel to the water on my right, about thirty yards from the edge, when I realised that the vehicle was likely to tip over sideways. I stopped. It seemed best to climb across into the uphill passenger seat while I thought about how to extricate myself and my boss's car from the tricky situation. But I hadn't applied the handbrake and was alarmed to feel the vehicle move forward and downhill as soon as I sat in the passenger seat. As it gathered a little speed it turned even more downhill towards the lake. At that point, with no access to the controls, I decided to abandon ship over the passenger door and watched in fascinated horror as the vehicle trundled down and into the lake, coming to rest a few yards offshore in about four feet of water.

I don't know whether I was more worried by the prospect of walking the few miles back through the bush to NUTAE or of arriving there and having to tell the boss what I'd done with his Land Rover. As luck would have it, shortly after I reached the road at the top of the hill, Doug Friend and a couple of labourers came along in a Land Rover. They were returning home after constructing a fenced experimental plot. They could see the Prof's Land Rover below them in the lake and found the whole situation exceedingly funny. I had to wade in and attach a rope, after Doug had assured me that there were no crocs in the lake. We towed the vehicle out backwards and found that, luckily, water hadn't got into the engine, probably because I had switched it off before shifting seats. It started first time on being pulled by Doug's car and I sheepishly followed him back home. Keith was actually quite unperturbed when I reported what I'd done, but the hostel inmates found Doug's Australian embellishments more than hilarious and the beers were on me.

I was puzzled by the absence of crocodiles from the lake and the park's other water bodies, but research showed that they had not occurred there for hundreds of years, although they have apparently become re-established since the 1980s. Other unexpected anomalies of QE Park were the absence of impala, zebra and giraffe, all species that are widespread and common in most other African protected areas.

A few of us would often call at Mweya Lodge for a snack or a drink, amusedly listening to the excited tourist banter at the bar. It was occasionally very funny, sometimes unbelievable, such as, "Do hippos really have legs?" or "Jeez Bill, Muriel thought all the warthogs were baby rhinos!"

On one occasion I was driving back to the NUTAE quarters at lunchtime and came across an elderly tourist couple, on foot, filming John Wayne from a few yards away as he dismantled a green shrub and nonchalantly stuffed it into his mouth. I stopped next to them and said fairly abruptly, "Get in the car!" They obeyed rather grudgingly, I suppose partly because I was at least fifty years younger than them, but the official badge on the vehicle's door gave me some authority.

"What do you think you're doing?" I admonished. "You could be killed. Don't you know that's a wild animal!"

The American lady replied quite tartly, "A wild elephant in a national park? – That's a disgrace!"

I couldn't think of a reply, so I just drove them back to the lodge and wished them a happy stay.

Towards the end of my stay one episode shed a different light on life in this tropical paradise. I was on my way to the Ishasha plains to measure the girths of as many of the large "lion-bearing" acacia trees as I could find and estimate the distances between them. The study was quite esoteric and had something to do with inherited traits compared with learnt behaviour in the area's lion prides. Another aspect of it compared prides that seemed to eat waterbuck almost exclusively, with prides that preferred buffalo meat.

Jacob was with me and as we entered the open grassland we passed a black Mercedes limousine. It appeared deserted. I couldn't think who would have brought a luxury vehicle into the park on such poor roads. Shortly afterwards we came across two army Land Rovers parked by the side of the track and about ten soldiers lazing about, smoking and chatting. They greeted us in a friendly enough fashion as we stopped. Jacob chatted to them for a few minutes and then we continued on our way and encountered a third military Land Rover on its way back towards the others. We both stopped. In the passenger seat, next to the soldier who was driving, was a man in civilian clothes carrying an automatic rifle. Standing in the back were two officers, who appeared unarmed. Also in the back were the fresh carcasses of two adult female topi and one yearling. In my naïvety, and to Jacob's great discomfort, I informed them that they were in a national park and that hunting was illegal. Thankfully something prevented me from belabouring the point. The civilian pointedly informed me that he was a government minister, that it was his park and that I was obviously a young foreigner with no rights whatsoever. Perhaps I would like him to shoot me as well as the antelopes? I summoned the required discretion and we drove on without any further humiliation, but it had been a very frightening interlude.

Back at Mweya, it was impressed upon me that I (and even more so Jacob) had been very lucky to escape so lightly. It transpired that the President, Idi Amin himself, would be addressing a political rally in Kasese the next day and the minister must have been one of his entourage. All the Ugandan park staff of any rank were expected to attend the rally and a bus duly came to collect them the next morning.

This was only a few months after Amin had come to power. He had been received quite well at first and was still looked upon, by foreigners anyway, as preferable to his predecessor (and eventual successor) Milton Obote. However, as the weeks went by we began to hear increasingly disturbing reports of Amin's capricious personality. When the incidents began to take on horror story proportions it became very clear that our status as expatriates would count for less and less with the authorities, even though the vast majority of Ugandans remained as friendly as ever.

It was almost time for me to write up and submit my dissertation to University College, so, with mixed feelings, I prepared to leave the park. I wanted very much to return and take up a long-term appointment. I had even discussed joining the staff at Makerere University in Kampala. The main consideration would be how the political situation developed. I was lucky to be able to fly with Keith in the Cessna 182 to Entebbe. Then I took the overnight bus from Kampala to Nairobi, which was quite an experience – uncomfortable, crowded and very noisy. There was a long interruption at the border where we all had to disembark in the middle of the night, identify our luggage and get our passports stamped, then repeat the whole process on the Kenyan side before continuing.

It was relatively easy and straightforward for me to leave NUTAE, after all I was just a short-term volunteer. For the others, some with families, a seriously deteriorating political and security situation was far more problematic, with far greater issues needing careful consideration. Some went "on leave", hoping that the situation would improve and they could return. A few weeks later I heard from Keith Eltringham that NUTAE would not carry on as before in QE Park and that it was unlikely I would be able to return. Then I learnt that all the expatriate scientists at Mweya had pulled out and NUTAE was no more, although it was later revived and continued as the Uganda Institute of Ecology until the late 1990s.

I spent a couple of weeks in Kenya before returning to England. My old *alma mater*, Glasgow University, played a prominent teaching and research role at Kabete, the Kenyan veterinary college in Nairobi and I quickly made contact with a couple of my old friends from Scotland. Pete Holt, the brightest student in my year class, was teaching there for a few months, and Max Murray, a staff member who had been conducting research at Kabete for years happily looked after me. They showed me Kabete's facilities and some of Nairobi's attractions, especially the Nairobi National Park, right on the edge of the city and filled with wildlife – where I saw my first impala, zebra and giraffe.

One evening they introduced me to John King, a veterinarian who was working at Galana Ranch, bordering Tsavo East NP. This huge ranch was an early attempt to farm with wildlife and has had a mixed history since it was established in 1968. He was keen to show me what they were trying to do and early the following day picked me up from Pete's flat and drove me to Wilson Airport.

We took off in his Cessna and swung east over Nairobi NP and the Athi Plains towards Tsavo and Galana. Flying low over thousands of square miles of arid bush gave me an unexpected buzz. All the same drab brown with a few groups of dry hills and an occasional thin green ribbon of vegetation signifying a watercourse, it was very different from Uganda. The vast amount of space, with seemingly very few signs of human settlement, intoxicated me and ever since I've preferred dry wilderness and desert to lush, green, softer environments; hence, I suppose, my lifelong passion for Botswana. During the two-hour flight John encouraged me to take the controls and try to keep the aircraft straight and level, which I found extremely difficult on my first attempt. We finally saw the Galana airstrip and John circled down to chase a black rhino mother and baby off the runway. They trotted quickly off the strip and disappeared into the scrub. I've seen many more rhino since, from various aircraft and up close on foot as I aimed a dart gun, but that first sighting was very special. We landed smoothly on the red gravel and pulled into the small parking area. A mix-up in communications meant we had to wait for half an hour for a vehicle to pick us up. Meanwhile John explained some of the things they were trying to achieve with the ranch.

Some of their aims had grown out of an ongoing severe drought in the region, which had killed thousands of cattle and, most famously, lots of elephants. Huge disagreements between various conservation factions were headline news in Africa and beyond. There was a strong argument for culling but, in the end, the anti-intervention lobby prevailed over contemporary, management-oriented scientists.

Galana Ranch shared a fairly permanent river, and therefore the elephants, rhino and other wildlife species, with the Park and also supported a large cattle population. Innovative ideas included dehorning animals such as oryx and attempting to herd them as domesticated stock. Early results showed impressive weight gains and production from these odd-looking animals that had to be constantly accompanied by local spear-carrying tribesmen to protect them from predators. Eland too were fairly successfully domesticated on the ranch. Alongside the experiments, safari hunting and beef production occurred on the ranch, demonstrating that a multi-use management regime could increase the animal-carrying capacity, protein production and financial returns for this type of semi-arid environment that covers millions of acres of Africa.

Some of the ranch was enclosed by fences and, as is their wont, elephants often pushed them down to access greener pastures. One of the reasons for John's visit was that a large breeding herd of elephants had broken into a main paddock and seemed intent on staying, despite the fact that there was no available water. This was odd because the Galana River was a mere mile or so from the fence line – a very short stroll for an elephant – and well within scenting distance. John and the farm manager assessed the situation by plane and tried to herd the sixty or so animals back towards the river through the cattle fence they had pushed down. After several attempts and low-level aerobatics it became clear that the elephants did not want to cross the fence, even though it presented no physical barrier to them. It was therefore decided to remove the fence wire from a stretch of about 200 yards, most of which they had broken anyway, leaving only the fence posts fixed at about twenty-yard intervals. This took the rest of the day and we hoped that the thirsty animals would leave through the gap during the night. But the herd was still in the paddock the next morning and further aerial persuasion was of no avail; the herd repeatedly turned back under the aircraft as they came close to the fence line. They had now been without water for four days and, under normal circumstances, elephants really need to drink daily. We resolved to try pushing them with vehicles and beaters on foot, making a tremendous racket and even shooting over their heads to drive them in the desired direction, but even with all that and the aircraft they would not cross the line. It was then decided to remove the remaining fence posts and try again, but even this was unsuccessful.

On the fourth day we resorted to fire. John decided that with the wind blowing gently towards the river, conditions were in our favour. We lit a line of bonfires behind the elephants. There was no danger that the fires would spread out of control because there was almost no grass or combustible material left in the paddock, merely bare ground and sparsely distributed thorn scrub. The smoke and smell of the fires seemed to have an effect and together with four vehicles, two guns, an aircraft and over twenty noisy beaters we finally watched them reluctantly cross the line and head for the river. None of us could come up with a plausible explanation for their behaviour but, as I found out several times in later years, that's elephants for you.

After a quick overnight visit to Diani Beach, a resort near Mombasa, John flew me back to Nairobi to catch my flight to London. It was a simple matter – amazing by modern security standards – to transfer the ticket into my name and board the East African Airways flight to Heathrow. I landed in a dull, wet city, the first rain I had seen since leaving months earlier. Jenny had spent the summer travelling and buying fashion for the House of Fraser group, given up our small flat in Golders Green and moved back to Bolton to work out of the Kendal Milne store in Manchester. She listened to my tales of exciting, exotic adventure and started trying to come to terms with the prospect of a different, unfamiliar life, far from everything she knew.

TWO

PENNINE PRACTICE

Back in London I busied myself writing up the dissertation for my master's degree at UCL. I had passed the necessary exams in the early summer before going out to Uganda and, to be honest, it didn't seem that too much store was set by the substance and quality of the dissertations. Some of my fellow students in conservation (there were only eleven of us) had finished their drafts several weeks before. "Stabilising mine dumps by promoting the growth of perennial herbaceous species" didn't sound like much competition for my exotic offering, so I was quietly confident that the HBLB would get value for its generous scholarship. I was more concerned with finding some way of returning to Africa and its wonderful wildlife and avoiding a lengthy spell of treating domestic animals and their insufferable owners in rain-soaked Bolton. What's more, since Nat Lofthouse had retired, Bolton Wanderers had slipped quietly out of the Football League's First Division and looked perilously close to repeating the feat from the Second Division.

After graduation I managed to get what I hoped would be a temporary job in a busy mixed practice in Ramsbottom, a Pennine village in the Rossendale Valley that would have qualified for Music Hall jokes even without its name. Situated on the valley road from Bury to Accrington and hemmed in on both sides by steep, bleak hillsides, it offered a less evocative image than Serengeti, Zambezi or Okavango. Even the practice seemed to enter into the joke – the vet's name was Peter Nut, his wife was Hazel and the receptionist was Mrs Almond! But it was convenient because Jenny and I could stay with parents in nearby Bolton and she could continue working in Manchester.

Peter seemed to have had a problem keeping his assistants; several young hopefuls had lasted only a few months. This didn't worry me because I had no desire to stay in general practice and hoped to be back in the African bush with the least delay possible. I had been interviewed by the Ministry of Overseas Development (ODM) with a view to being appointed to a project in one of Africa's many developing countries that received aid from Britain. The shortlist was Nigeria, Swaziland, Zambia and Botswana. I knew precious little about any of them, but after a few hours in the excellent reference library in Bolton's Town Hall I decided that Nigeria was out of the question for a great many reasons and that the other three countries, all in southern Africa, were more acceptable. I then ruled out Swaziland, on the grounds that it was far too small to have significant wildlife opportunities. The remaining two countries, which had only recently changed their names on gaining independence, seemed equally interesting. I knew slightly more about Zambia, formerly Northern Rhodesia, and it certainly seemed as if there was an abundance of national parks and other wildlife areas with a lot going on. I also knew it was a beautiful country with a wonderful climate and the only negative thing I had heard was that crime in the capital city Lusaka was extremely prevalent, especially housebreaking. Botswana, right in the centre of southern Africa, had been known as Bechuanaland until independence in 1966 and there was a puzzling dearth of information about the country. It was big, flat and very undeveloped, and relied mainly on producing and exporting beef to maintain its economy. There were about half a million people in a country as big as France and they were confined mainly to the narrow strip along the railway line in the east. Only one railway line and no tar roads; I needed to find out more about this tantalising wilderness.

The Commonwealth Club in London was kind enough to answer my letter of enquiry about Botswana. For more detailed information they referred me to a Mr Lawrence Tennant, a vet and Chief Game Warden in Botswana up until the late 1960s. Even better, Mr Tennant was now manager of the newly developed Knowsley Safari Park near Liverpool, just a short drive from Bolton. The stars were aligning.

I was rapidly finding out why Peter Nut's practice got through so many assistants. The Ramsbottom clinic operated two sub-branches in Haslingden and Rawtenstall. Daily surgeries in all three clinics entailed driving along narrow West Pennine roads, usually in filthy weather, at breakneck speed to open and officiate at each one. On arrival there was invariably a short queue of people with dogs, cats and other assorted pets waiting outside for attention. There were no receptionists and no appointments at the branches, so after I had unlocked the rooms and turned on the lights it was a bit of a free-for-all. Together with the house calls and visits to small, inaccessible farms, it needed a combination of rally driver and James Herriot on amphetamines to cope with the work. I was busy from 7.30 am until around 8.00 pm most days and on call until the next morning, which frequently meant call-outs in the middle of the night to anything from vomiting puppies to calving cows. My one night off during the week began after evening surgery at Haslingden, often 8.00 pm. I drove an average of over 100 miles a day – almost a job in itself under the local conditions.

I rarely saw Peter, only occasionally bumping into him at the Ramsbottom clinic. He was genuinely even busier than I was and I couldn't begin to imagine how he coped during his frequent single-handed episodes. One night he was arrested by the Bury police while knocking insistently at an old dear's house to vaccinate her three cats – it was 11.30 pm! Peter chain-smoked, even during consultations and surgical operations, and I clearly remember his technique of spaying bitches while they were hanging by their ankles from the surgery door. This had the effect of clearing the lower abdomen of intestines while leaving the uterus and ovaries easily accessible. Sadly, but not surprisingly, I don't think Peter made it to forty.

I lasted about three months, learnt what would normally take a year, picked up several speeding tickets, drove the practice's Mini Countryman into a bus at 2.00 am and confirmed that general practice in England was not my cup of tea. Luckily the local police were usually fairly laid back, especially the officer who waived the speeding ticket after accepting my explanation that I was rushing the budgerigar in a cage on the front seat for an emergency operation!

The hard work, chaotic conditions, and constant intellectual challenges were undoubtedly stimulating and the results were often rewarding, but the two big negative aspects were the general environment and the general public. People, even then, were just too evident – too noisy, too many, and often too unpleasant to make general practice what they now call a lifestyle choice. The exceptions that brightened up the job were too rare.

Peter tended to do most of the consulting sessions and surgery at Ramsbottom, while my territory was mainly up the valley looking after Haslingden and Rawtenstall. One day I was collecting some drugs from Ramsbottom and having a quick cup of coffee in the back room when Peter came through and asked me to deal with the next client. He quickly put on his raincoat and disappeared through the back door. I went into the consulting room to be met by a middle-aged gentleman carrying a large cardboard box.

"Can I help you?" I enquired in my best welcoming manner.

"Is Mr Nut not 'ere?" he asked.

"No, he was called out, I'm afraid."

"Well, I want to know when these rabbits'll go white. I suppose you'd know?"

"I'm not sure, let me have a look."

He hesitantly put the box on the table and began to open the perforated lid, which had been stuck down untidily with masking tape.

"I'm a magician you see," he announced.

"I'm sorry..."

"A magician, on t' stage you see. And these are for my act."

We peered into the box at a dozen baby rabbits. They were a nondescript grey, but it was difficult to be sure because they were soaking wet.

"They're wet through!" I stated the obvious.

"Aye, well. This were on t' box when I collected 'em from t' station." He rummaged in his coat pocket and produced a printed label that said: "Livestock: Water Well On Arrival".

"So I sprinkled 'em wit' th'osepipe."

Peter knew all his clients and, with his mischievous sense of humour, had every intention of giving me as hard a time as possible. I had to explain that the rabbits would not turn white and that our magician friend had been taken for a ride by the supplier. Mrs Almond had been trying to keep a straight face throughout.

On another occasion I was dispatched to an old folks' home up the valley to see a sick mynah bird. My training had been fairly lightweight on the subject of exotic cage birds and I had never been the most diligent student in our general poultry courses (after all they were not likely to be of much help to me when wrestling with elephants). Arriving at the rather fine old house, I parked on the gravel driveway, grabbed my bag and climbed the steps to the front porch. A group of elderly people were keenly watching my arrival through a large bay window. I was a little nervous as a uniformed carer welcomed me enthusiastically and ushered me into a sizeable lounge where the dozen residents I had seen were waiting. I determined to use my most charming bedside manner and improvise from first principles.

The patient was in a traditional bell-shaped cage in front of the assembled residents. Sounding surer of myself than I felt, I smilingly assessed the situation. The bird was obviously distressed and having difficulty breathing. From the group's comments it was clear that Joey was a great favourite who normally shouted and screamed a wide and dubious vocabulary. Now he was just sitting there and wheezing. It didn't need an expert to diagnose that some sort of upper respiratory infection was the most likely problem. Since Joey wasn't eating or drinking there was only one way to get some medication into him; I would have to inject him. The broad-spectrum antibiotic most widely used was a tetracycline called Terramycin and I had plenty in my medicine bag. The problem was that I hadn't a clue what dose was appropriate for a mynah and I knew that it stung like crazy when injected into a muscle. This latter property was sometimes useful if you wanted a moribund calf to jump up miraculously after treatment, but otherwise we tried to use it intravenously to avoid this side effect. How was I going to find a vein in a mynah bird? Well, I wasn't; it would have to be in the breast muscle and hope for the best. I drew up a tiny amount of the drug into the smallest syringe I could find and reached into the cage. Joey was too sick to care, so I easily gripped him gently and brought him out. I carefully inserted the needle through the feathers into his chest and injected the antibiotic slowly. So far, so good, I put him back in the cage and he gripped the wooden perch again. It looked like I had got away with it. Now only time would tell. I gave the gathering a guarded prognosis and left after asking the carer to let the practice know by telephone if there was any change in Joey's condition.

"You're a big hit with the old folk," chirped Mrs Almond the next morning when I called to get my schedule for the day. "Joey's much better."

I was very relieved and told her to dispense some Terramycin powder to continue the treatment for a few days in the bird's drinking water, but to be sure to check that he was taking it. A week or so later it was reported that Joey was back to normal and as rude as ever. Then the inevitable happened and a month later Peter remarked, rather sarcastically I thought, that "Joey's heroic saviour had better get up there and repeat the miracle cure" because he was sick again.

This time the elderly audience was a full house and I was indeed given a hero's welcome. Joey appeared to have exactly the same symptoms and I quickly decided that we would have to continue the treatment, for a longer period this time. I prepared the syringe and confidently reached into the cage to pull out Joey. I carefully inserted the needle into his chest. To my horror, at that very moment his head flopped over to one side in my hand. Joey was dead. I didn't speak, but my face obviously said enough. There was a moment or two of absolute silence, then one very old lady shrieked, "Murderer!" I had visions of a geriatric lynching mob. I got out as quickly as I could, dignity forgotten, with Joey in my left hand and my medicine bag in the other. I muttered something over my shoulder to the carer about a post-mortem and took off down the drive in a shower of gravel.

A sadder story involved an elderly couple and their dog, a Border Collie cross-breed. A large proportion of the dogs around the working-class villages in upper Lancashire seemed to have Border Collie in them, probably from the days when Pennine farmers used them to work the hill sheep and cattle. The breed's innate intelligence and sensitivity persisted in the mongrels derived from them and they made excellent companions.

Ted and Winnie Hargreaves and Matt had been regular clients at Ramsbottom for years. As with many older dogs, at fourteen Matt's kidneys were failing and his condition was deteriorating. The Hargreaves doted on their pet and they had been carefully nursing him and feeding him on a special diet and tonics that would be gentle on his ailing system. He had recently suffered a severe episode, which had required his admission to the clinic and stabilisation with intravenous fluids. A second collapse a few weeks later had caused them to call the clinic and request a home visit. I was on call that evening and duly arrived at their small terraced house, typical of the area and made familiar everywhere by the perennial TV soap opera *Coronation Street*.

Matt was lying on a blanket in front of the gas fire in the living room. He was obviously very weak and had been vomiting. He managed to wag his tail weakly as I approached. Ted explained that Mrs Hargreaves had gone out because she didn't want to be there if I was going to put Matt to sleep. They had obviously come to terms with Matt's condition and understood that he was never going to get well. They did not want to see him sick and suffering any longer and if I recommended euthanasia they would accept it. I explained sympathetically why I thought it best and Ted concurred. He wanted to be present and hold Matt while I did it. It was easy. Matt felt nothing as the anaesthetic entered his veins and a few seconds later he was gone. I wrapped him in the blanket, carried him out and placed him on the rear seat of my car. I said goodbye, reassuring Ted that we really had done the best thing for Matt, but his eyes were moist and he would never be absolutely certain.

As it was quite late I just went home and didn't take Matt's corpse back to the clinic. It was some way and I might have been called there anyway during the night. As it was I called in at Ramsbottom early in the morning and put the dead dog in the back yard where there was a pile of corpses waiting to be collected that morning by the knacker's men. In a busy week we might accumulate a dozen or so corpses from the various branches and they were all collected from Ramsbottom. I then left to get on with my morning rounds and visits.

I was on a hill farm later in the morning vaccinating some calves against contagious abortion, or Brucellosis, when the farmer's wife called me to the house to speak to the surgery. Apparently, a firm of pet undertakers had called to collect Matt for burial in the newly opened pet cemetery near Manchester. The Hargreaves had seen the advertisements in the local press and been persuaded to spend a considerable sum on a casket, service and gravestone with a contract to maintain the grave in a tasteful manner. The nurse on duty did not know which dog the driver should be given, so I described the black and white dog as best I could over the telephone and he was taken away to be prepared for burial.

One of the worst moments of my life was facing Mr and Mrs Hargreaves the following day. The old couple had gone by bus all the way to the pet chapel for Matt's interment service only to find a strange dog lying in the open casket. I can't imagine how they must have felt. Shortly after the undertakers had taken the dog from Ramsbottom, the remaining corpses, probably still including more than one black and white Collie-type, had been collected by the knacker's lorry and taken for processing. There was nothing that could be done to remedy the situation.

It was an unusually cold weekend in December with heavy falls of snow in the Western Pennines when I next had some time off. I had arranged to meet Lawrence Tennant at Knowsley Safari Park on the Saturday afternoon and I was very keen to hear more about Botswana. I drove down in the Nuts' Mini Countryman, and arrived about half an hour early. The snow, surprisingly for the low-lying Liverpool area, was quite thick on the ground in the Park where they had not cleared it from the roads. A selection of exotic antelopes seemed not to mind the wintry conditions, even though most of them must have been better suited to dry, sunny habitats. I drove around the extensive paddocks, reading the notices that indicated mainly African and Indian species. They seemed to be in good condition and feeding happily on the hay spread out on the snow. There were not many visitors, which wasn't surprising, and I enjoyed seeing the Park and the animals in such unusual circumstances.

I drove into the lion enclosure, which for obvious reasons was surrounded by a high security fence, to see how the big cats were coping. My first impression was that they appeared much more wide-awake than lions usually do in captive situations and they seemed to be actually enjoying the snow. They were romping around and playing in the manner of domestic cats. I stopped to watch. One or two seemed quite interested in my little pale blue car and came up close to investigate. A particularly large male with an impressive mane walked slowly around the Mini and rubbed against the corners as if he were a friendly tabby around my ankles. I felt far less secure when he approached the driver's door and gently pawed at the window close to my face, leaving a muddy smear. Next, he put a pair of huge forefeet on the tiny bonnet and peered down through the windscreen at me. I don't think he licked his lips, but it didn't need much imagination to visualise me as his next snack. I was never so relieved as when he seemed to lose interest after a few, very long seconds and dropped to the ground. Later, over a mug of steaming coffee in his office, I told Lawrence about my close shave with the lion. He seemed highly amused but, try as he might, I refused to be reassured that my tiny car was lion-proof.

As the Commonwealth Club had maintained, Lawrence confirmed that Botswana was indeed flat, dry bush, vast, empty of people and largely devoid of human artefacts such as roads, railways and fences. The Central Kalahari Game Reserve (CKGR), as big as Wales, teemed with all manner of wildlife, from springbok to giraffe and cheetah to lion – none of which had ever seen a Mini Countryman. Its only human inhabitants were a few hundred Bushmen. Developments were limited almost exclusively to a narrow belt of the country along the eastern border with South Africa where there were three or four small towns strung out along the country's only railway line. Only the capital, Gaborone, in the south, and Francistown, in the north, combined, boasted a total of three miles of tar roads. In the far north and west the wilderness of the Chobe and Okavango River systems was an unspoilt paradise, home to one of Africa's last great wildlife concentrations. Lawrence put into words dreams I had had since I was a small boy… space to breathe, adventures to live. My imagination was soaring as I drove back to Bolton in a tropical reverie.

The ODM was happy to recommend me to the government of Botswana for a post in the Veterinary Department, although they warned that they could not guarantee that I would be involved with wild animals. It was far more likely that I would be dealing with beef cattle, the mainstay of the economy and the target of much of Britain's aid programme. I would worry about that later, for now I just wanted to get back to Africa.

I left the Nuts in Ramsbottom just before Christmas, not without a pang of guilt. How would Peter cope with all the work on his own? He already had what is now called a 24/7 lifestyle and I had been equally busy – if not as productive. Young assistants were hard to come by, especially in industrial Lancashire. Rossendale found it hard to compete with either rural Gloucestershire or the bright lights of London and, despite my conscience, it stood absolutely no chance against the Okavango. After a festive seasonal round of goodbyes and almost two weeks at sea Jenny and I found ourselves disembarking from the good ship SA *Vaal* onto the quayside in sun-drenched Cape Town. Peter, no doubt, was turning up his collar in the drizzle as he dehorned another calf in wintry Ramsbottom.

The shipping office had a telegram waiting for me. It came from the Director of Veterinary Services in Botswana and instructed us not to get off the train in Gaborone, but to continue overnight to my posting in the village of Mahalapye, 120 miles further north. As Gaborone was already a day and a half away by train from Cape Town, the final leg of our journey, after eleven days at sea, was from Wednesday afternoon to Friday morning by steam-powered mail train across 1,000 miles of sun-drenched southern Africa.

THREE

BUSH VETERINARY OFFICER

The railway journey was relatively uneventful and extremely comfortable, with clean linen, excellent food and some entertaining fellow travellers in the bar. A majority of these (at least of the beer drinkers) were white Rhodesians on their way back home after Christmas holidays in Cape Town. Our destination provoked much mirth among these happy souls who claimed never to have seen anyone get off the train in Mahalapye. We passed through some spectacularly beautiful landscapes during the early part of our journey north through the Cape, but from waking up on Thursday morning the route traversed hundreds of miles of flat thorn bush, with little relief or variation, through the Northern Cape Province via Cecil Rhodes' famous diamond town of Kimberley, before crossing the border into Botswana at Mafeking during the evening. About 100 miles further on and late at night we passed through the tiny new capital, Gaborone, and continued to Mahalapye where the train stopped for water at 5.00 am on Friday morning.

None of the stations we had stopped at seemed to amount to much and there was none of the exotic, colourful commerce that had characterised the Ugandan railway stations, just concrete platforms with drab buildings and dusty surroundings. Kimberley and Mafeking, the setting for Baden-Powell's renowned siege during the Boer War, were a bit livelier, but not much. Mahalapye at dawn lacked any remarkable features, but I felt an excitement at finally arriving at a new chapter of my life. Jenny was not so keen. Her only comment was, "There isn't even a platform!"

As predicted, no one else alighted from the train and only a few passengers joined to travel north towards Francistown, Botswana's second biggest town.

Before the train had finished taking on water in a scene reminiscent of old Western movies, a battered Bedford pick-up truck pulled up next to where we were standing with our bags. As the dust cleared a cheerful sounding, middle-aged African man asked through the window if I was the new doctor. He seemed disappointed with my negative answer but cheered up immediately when I said I was a vet.

"Yes," he said. "I've come to pick you and take you to the hotel."

As we loaded our things into the back of the Bedford, Mr Marobela explained that he was the Senior Livestock Officer in charge of the district veterinary office and I was his new boss. Veterinarians in Africa, as in many places, are addressed as doctor, something it would take this Brit quite a while to get used to.

A short drive through the village on rough dirt roads, scattered with puddles from overnight rain, took us to the Chase-Me-Inn, a small hotel on the banks of the dry Mahalapye River. It consisted of a small central bar and separate dining room with some eight or nine rondavels around the grounds. These small, round buildings are ubiquitous in southern Africa and are either thatched or covered by a tin roof. They are usually bedrooms, sometimes with an en-suite bathroom. At 5.30 am the only sign of life was a nightwatchman who indicated that we should knock on the door of the nearest one to find the proprietor. He didn't seem too keen to do this – maybe he knew the owner's likely disposition so early in the morning. However, we knocked and were greeted from within by a growled instruction to enter. Jack Chase was still in bed and not overly sociable, but threw me a bunch of keys and told me to choose any unoccupied rondavel. Luckily the first one we tried was empty and Mr Marobela left us to unpack, saying he would "pick me" again at 7.30 am to take me to the office.

At 7.00 am we wandered up to the dining room and found breakfast being served to the only other guest. By happy coincidence he too was a vet, from Denmark but now on contract with Danish Aid to organise Botswana's artificial insemination (AI) service. He was on his way north to visit one of the AI camps under his management. He explained that farmers could take their cows to an AI camp and leave them there until they were pregnant by a bull of their choosing. The bulls belonged to the government and were of better quality than those available generally. It was one of many free services to cattle farmers.

Marobela took me to the district veterinary office, where I met the half dozen or so staff – secretary, cleaner, stores clerk, driver and three or four veterinary assistants (VAs). These last were the field staff who travelled the district vaccinating livestock and investigating reports of disease occurrence. There were ten VAs and a more senior stock inspector who worked under Marobela but several were out on field assignments. My arrival seemed to please everyone since the previous veterinary officer had left about nine months before. I hadn't the faintest idea what I was supposed to do and, although Marobela explained happily and enthusiastically, I thought I should at least telephone headquarters in Gaborone to report my arrival and arrange a briefing.

This proved more difficult than I had expected. The old-fashioned, wind-up telephone in the office was less than efficient and after about half an hour I had only managed to make contact with the local telephone exchange. The lady there was unable to put me through to Gaborone (or Gabs as everyone seemed to call it) and suggested I try on Monday morning. Marobela seemed happy with this, so who was I to argue. There was also an HF radio in the office with which to call HQ daily, but the schedule was at 7.30 am and Marobela said the radio had been broken for weeks anyway. I soon became resigned to this lack of urgency and fatalistic acceptance of breakdowns.

I was given a desk in an office all to myself and Marobela moved into another office shared with the stock inspector. We looked at the records of livestock disease incidence in the district. Names like anthrax, rabies, botulism, blackquarter and many others were familiar to me from college, although I had never actually come across them in my very limited clinical experience in Ramsbottom. It appeared that the next major task for the district team was a vaccination campaign to inoculate all the district cattle against anthrax – a free annual service to cattle owners. Mahalapye District (a subdistrict of Central District) is almost as big as Yorkshire and Lancashire combined, but largely without roads, and since we only had two Bedford pick-up trucks it would be quite an undertaking. My first day in the office gave me plenty to think about over the weekend.

Friday night at the Chase-Me-Inn was another eye-opener. After 5.00 pm the small bar filled with regulars bent on having a lively party. Almost without exception everyone was an expat. From behind the bar a much friendlier Jack Chase explained that Mahalapye was the headquarters of Rhodesia Railways in Botswana and that the majority of the revellers were railway employees who worked a "ten-day fortnight" in Botswana, returning to Bulawayo in Rhodesia for a four-day break every two weeks. These lively, hard-drinking folk included the stationmaster, workshop engineers and tradesmen of all types. There was also a sprinkling of British and South African expats holding posts at the small rural hospital and the two banks – Barclays and Standard Chartered. Botswana's population back then totalled only half a million people and qualified, skilled citizens were few and far between (only a small handful of university graduates existed at independence in 1966), so inevitably most senior positions in government and the private sector were occupied by expats.

The other Mahalapye expatriates numbered a couple of agricultural officers from the UK (including, surprisingly in a semi-desert country, a dairy technician), two American volunteers, a telephone technician and an older Canadian, who had volunteered to manage the government garage in the town after making his fortune running garages in Vancouver. The few other white residents were mainly of South African origin and involved in retail commerce or rearing cattle. As was and still is the case in many towns, the main storekeeper was of Indian origin, Goolam Arbi, who also played a prominent role in the tennis club, but otherwise did not engage socially very much.

By 9.00 pm the assistant manager of Standard Bank, Rob Hoets from Cape Town, was playing Beatles' songs on his guitar and everyone was howling along, and the drinks were still flowing. Mike Pyle, a railway engineer from Bulawayo and self-styled "182 pounds of fighting passion", interspersed with occasional rock 'n' roll favourites on his guitar to roars of approval and loud accompaniment. The party spilled over on to the veranda and made it pointless for anyone staying at the hotel to go to bed. Eventually a few couples shouted noisy goodbyes and made their way unsteadily to the car park – drinking and driving didn't seem to be an issue. Rob, Mike and a few bachelor diehards kept the momentum going until about midnight. Jack then decided that business at the bar had slackened off enough to close. The stragglers drifted off into the hot night, still clutching cans of Castle or Lion lager. It had been quite an introduction to Botswana and Jenny and I walked back to the rondavel in the now quiet night and slept like babies until early morning.

The world was soaking wet on Saturday morning. There had been a spectacular thunderstorm just before dawn, which I had been completely unaware of. January is the middle of southern Africa's rainy season but in Botswana this can be rather erratic. However, 1972 proved to be more than averagely wet and I learnt in my first few weeks that torrential tropical rain can play havoc with dirt roads. I determined that my first personal vehicle should be a Land Rover and arranged a government loan to buy one as soon as possible.

Our first weekend was spent happily getting to know a few of the town's residents over a succession of *braais* (barbecues) and ice-cold beers. In 1972, before the advent of Botswana currency, the price of a case of twenty-four cans was five South African rand, about three pounds then, and a single beer cost twenty-five cents at the bar. We were picked up after breakfast by Rob Hoets and given a tour of the Railway Club, the hospital, the tennis club, the two small banks, Tarr and Turk's garage and Goolam Arbi's general store near the station. There wasn't a lot more to see except for hundreds of traditional mud and thatch houses and winding, red, puddle-filled, dirt roads. Major features were the railway yards and workshops, full of steam engines, carriages and assorted vehicles. This was the domain of Ian Hayes, a sixtyish workshop manager from Bulawayo, who worked and partied very hard. He was undoubtedly the main protagonist when it came to the town's social life.

If an excuse could be found, usually at the end of a period of exceptionally hard work, he would declare a "Hayes Day". This could be any day of the week, but all of Rhodesia Railways' expat workforce would turn up at the pub at about nine in the morning and begin drinking and partying. This would go on for the whole day and many of the town's other more sociable inhabitants joined in these joyous occasions. One memorable Hayes Day was declared after the departure of senior management following a quarterly inspection. The party was in full swing by 11.00 am when the bosses returned because a bridge on the road north had been washed away. I feared for Ian's job but everyone was greatly relieved when the regional manager broke the uneasy pause by laughing and bellowing, "Drinks all round!"

The railway was central to life in Mahalapye, as were the Rhodesian staff who operated the workshops, offices and station. They must have numbered over fifty if families were included, by far the single largest component of the white expatriate community. A great event was the introduction of diesel engines on the Bulawayo to Mafeking line. This entailed much retraining of drivers, engineers and so on and disrupted the cosy ten-day fortnight routine. A computerised system for controlling the rolling stock was introduced. This was fraught with challenges in 1973 and the young Irishman charged with its installation and operation, Denis Coughlan, became a standing joke. In one move the management of Rhodesia Railways upgraded from the Morse code of Western movies to the only computerised system on the continent.

For many people this killed a great deal of the romance of the railways and even though a large number of freight trains were still pulled by steam engines, the gleaming new diesels marked the end of an era. Not that the new system made the trains any quicker or more punctual, they still suffered the problems of a single track system and frequently waited for hours in sidings for a train to pass in the opposite direction. Other delays affected the system too, such as weddings. The mail train to and from Cape Town twice a week was the flagship service and by far the best way to travel to that most beautiful of cities. As such it was occasionally used for honeymoon travel. On one famous occasion a full-scale wedding party, complete with band and bar, was taking place in Mahalapye station. It was an all-day affair and by the time the mail train pulled in late in the afternoon it had been in full swing for several hours. The music, dancing and drinking continued with many of the through passengers disembarking and joining the revelry. This delayed the train's departure but eventually the stationmaster managed to signal with whistle and flag and the steam engine pulled away in a huge white cloud – leaving behind the greater part of the train, from the buffet carriage back. It took quite some time for the engine and front part of the train to reverse and be re-coupled and meanwhile the party continued unabated. How this delay affected progress for the next 1,000 miles was never mentioned. Several wedding guests without tickets were dropped off at random stops south, such as Phala Road, Dibete and Artesia, but the happy couple made it all the way to Cape Town.

Jack Chase was a legendary character throughout Botswana. His father had been in the veterinary services of Bechuanaland Protectorate in the early 1900s, shortly after the Boer War. One of his tasks had been to vaccinate cattle in Ngamiland, in the far northwest, and an average vaccination campaign extended to at least six months. The service was based in Mafeking in the Northern Cape Province (Bechuanaland was unique in having its capital located outside its borders) and officers used to travel to Livingstone in Northern Rhodesia by train before crossing 500 miles of northern Bechuanaland by ox wagon to work in Ngamiland.

Jack grew up between the wars and joined the colonial service as a field officer in the Elephant Control Unit (the precursor of the Department of Wildlife and National Parks, DWNP). He was stationed near Francistown and was responsible for protecting farms from marauding elephants and other creatures, mainly lions. He joined the RAF at the outbreak of World War II and became a bomber pilot. He was shot down and taken prisoner, an event which the German forces probably regretted, since he caused more havoc in prison camps than his bombing raids ever did. Eventually he was repatriated via Sweden, where he made his mark by organising a huge party in Malmo's finest hotel. His father eventually paid for the band and the booze, but he told me "the girls worked for free".

One evening, during a busy session at the Chase-Me-Inn, a stranger asked if Jack was around. He claimed to owe Jack a favour from way back and had come from England to thank him. They had been prisoners of war together and the man had his twenty-first birthday in the camp. Somehow Jack had produced a bottle of champagne on the day and organised an unforgettable party. Jack was summoned and his old comrade produced his own bottle of champagne, which triggered a memorable celebration.

Life settled into a pleasant routine in Mahalapye, especially socially, with lots of tennis, beer and *braais*. The tradition of eating huge amounts of meat with copious alcoholic refreshment is a major feature of southern African hospitality. The men stand around the fire, often lit in half a forty-four-gallon drum, drinking beer or brandy and Coke, talking rugby, cricket or hunting, while the host grills a selection of meat over glowing charcoal. Heaps of thick steaks and *boerevors*, a spicy and exceptionally meaty sausage, are the heart of the meal. Chicken is often included, mainly as a concession to the women, who routinely segregate and prepare a selection of salads while discussing wider subjects. An habitual accompaniment is "pap" – boiled white maize meal served with an onion and tomato relish. This highly nutritious diet must be a factor in breeding the typical, giant Afrikaners who so often dominate world rugby tournaments. The flip side may be the national propensity to excessive blood triglyceride levels, resulting in a high incidence of heart attacks at a fairly young age. Nevertheless, *braais* remain extremely popular and the smell of meat over coals pervades most communities at weekends.

We became firm friends with the majority of the Mahalapye expats, both southern Africans and from further afield. They formed a lively if small community, fully self-sufficient in the absence of television, theatre and almost all other social entertainment and facilities. The Railway Club and the tennis club provided the main focus. The tennis courts were laid with material from the giant, red termite mounds that were so common in the bush. This was mixed with salt and a little sand and rolled out with copious watering. It made an excellent playing surface that Roland Garros would be proud of. One Wednesday afternoon the Deputy Director of Veterinary Services, Eddie

Bradley, called unexpectedly at my office on his way back to Gabs, only to be directed to the nearby tennis club. To be fair to him, although he disapproved he never brought it up again.

A local band played music with a strong 1960s flavour at occasional Railway Club dances. Rob Hoets and Mike Pyle were the core, aided by less accomplished musicians, such as Brian Frohlich (Jack Chase's son-in-law) and Dick Causton (the manager of Barclays Bank), on a tea-box bass and various percussion gadgets belting out Beatles, Rolling Stones and Rod Stewart standards. Every now and then, as a concession mainly to the Afrikaner farmers and their wives, a few *sakkie-sakkie* records would be played and they would take over the floor, dancing *langarm* in complete contrast to the contemporary styles. The club also housed the town's only swimming pool, a very popular feature and party venue.

Just outside town, along the dirt road heading east, was a golf course. Nine "fairways" connecting irregular clearings in the thorn bush where the "browns" – level areas of sand mixed with old engine oil – were situated. There was no clubhouse and the dilapidated fence allowed cattle to graze over the whole area. A few stalwarts played fairly regularly, with a cool box full of ice and beers on the back of their pick-up trucks or *bakkies*.

There were also occasional cricket matches, but their heyday was over. We could still raise a team, just, if we combined with the nearby towns of Palapye and Serowe and called ourselves Central District. About a year after I arrived we were invited to play a one-day match against Gaborone and I was drafted into the team to make up numbers, despite my complete lack of cricketing skill. We travelled the 120-odd miles of dirt road down to the capital in a collection of *bakkies* carrying our kit and the ubiquitous cool boxes. We arrived at the Gabs Golf Club on a Friday and spent a convivial evening at this well-appointed facility while we were introduced to the members and families who were going to host our players and companions. Gabs was a small town of single-storey buildings on dirt roads, with just a couple of miles of tar linking the centre with the railway crossing to the north. Reaching this on our way south was a major event, although Gaborone itself still could not be seen. Only the central shopping mall boasted any double-storey buildings, including the centrepiece President Hotel.

Jenny and I were billeted – along with Alistair Rutherford, our wicketkeeper, a large jovial agricultural officer from Northumberland – with a friendly South African couple whose home was in a nearby cul-de-sac. It was a typical four-bedroom detached bungalow with a garden lawn, a few shrubs and two dogs. A large friendly Rhodesian ridgeback bounded around the garden and a tiny Yorkshire terrier greeted us more suspiciously with high-pitched yapping.

We slept like logs and after a breakfast of toast and coffee drove to the cricket pitch at about 8.00 am. We won the toss and elected to bat. The difficulties of maintaining suitable grass in the near-desert environment necessitated the use of long mats as cricket wickets and the rest of the playing area was mainly sand, with an uneven distribution of coarse-grazed, short grass tufts. Even in Gabs the tell-tale spoor of the large greater kudu antelope was common in the red sandy soil.

We played as well as could be expected and although I didn't contribute to the score we managed a respectable total. Lunch was at 1.00 pm, after forty overs had been bowled. By then, our early batsmen had refreshed themselves, in a few cases excessively, from the numerous cool boxes. The picnic, provided by the host ladies, was accompanied by more cold beer. The Gabs team went out to bat at 2.30 pm and, although our two main bowlers had restrained themselves at lunch, won a comprehensive victory. The home side passed our total score with the loss of only two wickets in far fewer than forty overs.

A post-match party gained momentum and we returned to the golf club where the Central District team made up for our loss at cricket by inflicting defeat on our hosts at several drinking games. Alistair and I stayed to the bitter end, long after our hosts and Jenny had departed, and were taken home on the back of a *bakkie* crowded with extremely drunken cricketers.

We thought we knew where we were staying, but the layout of Gabs was quite repetitive and although we got to the right house it was in the wrong cul-de-sac. The occupants, not involved with either cricket match or golf club, were not amused by our noisy, boisterous group waking them in the wee small hours. They informed us that our hosts' bungalow was to be found in the same position but in the next street. Our approach to the correct address was more restrained and far quieter after our dressing down. We climbed off the *bakkie,* unsteadily opened the garden gate and peed in the bushes (a local tradition), despite the friendly, salivatory attention of the ridgeback. Alistair and I then entered the dark house as quietly as we could. A light had been left on in the bathroom by our thoughtful hosts and we managed to find our way without mishap to our respective rooms.

I was asleep in seconds and didn't hear a thing until Jenny shook me awake. It must have been just before dawn, about 4.00 am.

Alistair was standing by the bed. "Look!" he demanded in an agitated stage whisper, "Patterson, look! What am I going to do?"

I turned on the bedside light to see him holding a strangely still Yorkshire terrier. He had got up to use the bathroom and, returning to his bedroom in the dark, had felt that the door was hard to close, so pulled it quite hard. He swore he had heard nothing, but when he'd turned on the light had found he had trapped the dog's head. He didn't need a vet to tell him the animal was dead; its neck was clearly broken.

I tried to think of a plausible explanation for the tragedy, but the only suggestions either of us could come up with were hiding the corpse in his kit bag and pretending we knew nothing, or leaving it in the garden and blaming the ridgeback. Eventually sanity prevailed and Alistair plucked up the courage to face our hostess. We dressed as it was getting light and were in the kitchen when she surfaced. Alistair had placed the tiny dog on a cushion from the lounge. Her sheer disbelief and tearful hysteria roused her husband who, thankfully, was more understanding and able to calm her a little. Jenny made tea for everyone while Alistair and the grieving couple repeatedly went over the incident time and again. We had already packed our things and as soon as we were able to extract ourselves left on foot after refusing the unexpected, kind offer of a lift. Our relating of the episode was received with incredulity, manifested by gasps and giggles, from most of our team members and remained the focal point of accounts of that cricket weekend for years to come. Poor Alistair was paralysed with remorse, but some things are best left to fade; there was absolutely nothing he could do even to begin to remedy the state of affairs.

"Goldie" Goldstein and his best friend Louis Alberts were probably Mahalapye's most successful cattle farmers. They were both of South African origin and had become naturalised citizens of Botswana after independence in 1966. Goldie, whose nickname could also have referred to his sun-burnished skin, was in his early sixties and still lean, befitting the international sprinter he had once been. Louis, in his forties, was a typical Afrikaner, polite, stocky and very strong. They didn't own a farm, but raised stock in the traditional Tswana way with cattle posts. These were unfenced areas of bush (*veld*) centred around a borehole in the otherwise dry countryside. The grazing system was free range and the cattle mainly used an area of up to five miles from the borehole. West of Mahalapye the country was sandveld with sweet, nutritious grazing, as long as you could find water. Goldie and Louis had cattle posts near a village called Shoshong, some twenty miles west of town. They bred mainly local Tswana-type indigenous cattle, usually crossed with a Brahman bull. This provided a combination of hardiness, good mothering and fairly rapid growth. Alistair, a cattleman who had previously worked in Kenya, was continually impressed by the long-legged Tswana cattle and was very enthusiastic about their potential. Goldie and Louis lived with their families in Mahalapye and had other business interests, but their cattle posts were their main love and livelihood. They were constantly driving *bakkies* out of town overloaded with rations, stockfeed and drums of diesel for the borehole pump. They often spent nights out, sleeping in blankets around the fire at the cattle post. They were both fluent in Setswana and socialised like benign chiefs with the herd-boys who looked after the cattle in their absence.

They both knew far more than me about treating local cattle maladies and I learnt a lot on my occasional and thoroughly enjoyable visits to their cattle posts, particularly about traditional cattle husbandry on the edge of the Kalahari Desert. Those crisp, cold nights on the sand around the fire, wrapped in blankets and listening to the plaintive screaming of black-backed jackals still rank as some of the most evocative images of those early days in the bushveld. We always came across numerous herds of game, mainly red hartebeest and gemsbok, and at Lebung Pan there were always springbok and occasionally giraffe. The cattle had thinned out and ended by then because there was only ephemeral seasonal surface water between there and the Central Kalahari Game Reserve (CKGR). Bushmen workers at the scattered cattle posts told me that it was about three days to the game reserve – *ka dinao* – on foot.

On one Sunday afternoon Goldie and I were on our way back to Mahalapye and had a second puncture, and no spare wheel. We also had no pump. But Goldie, a real-life *MacGyver*, fixed the tube, then removed the overflow pipe from the radiator and managed to inflate the tyre sufficiently by using some air from each of the three good wheels. We got back late, on soft tyres, but we made it.

Two years in Mahalapye were fun and hard work with a great bunch of friendly people to learn from. Apart from local animal husbandry, there was the new vegetation, birds and wildlife. Although large wild animals had been largely depleted around the centres of human settlement there were still scattered pockets of bush that harboured such creatures as impala, kudu and ostrich. Black-backed jackal and steenbok, a tiny, delicate and beautiful antelope, were ubiquitous. So many varieties of birds of all hues, with an amazing number of raptors – eagles, hawks and vultures – could be seen daily in the skies and the bush. Guinea fowl and francolin constantly crossed the track in front of our vehicles.

One of my responsibilities was to supervise the Dibete quarantine station, one of a series around the country as part of the foot and mouth disease (FMD) control strategy. Dibete, about fifty miles south of Mahalapye, was the last in the series of quarantine camps from Makalamabedi in Ngamiland, via Francistown, which culminated in the Lobatse export abattoir. Cattle destined for the abattoir from Central District had to be kept for twenty-one days in the quarantine camp. They were inspected, or "mouthed", as they entered and again before they left. These inspections took place at the crush, a structure of parallel gum poles approximately twenty yards long with a narrow passage in between. The cattle were driven into the crush by a gang of labourers who packed them in tightly, herring-bone style, often by biting their tails. The vet then walked down past their heads, inspecting the tongues for blisters or other incriminating lesions. A couple of assistants would precede the vet, opening the mouths and pulling out the tongues. It was a very well-practised procedure and hundreds of cattle were checked in a few hours. Cleared cattle were then loaded on trains at Dibete station.

The Tuli Block, a strip of fenced freehold ranches in the Limpopo River Valley was a major beef producing area. The strip runs about 200 miles from north to south and averages about twelve miles – or one farm – wide from the Limpopo River, which is the country's border with South Africa. A dirt road about fifty miles long, going due east from Mahalapye, hits the middle of the block near a small village called Machaneng. Most farms were owned by Afrikaner farmers, a neat irony, because the land had been set aside around the time of the Boer War as a barrier to the expansion of the Afrikaner Transvaal Republic into Bechuanaland.

The farmers were very hospitable and phenomenally hard working and made a great success of raising their hardy cattle in the African bush. These cattle were sold to the parastatal Botswana Meat Commission (BMC) which ran the country's only authorised export abattoir in the small town of Lobatse, tucked away in the southeastern corner of Botswana. This entailed trucking them to Mahalapye and loading them on railway trucks for the 200-mile journey south. Their beef usually scored a *super* or *prime* grading, necessary for export to Europe under a preferential trade agreement. Cattle-post beef on the other hand usually didn't make these grades and was sold regionally at much lower prices. Because these ranch cattle were more valuable and the ranchers more professional I was frequently called out to Tuli Block to deal with problems and to help with breeding programmes by testing the bulls for fertility and the cows for pregnancy. On the freezing cold early mornings of June and July it wasn't unpleasant to spend a few hours with my arm deep inside a couple of hundred cows' rear ends.

The extensive form of ranching practised in Tuli Block (the paddocks, or camps, were normally at least two miles square) allowed space and habitat for quite large wildlife populations. Impala, blue wildebeest and kudu were the most common, but several other species could be encountered. These animals were largely tolerated, or even encouraged, by most of the ranchers, even though they competed with the cattle for grazing. Hunting was a way of life, especially for the production of biltong, the South African dried meat delicacy. Each farmer would have his own recipes for biltong and dried sausage and these formed a local social currency.

Visits to Tuli Block were some of the highlights of my work in Mahalapye, providing highly enjoyable breaks from the office. The frequently enormous Afrikaners were amused to find a diminutive Englishman in their midst at social occasions and I was constantly the butt of good-natured jests that reflected the huge disparity in our cultures and differences in our languages. Food was nearly always buffet-style, tables packed with all kinds of meat and vegetable dishes, many new to me. As an honoured guest I was always forced to be first in line and at one early birthday party I poured a brown sauce over my food, mistaking it for gravy. I gamely ate my way through a large plateful of steak and vegetables covered in chocolate! This produced a polite bemusement at first – maybe all *Engelsmanne* ate like this – followed by mass hysterical laughter at my embarrassment. Their almost religious devotion to rugby, brandy and biltong though wasn't so far from my northern English background of soccer, beer and pies. Religion played an enormous part in most of their lives. They were usually members of the Dutch Reformed Church, a Calvinistic faith akin to the strictest Scottish Presbyterian congregations. No matter how raucous the party, music and dancing ceased at midnight on Saturdays.

I managed to get further afield occasionally and these working safaris were undoubted highlights of my time in Mahalapye. Once I accompanied Ian Carmichael (more of him later!), an Australian vet who was attached to the disease investigation lab in Gaborone, on a field trip to the Chobe enclave in the far north. This meant travelling via Bulawayo and Victoria Falls in Rhodesia and re-entering Botswana at the confluence of the Chobe and Zambezi Rivers at Kazungula, because there was no road connection between Francistown and Chobe.

We spent a pleasant night at Greys Inn in Bulawayo and the next day travelled 300 miles north to Victoria Falls along a strip road, a big improvement on the corrugated dirt roads in Botswana. First used in the mid-thirties these roads consisted of two parallel strips of tar, each about a yard wide. Vehicles simply kept one wheel on each strip and happily drove along. It was a cheap and effective answer to road construction given the sparse traffic. When meeting an oncoming vehicle the drivers just shifted left and passed each other occupying only the nearside strip. In the 1970s these roads were still the main component of Rhodesia's communications and were the best roads in Southern Africa outside of South African highways.

Victoria Falls always takes the breath away at first sight and I was no exception. With hardly any tourists in those days it was free to enter and explore the Falls park – and absolutely awe inspiring. We spent the night in the well-appointed National Parks' campsite there and carried on to Kazungula border post early on the next day. Kasane, about eight miles upstream was a tiny, quiet backwater, with one general store and the Chobe River Hotel, which was being "upgraded" and re-opened as Chobe Safari Lodge at the time. We stocked up on beer and food supplies and headed west along the river bank through the newly proclaimed Chobe National Park.

The rough, winding dirt road followed the river bank where it could and descended into the floodplain at times, but there were also many stretches of fairly straight "improved" surface 100 or so yards back from the edge. Game was plentiful, especially the graceful kudu and impala. We saw the beautifully marked Chobe bushbuck several times, especially in the eastern section. These are completely gone from the park now because their habitat, the riverine woodland and understorey, has been removed by elephants. Ironically, they are still common in the privately owned plots and gardens along the river outside the park, including the large hotel grounds and the golf course that has replaced the old airstrip near the Kasane rapids.

I saw my first Botswana hippos, but only a few elephants, although giraffe were plentiful, especially around Serondela, where there was an abandoned sawmill. A few small herds of puku on the floodplain were also a first for me. It took several hours to reach Ngoma, the western park gate which was marked by a huge, hollow baobab tree that it was claimed had been used as a jail cell in previous times. The western section of the park was steeper and the sand largely gave way to rough stones, with many small, steep gullies to cross. There were many zebra, mainly on the floodplains, sometimes accompanied by red lechwe, which had apparently replaced the puku of further east – I wondered why. What were the ecological factors separating the two (to me anyway) very similar species? Also on the floodplains were some cattle, apparently across the border in Caprivi, but as the border seemed to be a narrow, very winding channel with many ox-bow lagoons they were occasionally within a few yards of the Botswana bank. The enclave was populated exclusively by Subiya people in a number of villages with their distinct thatched houses. They farmed cattle, but could not move them through the National Park to any southern markets because of FMD restrictions. Consequently the people were quite poor and relied on hunting and fishing for their livelihoods. A couple of Greek Cypriot-owned trading posts were the only signs of commerce.

We met up with a local stock inspector and his team in their Bedford truck and wandered about from village to village in the enclave, by vehicle when we could, and by dug-out mokoro to Satau and others when we couldn't drive. Although completely surrounded by the Park and the international border, the area had no official conservation status. It was a beautiful area with a striking escarpment overlooking huge floodplains shared with the Caprivi Strip in Southwest Africa (now Namibia). The fringes of the floodplains were covered with spectacular umbrella-thorn Acacia trees, bigger than I had seen in East Africa. Some of the cattle at the villages were suffering from streptothricosis or rain scald and apparently this wasn't previously documented in Botswana. However, it's a common worldwide disease with effective treatment by antibiotics and/or various management interventions like isolation and therefore Ian was able to advise the communities accordingly. After a fascinating few days in an extremely remote and spectacular area we made our long way back home again via Rhodesia.

I enjoyed another break from routine in mid-1972 when I was invited to attend a short course in wildlife immobilisation at the National Zoological Gardens in the South African capital Pretoria, a very Afrikaans city. One evening Jenny and I decided to see a film at the cinema, or *bioscope*, just across the road from our hotel. Unusually it was an English language film. We bought two tickets and made our way into the foyer and towards the door to the auditorium/*ouditorium* with its bilingual sign. A huge man, resplendent in a uniform befitting a South American general, stopped me and held out his hand.

"Car keys, *asseblief* (please)" I heard him say. He apparently wanted to park my car. I shook my head and said we didn't have a car and tried to pass him. He then moved in front of me again and repeated "Car keys!" a little more forcefully. Again, I said no and tried to get past him. Again he stopped me.

"Look," I said, "we just walked from across the road, I don't have a car!" I was becoming impatient with the giant and a small queue was developing behind us. Just then another filmgoer touched my arm and said, "He wants your tickets." *Kaartjie* (literally, little card and pronounced car key) is Afrikaans for ticket!

I stammered a thank you and handed the "General" my tickets. He ostentatiously tore them in half, handed me the stubs and then stepped aside to let us into the auditorium.

Back in Mahalapye life continued pleasantly enough through 1973, though it proved to be a drier year than the previous one. I had to get to grips with my neglected station and the more mundane duties of a veterinary officer in Africa. Files, duty rosters, stores queries, vehicle maintenance and personnel grievances made up most of my daily chores, enlivened by visits to investigate disease problems, mainly in the Tuli Block farms. Our house was just across the road from the railway stockyards and main line from Bulawayo to Mafeking. Cattle were loaded onto boxcars and waited for the southbound freight trains to deliver them to the abattoir in Lobatse. Their bellowing and the steam locomotives combined in a cacophony that gradually became a discordant, but somehow soothing background to home life.

Agreeable as life in Mahalapye was, I had no training or aptitude for office administration and after about six months I was summoned to Gaborone and given a dressing down and pep talk by the Director of Veterinary Services, Jack Falconer, a no-nonsense Aberdonian who had been there since before independence.

In a broad Scots accent Jack intoned, "Ye're a Veterinary Officer laddie and I'll thank ye to concentrate more on the office part."

I told him respectfully that I hadn't spent five years at vet school to fill out requisition forms for stationery and office cleaning materials and he could expect me to serve only my minimum two-year contract. We never really hit it off after that.

Fortunately there had been no detected FMD outbreaks for a few years. Whenever the disease was discovered the country's exports of beef to the lucrative European market were suspended until the outbreak was extinguished.

With no veterinarians of its own, Botswana relied upon expatriates, mainly provided by the UK, to keep the beef industry profitable. It could take many months before export approval was granted again and this had severe economic implications, mainly for the large commercial farmers, but with widespread trickle-down effects on most of the population. Apart from the economic aspect, cattle were extremely important socially and the Batswana people were almost without exception pastoralists. The vast majority of civil servants would decamp to their cattle posts on Friday afternoons, returning to the towns for work on Monday mornings. Far more cattle were kept under this free-range, extensive, communal system than were on commercial, fenced farms, which accounted for only five per cent of the land.

Already in the early 1970s this was becoming an environmental concern. In dry or drought years there was pressure from cattle owners to move their stock into new areas. Boreholes were drilled by the government to provide year-round water in hitherto seasonal grazing areas. This resulted in overgrazing and seriously affected the wildlife populations in those regions. In the Mahalapye District this meant that cattle posts expanded westwards towards the CKGR into areas previously only inhabited by Bushmen, who kept no livestock. Both the presence of new settlements and the activities of domestic stock had negative impacts on the environment. Although the new boreholes were initially designated as emergency measures for temporary use until the drought abated, they inevitably became permanent features and by the early 1980s the area between Mahalapye and the game reserve had become saturated with cattle posts. Grazing incursions into the reserve itself became common. Wildlife, such as the large herds of red hartebeest, springbok, gemsbok and blue wildebeest, which we frequently came across in the 1970s, pretty much disappeared outside the reserve.

Almost everyone owned at least a few cows. Consequently the Ministry of Agriculture provided all kinds of subsidies to the industry, from free vaccinations and veterinary care to artificial insemination services, boreholes and compensation in adverse drought spells. FMD vaccinations were limited to Ngamiland, but there were countrywide campaigns against anthrax and other diseases annually which took up a great deal of my time around Mahalapye.

Rabies was also prevalent and keeping the stray dog population down was an important factor in controlling the disease. Organising a rabies vaccination campaign meant informing the public in Mahalapye village and the District that there would be a "tie-up order" enforced on a particular date. For a couple of weeks prior to this the villagers were notified to bring their dogs to the vet office for vaccination and a dab of bright blue paint. After suitable notice all dogs not tied up and painted blue on the due date were shot. Firing an old single-barrelled shotgun in the confines of busy village streets was not for the faint hearted. For some reason we were only issued cartridges with light bird-shot, probably to encourage us to shoot only from close range to avoid accidents. I managed a reasonable success rate with only a few minor issues with stray pellets hitting pretty dilapidated motor cars, causing little or no damage.

Black-backed jackals were very common and extremely difficult to deal with. It was believed that they were the main reservoir of rabies virus and spread it by biting other species, mainly dogs, who killed them, but also other animals including cattle. I quickly learnt that rabies in cattle was usually not the well-known "furious" type, but the less easily diagnosed "dumb" type that often presented as a hind-end paralysis with the animal lying down. It could easily be mistaken for other conditions, notably botulism which was common because livestock would often chew bones owing to the chronic potassium deficiency in the Kalahari sand soils.

This was not always the case though and one afternoon I was called to the local agricultural station at Morale, a few miles south of town, because a bull appeared to have gone berserk. It had demolished a small building, turned over a tractor and was chasing people. I took my government-issue shotgun and some shells and drove there. The bull, a large Brahman cross-breed, was standing in a sandy kraal bellowing. I loaded the shotgun and walked cautiously towards it. It seemed not to notice me at first and I fired into the side of its skull from about three yards away, hoping I might hit the brain. It immediately turned and chased me through the sand towards the fence, which I vaulted, dropping the gun in the process. The bull merely pushed the fence down, but luckily I managed to scramble into a convenient, large thorn tree and get just high enough to be out of reach. The bull stood below me, within arm's reach bellowing and salivating. I managed to persuade an assistant sitting in my truck to venture out and retrieve the shotgun. He was then able to skirt around and approach my tree slowly from the other side without being seen by the bull. I got him to throw the shotgun and was able to catch it at the first attempt as he scampered away back to the truck.

I manoeuvred into a position that allowed me to fire into the bull's forehead from just a few inches away. It dropped to the sand, but got up again as if nothing had happened and continued bellowing as before just below me. Knowing my ammunition was merely light bird-shot I repeatedly fired at exactly the same spot on the bull's head four or five times. After I had "drilled" a hole in its skull in this manner the next shot put it down again and I jumped out of the tree and quickly shot it again at point blank range in the back of the skull, a much more vulnerable target, which had the desired effect. Despite all my warnings to the contrary the bull was cut up and eaten long before I was able to confirm a diagnosis of rabies at the laboratory. I learnt very quickly that meat in almost any form or condition was something that Batswana valued more than almost anything.

This episode earned me my second dressing down. According to the official bulletins Botswana was free of rabies – quite amazing really, considering it was surrounded by countries full of it. The only person who was allowed to report such cases was the Director, certainly not a very junior VO. It didn't help our already taxed relationship when I and another young veterinarian suggested that the reported absence of some infectious diseases might be due to the fact that there were precious few vets out there looking for them because they were all in the office most of the time.

One Saturday afternoon I was called from the tennis club because a motorist had collided with an ostrich on the dirt road south to Gaborone. His Land Rover was only slightly damaged but the bird had reportedly sustained a broken leg and was lying in the road. I drove about fifteen miles south towards Phalla Road, going quite fast, when a Mercedes saloon car approached at very high speed travelling north. Moving vehicles create dust clouds in their wake on dirt roads and these can be very large and dense at high speed. The Merc flashed past immersing me in an opaque red soup of dust and sand. I naturally applied brakes and tried to slow down without losing control on the loose road surface, but before I knew it there was a mighty bang and I struggled to keep a straight line as I came to a stop. I got out as the dust cleared somewhat to find that I had collided with a group of cattle.

Although, thankfully, I was unhurt my Land Rover was in a sorry state and obviously unable to be driven further. Three cows were dead and a fourth had two obviously broken legs. I took my shotgun again and put it out of its misery. Luckily I didn't have to wait too long in the midst of the carnage until a vehicle came by and gave me a lift back to town, but by then people had already magically appeared from the surrounding bush in numbers showing great excitement at the bonanza. By the time I returned with some friends to tow my vehicle there was scarcely more than a few piles of green-brown stomach contents and some bloodstains in the sand. My Land Rover was duly dispatched to Johannesburg by rail for repairs and I was relegated to a government-issue Bedford pick-up truck for the next few weeks. I never found out what happened to the ostrich, but it probably went the same way as the cattle.

This wasn't my only bovine accident. About a year later I was driving south down the main road to Gaborone for a meeting and saw a group of about half a dozen cattle in the road far ahead. There was no other vehicle in sight so I didn't slow down much, just hooted as I got closer to them, thinking that I could easily avoid them as they moved off. Unfortunately a couple of younger animals decided to play-fight and one skipped back into my path whereupon my Land Rover collected another "trophy". The front bumper was bent and the radiator was damaged and leaking badly, so I was going nowhere. The young bull seemed relatively unscathed and had disappeared into the bush. I still had almost fifty miles to go.

Luckily, not much later, another Land Rover appeared travelling in the same direction. The driver stopped and got out to see if he could help. It was Dave Gollifer, the head of the small agricultural college at Sebele on the outskirts of Gaborone (now the Botswana University of Agriculture and Natural Resources). We knew each other, but not well. It was decided that he would tow me and he produced a rope with which we duly attached my vehicle to the back of his, giving less than five yards of space. My bonnet clip had broken so I tied it shut with a small length of string. We set off down the corrugated sand road at a fairly sedate pace and I estimated that we would arrive in about two hours. Almost imperceptibly our speed increased until we were travelling at about 50mph, at which speed I was a little nervous about whether I would be able to stop if Dave braked suddenly, especially as his vehicle was churning up a lot of dust severely reducing my visibility. As there didn't seem to be much likelihood of this happening on the straight, deserted road, I relaxed a bit, until my bonnet suddenly flew up and became lodged against the windscreen. The string had broken and I could now see nothing except the vertical bonnet! Dave was apparently oblivious to my perilous situation as we kept on travelling at the same speed. I thought of hooting, but decided it might make him brake and I wouldn't be aware of it, with disastrous results. I was frankly terrified and at a loss for ideas, so just kept on steering and hanging on. Even if he noticed through the dust what had happened I wasn't sure what he would do. This alarming state of affairs carried on for what seemed like ages and I desperately tried to think of a solution.

Looking out of the side window I began to see that we were approaching Gaborone, so I decided to brake as hard as I could, hoping that the tow rope might break or the sudden deceleration might cause the bonnet to fall back into place. Neither happened but Dave finally noticed what was going on and responded to the extra drag by putting his vehicle in neutral and allowing me to bring us both to a halt. It was a piece of very bright thinking on his part and probably the only way a serious accident could have been avoided. As we stopped I jumped out, a nervous wreck, and we pulled down the bonnet and refastened it before continuing at a slower speed for the remaining few miles.

FOUR

BUFFALO FUN AT SAVUTI

By far the most enjoyable interlude during my time as Mahalapye Veterinary Officer began in August 1972 when I was asked to join a team of vets and technicians who were going to the far northwest of the country to test buffalo for FMD. This would be a six-week safari into the vast Chobe National Park and the Okavango Delta. We were to base ourselves in Savuti and immobilise buffalo to take clinical samples for testing at the World Foot and Mouth Disease Reference Laboratory at Pirbright in Surrey, England. While we vets sampled the buffalo a team from DWNP would also collect information on the animals, especially tagging them to try to establish their seasonal movements. It sounded like an opportunity of a lifetime to me and definitely too good to miss!

Botswana's beef exports were continually at risk of being closed down because of outbreaks of FMD. The disease is comparatively innocuous in Africa, but extremely contagious under European conditions and can cause economically devastating epidemics. It was known that African buffalo harboured the virus, showing no symptoms, and could possibly infect cattle under certain conditions, giving rise to damaging outbreaks of the disease. The evidence for this in Botswana was almost completely circumstantial and based on the fact that most FMD outbreaks originated in the northwest of the country, where the buffalo population was found and where they might come into contact with cattle. The situation needed more thorough investigation.

Savuti is a shallow marsh in the southwestern section of Chobe National Park, about 100 miles north of the regional capital Maun. Fed by a channel from the Linyanti Swamp on Botswana's northern border with the Caprivi Strip in Namibia, the marsh is approximately twenty miles long and ten miles wide, but it's not always like that. It can be much longer (never much wider) or it can be completely dry, sometimes for years at a time. Nowadays it is renowned as one of Africa's premier wildlife tourism destinations, but in 1972 there were no tourists – just wildlife. I was thrilled beyond words. Jenny was less enthusiastic and decided a six-week camping trip in the remote bush was not for her. So I packed my Land Rover and set off, taking the main, dirt road from Mahalapye parallel with the railway line to Francistown where I spent the night with Senior Livestock Officer Ken Ward and his wife Beryl.

Ken was a Cornishman, a World War II veteran and an experienced Africa hand, mainly in Malawi. He had become my mentor and, although officially I was ranked above him, he guided and advised me from afar. He extricated me from a number of difficult situations, rather like a benevolent sergeant major with an inexperienced lieutenant. Most notably, he came to the rescue when my poor performance at office matters had come to a head and the Mahalapye Veterinary Office was to be subjected to a stocktaking inventory.

Apparently I should have completed an inventory on taking over the station from the previous veterinary officer, or in my case Marobela, who had been in charge for nine months before I arrived and had managed to avoid taking responsibility for anything. I panicked when I discovered how much was missing from the previous inventory a couple of years previously and what it might cost me if I was surcharged. Items listed as being in the stores, but which could not be found, included tents, groundsheets, shovels, brushes, buckets and even an anvil! Marobela suggested I contact Ken, who would surely know what to do.

Ken duly caught the train down from Francistown and the three of us spent a whole day with scissors and saws creating two buckets from one and two or even three groundsheets from one. The really impossible missing items, such as the anvil, were listed as being in a "missing" fourth fitted cupboard, which was an obvious typing error as there was one in each of the three offices. Amazingly, this brilliant bit of imaginative accounting was accepted by the stock verifiers on their visit the following week.

Ken's many talents included playing the piano to concert standards and we spent a pleasant evening with music and an excellent dinner before I left early the next morning to head west for Maun and the Okavango Delta.

This was a new and exciting adventure along a very straight, wide, sand and gravel road almost devoid of traffic, nothing going my way and only a couple of five-ton government trucks heading east. One exception was a "bush-drag". This simple but effective method of maintaining a relatively smooth and corrugation-free surface was widely used on Botswana's dirt roads. A tractor pulling a large thorn tree scraped the road surface and created a huge plume of reddish dust that could be a serious hazard when trying to pass it, inevitable if you wanted to proceed at more than a tractor's snail-pace. The first 100 miles was largely similar to the road to Francistown from Mahalapye, but flatter. There were patches of mixed woodland, but mainly the road traversed mopane forests. This tree covers vast areas of northern Botswana in a kind of monoculture, but it can vary from short scrub to tall "cathedral" woodland, probably owing to differences in soils and drainage.

About eighty miles out I came to a veterinary cordon fence, Dukwe, with a couple of cheerful veterinary assistants sitting outside a tin hut, manning the gate. Nearby was the quarantine station where any cattle from further west were held for three weeks and checked for FMD before they could continue on to the railhead at Francistown. No checks were required going west, but they were glad to see me and their only enquiry was the usual request for *motsoko* (tobacco).

Just before the village of Nata the landscape opened up into flat grassland, punctuated with groves of *Hyphaene* fan palm trees. On the left was the northern end of Sua Pan, a huge salt pan stretching over 100 miles to the south and linked to the west with another massive salt pan called Ntwetwe. These, and dozens of smaller pans with the intervening grasslands are the Makgadikgadi, which, together with hundreds of square miles of grass plains to the west, formed the Makgadikgadi Pans Game Reserve, now upgraded to national park status. This enormous uninhabited area, enclosed in the far west by the Boteti River, abounded with large herds of zebra, blue wildebeest, gemsbok and springbok. For spectacle it rivalled the famous Serengeti, far to the north in Tanzania, but was largely unknown outside Botswana. The main road crossed the northern edge of this magnificent wilderness and even from here herds of wildlife were a common sight. Ostriches, also numerous, frequently raced the Land Rover along the road before peeling off into the plains.

Nata was a small, scruffy village with a mixture of traditional thatched huts and a few brick or block-built dwellings scattered under palm trees mostly along the west bank of a dry riverbed, across which was a low, pot-holed, concrete causeway. All the rivers in Botswana, apart from the Chobe and Okavango are seasonal, mainly ephemeral, flowing only for a few days after heavy rains. In the village there was one trading store, part of a chain owned by R.A. Bailey based in Palapye, and nothing else of note. After Nata was another 100 miles of unbroken plains, palm trees and salt pans before woodland began to close in on either side. The huts of the small village of Gweta and another R.A. Bailey store were clustered among a few islands of palm trees and stunted mopane about halfway along this stretch. The final 100 miles before Maun followed the unseen Boteti River, half a mile or so away to the left. A few small settlements became evident, mainly through the appearance of thin, straggling cattle, small herds of goats and numerous donkeys. I saw no wildlife on this stretch. About thirty miles before Maun I came across a large manned gate across the road and a sign proclaiming the Makalamabedi Veterinary Cordon Fence. Here I was required to stop and sign a register before being allowed into Ngamiland proper.

Vehicles coming the other way were subjected to searches for meat and fresh animal products, none of which were allowed out of Ngamiland because of FMD restrictions. Travellers sometimes complained of abuses, such as corned beef being removed from sandwiches and the bread being handed back. Even eggs and canned meats might be confiscated, a ludicrous state of affairs that lingers on today. Whether it's the result of poor training or a scam to obtain free food is still hotly debated by regular travellers and lots of modern tourists, some of whom go to elaborate lengths to hide items and outwit the gate guards. Honest veterinarians will tell you that the measures are now mainly a public relations exercise, but in the 1970s they were very serious.

The last hour into Maun was uneventful; more straight, flat, dusty road and a parade of small hamlets with their attendant livestock.

About eight hours after leaving Francistown, with a short break under a giant baobab tree to eat Beryl's sandwiches, I found myself on a short downhill slope towards a concrete bridge over the Thamalakane River. The deep, green, slow-moving water, fringed with reedbeds and decorated with hundreds of colourful water-lilies, was the most delightful scene after 300 miles of dusty driving on an almost dead straight road. Most of Maun lay on the opposite, western bank and crossing the bridge for the first time was a defining moment for me. This river, flowing along a fault line that represented the most southern element of Africa's Great Rift, symbolically separated the northern wonderland of lush, green, truly tropical wild Africa, with its incomparable and spectacular biodiversity, from the drabber, monotonous and often adulterated land to the south. I had heard so much about Ngamiland, especially the Okavango Delta, and I couldn't wait to start exploring and experiencing it for myself.

I slowly traced my way through Maun's confusion of sandy tracks, past the post office, a few small stores and a Shell petrol station next to the historic Riley's Hotel, to the offices of the Veterinary Department. At first sight, this shambolic, oversized village was a disappointment. Mainly consisting of hundreds of traditionally built mud and thatch huts, most, it seemed, in various degrees of dilapidation, it was crowded, scruffy and chaotic. Scrawny yellow dogs and scores of oblivious donkeys wandered everywhere. Away from the boma, a collection of government offices and houses, very few brick or more substantial buildings were evident. The boma itself consisted mostly of offices for the District Commissioner, police, agriculture, tsetse fly control and the Game Department – and the half-dozen old colonial-style bungalows along the river bank that housed the senior officers, all expatriates.

The river bank was a revelation – so many huge trees, in complete contrast to the vast areas of bushveld that made up most of Botswana. In the gardens were beautiful specimens of flamboyants, jacarandas, frangipani and other exotic species, which, if ecologically questionable by today's standards, gave a vivid, tropical boost to the local environment. Indigenous species like jackalberry, leadwood, mopane, knobthorn and crotons were also much bigger than elsewhere. The river itself was flanked with tall reedbeds, busy with birds and laced with colourful lilies. From my Uganda days I immediately recognised the piercing cry of the fish eagle, but apart from the colourful jacana, or lily-trotter, and the pied kingfishers, the myriad other birds were a fascinating mystery.

At the office I met Norbert Drager, a slim, blond, earnest German, a few years older than me. He was a research veterinarian, mainly concerned with rabies, and a very keen and knowledgeable wildlife enthusiast who had travelled overland from Europe with a stint in Kenya as a veterinary officer. He had been put in charge of the buffalo sampling exercise. After a brief introduction to the office and staff he took me to his house for tea with his Scottish wife Kate. The Dragers took me under their wing immediately and Kate made me feel completely at home. She was a former airhostess with BOAC and had met Norbert in Kenya. Her generous and exuberant personality belied her Aberdonian origins and she ran a lively, friendly and very welcoming home.

That evening they took me out for supper at AfAm Safaris, a rustic lodge on the east bank of the river a few miles upstream outside town, with the fabled

Crocodile Camp next door. These two casual bars formed the basis of expat social life in Maun. There was also Riley's Hotel in the middle of town, but that was more raucous and somewhat run-down. Otherwise, folks ate and entertained at home, but in a less South African and more European style than in the southern towns I knew. This was undoubtedly because there were very few South Africans in Maun in those days.

AfAm, short for African American Safaris, consisted of a large open-fronted bar cum dining room with a gently sloping sandy bank down to the river. Local reeds figured prominently in its construction and the roof of the bar and other buildings was thatch. Tony Graham, the manager, was a cheerful, chain-smoking, ruddy-faced character of about forty. He had earned some money as a mercenary in the Congo troubles and, rather than return to his native South Africa, had decide to invest in Botswana. He was building a fairly substantial lodge of his own across the river, about 400 yards upstream, to be called Island Safari Lodge. In the meantime, mainly to have a place to live, he was running AfAm. He was married to a tall Englishwoman, an ex-model, whom he claimed to have met in the Caribbean. Yolande (Yoey) Graham gave the impression that she was from a well-to-do background, but never elaborated. Tony was a practical guy who could build, plumb, weld and fix most things electrical or mechanical. He was also a convivial host who joined in drinking and storytelling with the customers, most of whom he knew well because Maun was a fairly small community. There were few tourists, but Tony was adamant that there would be an explosion in numbers in the near future and hence his investment in a new lodge. How right he was.

The next day our team gathered for the final preparations for our exercise. The timing was crucial for a number of reasons. At the office Norbert explained that, towards the end of the dry season, the buffalo population would be concentrated in a few places that provided water. Prime among these was the Savuti Marsh, which, with its associated grasslands, provided not only an ideal habitat for the buffalo, but also a relatively easy area for the work we planned. The rainy season was due to arrive in late September and with it the buffalo would scatter far and wide through northwestern Botswana in search of sweeter pastures made available by the accumulation of rainwater in hundreds of small pans and waterholes. Working and travelling conditions then would become almost impossible.

The logistics for the exercise were unprecedented in a field operation in Botswana. A team of six vets with three or four technicians would form the scientific core. Other aspects were covered by game wardens, trackers, drivers and field assistants drawn from district offices all over Botswana. Kate had been roped in to supervise the catering and she had organised cooks from the safari-hunting companies in Maun and food for thirty people for six weeks, quite a task. Maun was poorly supplied with stores and most basic fresh produce and provisions had to be sourced from Bulawayo, 500 miles away in Rhodesia. Luckily, the Veterinary Department was equipped with enormous, black, 200-litre cool boxes, normally used to keep vaccine on ice for up to three weeks. Several of these were commandeered by Kate and one or two were diverted to the important function of keeping beer cold.

A number of six-ton trucks would carry all the equipment and provisions. A small fleet of 4x4 vehicles, mainly Land Rovers, had been provided for the actual fieldwork. They, like the bigger trucks were mainly new, a testament to the importance placed on our task and the substantial budget available. Most of the funding had been provided by the British Government and Bob Hedger, a leading expert in FMD from Pirbright, accompanied the team. Tents, marquees, tables and chairs, cooking pots and implements, 200-litre drums of diesel, petrol and avgas, scientific equipment and much more were loaded into the trucks. Finally, the huge, black, insulated cool boxes were filled with ice and perishables. The most critically sensitive scientific chemicals and reagents were submerged in boxes filled with dry ice (solid carbon dioxide) and special inert packaging at minus seventy degrees Celsius. The loading process took most of the day and as it was at least a six-hour drive to Savuti, the departure was scheduled for early the next morning.

Everything was ready. The only thing still to arrive was a helicopter. None of these wondrous machines had ever been used, or even seen, in Botswana – as far as anyone knew. We were all anticipating its arrival with great excitement. A radio message was received with a revised ETA for the helicopter of noon the following day. That evening most of the vets and other expats on the team retired to Crocodile Camp. Norbert remained sober and at home, reflecting his serious sense of responsibility concerning the upcoming exercise. For the rest of us it was an extremely lively evening of getting to know each other and looking forward to the coming adventure. "Bluey" Carmichael was the stand-out social performer, with supporting roles for Stan Hall and Ron Anderson, a double act of Glaswegian meat inspectors drafted in as technicians during the annual maintenance closure of the Lobatse export abattoir.

The helicopter had been chartered from Cape Town, almost 2,000 miles to the south, and needed a few days just to get to Maun, having to plan a careful route according to the availability of fuel (avgas). Court Lines, the operators, specialised in servicing oil tankers and other shipping rounding the Cape, so the Kalahari Desert was probably as strange and exciting to them as their machine was to us. The veterinary convoy left town early – but not quite as early as planned given the rather frail condition of several "senior officers". Norbert had asked me to stay behind because he would have to fly in the helicopter to show the pilot the way to the Savuti base, so I would drive the engineer accompanying the pilot. I was assured that it would be easy to follow the spoor (tracks) made by the convoy.

Just before noon Norbert and I were at the Maun airstrip eagerly awaiting the chopper's arrival. Quite a few interested local residents were also at the airstrip – the news of a helicopter arriving had leaked out and it was not to be missed. The airstrip was fairly central in the village and roughly parallel to the river on the north side. It was just a flattened and gravelled stretch of harder sand, very white in the sunshine. There was a low, not very confident, fence that struggled to keep out donkeys and the odd cow, but failed completely to exclude goats. A tin-roofed hut functioned as a passenger terminal and was flanked by a small, cleared parking area.

The only official was a caretaker who mainly tried to keep the strip free of livestock and also kept a scruffy exercise book in which pilots sometimes recorded their comings and goings. There were columns for date, time, aircraft registration, pilot's name, number of passengers, origin and destination. It made for quite interesting reading. The local fleet consisted of a handful of single-engine light aircraft, four and six seaters, mainly Cessnas and a couple of Pipers, with two twin-engine, slightly larger planes that were owned by the local big-game hunting companies. The only really impressive aircraft that landed in Maun were the twice-weekly scheduled flights from the capital Gaborone, operated by Desert Airways. These were usually flown by a Britten-Norman Islander and could take nine passengers. Otherwise, there was only the occasional visit by an ancient DC-3 operating the flights for the mine labour organisation Wenela, to the South African gold mines.

A slight, strange noise from the south was heard, getting louder and becoming a clatter, and then a small helicopter came into view, fairly low over the village. After a brief circuit the machine landed in a huge, deafening cloud of dust a few metres from the "terminal building". By now dozens of villagers were running from all directions towards the scene. The pilot allowed the engine and rotors to cool and slow gradually for a couple of minutes and the dust cleared. Out stepped a large, dark-haired, middle-aged man, immaculate in khakis and shiny boots. Cor Beek was a Hollander who had been flying helicopters for many years in Europe and latterly in South Africa. He sported a neat goatee beard and a sidearm in a holster at his waist. From the other side emerged a young, more casually attired man, Greg, who was the flight engineer. We were impressed, but not half as much as the gathering of locals who were being kept at bay, outside the fence, by the caretaker and a couple of policemen who had arrived to see the goings on.

Introductions were made and we took the crew for a drink and snack at Norbert's nearby house, leaving the helicopter, a Bell 47, locked and in the safekeeping of the now immensely proud and newly important caretaker. The flight to Savuti was expected to take at least an hour and take-off was planned for 2.00 pm. We all returned to the strip and Cor, assisted by Greg, prepared for departure. After filling the tank from a drum of avgas on my Land Rover and completing the formalities required in the caretaker's book, Cor and Norbert were ready for off. A few remaining onlookers were joined by scores more as soon as the machine started its engine. In another blast of sand and dust, and with a deafening roar, it took off, tilting its nose slightly forward and then climbing into the clear sky on a northerly course. The excited clamour among the audience as the machine became airborne matched the engine's roar decibel for decibel.

Greg and I had a five-hour drive ahead of us, so we packed our bags into the Land Rover and headed out of town on the sand road towards the old bridge at Matlapaneng. We had planned to get to the camp at Savuti before dark, but there were obstacles along the track north and the first of these was just beyond the bridge in the form of Crocodile Camp. I had been so impressed by this establishment the previous evening that I decided to introduce Greg to its charms. We pulled in through the reed fence, parked and walked down to the bar near the riverbank. Like most of Ngamiland's structures it consisted mainly of reed and thatch. A few local residents were enjoying lunchtime beers and I recognised a professional hunter called Cecil Riggs, a serious contender for the previous evening's party champ. He had apparently slept in one of the cottages and was now continuing where he'd left off.

I was yet to become familiar with the safari hunter lifestyle during the season; on safari for a few weeks and then non-stop partying for a few days in town between safaris. Cecil was in full flight – loud, garrulous, genial and full of fun (and beer). He recognised me from the previous evening and welcomed us into the circle of revellers with great bonhomie. His safari tales of camp life with charging buffalo and close encounters with lions were endorsed, echoed and embellished by his drinking companions, also mainly hunters, and the afternoon passed very enjoyably and quickly – too quickly! It must have been about 5.00 pm when Greg and I left the bar, slightly worse for wear, and headed up the path to where the Land Rover was parked. I remember it was dark well before we reached the entrance gate to Chobe National Park at Mababe, but luckily there was only one possible turn-off before then and we managed to avoid it. The game scout on duty knew of the Savuti exercise because of the fleet of trucks that had gone through earlier, so he was happy to let us into the park despite the late hour and gave us helpful directions to the camp, still some fifty miles or so to the north.

Finding the camp a couple of hours later proved more difficult than expected. There seemed to be a network of sand tracks around the Savuti area, and we undoubtedly followed some more than once. The sand was deep in places and we were very grateful for the four-wheel drive capability of the vehicle. Eventually we drove into a clearing near the bank of a river. We could see a very large tent in the headlights and headed towards it, but unfortunately didn't see the many guy-ropes holding it up – until we drove through and pulled most of them out of the ground. The huge tent partially collapsed and enveloped our Land Rover. By the time we had extricated ourselves from the canvas shroud we were met by a group of people who had been sleeping in nearby tents and were mostly not amused to be rudely awakened by our arrival. A few, like Bluey Carmichael saw the funny side, but Kate Drager, the "camp commandant" was incandescent. Luckily, with a little help and torchlight, Greg and I managed to free the vehicle and repair the damage sufficiently for Kate to allow us to put up our own small sleeping tent among the lines. We were awakened at dawn by a gunshot – Norbert's way of heralding a new day – and, suitably embarrassed, joined our fellow campers for breakfast in a slightly sagging mess tent.

The camp was quite something. Next to the enormous mess tent was a series of store tents and a kitchen. The sleeping lines stretched a couple of hundred yards along the bank of the river, perhaps twenty tents for vets, technicians, drivers, visitors and even a couple of journalists. The labourers had their own encampment behind. There was even a laboratory tent for processing the samples. Next to the mess tent, parked in a neat line, were the six new Land Rovers, all provided by the UK Government. Pride of place went to the Bell 47 helicopter in a cleared landing zone, with Cor's tent fairly close by under a shady apple-leaf tree. No one warned us that this species has a habit of losing large branches unexpectedly and is not ideal to camp under.

The normal camp routine, after Norbert's reveille, was for Greg to check the helicopter, before Cor, resplendent in his immaculate khaki uniform, pulled on white gloves and took off with one observer to look for suitable buffalo herds. The rest of us would have coffee and rusks provided by Kate and her crew while we waited for the helicopter to return. Then the four ground crews, each with a vet, a lab technician, two labourers and a driver would leave for an agreed rendezvous close to the selected buffalo herd. One of the vets, initially Norbert, would take his place in the helicopter with a dart gun and also meet us there.

Savuti was an ideal place for our darting exercise. The channel was flowing strongly and the wet central part of the marsh attracted huge herds of buffalo from the thousands of square miles of dry bush around it. Large dead acacia trees, a species that cannot survive in water, were dotted along the centre of the channel, indicating that at some time it must have been dry for over fifty years. After the mid-1970s the channel was again dry for twenty years. Even in 1973 it failed to flow, causing us to move the second buffalo sampling exercise to another location, although it filled the marsh again in 1974.

The preferred *modus operandi* was for the marksman to dart up to six buffalo together and for the helicopter to try to keep them bunched until they went down, to facilitate the task of the ground crews. This was also safest for the buffalo because a straying narcotised animal would be susceptible to predation by hyaenas and lions or to accidents such as drowning. Ideally all six animals would go down within a fifty-yard radius in an area easily accessible to the ground crews' vehicles, but this was rarely achieved. The many unpredictables – from the placement of darts, to the animals' variability in size, age and susceptibility to the drugs – ensured that some of the darted animals were widely separated and the ground crews often had exciting chases to obtain their samples. Down times (the time between the dart hitting and the animal becoming recumbent), theoretically about eight minutes, varied widely depending on whether the dart hit deep into a muscle (short down time) or injected the drug into tissue with less blood circulation (like gristle) or just under the skin (long down time). Often, although the animals were affected they would not go down without being roped and thrown, which led to many thrills and spills, not to mention minor injuries, among the ground crews. Several photographs were taken of a buffalo dragging two or three intrepid vets and technicians like water skiers hanging onto its tail. Luckily no one was seriously hurt, but underestimating an animal's degree of narcosis led to some quick reversals, narrow escapes and occasional damage to vehicles – and a rich vein of hilarity over cold beer around the evening campfire.

As in Uganda, we used M99 as the main immobilising drug. A few milligrams will put a buffalo down in six or seven minutes. We usually added some tranquilliser to the dart as well. This helped to calm the buffalo and made it easier for the ground teams to handle them when taking biological samples and body measurements. The tranquilliser, acetylpromazine (ACP), was cheap and effective. It did have the unwanted side effect of interfering with the body's temperature control mechanisms, but this was minimised by working early in the morning. Unfortunately, it could not be reversed and was still active for a few hours after the buffalo had been given the antidote to M99. The animals could seem dozy for some time after, especially, as sometimes happened, if they received more than one dart. Savuti's now-famous lions and hyaenas were quick to notice if a buffalo was slow to rejoin the herd, especially if it appeared lethargic, and we had occasionally to chase away inquisitive big cats and perceptive hyaenas. Our official figures reported a very high success rate with almost no casualties, but a few of us had some misgivings about the later survival of some individuals.

Norbert and I shared most of the darting. Most of the vets wanted to give it a try but not all were equally successful with a dart gun and individual temperament made a difference. It was essential to be relaxed and take enough time to shoot accurately at a group of moving targets, even though the distance from the helicopter to the rump of the targeted buffalo was rarely more than twenty yards. On one occasion the helicopter landed next to my Land Rover and Derek Breton, a tall gangly Englishman, jumped out and ran towards me in a highly agitated state. He had missed with several darts and couldn't get the hang of it. He told me to take over and he took my place in the ground crew. When we were airborne I asked the pilot what the problem had been, but he had no idea where the darts had been going. On approaching a target group I pushed a dart into the breech of the rifle. I was amazed to see another dart protruding from the end of the barrel. Derek had been loading the gun and pulling the trigger without cocking the mechanism – the barrel was full of unfired darts. He hadn't been missing – he hadn't even been shooting!

Someone once described Derek as "all elbows and knees" and he was forever tripping over tent guy ropes and dropping things. After a couple of years he moved on to an abattoir job in New Zealand.

Once, on a later exercise, after taking over the darting, I loaded the gun, fired and was amazed as two darts flew through the air and hit two separate buffaloes! The previous marksman had loaded but not fired the dart gun and had forgotten to tell me. The Portuguese pilot was completely incredulous and refused to believe that I routinely darted two at a time.

When a ground team approached a darted animal the vet had to ascertain that it was safe to handle before the rest of the crew left the vehicle. Usually it was already lying down, but occasionally it was necessary to jump off the Land Rover and grab it by the tail to immobilise it and pull it down. The drugs slowed it down enough to prevent it kicking, but a few wild rides were had. Once down, a rope was tied between the horns and a hind leg to help keep it in a suitable position for sampling. This entailed: scraping the lining of the throat in an attempt to isolate any virus; taking a blood sample from the jugular vein to check for FMD antibodies; estimating the animal's age from its teeth; measuring its chest girth to estimate its weight; checking females for pregnancy by performing a rectal examination and applying numbered brass ear tags to identify the animal. Finally, they were given an antidote to the immobilising drug, which revived them after a couple of minutes. They would normally then trot away to rejoin the herd, although once or twice, if a buffalo became aware of a vehicle it charged.

Some buffalo were fitted with bright red collars, easily visible at a distance and especially from the air. This was to gather information on the seasonal movement and range of the buffalo herds. Information would be fed back from sightings by hunters, game scouts, biologists and the gradually increasing number of tourists.

Once, a darted buffalo strayed through some deepish water and went down on a tiny, bare island. Norbert had been darting and the chopper landed close to our vehicle to tell us we couldn't drive through the water. I grabbed a small sample kit, joined him in the helicopter and we flew the short hop to the island. It was a young bull and the two of us managed to take the blood and throat scraping while Cor kept the helicopter running about ten yards away. After giving the antidote to revive the animal, Norbert jumped into the helicopter after me. His favourite Bavarian military hat fell off and he got out to retrieve it. Cor didn't notice because I was obstructing his vision and, anyway, he was watching the buffalo getting up. Unusually, it charged the helicopter and Cor immediately got airborne vertically, causing the lumbering buffalo to pass directly under the machine and collide with Norbert, who was now in its path. Luckily the bull merely brushed past him and kept going, nevertheless, much to his Germanic displeasure, it did knock him over and left a few bruises.

By late morning it was too hot to continue, mainly for the animals' safety, and the teams returned to camp and the lab tent. Here samples were processed, throat scrapings were carefully labelled and stored deep-frozen in dry ice, blood and serum samples were spun down in centrifuges and stored on ice in cool boxes. The lab tent became a social space where technicians and vets swapped stories and would hang out through the hottest part of the day, when temperatures reached forty degrees Celsius and above.

We had a succession of helicopter pilots during the series of sampling exercises and discovered that not all were as rigid and straight laced as Cor Beek. Undoubtedly our favourite was a young ex-military pilot called John Eccles, who was as different from Cor as could be imagined. The first time he arrived in Maun most of the team were waiting at the airstrip, it was late afternoon and we were beginning to worry. The little machine, a Hughes 300 this time, swooped down from the south and flared directly above the small aircraft parking area next to the fence. As the dust cleared Norbert and I walked towards the chopper. We glanced at each other after spotting the words *Midnight Cowboy* in white on the front of the black aircraft. We did a real double-take a moment later when the pilot got out. He was very young with a shock of long curly hair, not quite an Afro, several days' growth of straggly beard, wearing an old, grey T-shirt with oil stained khaki shorts and boots without laces or socks! This was no Cor Beek!

His flying was also very different. As we got used to him he charmed us with his laid-back style and thrilled us with his unorthodox flying. He would occasionally push a stubborn buffalo down with the helicopter skids if it wasn't responding well to the dart and enjoyed tailgating a vulture for as long as possible, with the poor bird looking over its shoulder and doing everything it could to escape. He also landed the machine in the most impossibly small clearings, sometimes even using the main rotors as giant bush strimmers to cut a way down through the trees. He was undoubtedly a consummate operator whose hundreds of hours of military training had given him astonishing confidence in the machine and his own skills. He brought a totally new dimension to the job and we worked together for two seasons.

Stan and Ron, the technicians from the Lobatse abattoir, were responsible for our field laboratory, preparing fresh sampling kits and storing the collected samples. As senior meat inspectors they were not only frighteningly expert with a knife and experienced in laboratory techniques but they were also an extremely funny double act, as long as you understood their rich brogue. As a recent Glasgow graduate I became a favoured chum.

Other species susceptible to FMD had to be sampled too, though in much smaller numbers. These were mainly shot and provided the camp with a regular supply of fresh meat. In the afternoons a couple of vets went out by vehicle or on foot to shoot warthog, kudu, impala or other antelopes. One day, Norbert, the best shot, returned from a long, hot walk with a couple of samples from a kudu. Entering the lab tent, he picked up a full glass of "water" from a table and, before anyone noticed, took a deep swallow of Jik bleach, with spectacular effect! Luckily, the colourless, clear fluid, used for sterilising instruments, was a fairly dilute solution, but he was in considerable distress. The occupants of the lab were in hysterics while trying to help him. Fresh water was quickly provided with lots of advice on the best way to induce vomiting. Stan and Ron's witty, Glaswegian comments about bleaching were very funny, except to Norbert, who suffered no lingering after effects – but there was a tightening of lab procedures.

One of my hunting forays, also for kudu, was more exciting than I needed. I tracked a male kudu that I had shot for about 400 yards through the bush along the Savuti Channel. I eventually saw it lying at the far side of a small clearing and ran to it to try to ensure that I obtained really fresh samples. I leant my rifle against a small hill a few yards away and proceeded to try to get blood from the kudu's jugular vein. Hearing a clatter, I turned to see the small hill running away – I had leant my gun against a sleeping hippo!

Malte Sommerlatte was a young German biologist working for the UN's Food and Agriculture Organisation (FAO), studying elephants and based at Kasane on the Chobe River. He joined us at Savuti to help out with data collection. His supervisor was another German, Wolfgang von Richter, who headed the Wildlife Department's research section in Gaborone. Wolfgang wanted information on sable antelope, a beautiful species found throughout northern Botswana and further north. We were also keen to catch some and take samples for our FMD survey. Malte decided to obtain some plastic sheeting and steel cables to try and catch a herd in a boma, using the newly described Oelofse method that had been recently pioneered in South Africa's Kruger National Park and is now used widely in commercial game capture.

This method involved building an extensive trap (boma) – a triangular funnel about 200 yards across the mouth and 400 yards deep, terminating in a kind of holding area roughly fifty yards square. Its walls were curtains of woven, beige, plastic sheeting, about eight feet high and hung between tensioned steel cables. Animals reacted to the curtains as though they were solid walls. The outer curtain closed off the entrance and successively shorter cross-curtains were placed at suitable intervals down the funnel and could be closed when the animals had passed by. Some of the main cables were over 100 yards long and were pulled tight by powerful winches. We only had a few winches and they were crucially situated to hold the curtains in place. This whole construction, anything up to ten acres in extent, had to be strategically positioned out of sight and downwind of the target animals. Malte achieved this by building the boma just below a high sand ridge and between two of Savuti's prominent *kopjes,* a task which took him and a small team of labourers almost two days.

Malte proudly showed us around the boma on the evening before we planned to use it. There were about six vets and a few interested visitors, including Wolfgang who didn't spend too much time in the bush and was much more inclined towards administration than practical assignments. In querying what the odd contraption was he pulled the handle of one of the winches. Several hundred yards of highly tensioned cable were suddenly released and the billowing curtains disappeared into the bush. We were all speechless until Malte screamed something in German that made Wolfgang take off at high speed down the sandy hill, closely followed by Malte wielding a heavy pair of fencing pliers. We feared the worst, but sanity prevailed and Malte was eventually persuaded not to bludgeon his senior colleague.

Early the following morning Malte's boma had been repaired and we took up our allotted stations to close the curtains on command. After a few trial runs we dispatched the helicopter to go and find a suitable herd of sable. It took an hour or so for the radios to crackle with the news that twenty animals were being herded towards us and that we should take up our positions in silence. A few minutes later the sable herd trotted down the centre of the funnel and was easily trapped in the holding pen. As we found later, we were unusually fortunate. The sable were darted from behind the plastic and lay down without any problems. Blood and saliva samples were collected and Malte supervised the measuring and recording of other biological information. On completion they were all revived together and the curtains were opened to allow them to run free.

It had been an impressive success as an exercise in mass capture and we determined to try it with buffalo. If it worked it would obviously save time and, especially, economise on very expensive helicopter usage. We reinforced the holding pen with nets behind the plastic sheets and beefed up the teams who would close the curtains. I was stationed on one of the shorter curtains near the holding pen and I co-opted Jeff Dawson, a bespectacled American Peace Corps volunteer, to help me run with the plastic.

Jeff's main interest was ornithology. He had recently arrived from the USA and was still pretty nervous of Africa's wild animals. This was hardly surprising since on his first night in the bush, on his way to Savuti, he had been pulled out of a tent by a lioness tugging at his sleeping bag. He had been sharing a tent with Tom Butynsky, another American biologist, and his girlfriend and had felt the first exploratory tugs, but thought it was the girlfriend who had mistaken him for Tom. The subsequent uproar apparently persuaded the lioness to let go and take off into the night. Jeff's bad luck continued when the first buffalo passed our station and I gave the call to run like hell with the curtain. He was so worried about being in such close proximity to the beasts that he ran straight into a tree trunk holding up the cable and knocked himself out cold, while three or four other people ran over him in their haste to close the curtain without being gored or trampled. We did get a few buffaloes into the boma, but they broke out through the side curtains and were not sampled. We abandoned the idea of boma capture for buffalo and reverted to darting directly from the helicopter.

After Savuti's buffalo had yielded enough data we moved the whole circus (minus one or two fringe participants and observers) to the northeastern edge of the Okavango Delta near the Khwai River. This area had less open grassland and so the *modus operandi* was changed to take into consideration the more difficult terrain. Smaller numbers of buffalo were darted in each sortie and fewer animals were sampled overall. Otherwise the operation was similar except that yellow collars were fitted instead of the red ones used at Savuti. At a third sampling site, Matsebe, a stunning area on the western side of the Okavango, we fitted blue collars.

It was a very enjoyable few weeks in beautiful, wildlife-rich locations for everyone involved. Kate's kitchen provided excellent food and the copious amounts of ice for scientific purposes ensured a liberal supply of cold beer. Trucks made frequent trips back to Maun for stores and more urgent items were brought back by air, making full use of the chartered light aircraft flown by Ivor Scott of Selebe-Phikwe, who regularly took the samples to Gaborone to be dispatched overnight to Pirbright in the UK. It was such a groundbreaking event that among the many visitors who flew in was a well-known reporter for a major Johannesburg newspaper, Wilf Nussey, who published a long article with photographs. We were even visited by a Japanese film crew for a few days and by Marlon Perkins and his team from the famous American television series *Mutual of Omaha's Wild Kingdom*. Such interest seems extraordinary now, since immobilising wild animals is an everyday, routine procedure on thousands of game ranches and reserves all over the world. But in 1972 it was an exciting new technique, with untested drugs and equipment that few people had tried.

While we were working at Khwai one or two of the team started to show signs of irritability – not everyone is equally suited to long periods under canvas in a tiny, remote community and the tsetse flies along the river were also a serious annoyance. They were particularly attracted to large moving objects and our Land Rovers were prime targets. The people on the back were continually tormented and bitten painfully hundreds of times every day. Barry Bousfield, a young vet whose father was a legendary crocodile hunter, left us to go back to Gabs and ultimately spent most of his life in practice in Hong Kong.

Bluey was irrepressible throughout, although even I was stretched by one of his jokes when we were fly-camping upriver. Five of us had been out for a couple of days collecting samples from kudu, warthog and lechwe. We were camping without tents, sleeping on light camp beds around a fire. The skins of some of the animals, especially kudu, were valuable and we kept them salted in a wet pile near the fire because hyaenas were a nuisance. One night a number of them circled our camp for hours, whooping, giggling and laughing. Whenever one got too close we would chase it away by throwing beer cans and sticks, eventually going to bed after throwing more wood on the fire. One night I awoke to see a hyaena skulking in the firelight a few yards from my bed. I yelled and jumped up, grabbed the fire shovel, and chased it away. Nobody else reacted. I went back to bed and was almost asleep again when I heard a scraping sound and felt my bed move slightly. I sat up and saw a hyaena's head tugging at a skin just a couple of feet from me. I yelled and screamed and waved my arms and it retreated again. This time I heard a few giggles that weren't a hyaena's. Beneath my bed was a fresh kudu skin, put there by Bluey after I had fallen asleep. Norbert, Ron and Stan all found it hysterically funny.

Leaving Maun after a couple of days off to reposition the exercise at Matsebe, Norbert was to fly to camp in the helicopter and I was delegated to make sure the caravan of vehicles all made it to camp. The campsite had been chosen by Cecil Riggs, who knew the area well and had been co-opted onto the team. Cecil, as the guide, left the vet offices in the leading vehicle followed by about a dozen trucks and Land Rovers full of equipment, stores and staff. I was to bring up the rear to prevent any stragglers and Kate was travelling with me. We agreed that Cecil would wait on the Ghanzi road a few miles south of Maun where the track branched off towards the Delta. The whole caravan was strung out on the white calcrete road, each vehicle hanging back to avoid the dust from the one in front. Kate and I slowly followed the billowing clouds. At the rendezvous we were taken aback to find only Cecil sitting there in his car – the whole convoy in the middle had disappeared! Kate and I dissolved in hysterics and Cecil saw the funny side, but it wasn't the sort of thing that Norbert would have found amusing. The other drivers had all turned off at various points in town to buy last minute cigarettes and soft drinks and we hadn't noticed. The stragglers duly arrived and were given a dressing down in fluent Setswana by Cecil but we all made it to the new camp by lunchtime, through thick sand and a couple of deep river crossings.

Norbert once lost his sense of humour completely in Matsebe. He and I were fly camping and trying to collect samples from other species, mainly kudu, the almost ubiquitous and most stately of antelopes. We had two technicians/labourers and two new trackers, the latter recruited from the local village of Tsau. Kate had tagged along, which made life much more bearable in terms of meals and campfire banter.

Over two days of hunting Norbert had come home empty-handed, while I had shot two impala and three kudu, which was strange because he was the better hunter. At the end of the second day he arrived back at camp in a furious, black mood.

"It's f…ing impossible!" he yelled. "This bloody tracker must be blind! I saw at least four groups of kudu while driving and he didn't say a word!" The rest of his outburst seemed to be in an ancient Bavarian dialect.

I knew the tracker must have seen the kudu, they weren't scarce and he had excellent eyesight. I asked him why he hadn't alerted Norbert and he explained that he had been instructed to look for tortoises. In Setswana the word for tortoise is *khudu*, pronounced almost the same as the English kudu, the word for kudu is *tholo*. Kate and I were reduced to tears of laughter, imagining

Norbert driving for hours through the bush searching for tortoises. I did wonder why on earth the tracker thought Norbert needed a high-powered rifle to hunt tortoises.

Working in the Okavango was a dream come true. Spectacular and rich in wildlife as Savuti was, the Okavango was the paramount unspoilt African wilderness. Its vast mosaic of habitats – islands, channels, floodplains, forests, reedbeds and lagoons – was the ultimate in enchanted ecology. The diversity of wild species – mammals, birds, reptiles and vegetation – was, and still is, bewitching. This was where I wanted to be.

Eventually the job was done, for that year at least. The imminent rains would have made conditions impossible and the big buffalo herds would fragment and scatter with the first storms. But thanks to the collars and ear tags we had put on over 200 buffaloes we would at least know where they went. We received feedback from professional hunters and tour guides for years to come, allowing us to build up a picture of the seasonal movements and migrations of the buffalo herds. The exercise was repeated three more times in the next four years, enabling us to tag over 1,000 animals. Two of the early cows that were marked in Khwai migrated as far as Hwange National Park in Zimbabwe during the wet season, a distance of over 200 miles and back. But strangely none of the tagged buffaloes ever crossed the Boro River in the central Okavango Delta; the Matsebe and Khwai populations seemed completely separate. Unfortunately the study did not continue into the drier 1980s, when a different picture might have emerged.

Cattle vaccination campaigns took me back to Ngamiland, but not into the Okavango. All cattle in Ngamiland were vaccinated annually against FMD because it was believed that buffalo coming into contact with susceptible cattle on the fringes of the Okavango were responsible for the sporadic outbreaks of the disease, which almost always started there. Most of the district veterinary officers looked forward to the annual vaccination campaign as a chance to meet up with colleagues from other stations and to spend a few weeks camping in the bush. It was also a good opportunity to visit some of the northern areas rich in wildlife, eat a little venison and do some fishing.

Starting in the north around Shakawe we would work our way gradually back towards Lake Ngami and then Maun. If more than a certain proportion of the cattle were protected by vaccine, often claimed to be about eighty per cent, then this herd immunity would stop the disease spreading. Unfortunately, local tribesmen were often uncooperative and would hold back cattle in the bush, refusing to bring them to the communal crushes for vaccination. The main culprits were undoubtedly the Herero people, who were the most successful farmers and owned the most cattle. They were relative newcomers to Ngamiland, having arrived as refugees from South West Africa (Namibia) in the early twentieth century, and there was some resentment from the local Batawana about their cattle numbers. Consequently they were loath to have their cattle counted by outsiders and some even spread stories that the vaccinations were meant to stop their cows breeding.

One year we decided to do some detective work to try to establish what proportion of their herds were actually presented for vaccination. We painted the horns of all vaccinated cattle bright blue. Over the following day or two we visited several cattle posts unannounced when the cattle came to drink and tried to estimate what proportion had blue horns. In some areas the figure was as low as thirty-five per cent. This would have been next to useless in preventing FMD outbreaks and some of the more dissident of us postulated that maybe the virus was permanently present among the cattle, especially in more remote areas where veterinary staff were rare visitors, and that the buffalo thesis might be a red herring. This was dismissed as heresy by our superiors. Nevertheless, experimental attempts in neighbouring Rhodesia to infect cattle by exposing them to virus-carrying buffalo repeatedly failed for many years, further inciting our scepticism.

In the general absence of telephones, headquarters in Gaborone used to hold a radio schedule every morning to check on business at each district veterinary office. Being in Mahalapye and in telephone contact I was never involved in the ritual. The schedule, normally hosted by an officious deputy director, Eddie Bradley, would start by calling Ghanzi and work its way clockwise around the country for half an hour, calling Maun, Francistown and Serowe in turn and any field camp that also happened to be operational at the time. The story goes that at the end of one FMD vaccination campaign, four young vets, enjoying their spell in the bush, diverted to Nxai Pan, a beautiful wildlife area, for a couple of nights before returning to their various stations. These delinquents used the same radio in turn to talk to Eddie, making out that they were in their respective stations, hundreds of miles apart, while sitting together around the campfire drinking morning coffee!

FIVE

A JOB IN PARADISE

When the long-delayed rains finally began in late 1973 I began to consider my future. I enjoyed Botswana, especially its wilderness and the opportunities for working with wildlife, but I was not cut out to be a veterinary administrator responsible for a district; my uneven relations with a couple of senior officers in Gabs Headquarters were testament to that. I was certain that I didn't want to return to England and domestic veterinary practice; the animals were fun and the science was interesting and rewarding, but dealing with owners was not for me. To be honest, I also found it difficult to justify the expense and professional effort sometimes involved in treating pets, much of which was more often psychological therapy for the client than medical therapy for the animal.

Jenny, on the other hand, was keen to return to life in England. For her the rustic living conditions and limited social and cultural opportunities in Mahalapye were not compensated by a deep interest in the wildlife and surrounding wilderness as in my own case. My frequent and sometimes quite prolonged absences on working trips in the bush had also put strain on our relationship, but as is often the case, we were reluctant to make any definite resolutions about the future.

My contract with the Botswana Government stipulated twenty-four to thirty months of service so I could move on in January 1974. In those days before electronic communication, letters and applications took forever, especially from a place like Mahalapye. Christmas came and went without a plan materialising. Nevertheless, slightly reluctantly, I handed in my resignation and determined to return to England in February, as a better place from which to pursue opportunities. I was communicating with Ken Tinley, an ecologist working in Southern Angola, about joining him on a major wildlife project in Cuando-Cubango, although having to learn Portuguese before being appointed seemed a serious obstacle.

During the buffalo sampling project at Savuti we had worked with the DWNP, referred to for convenience and historical reasons by everyone as the Game Department. They had provided wardens and biologists to collect data and extract as much information as possible from the immobilised buffalo. The scientist in charge of the Game Department's research section, Dr Wolfgang von Richter, seconded from the UN, heard that I was proposing to leave Botswana and he asked me to meet him in Gaborone after the New Year holiday to discuss a project.

The UN was sponsoring a major four-year investigation into the Okavango Delta and its potential as a source of fresh water for development in Botswana. The lead scientists, drawn from all over the world, would be hydrologists, hydraulic engineers and the like, but there would be a strong environmental component with a general ecologist and a wildlife ecologist. Botswana was expected to provide two counterpart scientists to work alongside the ecologists. The Game Department had no suitably qualified candidates and Wolfgang wondered if, given my MSc in conservation, I might be interested in transferring to them and being seconded to the Okavango project. He also wanted me to take over the biological data collection from buffalo when the vets resumed sampling – this project was now planned to continue for at least another three years.

It was the easiest decision of my life and even Jenny, who had never really enjoyed life in Mahalapye, agreed that it could be the fresh start that our relationship needed. We flew back to England for a few weeks of wet winter weather that reinforced my enthusiasm for the new post and returned to Gabs in mid-March 1974. We completed my transfer from the Veterinary Department to the Game Department and our move from Mahalapye to Maun on a permanent basis. Although an ecologist with the DWNP was a lower rank in the Botswana civil service than a veterinary officer, the news that I would still be paid as a vet was the icing on the cake.

By the end of March 1974 we were settled in Maun between the river and the airstrip in one of a group of brand new houses built specially for the project. Jenny had briefly visited Maun once before and we quickly renewed our acquaintance with Norbert and Kate and met more residents, mostly government officers or hunting safari outfitters. The latter were the largest employers in northern Botswana and Maun was the industry's main centre. There were two major safari companies – Safari South and Ker, Downey and Selby (KDS) – who leased huge areas of wilderness in the Okavango Delta for their exclusive use. Safari South operated mainly in the west with KDS in the east, divided by the central Boro River.

As is so often the case, the UN project, scheduled for April, was late starting. In the meantime my instructions from Wolfgang were simple: learn as much as possible about the Okavango Delta. The best starting point was Pete Smith, a reserved man of about forty who worked from his house on the river in Maun.

Pete had been working in Botswana since 1956, ten years before independence, first as a bookkeeper for the Colonial Development Corporation (CDC) in Pandamatenga on the Rhodesian border, one of the few areas in the country with soils thought to be suited to commercial agriculture. The CDC had initiated an ill-fated farming project that hadn't reckoned with the environmental extremes of drought or too much rain, either of which made growing crops on the vast cotton-soil plains extremely challenging. The depredations of various wildlife species also plagued the project and, like so many others in Africa, it terminated in an early failure.

In 1959 Pete had moved to Maun and after a year at Riley's Garage, he joined the Tsetse Fly Control Department (TFC), a subdivision of the Veterinary Department, as one of three expat field officers based in Maun, along with Ronnie Ridge and Ryland Wallace. They were responsible for supervising staff on tsetse fly surveys and for shooting game in an effort to reduce the fly's feeding hosts. All three spent long periods in remote camps and developed a deep knowledge of the bush, its vegetation and wildlife, and the influence of the annual flooding regime of the Okavango Delta. Pete became an acknowledged expert on the vegetation, especially aquatic species, and was extremely skilled at interpreting aerial photography for mapping and ecological planning. He received an MBE in recognition of his work.

As a confirmed bachelor, his house was quite spartan; one bedroom was an office and another was a herbarium, where he had a comprehensive collection of Okavango plants and an extensive library. He rarely cooked and seemed to exist on canned food, biscuits and tea. Occasionally he would appear at Island Safari Lodge to watch a Friday night "bioscope" and enjoy chicken in a basket.

This was where I was first introduced to him by the proprietor, Tony Graham. Pete was tall and slim with thinning hair and spectacles; he always wore long trousers and a sports jacket over a checked, long-sleeved shirt. By Maun standards this was formal dress and he still appeared more like a bookkeeper than the field officer he had been for the past ten years. He was not a heavy drinker or a party animal, like many in town. Almost everyone drank Castle lager but Pete enjoyed the less bitter Lion lager to which he would often add a tot of Mazoe orange squash – a legacy of his Rhodesian youth.

At first Pete was polite, but not overly welcoming. He was obviously a loner who protected his privacy. I explained what I had come to Maun to do and my desire to learn as much as possible about the Okavango. We did have something in common as he too was going to be attached to the UN project as a counterpart to the general ecologist. I sensed a slight wariness of newcomers on his patch, as if he was a little reluctant to share the information he had accumulated over so long. I grew to realise that this type of territoriality is common among field researchers and that Pete's was a very mild case.

He was planning a trip by boat from Maun through the Delta to Shakawe at the northern end of the panhandle where the Okavango River enters Botswana. En route he would be collecting plants and taking hydrological readings – flow rates, water depth and quality – and also delivering the components for a basic meteorological station on Chief's Island in the heart of the Delta. The whole trip was expected to take about ten days. Pete spent most of his time on a boat in the Delta and few others had done a trip like this. I couldn't think of a better way to gain a valuable introduction to the workings of the place and was over the moon when he suggested that I accompany him. This was not as enthusiastically received by Jenny, who could already see the writing on the wall and was concerned that she was going to be deserted as much in Maun as she had been in Mahalapye.

A couple of days later I pitched up at his house with my sleeping bag, mosquito net and a few personal items. Pete was catering and I had only to provide a case of beer. His sixteen-foot aluminium boat, moored at the bottom of his garden, was as spartan as his home, and we packed it to its limits with equipment and stores for the journey. I found a cramped seat at the back, on top of a fuel tank, next to where Pete – still dressed as if in an office with the addition of a battered, brown trilby hat – sat to operate the 30hp outboard engine.

We didn't get away until early afternoon, when we poled through the reeds and water-lilies into the open water of the Thamalakane River. Pete started the engine and we headed upstream towards the old Matlapaneng Bridge, past Croc Camp and AfAm Safaris and turned left up the Boro River at Island Safari Lodge. The Boro was a much narrower, well-defined channel and seemed to flow faster than the Thamalakane. This was partly because sections had recently been dredged and straightened in an unsuccessful attempt to boost the outflow into the Thamalakane and ultimately down the Boteti River to supply the new diamond mine at Orapa. After about eight miles the banks receded and we abruptly entered a wide, shallow, almost lake-like area dotted with small islands and filled with emergent aquatic vegetation, mainly low sedges, but with numerous patches of taller reeds and grasses. Pete explained that we had just passed the edge of the Kunyere fault line and were now in the Tokatsebe Flats. This fault line, along with a parallel one back at the Thamalakane, had caused the formation of the Okavango Delta by creating barriers at a right-angle to the flow of the river. These fault lines were considered to be the most southerly part of the Great East African Rift responsible for the striking landscapes and lakes so famous in Kenya and neighbouring countries and very, very slowly splitting the continent in two.

We meandered slowly through these flats, following an almost indiscernible, shallow channel marking the course of the Boro River. Quite late in the afternoon, out of sight of any land, the engine abruptly stopped and refused to restart, despite Pete's best efforts. I had no knowledge of outboard motors, so we were stranded with no likely chance of assistance. The sun set and it quickly started to go dark. We tied the boat to a clump of reeds and prepared to spend the night. I knew it was going to be unpleasant when the vanguard of hordes of mosquitoes emerged. Cooking was out of the question and supper consisted of ginger nuts and river water. Pete didn't seem too phased and made himself comfortable, wrapped in a blanket at his driving position. I was too cramped and made my way to the front to stretch out on the rolls of chicken wire and barbed wire intended for the weather station. My sleeping bag did very little to cushion the dozens of sharp points and edges and caused me to overheat, but it was a marginal improvement on being eaten alive by mosquitoes.

At first light we had breakfast – the same menu as supper – and tried to figure a way out. The surrounding floodplain was inundated to at least chest deep, probably more, so wading a couple of miles to dry land was not an option, especially as crocodiles were common. Poling the heavily laden boat back downstream for hours was also an unattractive idea, but seemed the only solution. Pete's toolkit was rudimentary, to put it kindly (a small shifting spanner and a screwdriver), to which could be added my small Swiss Army pocket knife, hardly more than a blade and a bottle opener. Undaunted, Pete pulled components of the engine to pieces and then reassembled them. After each fix we duly blew out the fuel line, reattached and primed it, before pulling the starter, at first enthusiastically and later quite desperately. Amazingly, the engine eventually coughed into life for no reason that we could fathom. We were soon on our way against the slow current and I fell into a pleasant reverie watching the herons, kingfishers, other birds and bright dragonflies against the crystal-clear water, green vegetation and blue sky. After an hour or so we came to an island and Pete beached the boat on its empty sandy bank. We lit a small fire and Pete produced some Five Roses tea bags for a welcome morning drink with condensed milk – and more ginger nuts.

A short while later we were on our way again with Pete describing the passing island vegetation: various fig trees, ebony, palms and the amazing sausage trees, with their pendulous, long, heavy fruits. They all had Latin and Setswana names, with which Pete was entirely familiar, but which I found challenging; sausage tree was unforgettable, but neither *Kigelia pinnata* nor *Moporota* stuck in my mind. However, by the time we got back to Maun I recognised many of the most common species and knew their vernacular and scientific names. At intervals we came across lagoons from the size of a tennis court to double the area of a soccer field, where the water was still and deep containing two or three different types of bream, all edible. We used lures on reels and although we were far from expert fishermen we ate well. It certainly boosted our diet beyond the bully beef, tinned fish, baked beans and ginger nuts that seemed to be Pete's staples. Camping on tiny, remote islands in a tropical paradise, eating freshly caught bream and enjoying a cool can of lager was something I could get used to, especially when I was being paid for it.

As we made our winding course along the Boro channel, up through the centre of the Delta we came across more and more game animals. Hippos had to be avoided in the channels and crocodiles, some huge, would explode into the water from sandbanks as we came into view around bends. Most of the time our immediate view was blocked by the high reeds and tall emergent grass, but when we could see any distance palm trees and others revealed the position of islands and herds of red lechwe were ubiquitous in the shallow floodplains, often hundreds strong. Sometimes, fleetingly, we would see two or three reedbuck and, on larger islands, herds of impala, families of warthog and groups of kudu – the males sporting magnificent spiral horns and the females with huge swivelling ears. Troops of baboons were common and as noisy as they were visible. We also saw a number of giraffe, either peering curiously from thick cover or marching across inundated floodplains en route from one island to browse on another. Evidence of elephants was scarce and we only heard, never saw, buffalo splashing through the shallows, leaving a muddy path through the wet grass and reeds. At night we frequently heard lions proclaiming ownership of their territories and spotted hyaenas whooping at a distance. Only once did one venture close to our camp, but lost interest after a cursory inspection from the edge of the firelight.

We unloaded the wire and other materials for the weather station on a small island close to the northern end of Chief's Island, near what became known as Lechwe Haven. Its construction and the installation of instruments would be undertaken by the Meteorological Department later, so we merely dumped everything a few yards above the water line. In five days and nights on the river we met no one else. But even then some of the island landing places bore evidence of human use as campsites, fireplaces or toilets. There was little obvious littering, even though hyaenas, mostly, had dug up buried refuse in some sites.

Upstream from Chief's Island we soon entered the permanent swamp zone where the channel was deep and swift and bordered mainly by thick papyrus, ten or twelve feet high. This restricted our field of vision completely and only rarely could we see beyond the main channel or lagoons. We still needed to be aware of crocodiles and hippos but we didn't see any sitatunga, even though Pete assured me that they were plentiful throughout the upper Delta. Bird life was varied, with different herons, waders and raptors all abundant. Ducks and geese were restricted to lagoons, from the tiny, vivid pygmy geese that splattered into the air as we passed to the enormous black and white spurwing geese that ignored us. In this zone the channel meandered crazily and we often found ourselves just a couple of hundred yards from where we had passed hours before after following huge loops in the river. Of course we only knew this because Pete had a series of 1;50,000 aerial photographs of our route and was expert in their interpretation, a skill that took me some time to master.

The channel straightened and widened considerably when we entered the panhandle and made our way up the Okavango River proper. By then I was less in awe of my surroundings and was glad to meet the local fishermen paddling mekoro, the dugout canoes used throughout the Delta. At first I thought they all knew Pete, undoubtedly some did, but I soon learnt that the friendly, excited chatter was their normal, everyday mode. They were mainly from the baYei and Hambukushu tribes, the former powerful polers and swamp dwellers while the latter were more recent immigrants from the north.

It took us a full day and a half to motor upstream to just below Shakawe and we landed on a grassy bank below a newly built fishing camp just after midnight. The owner was Peter Becker, a businessman from Francistown who also owned Botswana Game Industries. No one was around and everything was quiet and dark. A fairly large tent was pitched at the top of the bank. We moored the boat and slept about fifty yards from the tent where the bank levelled out and a safe distance up from the water's edge to avoid any crocodiles. I awoke just as it was getting light and gathered together two or three logs to make a fire from quite a number that were scattered around the bank. I made tea as Pete roused from his slumbers and placed his camp chair next to mine by the fire.

We were startled by an angry outburst from a white man approaching at a trot from the tent, a rumpled-looking young guy with spectacles shouting in an American accent, "My crocodiles! What are you doing?"

He was a student researching crocodiles and had cut a number of logs to lengths of four up to about fifteen feet to represent different lengths of crocodile. The logs were scattered around the bank, rearranged at random by his assistant after he had gone to bed, and every morning he would estimate their lengths as soon as he emerged. He was very upset that we were making morning tea by burning his "crocodiles". However, he was soon placated and pleased to meet Pete, who was going to help him identify plants he'd collected.

Goran Blomberg was from a small town in Massachusetts, where his Swedish parents had settled when he was a small boy. He struck me as an unlikely crocodile student, very different from the hunters who told crocodile stories in Maun, such as John Seaman and Willie Phillips. We spent the day with him as he explained some of the questions he was trying to answer, mainly concerning the stones and other objects that crocodiles apparently ingest as ballast or as tools for grinding their food.

In the evening we ate a proper meal at the fishing camp (our first since Maun) and invited Goran to join us to make up for damaging his practice materials. Over a beer he explained how he came to be in the wilds of Africa studying crocodiles. Apparently, as a very small child in Sweden his mother tasked him with collecting eggs from the family's chickens every morning. He hated doing it because some of the chickens were aggressive and used to chase him. He developed a real fear of these and other birds. As a teenager and young man this irrational phobia persisted and he was advised by an analyst in Boston to try to work with some truly dangerous animals as a form of therapy, hence his interest in crocodiles. I don't know if he was ever cured, but after Shakawe he apparently continued with his academic career on various other crocodilians.

The river trip downstream back to Maun was even more enjoyable than the upstream journey. We travelled much faster through the swift-flowing upper channels, which could be a fairly monotonous tapestry of papyrus. Once we left the panhandle we headed for the Ngokha River then the Moanachira and Santantadibe, which took us down the northern and eastern edges of Chief's Island, as opposed to the western side which was skirted by the Boro River system that we had followed on the way up. How Pete found his way through the myriad interconnecting channels, all seemingly identical green tunnels of papyrus, was a mystery. Only intermittently could I locate our course on one of the aerial photos, but Pete easily located every bend and even most of the big trees.

We called in at Xugana, a luxury lodge situated on a beautiful lagoon. This had been constructed in the late 1960s by KDS and was one of only three tourist lodges in the whole Okavango. The manager of course knew Pete and we were treated to a free lunch in the company of two Texan couples who, at the insistence of the wives, were taking a couple of days' break from three weeks in a hunting camp. Their professional hunter and guide was a large, loud, jovial man called Tony Henley, a throwback to the "white hunters" of Kenya's heyday, who now lived in Natal. These were the first hunting clients I had ever met and I enjoyed their lively bonhomie. I was surprised to hear from the older of the two that he only wanted to shoot a good specimen of a sitatunga, nothing else, unlike his companion who had bought licences for a variety of species. He explained that he had collected most of the others on previous African safaris. It seemed to me that it was a hugely expensive undertaking for one trophy, but he assured us that he was really along for the wilderness and fun of it. The following day the four of them were flying by charter plane to see Victoria Falls. After that he had one more week to "bag" his elusive swamp antelope.

Downstream from Xugana the mosaic of islands, water and vegetation became more beautiful still. I decided that I preferred the Santantadibe over the Boro, a bias I still hold forty years later. Progress was easy and game was plentiful in the floodplains or maybe just more easily seen than on the other side of Chief's Island. We came across two baNoka polers in a mokoro and the older one greeted Pete like a long-lost brother. They had some buffalo meat, probably illegal, but so what – there were plenty of buffalo and very few truly traditional hunters. Pete explained that the baNoka, or River Bushmen, were present in the Okavango before the Batswana came to Ngamiland from the south. They were true swamp people who lived mainly by fishing, hunting and gathering edible wild plants. Although most now lived in villages on the fringes of the Delta and had mixed with later arrivals, such as the baYei and Hambukush tribes, there were still a few small communities deep in the swamp proper.

We eventually arrived back at the Thamalakane River just upstream of where we had turned up the Boro ten days earlier. It was late in the afternoon and we called in for a sundowner with Tony Graham at Island Safari Lodge. It had been a memorable trip and the best possible appetiser for a newcomer hoping to experience the amazing Okavango and make a success of a new life. Now these so-called "trans-Okavango adventures" are available commercially and many of the accessible islands are littered with tents and camping paraphernalia with boats and canoes parked on the bank. Participants have a great experience I hope, but I shall always be grateful that I was lucky enough to do it in 1974.

I did several more trips with Pete – mostly by boat, but occasionally in his Land Rover – and soaked up as much information as possible about this unique environment. He took me to Moremi Game Reserve many times. He kept a cache of boat fuel in drums at Mboma and we would use this tip of the Moremi mainland as a base for boat trips into and beyond the great lagoons of Gadikwe and Gobegha, with their islands of swamp figs festooned with heronries and nesting colonies of hundreds of marabou storks. Only rarely did we meet another motor boat, usually staff from the Department of Water Affairs office in Maun. We would also walk for miles in Moremi and on many large islands, including the huge Chief's Island. Pete would point out a vast array of plants, from grasses to trees, and I would make notes and do my best to remember a fraction. He was also a knowledgeable bird enthusiast and introduced me to dozens of new species of all kinds.

All this time Pete wore the same outfit of brown town shoes, check shirt, trousers and often a jacket, as if he were in an office – I suppose in some sense he was, at least in his workplace. He never carried a gun, even though we often came across buffalo and lions, occasionally elephants and other nominally dangerous animals, sometimes unexpectedly at close quarters. He did know how to use a gun because he told me that one of his tasks at Pandamatenga had been shooting rations, more often than not sable antelope because they were the most common species back then. However, he wandered, mostly alone, across every inch of the Delta for fifty years unarmed and unharmed – a truly unique man.

I like to think that Pete and I formed a bond, personally and professionally, if rather unequally, he as teacher and I as keen pupil. He was definitely a huge influence on my life in the Okavango and I never met anyone whose range and depth of knowledge of the plants and ecological functioning of the Delta could match his. He was the first person to travel from the source of the Okavango River in the Angolan highlands to the Delta and then from the Delta to where its outflow terminated in Lake Xau and the Makgadikgadi Pans. He would undertake these journeys while he was "on leave", for he seemed to have few other recreational pursuits. Also on leave he visited Kew Gardens in London to study at the world's greatest herbarium, to which he contributed many specimens. Once, while Jenny and I were on home leave and happened to travel to London, we were crossing the road at Piccadilly Circus when I heard my name called loudly. It was Pete, dressed as he always was. He was working at Kew and going to the theatre to watch the musical *Cats*. We had a drink in a nearby bar and ended up as his guests at the theatre – a memorable and entirely coincidental evening.

I did test our friendship on at least one calamitous occasion though. After a particularly hard party on a Friday night I was a bit late getting organised to accompany him to Moremi the next morning. Pete decided to go on ahead and I would follow when I was ready. We agreed to meet in Moremi where the turning to Mboma took off from the Third Bridge Road. It was during the rains in February and we were pretty certain to be the only people in the Reserve. Feeling still a little under the weather I drove as fast as I could along the sandy roads, splashing through dozens of water-filled depressions, which slowed me down quite a lot. After about two hours I went through the Moremi South Gate, forked left and continued more slowly through the mopane woodland towards Second and Third Bridges. I came around a bend in the track and saw Pete's Land Rover waiting about 400 yards in front of me. The next thing I knew I was crashing into the back of Pete's car! I must have fallen asleep while the vehicle carried on, with the deep spoor holding the wheels on the track. I jumped out and Pete met me with a very calm, "What did you do that for?"

I was at a complete loss for words and stuttered an inane apology. There was considerable damage to the two Land Rovers. Pete's rear bumper was bent badly and the fuel tank was punctured; my front bumper was equally damaged and my radiator was leaking seriously. Pete had been reading in the cab and was lucky not to suffer any whiplash, while I had bashed my forehead on the windscreen but was otherwise fine. The odds against hitting the only other vehicle in a 1,000 square mile wilderness must have been astronomical, but I managed it. We made a temporary repair to Pete's fuel tank with the old bush remedy of a paste made from green soap, but our attempts to fix the hole in my radiator were less successful. We tried melting plastic sugar bags, mealie-meal and green soap, but nothing worked, so, to add insult to injury, Pete had to tow me to camp.

By the middle of 1974 most of the UN team had arrived and settled in. The project leader was a Sinhalese, Mac Ernest; his deputy, the main hydrologist, Turgut Dincer, was a Turkish mathematics professor at Chicago University; there was a Swedish hydraulic engineer and a Danish sociologist; the general ecologist was British, Bill Astle, married to an attractive Brazilian dentist named Mercedes. Bill had spent most of his professional life working in Zambia and was mainly interested in botany.

The wildlife ecologist, my "boss", was Alistair Graham, a bespectacled, long-haired Kenyan who was an expert pilot and had a reputation as both a practical hands-on wildlife manager and a scientist. He had written two books: a controversial critique of wildlife conservation in Africa, *The Gardeners of Eden*; and a pictorial account of Lake Rudolf (now Lake Turkana) and its crocodiles, *Eyelids of Morning*, with photographer Peter Beard. Alistair and I got on famously from the start. He was very experienced, formidably intelligent and lots of fun. His blonde wife Jane, a free-spirited individual, also immediately fitted in with and stimulated the bohemian elements of Maun society.

Alistair's main contribution to the project was to devise and implement a sophisticated series of aerial wildlife surveys covering the Delta. Aerial census techniques were in their infancy, and had been largely confined to well-studied places in East Africa, such as the Serengeti. After putting together a composite map of the Delta from existing aerial photography, we designed a pattern of parallel flight lines aligned northeast to southwest across the main axis of the Delta. A small area right in its centre near Xo Flats was difficult to reconcile, so we merely threw away those two or three photographs and drew a few features freehand! Our map was subsequently adopted and reproduced in many forms over the years by the Government Department of Lands and Surveys and I don't know when it was eventually corrected – with the advent of GPS data I suppose.

Census flights are inevitably always a compromise between available time and funds and the accuracy of the data to be gathered. The Okavango is a very complex mosaic of wildlife habitats, with different usages by many species and dramatic seasonal variability. Consequently, it's an exceptionally difficult subject for effective aerial surveys. Flying transects at right angles to the main distribution of water flow seemed the best way to maximise the precision of the results.

By signing a deal to guarantee a certain number of hours flying every year, Alistair persuaded Dave Sandenbergh (a professional hunter and businessman who owned Aerkavango, a small air charter company), to buy a Helio Courier aircraft. He considered this aircraft to be ideally suited to our survey needs. It was a long, six-seater taildragger, with unparalleled slow flying ability, remaining controllable at twenty-five knots, and superb short take-off and landing (STOL) performance. It also had almost thirteen hours' endurance, making refuelling stops during surveys unnecessary. We had all been very impressed by a promotional film showing the aircraft descending to within three feet of the ground without landing, one man jumping out and another getting in before it climbed away. The Helio also had no stall warning indicator, but slats on the leading edges of the wings dropped into place to provide extra lift when the flying speed dropped below about fifty knots.

It was not a plane for a novice, but Alistair, who should have been born with feathers, could perform amazing feats. With the cargo doors removed I would often sit on the floor for hours, with my legs dangling in space, secured only by a piece of ski rope round my waist, taking vertical photographs of elephant herds and crocs on their nests. Both species grow throughout their lives, so accurate photography can reveal their ages. Alistair would circle very slowly, with the aircraft almost hovering if the wind was in our favour, and I would try to fill the viewfinder with the desired target.

On survey flights, with Alistair flying and me in the right-hand seat navigating by aerial photos, we covered the whole 6,000 square miles of the Okavango at 90mph and 300 feet above the ground. The transects were spaced one mile apart and the two observers sitting in the rear seats counted all the animals they saw inside strips 150 yards wide on each side of the aircraft. These strips were demarcated by fixing rods to the wing struts at a calculated distance apart. Thus, we were counting the animals in approximately seventeen per cent of the Delta and the total numbers could be derived by simple proportion. For example, if we counted 120 giraffes, the estimate of the population was 705. This is a huge simplification, but by recording actual speed, accurate height above ground, detailed position and other variables for each observation, the estimate can be statistically improved to, say, 705 plus or minus eighty. That is to say the population of giraffe was between 625 and 785 with a degree of confidence. It was important to repeat the survey as often as possible in exactly the same way and in various seasons. We carried out six censuses over two years and arrived at population estimates for sixteen different species in both dry and wet seasons. We also derived distribution data for the animals by assigning each observation a time, which could be plotted back to a position on the ground. The results were admittedly fairly crude and inaccurate, but for the first time they at least painted a rough picture of animal populations and their distribution throughout the Delta. This could be related to the ever-changing annual flooding regime. To paraphrase Churchill's quote about democracy: aerial wildlife censuses give the worst results, apart from all the other techniques! It was a start.

Each survey took three or four days to fly, allowing for adverse weather conditions and factors such as poor visibility caused by bushfires. We only flew in the mornings to take advantage of smooth conditions, consistent lighting and animal behaviour – many species seek shelter from the heat during the middle hours of the day and become harder to see. Cryptic species such as kudu are also far less suited to aerial counts than say wildebeest that stand out in the open most of the time. The data recordings on audio tape were then "cleaned" by the observers before any analysis was attempted. There was a great deal of data – thousands of observations for each flight – and it was decided to use a computer to analyse and map the results. A consultant from Kenya, David "Jonah" Western, flew down to Maun, sold us some advanced software and instructed us how to prepare the data and carry out the analysis. Jonah later headed the Kenya Wildlife Service and was an unlikely aerial survey expert because he suffered from severe airsickness – we had to put him down on various remote airstrips, to be picked up later, while we carried on.

In the early 1970s there was only one computer in Botswana and this was housed in a large building in Gaborone, the Government Computer Bureau. The machine was larger than an average bedroom and installed in an air-conditioned room with access allowed only to a few senior personnel; we could watch it operating through large windows from an anteroom. Its main function seemed to be to calculate civil service wages. The helpful man in charge, Mike Small, a stalwart of the rugby club, was interested in what we were doing and kindly allowed us to use the computer late at night, after government business had been completed.

First, the data tapes had to be transferred to punched cards by a team of ladies who "typed" the information over several hours. At 11.00 pm Mike arrived back at the Bureau to oversee the analysis. Hundreds of cards, with masses of tiny holes, were fed into the computer's card reader in a relatively quick process. Alistair and I waited expectantly, but it became clear that the results would only be available after 5.00 am! When we arrived back at daylight Mike proudly handed us a large pile of folded computer printouts.

On each printout was a stylised map of the Delta with all of the sightings of one species. The relative densities of the species in each grid cell were indicated by different sizes of circle. There was also a printout combining all the species' sightings on one map. Finally, there was a list of the population estimates for each species, with calculated variances, standard errors and other measures of the reliability of the estimates. It was all very impressive in 1974. The average laptop computer could do the same in a matter of seconds now, directly from the recording tapes and probably while still flying!

Comparing the results with today's situation the most startling observation is the relative paucity of elephants in the Delta then. There were, at most, fewer than 2,000 and these were almost completely confined to Moremi and the half of the Delta lying to the east of the Boro River. Recent censuses reveal more than a ten-fold increase in elephant numbers and a much wider range. This has had a striking effect on certain species of trees, in particular baobabs, fan palms and knobthorns, which have been drastically reduced. In some areas even the hardy mopane woodland has been transformed into short scrub.

Because some of the other commercial pilots were not comfortable flying the Helio (A2-AAK), mainly because of its idiosyncrasies as a taildragger on take-off and landing, Alistair flew the aircraft on many other tasks outside a wildlife remit. He designed a highly visible water depth gauge that could be photographed from the air. When these were deployed throughout the Delta we could measure the depth of water at dozens of points in an hour or so, compared with the days it took to visit each traditional gauge by boat teams from Water Affairs.

We also spent many hours assisting Bill Astle and Pete Smith to identify and photograph hundreds of exact locations throughout the Delta. This was to establish accurate ground truth (pre GPS) to interpret earlier series of aerial photographs depicting changes in flooding and vegetation. This was an important indication of the way the Delta functioned both hydrologically and biologically.

As part of our study of the Delta's wildlife populations Alistair had taken a particular interest in crocodiles. He had lots of experience working with them and took on a supervisory role over Goran Blomberg's study in the panhandle area. He improved on Goran's estimation of croc sizes by using an aerial technique of placing black and white boards, rather like his water depth gauges, of known lengths next to croc nests and then photographing the females as they lay by the boards. We struggled on foot, carrying these long boards, through the dense reeds and papyrus to find croc nests that we had identified from the air. We also dug up the nests to count the eggs, before carefully replacing them. This worked very well except for one large female who chased us every time we came near – unlike all the others who slipped quietly away as we approached noisily.

We often went out in our sixteen-foot aluminium boat on dark nights to catch and tag crocs in the Thamalakane River where it flowed through Maun in front of our houses. They were pretty easy to catch with flexible stainless-steel nooses, obtained from the Louisiana Department of Wildlife and Fisheries, with one end tied firmly to the boat. Alistair would sit at the back controlling the outboard motor while I searched the river with a powerful spotlight for the tell-tale red eyes of the beasts. Without speaking, I would signal by shaking the spotlight when I saw a croc and Alistair would slowly approach the spot as I got the noose ready on the end of a forked stick. The crocs seemed mesmerised by the light as long as it was held out in front of the boat. It was usually possible to get within a yard or so, carefully place the noose over their snouts, then touch the croc lightly under the chin with it, which caused them to lunge forward and downward, catching them around the neck as they tightened the noose. We caught dozens like this and hauled them into the boat after getting them to bite on a towel that closed their jaws as they spun. By the time we had them next to the boat they were pretty tired from trying to pull against the noose and we could hold them safely to measure them and ascertain their sex before marking them by cutting off scutes from their backs and tails in a unique code. They were then put back in the river, hopefully to be caught again a year or two later when their new measurements would tell us their growth rates. Youngsters, up to about two years or three-feet long, we would catch simply by grabbing them behind the neck by hand, but we quickly learnt that over about nine feet they were usually too strong for us, even with the noose, and we avoided them. When we did occasionally catch bigger ones we had to let them exhaust themselves pulling the boat before we could handle them well enough to get the noose off.

Alec Campbell, the former Director of Wildlife, became Director of the National Museum in Gaborone. The museum's live crocodile exhibit had been vandalised and he needed a couple of new animals. On one promising, moonless night, along with Norbert Drager to give a hand, we took the boat out and caught two crocs, one about seven and a half feet long and a larger male of almost nine feet – a record for us. We hog-tied them and took them back to Jeff Bowles' house. Jeff, also a vet, was the Chief Tsetse Officer and he and his family were on overseas leave. Theirs was the only house with a fairly large swimming pool, but it was old and needed a lot of maintenance so was often empty, or nearly so. At the time there was only a foot or so of dirty water in the deep end, which was ideal for our purpose. We put the two crocs in and used it as a holding pen until we had a better plan. Alistair called the museum, who agreed to take the crocs even though they were a little bigger than planned. Alistair also persuaded the chief pilot of Desert Airways, Brian Whitley, to take them to Gaborone. The problem was going to be how to get them out of the swimming pool and into the aircraft.

A few days after the capture, Alistair's powers of persuasion were turned on me and I agreed to jump from the side of the empty pool down onto the back of the bigger crocodile, basking in the dry shallow end. He assured me that if we could get it to bite a large towel it wouldn't release it to bite me! What I didn't realise was how strong the croc was after a few days' rest compared with when it had exhausted itself pulling our boat. I was effortlessly flipped against the pool wall before I could get a good hold and I scrambled out with Olympic agility and decided it was a two-man job. Jonathan, my Malawian foreman, reluctantly agreed to jump on the croc with me, as long as I had the front end. Our next attempt worked well, the animal fell for the towel trick again and once we had overpowered the croc we were able to tie its jaws closed with strips of rubber inner tube and lift it out of the pool with more help. Crocs have a powerful and quick bite, but can exert much less force to open their jaws. The smaller croc was much easier to restrain and we soon had them both tied securely to planks that almost completely prevented them from moving. They were duly loaded onto the back of our Land Rovers and driven to the airstrip.

Brian was waiting next to the Britten-Norman Islander aircraft ready to board for the scheduled flight to Gaborone. He baulked at the size of the two reptiles but after being assured that they could not move or, especially, open their jaws, he asked the only two ticket holders if they would mind having the crocs as fellow passengers. Luckily, they were good sports and agreed, so we loaded them on the floor along the narrow passageway between the seats. They arrived without incident at the old Gaborone airport and were driven off to the nearby museum and the waiting, newly cleaned pond. The only problem was the museum staff were too frightened to take off the inner tube holding their mouths closed. Luckily crocs don't need to eat every day because it wasn't until much later that Alec managed to cut the rubber with a razor attached to a long pole!

SIX

AFRICAN SKIES

Maun's remote location and the undeveloped state of the access roads made flying an attractive proposition. Botswana's normally clear blue skies and almost complete lack of any hills that you couldn't see over also helped. In 1975, Norbert Drager, together with Maun's new veterinary officer, Michael Maher, and an ex-TFC field officer, Ronnie Ridge, bought an old Cessna 172 aeroplane with the intention of learning to fly. Although there was no fully qualified instructor in Maun, there were a number of pilots with assistant instructor ratings and lots of enthusiasm. Also, the chief flying instructor from Wonderboom Airport in Pretoria, Neville Austin, a slim, cheerful and energetic man, used to visit Maun quite often because he shared a small camp off the southern edge of Chief's Island with the Wilmot family.

The Botswana Department of Civil Aviation (DCA) was fairly easygoing, especially when it came to bush flying in remote areas like Ngamiland and, in the absence of any other suitably qualified pilot in Botswana, Neville was appointed to certify student pilots to go solo and to perform essential flight tests before they were granted a full licence. In between his visits to Maun he authorised a couple of our resident assistant instructors to teach students both practical flying and ground school subjects, such as meteorology, air law and navigation (although, in truth, the bookwork wasn't taken too seriously).

Our perceived remoteness was illustrated by the rule that qualified pilots of any level were required to fly in corridors across the Kalahari until they had logged 200 hours in Botswana. This meant that most pilots had to fly from

Gaborone via Francistown, following the railway, and then northwest to Maun close to the road – a lengthy dog's leg. Like most rules it was not always adhered to, especially by old Botswana hands.

The proud new owners of A2-ZHD were keen to recruit other student pilots to contribute to the running costs of the little Cessna. I thought it would be both fun and useful, so I enrolled at a cost of R25 per hour (Botswana used the South African currency then). A licence required a minimum of forty hours flying so, with free ground schooling, it was possible to get a pilot's licence for R1,000. I was even luckier than most because Alistair was appointed an assistant instructor, so I was often able to gain experience for free by taking the controls of the survey aircraft on "ferry" flights while he caught up with book work, or just snoozed.

As soon as I could I logged the mandatory eight hours of dual-control flight in A2-ZHD under Alistair's instruction and was ready to go solo. On Neville's next trip through Maun I cornered him at the airfield on Christmas Eve 1975 and asked him to check me out. He kindly jumped into the right-hand seat of the Cessna after parking his own Piper Cherokee and we flew a few circuits of Maun's dirt airstrip (there was no control tower). After about ten minutes of "touch and goes" he instructed me to stop, got out and said brightly, "All yours." Suddenly I wasn't at all confident that I could repeat all by myself what we had just done. However, I managed to complete two more circuits and landings without any damage to myself or the aircraft and Neville duly signed my logbook.

Regulations demanded that until they'd logged fifteen hours, student pilots must fly one circuit with an assistant instructor before each solo flight. This was no problem when Alistair was around, so I quite quickly accumulated the hours. The only incident was when I asked another friend and assistant instructor, Mark Muller, to do a circuit with me. Mark was a young commercial pilot with Aerkavango. He and his best friend Brian Bridges were both keen, skilled fliers and always willing to help. On the morning of New Year's Eve I performed all the pre-flight checks, Mark climbed into the old aircraft and I taxied to the threshold of runway 08. We were accelerating down the runway and I had just raised the nose and felt the aircraft leave the ground when the engine cowling flew up in front of the windscreen, completely blocking our view. I instantly closed the throttle and we settled back down, thankfully in a straight line. I braked quite hard and there was a loud bang, after which we slowly decelerated and came to a stop. Mark jumped out to investigate: a couple of the engine cowling clips were broken; the others had vibrated loose; the loud bang was the brake pad on one wheel disintegrating because it too had become loose and trapped against the wheel. My hard braking had been too much for the worn components. Mark proclaimed that he didn't care what he signed, but no way was he getting back into that aircraft!

There was no maintenance facility in Maun and most basic stuff was very much do-it-yourself, so we just replaced the brake pads and fastened the cowling with fencing wire until we could obtain proper clips from Johannesburg. The C-172 was pretty old and had a sketchy history, but our enthusiasm was such that we were happy to fly it and there were very few alarming incidents, at least any due to the aircraft, except for one near-tragedy that occurred several months after I had qualified as a pilot.

Our daughter Samantha had been born in August 1974 at the single-bed maternity unit in Maun hospital. Jenny was rhesus-negative blood type so there could have been complications but the two missionary midwives in Maun had made excellent provision for any possible outcome. Sammy was born healthy, a day after the bed had been vacated by Hazel, one of the renowned Wilmot sisters, after the birth of her daughter Natasha.

Sammy loved to fly in the little aeroplane and often accompanied me, at first with our maid Sarah to control her, but later on her own. She nearly always fell asleep soon after take-off and often only woke up as we landed, so the attraction was a little puzzling. Coming up to her second birthday she had been standing on the passenger seat, without a belt, looking out of the window and shrieking in recognition of the hippos, buffaloes and elephants below. Shortly after landing the right-hand passenger door fell off onto the runway! The hinges had rusted through but had been covered with blue paint. I still shiver when I think how the door could have come off as she lent against it in mid-air.

After about ten hours of solo "experience", mainly circuits and bumps in Maun, with some stalls and forced landing practice thrown in, Alistair considered me ready for my first solo cross-country flight. From all my survey flying with Alistair I knew the Okavango and surrounding areas pretty well, so navigating the triangular course should have been easy. I was to fly north from Maun to Savuti, land there and then fly southwest to Xugana, land again and then fly southeast back to Maun. In the fairly slow C-172 this should have amounted to approximately three hours' flying.

I left Maun at about 8.00 am on April 4th in good weather and full of confidence. At 7,500 feet I could see the *kopjes* at Savuti after about forty minutes, shortly after passing east of Khwai River Lodge, and I was over the Savuti airstrip just after the hour. Everything looked good as I joined my landing circuit for an easterly approach into the prevailing breeze. There were no animals on the strip and it looked smooth. Only when I was over the runway threshold did it occur to me that the grass seemed very long, but I was committed and continued down with full flaps and flared to touch down. The little aircraft just about disappeared in the grass and came to a halt extremely quickly. I then realised that no one had landed at Savuti since before the start of the rains, at least four months earlier. There were very few tourists in 1975 and none at all during the wet summer, so Savuti, unlike today, was closed and deserted.

Getting airborne again was going to be a struggle. Using pretty much full power I managed to cut a swathe through the long grass along the midline of the airstrip. Luckily, there were no warthog burrows or other holes. My first effort was about 250 metres long and I taxied up and down, making it a bit wider each time. When I tried a take-off run it was obvious that I wouldn't get airborne without a lot more "mowing". This took some considerable time and a great deal of worry. I couldn't call Maun by radio to tell Alistair about my problem because I was out of VHF range on the ground and there were no other aircraft flying in the vicinity. Eventually, using extra flaps and some unorthodox manoeuvres I managed to get the aircraft off the ground and was mightily relieved to clear the grass and get on my way to Xugana.

I climbed out and turned left on a southwesterly heading towards the Okavango and Xugana and calmed myself down for a routine flight. I knew the Xugana airstrip was OK because we'd used it on a survey a few days before, so I was soon pretty relaxed. After a few minutes I could see a fairly big river in front. This puzzled me because I should still have been too far from the western reaches of the Khwai to see it. As I reached the water I saw a large lagoon far away to my left, and with a start I recognised Zibadianja, where the Savuti Channel takes off from the Linyanti. We had camped next to it for a couple of weeks on the previous year's buffalo sampling exercise. Across this was the Linyanti Swamp, a much smaller version of the Okavango in the Caprivi Strip of Namibia. This was quite a shock because it meant that I was flying north of my intended route by about forty-five degrees. It took me a while to realise that I had been careless with my take-off checks and had not aligned my direction indicator (DI) with the magnetic compass after all the backwards and forwards movements on the ground. I consulted the magnetic compass, reset the DI, worked out my true heading and then adjusted my course to the south and Xugana. Had I not been familiar with the area I might not have noticed my mistake until I was over Angola!

A half hour later I saw the northern edge of the Delta and soon landed with considerable relief at Xugana. I still hadn't been able to contact Alistair, or anyone else, by radio and was now well behind schedule. Wasting no time, I took off again without any problems and headed across the familiar mosaic of islands and streams that make up the Delta towards Maun. I finally made radio contact with Alistair about halfway there and landed safely at midday, slightly more than an hour overdue. I expected him to be frantic, but he seemed pretty matter of fact about my adventure. He must have been relieved to see me return though, not least because the C-172 only had about four hours' endurance on full tanks so, although I had spent some time on the ground, it was getting pretty close to empty.

A month or so later I flew another cross-country flight. This time an hour or so south to Deception Pan in the CKGR. Mark and Delia Owens, young researchers from America were camping there, studying brown hyaenas and lions. They subsequently became quite famous by writing *Cry of the Kalahari*, an emotional and exciting, if not strictly accurate, account of their time at Deception Valley.

In their early days I was partly responsible for them because of my position as Senior Biologist in National Parks. Alistair authorised the flight and I used the opportunity to take Mark and Delia their post and a few fresh supplies from Maun. The flight to Deception Valley was uneventful and I landed on the flat surface of the pan, where they had marked out a short strip by driving up and down with their Land Rover – avoiding holes. They were excited to see me and to receive the unexpected post and goodies. They existed on a shoestring and were constantly writing letters to try to obtain funds to continue their research. If it hadn't been for the generosity of the Maun community they would not have been able to continue. In the post, however, was a letter from the National Geographic Society informing them that they were to receive a research grant – their first – so they were overjoyed.

After a celebratory mug of their precious coffee I climbed back in and took off across the pan. I flew around at low level for a few minutes to see the hundreds of springbok and gemsbok that congregated in the valley. In early May it was green and beautiful and I was a little envious of the Owens' idyllic situation. It was easy to forget the harsh, brown, dusty wasteland it became in

September and October, towards the end of the dry season, when temperatures are in the forties Celsius and there are constant hot, dry winds.

I turned and headed just west of north towards Maun. I intended to climb to 4,500 feet, but after a couple of minutes the engine abruptly stopped. I was about 1,000 feet above the ground so I turned back along the pan thinking that I would be able to land safely almost anywhere, but preferably on, or at least close to, the Owens' makeshift airstrip. I started a glide down towards the pan floor and the engine started again. Very strange; I investigated by flying fairly level along the flat valley and everything seemed OK, the gauges were all normal, the switches were in the correct position, there was plenty of fuel and so on. Turning once more towards Maun I started to climb over the dunes and the engine stopped again. This time I single-mindedly followed the training procedure for a precautionary landing and put the aircraft down on the strip without taking any more chances.

I didn't make a Mayday call because the Owens had a radio to communicate with Safari South's office in Maun. I asked the manager, my friend Ryland Wallace, to get hold of Alistair to give me some advice. Half an hour later Alistair was on the radio and I described the events. He thought it might be a carburettor problem, perhaps caused by dirty fuel. He and Wally Johnson, a professional hunter and experienced pilot, agreed to fly down and assist, but not until the following morning. I spent the night in a spare tent, made memorable by the attentions of one of Mark's study lions who kept us awake for most of the night, despite a few tots of whisky in further celebration of their new financial support.

Alistair and Wally arrived early the next day in a Cessna 206. They stripped and cleaned the 172's carburettor. Alistair flew it around the pan a couple of times and then announced over the radio that he was heading for Maun and that Wally and I should fly behind him and keep in touch. Both aircraft flew back to Maun without further incident. In theory all this was illegal, I should have contacted Gabs and reported the problem, whereupon a licensed engineer would have eventually been sent out. This would in all probability have cost a small fortune and taken several days.

My flying progressed well thanks to advice and demonstrations by Mark, Brian and Wally. I also continued to take control of the aircraft on ferry flights to and from survey areas, although Alistair always took over for the survey transects themselves. I finally passed my flight test in September 1976, but not without causing Neville some consternation at Xaxaba airstrip, where he asked me to simulate a forced landing. We used his Piper Cherokee 140 for the test and I'd never flown it, or any other low-wing aircraft, before. He thought I was going to put it down in the Boro River, just short of the airstrip, but I managed to caress the reeds and just make the runway threshold. I passed, and collected my Private Pilot's Licence (PPL) on my next trip to Gabs, two months later. It was time to start some useful flying.

The Game Department had obtained a Maule Rocket aircraft to fly some surveys of their own. This was a four-seater canvas aircraft with a taildragger configuration. It was far less forgiving than the Cessnas I was used to. It had lots of power but relatively small wings, so it didn't float like a Cessna. If you reduced power it dropped like a stone. I also found it quite tricky to master the tail wheel, especially on landing. There were lots of exciting moments and many high bounces, requiring go-arounds and new approaches, but I gradually got the hang of it. There were fewer pilots around who had taildragger time, but Alistair, Mark and Brian were all very helpful, experienced bush pilots.

My conversion training was completed in Gabs under a Swiss instructor called Roald Nanni, an airline pilot with years of experience. Once, seeing my difficulty with landing, he laughed, said, "Watch me," and took over control. With his arms folded he landed the aeroplane dead straight and very softly, using only the pedals. This convinced me that my tension and nervousness was causing me to fight with the aircraft instead of letting it fly naturally. After that, it became quite simple to control, although I still had one or two hair-raising moments over the years.

Shortly after I had obtained my PPL, Martin Mercer, the Swiss Veterinary Officer in Ghanzi, announced he was to marry Rosemary Alberts, a pretty, dark-haired girl from Palapye. He asked me to be his best man at the wedding in Johannesburg. He also asked Michael Maher, the Irish Veterinary Officer in Maun who was also a Catholic priest and one of the co-owners of the old Cessna 172, to officiate at the wedding. This was an opportunity for a real, international, cross-country adventure.

We estimated that it would take about seven hours to fly from Maun to Rand Airport in Johannesburg, which sounded a whole lot better than the seventeen hours' minimum driving time. Father Mike had also just qualified for his PPL and, with only forty-four hours' flying time, he demanded that I fly there and he fly back because I had just over fifty hours experience and was therefore the senior pilot. Mike was much older, probably in his early fifties, with a marked Irish brogue. He was also an extremely scandalous, but popular, individual, given to carousing and causing consternation completely out of character with his religious vocation. Somehow, whatever state he'd been in at a party in the wee small hours, he would turn up to conduct early mass every Sunday morning. No one seemed to know his exact background and many entertained doubts about the veracity of his qualifications but, whatever the truth, he performed his dual role competently, even though he could be a little unorthodox at times.

The day before the wedding weekend, Mike and I took off in the Cessna and headed for Selebi-Phikwe, a new copper-mining town in eastern Botswana and roughly on track for Pretoria, our destination for that night. It was about two-and-a-half hours' flying from Maun and we planned to refuel and clear customs and immigration there for the onward cross-border flight. The landing on a tar runway was a first for both of us and I had difficulty judging the height of the aeroplane as we descended on a short final approach, which led to a rather high flare and quite a heavy bump onto the tar. No damage done however and we quickly refilled the tanks and cleared customs and immigration before filing a flight plan (another first) for the journey to Wonderboom Airport, just north of Pretoria.

After take-off we settled into a course just east of south, at an altitude of 7,500 feet above sea level, about 4,000 feet above the ground. The weather was clear and after about half an hour we could clearly see the Limpopo River forming the border below us. We estimated that we had another hour and a half to Wonderboom. I had the radio tuned to the approach frequency of Wonderboom, but hadn't heard any transmissions. However, this was pretty normal for flying around Maun, our only previous experience, so we thought little of it. About halfway there we tried to call them, but got no response, so we assumed we were still out of range and carried on. When we estimated that we were about half an hour out we tried again, several times, still without any response. I then became a little anxious about flying around *incommunicado* in a foreign country with more air traffic than I was used to. With Approach not replying, we tried to call Wonderboom Tower, but again drew a blank. Mike suggested that "the boggers are ignoring us because we aren't speaking Afrikaans." But neither he nor I could say more than the odd greeting in that language and certainly not enough to converse with a flight controller.

We were in a bit of a fix and tried repeatedly, getting more and more worried. I didn't buy Mike's prejudiced explanation and suspected that our radio had developed a fault. When we could clearly see the airport (we knew it because it was next to Onderstepoort Veterinary School) we were frankly quite panicky and I began a very nervous descent, calling on the radio all the time in the hope that we were transmitting, if not receiving. Mike was still colourfully cursing the controller and, indeed, most of the Afrikaner nation. I urgently interrupted him to ask his advice about landing at a controlled airfield without radio communications. Neither of us could remember anything about it in our ground-schooling. Mike thought there had been something about buzzing the control tower, but wasn't sure of the details. Bereft of any better idea and too close now to try anything else I aimed the aircraft at the tower and flew in a steep dive pulling up fairly close to the roof of the building, rather like we sometimes buzzed camps in the Delta to announce our arrival. I then pulled a fairly tight turn and repeated the manoeuvre from the opposite direction.

People appeared on the parking apron, running around and waving their arms at us. Two men ran for parked aircraft and quickly climbed inside. I was terrified by now, but Mike was shouting gleefully, "Now we've got the boggers' attention!" I just wanted to get the aircraft on the ground as quickly as possible, but a further complication lay in the fact that there were two runways crossing each other (yet another first). In a complete panic I quickly checked that I couldn't see any other airborne aircraft and without further formality I landed on what appeared to be the major runway. I hadn't checked the wind or the sign indicating the runway in use and landed downwind, the opposite direction to that required. The little Cessna found the tarmac and easily stopped without using most of the unaccustomed long runway. I was never more relieved, and started up the taxiway towards the apron under the control tower. Now safe, it occurred to me that of the two people in the aircraft it was me, an avowed atheist, that had been doing the only praying, not the priest!

As we made our way between the rows of parked aeroplanes we realised that we were the centre of attention and a small welcoming party awaited us as I turned into a parking bay.

"The boggers don't look all that friendly," commented my co-pilot.

The prop stopped and we opened the doors to get out. We were confronted by a small posse of Afrikaner officials, wearing regulation uniforms and moustaches and appearing, as most of them do, to be well over six feet tall and of generous girth.

"What do you think you're f… doing!" was a rough and bowdlerised translation of their leader's furious opening question. Afrikaans is a wonderful language to swear in.

I glanced at Mike and stammered, "I don't think my radio is working properly. I'm sorry, I couldn't hear any of your transmissions."

I was immediately shouted down, this time in English, but with the same Anglo-Saxon inclusions.

"This is a f… radio-controlled airport! You can't land here without a f… radio!"

"I'm sorry, but I didn't know where else to go."

"For Christ's sake, you should've landed at Warmbaths."

"Where's that?"

"Look at your f… map, for f…'s sake!"

"We don't have a map."

"What the f…! I don't believe it! Where have you come from?"

"Botswana."

By now quite a crowd had gathered, all Afrikaans, and mainly fliers I supposed.

"Can you f… believe these guys? They've flown here from Botswana with no f… map!"

This brought a few giggles from the audience, most of whom probably thought Botswana was the other side of the Congo up in "black Africa", as it was then known.

"You'd better come up to the tower, now!" ordered the man in charge, turning to stride away.

Most of the spectators were fairly good humoured and began to disperse, leaving Mike and I to sheepishly follow the official. As we climbed the stairs to the tower Mike was muttering pseudo-ecclesiastical protestations concerning the South African administration and its presumed lack of authority over foreign aircraft and nationals such as us. I wasn't at all sure just how many laws and regulations we might have transgressed and my head was full of thoughts of an impounded Cessna, nights in gaol and deportation. It was OK for Mike to be obstreperous, but I was the pilot in-charge and likely to bear the brunt of any sanctions.

Up in the tower, the flight controller was much calmer, perhaps because his audience now consisted of only one other official, who was kept busy dealing with radio communications from several aircraft, or maybe, as Mike had hinted, he was also unsure of his ground with respect to international flight crews. I explained that we were veterinarians with an appointment at the next-door faculty and that a senior professor was meeting us (Bluey Carmichael had recently joined Onderstepoort Research Institute and was putting us up for the night). Being "Doctors" instantly raised our standing in the controller's eyes; something deep in the Afrikaner psyche causes them to treat uniforms, rank and all things official with respect bordering on awe. We further explained that Mike was also a priest and on his way to officiate at a wedding. Mike turned on the Irish charm and in no time we were on friendly terms with our inquisitor. He called a resident radio technician to check and repair our radio and took us downstairs to the airport shop to obtain a map, the two things he insisted on before he would let us continue our journey the following morning to Rand Airport in Germiston. The radio was duly fixed (without charge), but the shop didn't have a map. No problem, the controller drew us a sketch map of the route to nearby Rand Airport and extracted from us a promise that we would buy a map there before our return journey.

Bluey was waiting and escorted us through customs and immigration with a minimum of fuss, bamboozling the officials that our various bags contained specimens for veterinary research and were the property of the South African Government. He then drove us to the nearest bar for a couple of swift gin and tonics while we described our adventure. He had witnessed our highly unorthodox approach to the airport and the effects on the airport staff of our buzzing the tower and landing from the wrong direction.

"Jeez mate, they must've thought it was a bleedin' air raid!" he laughed, and we enjoyed his exaggerated and colourful description of the commotion we had caused in the usually sleepy airport, feeling very lucky to have got away with it.

Quite early the following morning Bluey dropped us back at Wonderboom Airport and I left Mike to do the pre-flight inspection while I went to the briefing room to file a flight plan to Rand Airport, a very busy airport just on the southeastern side of Johannesburg in the suburb of Germiston. Our friend of the day before was on duty in the tower again and repeated his directions: "Fly over Atteridgeville and head for Sandton City, a very big building, you can't miss it. Then take a heading of 125 and it will take you directly to Rand."

We were quickly airborne and the weather was wonderfully clear, so we easily picked out Atteridgeville to the west of Pretoria. It was a huge featureless township, like many others in apartheid days, and was home to over 100,000 black South Africans, who daily made their way to work in the "white" city of Pretoria. We then turned our attention to the skyline of Johannesburg, about forty miles to the south, and headed that way, looking for a "very big building". To residents of Maun, a very big building was a different concept and Mike and I soon realised that they were as common in Johannesburg as mud huts were in Maun. It seemed to us that the whole city comprised very big buildings. As we got closer – flying over affluent suburbs, judging by the housing styles and swimming pools – I began to feel nervous again. We had been told to remain under 6,000 feet above sea level because higher altitudes were apparently reserved for controlled flights – a little challenging when the centre of Johannesburg is at least 5,500 feet.

Eventually we settled on what appeared to be the highest building near the city centre and headed for it. Later we found out that this was the Hillbrow Tower, the tallest building in the southern hemisphere at that time. It was clearly higher than we were and we flew around the south side, well below its summit. This was an extremely nerve-wracking experience in the ancient little Cessna because we seemed perilously close to some of the surrounding buildings. Turning onto a heading of 125 degrees we left Hillbrow behind and started to look for Rand Airport. We had been told it also had cross runways and was situated next to a lake, surrounded by large spoil dumps from the ubiquitous gold mines. We expected it to be about fifteen minutes flying from Sandton, but of course we weren't aware that we hadn't been to Sandton and that Hillbrow was much closer.

I called the Rand Airport approach frequency and explained that I was unfamiliar with the area, but that I was inbound from Sandton. The calm voice said, "No problem, continue and call 'field in sight'." He then continued to talk to a number of other aircraft that were converging on the airport. Mike and I were desperately looking around for the airport or lake, or anything to give us a clue. I eventually saw an airstrip in the distance, but as I was turning towards it I asked Mike if he thought it might be Jan Smuts, the huge international airport east of Johannesburg, full of jumbo jets and similar terrifying traffic. Mike had flown into Jan Smuts, unlike me who had arrived in South Africa by ship.

"Now, I suppose it just could be," Mike replied, which made me want to weep and jump out.

In a panic I turned the plane back the way we had come. As he looked down Mike yelled that there was an airstrip directly below us. Banking steeply, I could make out the "X" layout of the runways and a lake close to some small, yellow hills. I called the controller and excitedly told him I thought we were overhead. He merely droned that I should switch to the tower's frequency and call “field in sight”. I complied and, after a few attempts, managed to interrupt the transmissions and report what I guessed our position to be. The tower instructed me to, “Join downwind for runway 36,” adding that I was, “number three behind a Baron and a Chieftain.” This meant nothing to me, except that they certainly outranked a mere vet, and I couldn’t see any other planes anyway.

Mike was scribbling on his palm with a biro and said, “Downwind for 36, that’s zero degrees.”

In another blue funk I manoeuvred to descend to circuit height, heading due north. When I was level with the tower I called, “A2-ZHD downwind for 36.”

“I don’t have you visual,” replied the tower. “Continue your approach and call left base.”

I couldn’t understand why he was unable to see me and worriedly wondered again if we were at the right airport. All I could do was follow instructions and hope. I duly turned left and reported left base, but the tower still insisted that he couldn’t see us.

“Turn on your landing lights and call finals,” was his next instruction and he continued to direct other aircraft that were in, or close to, his circuit.

When I turned and began my final descent and approach I called him as instructed, “Zulu Hotel Delta on finals 36.”

Just then Mike exclaimed, “Will ye look at that daft bogger, he’s taking off towards us!”

Almost simultaneously the controller screamed, “ZHD turn right immediately and climb out!”

I did as I was told and watched with horror as a light twin aircraft hurtled down the runway and took off down to my left and behind us.

“Climb to circuit height and report,” came the curt instruction.

The poor little Cessna was a bit short of power to climb abruptly at 6,000 feet, but I called as instructed a minute or so later.

“Turn left and maintain,” was the next equally sharp order.

I obediently flew parallel with the runway until I was instructed to turn left again. A minute later the controller again ordered, “Turn left again.” As I did so he barked, “You are *now* on finals for runway 36! Cleared to land.”

When we touched down I was in a worse state of near-hysteria than the previous day at Wonderboom. The controller told me where to park and to report to the tower forthwith. I had nearly managed to land the wrong way round for the second day running – this time *with* a radio. I couldn’t blame

Mike's geometry or the diagram he'd drawn on his hand, but I will never ever forget again that the opposite of 360 degrees is 180 not zero.

This time the controller was English-speaking, much less intimidating, and behaved as if he came across dangerous idiots flying every day. He merely advised me to practise my radio procedures a little more and, of course, obtain a map without delay. In fact I got to know him quite well months later when I began to fly the Maule Rocket taildragger to Rand for maintenance. It was an unusual aircraft and attracted attention. One unforgettable landing I made on his watch resulted in a ground loop and I spun off the runway at high speed onto the grass. When I had finally fought and regained control he calmly said, "A2-WNP you may rejoin the runway at your discretion."

After grabbing our bags Mike and I had a couple of drinks at the airport bar, discussing how lucky we were to still be in one piece, safe on the ground, and how different it was flying in "civilised" places with lots of air traffic. We eventually took a taxi to the Milpark Holiday Inn where most of the wedding guests would be and checked in. I quickly showered and changed my bush shorts and flip-flops for jeans, a shirt and socks and shoes, in an effort to dress for the evening. I then caught the lift down to the cocktail bar to meet other wedding guests. As I was walking through the door I spied a few friends at the bar and headed towards them. The neat, Italian-looking barman pointed at my jeans and started to say they weren't allowed in the cocktail bar when I felt an excruciating pain in my groin – just where he was pointing. It felt like being stabbed with a red-hot needle. I dropped to the floor as if I'd been shot, clutching my crotch, leaving the barman staring at his pointing finger wondering what had happened. Two more agonising shots made me rip off my jeans as fast as I could. A scorpion scuttled across the carpet before being smashed by someone's boot! I gingerly got to my feet and did up my clothing while the assembled crowd laughed, oohed and aahed. A cold Castle lager was thrust into my hand and I was tempted to pour it over my groin, but managed to drink it instead. The bar's dress regulations were forgotten and we had quite a party, although I was in some pain for the best part of half an hour. This was only the beginning of a calamitous weekend I've always been ashamed of, which resulted in the bride and groom not speaking to either Mike or me for many years.

To begin with we got very drunk at the hotel that evening and went on the town with a group of male guests, but without the groom, who obviously saw what was coming. We finally got to bed just as daylight crept into the city.

Mike woke me at about 9.00 am because I had to buy a suit and trimmings for the wedding at 1.00 pm. Thanks either to the leprechauns or his multivitamin remedy he seemed fine. He had a small sample of the cloth the bridesmaids' dresses were made of and that my suit had to match. We went to the biggest department store we knew, Stuttafords, and I sat down in the menswear department feeling rough. Mike produced the cloth and together with the sales assistant produced a suit that was about the right colour and size. Being colour blind I couldn't have helped much anyway. They quickly provided a matching shirt and tie as well as acceptable shoes and socks and I was ready to go, after forking out what seemed like a month's salary. We then returned to the hotel and decided to have a couple of gin and tonics to brighten us up and by the time we dressed to go to the church we were feeling pretty good.

The first problem was that we didn't know the address of the church and everyone else had already left the hotel. The taxi driver wasn't much help and, being pre-cell phones, it was a mission to locate the place. We eventually arrived and retired to the priest's house in the grounds of the church for Mike to borrow his vestments and the other paraphernalia, all quite alien to me. Father McCormack insisted on opening a bottle of good Irish whiskey "to bless the wedding", so the three of us had a couple of measures. By the time we finally made it to the altar the bride and her father were waiting to enter the church. The service was mostly fine, except for Mike's "hope that the couple would have as happy a marriage as Martin's parents," (whom he falsely claimed to know well), unfortunately they had gone through a bitter divorce some years previously.

Mike was quite garrulous during the blessing, but that was put down to Irish blarney and eventually the service and accompanying formalities were completed. The wedding party left the church in a shower of confetti and good wishes from the congregation and everyone headed off to the reception after the usual socialising and wedding chatter in the sun-drenched churchyard. We had to go back to Father McCormack's house for Mike to change and for me to hand over a generous cheque for the use of the church from Mr Alberts, the father of the bride. This led to more tots of Irish whiskey and we didn't leave until the bottle was finished. The next problem was to find the reception. Neither of us knew where it was being held but we eventually arrived, very drunk and much too late to participate in the speeches and other formalities. We mumbled apologies, but it was obvious that we'd let the newly-weds down very badly and our relationship never recovered. Martin and Rosemary left

Botswana shortly after to take up a post in Bujumbura, Burundi. I saw and heard nothing from them until one Saturday morning, ten years later, when Martin turned up at my clinic in Gaborone and suggested that we shake hands and make up, which was very gracious of him.

The Botswana Department of Civil Aviation (DCA) in those days consisted mainly of two expatriate commercial pilots with many years of flying experience in Africa. Bill West and Tony Vise were both reasonable and accommodating men who didn't take rules and paperwork all that seriously. There were, after all, only a handful of light aircraft operating in the country, mostly out of Maun as it developed as a centre for safaris. Another one or two were based in Gaborone and Francistown. The total number was probably fewer than twenty single-engined light aircraft and half that number of twins. Most of the DCA's work involved the regulation and development of scheduled services between Johannesburg and the fast-growing Gaborone, and of the internal carrier, Desert Airways, which operated scheduled flights from Gaborone to Maun three times a week and to a couple of other centres intermittently. A visit to Maun was an enjoyable excursion for them and they normally "held court" in Crocodile Camp on the Thamalakane River after a day of inspections at the Maun airstrip.

Bill West stood about six and a half feet tall and was known as Lofty. He was a popular, avuncular character who liked a few drinks. Tony was of average size and a little more serious, although responsible might be a better word, but he also enjoyed a drink. They liked to fly together around the country, inspecting airstrips and getting to know the flying community. By mid-1977 I was regularly flying the Wildlife Department's Maule Rocket to count wildlife and to survey game areas in an effort to come up with hunting quotas based on some form of scientific methodology. It was impossible to file accurate flight plans and my returns to Maun were erratic, to say the least. One day I had been flying in the Khwai concession, north of Maun, and decided to call in at Savuti to check on Chris McBride, a lion researcher who was based there and who, like the Owens in the Kalahari, fell under my loose supervision. I eventually took off from Savuti at last light and headed for Maun. There were no lights on the Maun airstrip, but I called my friend Ryland by radio, who arranged for a couple of vehicles to shine headlights down the strip for my landing. This was highly illegal, and I didn't have a night rating, but I wasn't the only pilot to push the limits and a number of us landed on bush strips out of hours. I found my way easily to Maun by moonlight and approached at low level down the

Thamalakane River, which reflected the moonlight and led me directly to the airstrip. I turned onto finals and was happy to see the converging beams of the headlights on the pale gravel surface before landing safely and taxiing to the parking area, halfway down the strip by the fence.

One of the Land Rovers drove up and Ryland greeted me with the news that Bill and Tony were at Croc Camp and it would probably be best to go there and explain myself. This was a bit worrying, but there was nothing for it but to try to come up with some plausible excuse for breaking the rules. As I drove out to Croc Camp I racked my brains but could come up with nothing that would mitigate my irresponsibility, particularly as I had just about taken the roof off the bar as I flew past down the river.

The bar was pretty lively and one or two drinkers laughed and shook a finger at me in mock admonition. I took a deep breath and walked up to stand between the bar stools of the two DCA officials, who were engaged in jovial banter with a few professional hunters and pilots. I greeted Bill and Tony respectfully and admitted that it had been me who was flying the aircraft in the dark about an hour ago, which they and most of the bar were well aware of.

There was a significant lull in conversation as Bill turned to Tony and asked, "I didn't hear an aircraft, did you Tony?"

His colleague replied, "No. A very loud speedboat went past though."

A fresh round of drinks was on me.

Brian Bridges, one of Aerkavango's first pilots, was a gifted flyer who quite quickly became competent with the Helio Courier (A2-AAK) and had it endorsed on his licence. Brian wasn't one for rules and regulations and his reputation was known to the DCA bureaucrats who eventually replaced Bill and Tony, especially a British expat called Bob Hampshire, the Chief Flight Safety Officer, every inch the old-school aviator, right down to the RAF-style handlebar moustache. When Brian certified me to move up from a C-206 to a C-210, Bob quipped, "No doubt the flight test was conducted in the bar at Croc Camp."

He once came across Brian smoking his pipe while seated on a plastic jerrycan next to Aerkavango's Super Cub. The tiny aircraft was so slow that pilots habitually took an extra jerrycan of fuel. Brian replied to Bob's sarcastic, "I don't suppose that's Avgas, Mr Bridges?" by knocking out his pipe on the jerrycan and saying, "Of course not, Mr Hampshire, never." Upon which the official walked away, shaking his head in exasperation.

Ironically, Brian and his boss, Dave Sandenbergh, inadvertently demonstrated just how slowly and safely the Helio Courier actually could fly, by crashing it into the papyrus swamps. They had been away all morning flying in the upper, wettest part of the Delta. The story goes that Dave was actually flying, but for "official" reasons (Dave wasn't checked out on the aircraft) Brian claimed to be in control at the time of the incident. The cargo doors had been removed and they were flying low and slow looking for bull elephants. It was said that they had a .458 rifle in the aircraft, but maybe that was just speculation. During one tight descending turn the aircraft went into an irrecoverable situation where there wasn't enough power to climb out. The Helio sank gently into the papyrus, like landing on cotton wool. There was remarkably little damage and Brian and Dave were completely uninjured, despite not wearing seat belts. They were, however, in a remote and inhospitable situation, with little chance of a speedy rescue. After an uncomfortable night in the small aircraft, plagued by hordes of mosquitoes and surrounded by wild animals, most notably crocodiles, they were picked up by helicopter the following day after the South African military from the Caprivi Strip were alerted. A2-AAK remained in the papyrus swamp for over a year until drier conditions allowed it to be pulled onto a tiny, sandy island fringe, patched up, mainly with duct tape and, incredibly, flown out, demonstrating its incomparable STOL abilities.

All the bush pilots operating from Maun in those days have tales to tell, although most of them seemed far more competent and skilled than I would ever be. Many were professionals or commercial pilots who had accumulated years of experience, including John Allott, who earned the nickname Captain Cool after landing safely on a small pan in the bush with his employer Harry Selby and family on board. His propeller had disintegrated, but he didn't bat an eyelid, merely shut down the engine and glided into the dry pan. There was a larger pan close by but John maintained that he knew from bird shoots that the surface was quite rough. Brian Bridges and Mark Muller continue to expertly fly all manner of machines, but now do it for fun as retired businessmen who still love the bush. In the twenty-first century Maun boasts several large air-charter operators, with dozens of aircraft and a host of young pilots from all over the world keen to accumulate flying hours over the incomparable Okavango Delta. Over eighty tourist lodges, many with their own private airstrips, now keep the Delta's skies so much busier than those over Johannesburg that so terrified me in the 1970s.

Some flying incidents were serious and there were inevitably one or two tragedies, some caused by irresponsible behaviour, but not always. Two instances that could have been disastrous, but ended happily, occurred between

Gaborone and Maun. One involved an old friend, Andy Saunders, who often flew a Cessna 206 from Gaborone while he was supervising the construction of Maun's first stretch of tar road, along the main road past Riley's Hotel.

Andy would arrive in Maun loaded with fresh groceries in cool boxes for the housewives, among whom he was extremely popular. One morning his aeroplane failed to show up and as the time passed we realised that there had to be a serious problem. The DCA in Gaborone was notified and they instigated a search and rescue operation. There had apparently been no Mayday call and the aircraft had not been heard from after leaving the Gaborone control zone. The official search was carried out first along the flight corridor dog's leg.

Alistair and I had a hunch that Andy might have flown a direct route, against the rules, because he knew the country exceptionally well, even though he had fewer than the required 200 hours as a pilot. We therefore flew two aircraft from Maun on a direct track southeast towards Gaborone. I was on Alistair's starboard side, about half a mile away, in the Maule with Jeff Bowles, the Chief Tsetse Officer, in the right-hand seat. About half an hour out of Maun, heading for Kuke Corner, a well-known landmark where three veterinary fences converged near Rakops, Jeff suddenly shouted that he had seen something unusual and white some distance off the starboard wing. Alerting Alistair, who was flying a Cessna 210, I turned sharply to the right, into the sun and started to descend. We soon saw an aeroplane in the bush, no more than two miles from Kuke Corner to the northwest. It was definitely Andy's C-206 and we were briefly elated that it obviously had not burned, but then we saw it was upside down and our fears returned. We flew a low pass and thought the aircraft looked relatively undamaged with the doors open. We then saw Andy and his passenger standing in a small clearing waving frantically. Another slow and lower pass and we could clearly see Andy giving a thumbs up; behind him were two of the Cessna's seats and some cool boxes, so we knew they were unhurt and had more than enough provisions to spend the night in relative comfort while we got a vehicle to them. Very early the next morning Jeff and Ryland drove out before daylight to get close to the crash site along the veterinary fence. Alistair and I flew together in the C-210 to intercept the vehicles and slowly guide them through the bush to find Andy and his companion. They had spent the night quite happily eating prawns and drinking champagne from their freight, happy to be alive and uninjured.

The second occasion was a forced landing made by the scheduled flight returning to Gaborone from Maun. The Twin Otter, which carried about twenty passengers, went down fairly close to the same spot where Andy had crashed a couple of years earlier. I had rushed my old friend and next-door neighbour from Mahalapye, Alistair Rutherford, to the airport to catch the flight after a long, boozy lunch. The plane was already taxiing when we arrived and we actually chased it in my Land Cruiser as it was backtracking down the runway. The pilot, another friend, stopped and allowed Alistair to climb aboard. Alistair had become the boss of BLDC, a large cattle production company that operated a huge ranch at Makalamabedi, about thirty miles outside Maun on the road to Francistown. He came up to Maun every month to pay cash for all the cattle the company bought from local farmers.

When the news came through that the schedule hadn't reached Gaborone, it was already dark and we spent a very worried night. I felt especially gloomy, wishing I had forced another drink into Alistair that would have meant he missed the plane. He had very young twins and his wife Sue often upbraided me for leading him astray, but that night she tearfully berated me for not getting him too drunk to go home. Early the next morning a major aerial search was begun with our Cessna 210 as the focal point in the grid system of several aircraft. This was because we had fitted an extremely expensive global navigation system (GNS) to the Cessna in order to fly very precise surveys. This precursor of the now ubiquitous and cheap GPS (global positioning system) received very low frequency radio signals from a series of US military installations around the world (there were very few satellites then) and calculated the aircraft's accurate position. After a couple of hours searching we were able to pinpoint the downed Twin Otter and ascertain that it appeared undamaged. From there we left the rescue to the relevant authorities and everyone was recovered unhurt.

I was now mostly flying the Maule and it was giving me more than the occasional trial. I made a trip up to Kwando, a hunting concession bordering the Caprivi, to pick up Jeff Bowles, who had been checking on his tsetse fly surveys. There was a heavy thunderstorm while we were on the ground at Horseshoe Bend so we had to wait it out. When the weather cleared, the airstrip was seriously waterlogged and covered in puddles. I thought maybe we could take off by swerving between the larger pools, so Jeff climbed in, I fired up and taxied the length of the airstrip, avoiding the water whenever possible. After performing the normal checks I opened the throttle and tried a take-off run, but there was no chance of attaining enough speed to raise the tail. Each time we almost made it we would splash through some water and slow down abruptly, so we went for more coffee while the sun did its work.

An hour or so later we tried again. Jeff was a heavy man with a big girth and although we were only two-up, it was touch and go whether we'd get off the ground. After two more aborted runs I said to Jeff, "Hold tight! We're going this time."

I gave the machine full throttle, used extra flaps to get the tail off the ground and careered down the airstrip dodging some puddles, splashing through others and we were just about to get airborne when there was a loud bang. Jeff disappeared backwards and his feet came up and hit the control column on his side. I managed to stop the plane without doing any damage and we climbed out to investigate. Jeff had been bracing so hard for the take-off run that the steel frame of the co-pilot's seat had snapped in two. We had to cobble it together and eventually managed to take off and fly back to Maun with him lying almost flat. I had the seat welded at Riley's garage in Maun, which caused Bob Hampshire to read the riot act, yet again, at the next annual airworthiness examination. According to regulations Riley's was not authorised to work on aircraft; mind you, no one in Botswana was authorised to weld an aircraft seat.

Once I was flying to Tuli, in the Limpopo Valley close to the South African border, with a game warden called David Peacock. He was qualified to fly the Maule and had been trained to use the wheeler landing technique, while I was more comfortable with the three-pointer landing. Coming in to land at Tuli Lodge, I pulled the stick back to flare and he panicked a bit and pushed it forward on his side, I responded instinctively by pulling back hard and we hit the ground bouncing down the airstrip like a crazy kangaroo. The next day, during pre-flight checks, we found that we had bent about three inches of the propeller tips back at right angles. Then bureaucracy really kicked in!

We obviously couldn't fly the aircraft like that. It needed to be checked by an aircraft engineer, who would doubtless require extensive tests to see if any engine components had been damaged. Bob Hampshire at the DCA said he would allow me to fly it to Johannesburg for tests and repairs as long as an engineer had inspected it first. There wasn't a suitably qualified engineer in Botswana, so we would have to get one to fly up from Joburg to Tuli. The flight to Joburg was international and the South African DCA stipulated that the pilot had to hold a commercial licence, which I didn't. There was no pilot in South Africa qualified to fly the Maule Rocket (because there were none in that country), and anyway, the aircraft was registered in Botswana and couldn't be flown in Botswana by a foreign pilot – talk about red tape! The only commercial pilot in Botswana who was qualified to fly the Maule was Mark Muller in Maun, and he was away on leave.

We sat at Tuli Lodge for just over a week while the two sets of officials squabbled. Eventually, the South African authorities relented and gave me a special dispensation, as a private pilot, to fly the Maule to Rand Airport, as long as the South African engineer accompanied me. When the engineer arrived in a Cessna 210 from Rand Airport he refused point blank to fly back in the Maule, but after checking it out he declared it safe for me to fly it by myself!

"After all," he said, "what am I supposed to do from inside if something does go wrong?" We flew (illegally) back to Rand, together but in separate aircraft.

Many years and thousands of hours experience later, after holding licences from Botswana, Zambia and Tanzania I still maintain that those early days in Botswana's clear skies, free from traffic and controllers, and shared with a handful of laid-back pilots, nearly all more skilful and more competent than me, were as enjoyable and fun as flying can be. I take my hat off to all those casually intrepid pioneers.

SEVEN

FRONTIER TOWN

Maun in the early 1970s was still very much an outpost. It required an effort to get there and a certain self-sufficiency to make a go of it. Just a few years earlier it had been a real backwater, at least a two-day drive on a bad dirt and sand road from the nearest town, the railhead of Francistown. (Ghanzi was a bit closer, but had little to offer.) The Batawana tribe had made it their capital in 1915 and settlers had formed and developed its rudimentary infrastructure. But its commerce and character had been formed for the most part by adventurers of one sort or another: hunters, cattlemen, traders, missionaries and colonial administrators who preferred remote postings.

The second generation was dominated mainly by those who had been born there before independence; white citizens who had opted to remain after 1966 and take their chances with the new Botswana. One such was Tom Kays, who had arrived in Ngamiland as a boy on horseback from Windhoek just before World War I. In his eighties, he told me his father had sent him to try his hand at ivory hunting, but had soon followed him to farm cattle near Tsau, eventually settling in Maun in the 1920s. In the 1970s his son Ronnie was the owner of Riley's Hotel and Garage but the old man still did a few mechanical repairs, mainly bicycles. Hearing that I had studied briefly in London and lodged in Golders Green, he asked if the number twelve tram still ran there from King's Cross; he meant a tram pulled by horses!

Riley's was still the busiest bar and social hub of Maun, although the out of town lodges (Island Safari Lodge, Crocodile Camp and Okavango River

Lodge – formerly AfAm Safaris) were attracting the newer residents and the few early photographic tourists travelling with companies such as Penduka Safaris, Afro-Ventures and Gametrackers. As Tony Graham had predicted, the Okavango was duly discovered! Camps had started in Moremi and Savuti to cater for non-hunting visitors. The earliest ones, such as Xaxaba, Xaxanaka and Savuti were mostly fairly basic tented facilities, but soon more upmarket lodges, like San-ta-Wani, were constructed to cater for the increasing influx of fly-in photo-tourists.

The safari-hunting industry also expanded dramatically in Botswana in the early 1970s. Pioneers from the long-established East African industry, such as Harry Selby, had moved to Maun in the 1960s and were joined by local men: Lionel Palmer, married to Tom Kays' daughter Phyllis, and a government stock inspector before independence; Dougie Wright, born in Nokaneng; Cecil Riggs; Willie Englebrecht and Kenny Kays, Phyllis' brother, all became successful professional hunters. A smaller hub was based in Kasane, but Maun was the real heart of this burgeoning industry, with Safari South and Ker, Downey and Selby (KDS) most prominent.

The hunting fraternity made Maun a lively place, full of hard partying. The bar at Riley's hosted regular Saturday lunchtime drinking sessions, attended by any professional hunter who was in between safaris or passing through to a new camp. As businesses in town closed at midday on Saturday, other prominent residents were regulars – such as "Ribs" Bateman, from Ngami Motors, and Willie Phillips, a transport operator. Often foremost among the noisy throng at the extended sessions on the hotel veranda were Lionel Palmer or Darryl Dandridge. Darryl hunted with KDS, but seemed to party most with those who hunted for Safari South.

Another pal was Malcolm Thomas, a Welshman who worked with the Hambukush community at Etsha in the upper Delta. He had a pet vervet monkey that generally sat on his shoulder at such gatherings. Malcolm was an expert left-handed darts player and therefore often drank for free. Once, Lionel left his wallet on the metal, mesh table among the drinks and the monkey grabbed it. The hilarity escalated, except on Lionel's part, when it climbed up a nearby shade tree and proceeded to trash the contents, tearing up banknotes and scattering them across the garden below.

Lionel, generally known just as Palmer, was probably the highest profile professional hunter in Maun, with a reputation as a superb shot and a prodigious drinker. A client had presented him with a bronze goose after he shot a flying spurwing goose with his rifle, as opposed to the shotguns used by everyone else. Exceptionally good looking, if a little careworn by then, stories about his exploits on safari and at hunting conventions were legion. An island in the western Delta became known as Wireless Island because on one safari during lunch he silenced an offending radio with his .458 hunting rifle from a distance of about fifty yards. The staff member, whose radio had been on the end of his ironing board, complained to the authorities that Palmer had tried to kill him, but settled for a new radio when the police told him that if Palmer had meant to hit him he would have. Once, during the rainy off-season, Lionel consumed enough vodka at Riley's to overturn his Land Rover in a deep puddle in the sandy main street outside the police station. We were called from the bar by the police to find him still sitting in the driver's seat arguing that if someone would help him put it into four-wheel drive he would be OK; the fact that all four wheels were in the air and he was lying in a big puddle of water didn't seem to phase him. With help from a few policemen we managed to right the vehicle and persuaded him to let Darryl, who was scarcely more sober, drive him home.

The safari season was from early March to the second Tuesday in September. Out of season, during the rains, was time for maintaining camps and vehicles, for spending time with families… but mostly for intensive partying.

Jenny and I settled into our newly built detached house on a small development close to the old colonial boma. Jenny got to grips with the practical side of life in Maun, with extremely limited shopping facilities and intermittent power supply, but seemed to enjoy the company of new friends and the fairly bohemian social life. In August 1974 she had our daughter Samantha in the small cottage hospital and settled into fairly demanding motherhood, given the conditions.

The Palmers' house on the west bank of the Thamalakane near Matlapaneng was the scene of unforgettable dinner parties and more often than not the venue for all-day (and night) revels at Christmas, weddings and other big social occasions, when the whole Maun community would be there. Lionel would lead the drinking and singing with his own out-of-tune renditions of 'Cotton Fields', then 'Green, Green Grass of Home' and, in later years, 'Rhinestone Cowboy'. The diehards would often be going strong as the sun rose over the river and, crocodiles forgotten, skinny dipping would be the order of the day.

Other celebrated hosts were the Wrights and the Sandenberghs. Eustace, Dougie's older brother, and Daisy Wright lived close to the Palmers, slightly downstream. Daisy was a Motswana, a cousin of the President, Sir Seretse Khama, and came from Serowe. Every year they would invite everyone to a lunch party on Boxing Day. It was a big occasion with crazy games on the lawn, based loosely on cricket or touch rugby. Eustace, the unofficial "Lord Mayor of Maun" and an enthusiastic drinker, would wander around the gathering with a two-litre bottle of his own "ready-mix" tied around his neck – based on, among other things, rum, vodka, fruit juice and lemonade. He claimed that prevention was better than cure and would often add a liberal dose of Disprin and/or Alka-Seltzer to the mix to ward off the expected hangover.

The Sandenberghs, Dave and Anne, traditionally threw a New Year's Eve party at their house across the river. It was attended by everyone and was often the wildest party of the year. One unforgettable afternoon two of Dave's young pilots left the party, collected a company aircraft and proceeded to buzz the house, getting lower with every pass. Revellers, including Dave, threw beer and Coke cans at the aircraft as it skimmed the mapororo trees. They got close but luckily never made contact.

Dave's father, Colonel Sandenbergh, had been married two or three times and Dave had a half-brother, Peter, who was at least fifteen years his junior. Peter had been a bit wild at the University of Cape Town and left before he got a degree. Typical of the times, he had long black hair, an earring and wore no shoes. He was tall and slim and, at twenty, was an unruly, pot-smoking, anti-apartheid activist. When at a loose end, he would come to Maun and usually stayed with Dave and his wife. Anne was not impressed with this outlandish youth, fearing he would be a bad influence on her two young sons, John and David. He certainly influenced Maun's growing hipster community and when, in 1977, it seemed that Peter would probably stay permanently in Maun it was too much for Anne.

This was shortly after Jenny had moved back to England with baby Samantha and I was living alone in a large house. One night at Croc Camp Dave explained Anne's concerns and asked if I would consider letting Peter move in with me. We shared bachelor accommodation for a year or so and he moved my musical appreciation on from the Beatles to Bruce Springsteen. We remained firm friends and, although we saw much less of each other after I left Maun, I was pleased to follow his progress as a successful, barefoot entrepreneur with several businesses in retail and tourism, including two lodges upstream on the Boro River: Delta Camp and the unconventional Oddball's, which pioneered backpacking in the Delta.

One evening Peter and I got back from Croc Camp to find a broken window and quite a lot of our belongings missing, mostly electrical items – our transistor radios and cassette tape recorders (then the latest in music technology) – plus cameras and binoculars. The police arrived and combed the house and garden for footprints and fingerprints. A couple of days later I was called to the police station to identify a cache of suspected stolen goods. The police had arrested the young black-sheep of a prominent local family, the Wellios, with some unlikely possessions. His fingerprints matched some found in the house and on the broken window, which made him a pretty firm suspect as he had never been there as an invited guest. I duly checked out the items in a back room of the police station in the presence of the young delinquent and sure enough they were mostly things from my house. I formally identified everything, noting that my radio-cassette was the only item missing. It appeared to be a cut and dried case and Peter and I were very happy to get our possessions back so quickly. On the way out a radio-cassette was on the front desk, playing loudly, being happily examined by the desk sergeant and another policeman.

"Oh great, you've found that as well," I said to the investigating CID officer who was seeing us out. "That's mine."

"No sir," the sergeant replied, "it's mine."

The CID man asked, "Where did you get it?"

"I bought it from him yesterday," answered the sergeant in all seriousness, pointing at young Wellio!

Throughout the 1970s the rains were usually good and it must have been the same in Angola for the Delta was regularly heavily inundated and the Thamalakane River in Maun was a deep, permanent feature. River traffic varied from the ever-present mokoro, the traditional dug-out canoe, to aluminium boats of various sizes and capacities with outboard motors, used mainly by safari companies and government departments. There were also a few fibreglass pleasure boats, owned mainly by expatriate residents.

Water skiing was a popular weekend activity and the giant sycamore fig trees next to the old Matlapaneng Bridge were the main venue for a fun day in the water. Crocodiles were never a problem, but on one of my first novice runs, I couldn't understand the urgent hand signals Norbert, who was driving the boat, was giving me; they weren't anything like the ones he'd briefed me with. Suddenly, very close to the boat, a hippo surfaced with a loud snort, necessitating an immediate slalom, uncomfortably close to the huge beast, which I accomplished expertly, to everyone's amazement and my great relief. A safer swimming site was south of town, where the road to Ghanzi went through the Shashe River before it flowed into the Thamalakane. This was an excellent picnic spot and many children, including Samantha, learnt to swim there on social Sundays, when half a dozen families would gather for the day with cool-boxes full of food and drink.

One of the first swimming pools in Maun was constructed in the Safari South compound in the mid-1970s. The company, by then owned by Californian multi-millionaire Tommy Friedkin, amalgamated with KDS and invested substantially in property, aeroplanes and concession developments. They employed a retired professional hunter from Tanzania, Norman Read, to help with camp construction and other odd jobs, including developing their new office compound. Norman was a very big man, tall and heavy, and had reportedly worked as a stand-in for John Wayne in 1962, during the production of the famous film *Hatari* in East Africa. Norman built a large swimming pool in the office compound, surrounded by lawns, and Safari South, largely due to the popularity of some of its staff, notably Ryland Wallace, became the hub of Maun's social life.

Sadly, Norman died soon after in Maun Hospital and his funeral will never be forgotten by anyone who attended. There were no undertakers or mortuary facilities in Maun then and funerals were a strictly do-it-yourself business. Alan Hill, a former agriculture officer and the founder of Northern Construction Company, normally supplied simple pine coffins and Europeans were mostly interred behind Riley's Hotel in the Kays family's private graveyard.

Norman's body was kept on ice by the Veterinary Department for a couple of days while relatives gathered from far and wide. On the day of the funeral I was one of the six pall-bearers who arrived with the empty coffin to discover that there was no way Norman was going to fit into it. Alan was called and asked to produce a much larger box in a hurry, with eight handles for two more bearers. The funeral congregation was already assembling at Riley's. An hour or so later we had a coffin large enough to squeeze Norman's body into. We loaded it on Willie Englebrecht's hunting car and proceeded to Riley's. We carried the coffin through quite a crowd and placed it next to the grave, when it became obvious that it was now too long to fit in the hole. The mourners decamped back to the hotel while Ronnie Kays arranged for labourers to enlarge the grave. The event was an unusual mixture of sadness and jocularity, especially in the bar after the funeral, and I'm sure Norman would have appreciated it.

Willie Englebrecht was a top hunter and one of Maun's most popular and unforgettable characters. Slim and extremely handsome, he'd developed a shock of silver hair in his twenties. Although he was extraordinarily polite and courteous, and somewhat reserved until you really got to know him, he was best known for his exceptional Afrikaans-based fluency at cursing. Anything or anyone could be the target of his ire: a wounded animal, his vehicle, his trackers, even his clients. The outbursts were so amusing no one was ever offended. One of my favourite Willie outbursts was when I was flying him back to Maun from camp with Wally Johnson, a professional hunter, mutual friend and much more experienced pilot. Wally winked at me and took over the controls of the Cessna 206 as Willie was quietly smoking his pipe in the rear seat. Wally carried out a barrel roll and the manoeuvre caused Willie to drop his pipe and thrash about recovering it, all the while reciting an extensive litany of Afrikaans profanities.

I was often an overnight guest at safari hunting camps when I was doing my buffalo study and became friends with many of the professional hunters. Amid the drinking, joking and macho atmosphere of most safaris I gradually became aware of these men's deep, hard-earned knowledge of the bush and its plant and animal components; it might have had a different slant to Pete Smith's, but nevertheless, they were truly committed to the wild. Whilst they were no angels, they were dedicated in their way to its preservation. I have argued ever since that properly managed professional safari hunting is one of the most effective and valuable tools for conservation.

Safari hunting takes relatively few animals and has no discernible effect on wild populations – years of data from hunting quotas and wildlife censuses confirm this. Quotas should be scientifically set and limited to insignificant levels, so even a small population can be safely hunted, but the rules must be tighter. The daily activities of a safari operation deter poachers and other illegal and damaging activities such as timber extraction, burning and fishing. Most of all, safari hunting occupies land and precludes unsustainable developments, among which livestock farming and informal human settlement have been the worst, but are now being surpassed in many areas by unregulated and poorly planned photographic tourism. City-dwelling Westerners may find it difficult to believe that any activity resulting in the death of any animal can be beneficial for wild populations, but it is the truth. Tragically their ignorance and their influence through so-called green lobbies are condemning the wilderness and wild populations to impoverishment and extinction.

In those pre-digital days, telephones in Maun operated from the telephone exchange behind the post office. Although we could only dial other Maun numbers and there was no connection to the outside world, there was an expatriate telephone engineer provided by the British Government. Mel Thurgood lived in the house opposite us with his wife Joyce and young son Kieran. Keeping a mere handful of telephones functioning was not the most onerous of tasks and Mel had lots of spare time to be sociable. We always knew when he was around because he sang opera very loudly – and fairly badly I think. If you booked a time Mel could somehow, "unofficially" connect you with numbers outside Maun. It was a great boon for us expats to be able to speak to relatives overseas on special occasions. The only other way to call out was via the government's high-frequency radio-telephone service, a tedious procedure that entailed whistling into the microphone for ages, trying to "break the pips" and attract the attention of an operator in Gaborone.

Mel became great friends with Phil, the sergeant in charge of a small band of British Army surveyors who were based in Maun for a while. Phil was a big, jovial, beer-drinking chap and he and Mel were often the life and soul of lunchtime *braais*. Their friendship was sorely tested one day though when Mel was taking Joyce and Kieran on a shopping trip to Bulawayo. Mel drove a Peugeot 404, a very popular car in Africa that coped pretty well with the rough dirt roads. They set off quite early for the six- or seven-hour drive to Francistown. All was well for the first 200 miles, past Nata village and the Dukwe veterinary gate. Then, mid-afternoon, the car stopped. Mel was unable to get it going and had no idea what was wrong. They could only sit and hope that someone helpful would pass by.

After about two hours Phil's Ford F-250 pick-up truck came along. He was also on his way to Francistown and, as was his custom, he was about halfway through a case of Castle lager. He was happy to tow them and produced a chain from his truck, which was fully loaded with equipment and stores for his army colleagues in Francistown. It began to rain as Phil got under the Peugeot and fastened the chain around the front axle. He gave Mel one of his beers, "for the road", climbed back into his truck and off they went. It was now late afternoon and beginning to get dark.

They made slow but steady progress along the rough road. Mel's headlights lit up the back of Phil's vehicle until first one and then the other was smashed by flying debris from the truck's large wheels. Phil's windows were closed against the rain so he neither noticed nor heard Mel hooting desperately. They seemed to be gaining speed and Mel and Joyce became very worried, even more so when the windscreen cracked and their vision deteriorated further. Joyce climbed over into the back seat with Kieran and they lay down just as the windscreen took another blow and disintegrated. Mel struggled on, terrified, trying to keep control of the steering as he was showered with rain, dust and stones. The road just got worse as they hurtled, almost blind in the dark, behind the speeding Ford truck. Then there was a huge bang and a scraping sound and the car shuddered to a halt as Phil's tail lights disappeared. Mel couldn't find his front wheels!

When Phil reached the outskirts of Francistown, the mud and sand gave way to tar and he pulled over to check on Mel and the Peugeot. All he found was the front axle and wheels attached by the chain, so he dropped the axle and turned back towards Maun. The Thurgoods and the rest of their car were about twenty miles back when he found them, sheltering from the downpour in the back seat of the wreckage.

Another of Mel's best friends was Mike Dance, the bookkeeper at Safari South. Mike had been in Maun for a long time, married twice and had a son and daughter away at school. He rarely, if ever got into the bush despite living on its doorstep for years and mixing socially and professionally almost exclusively with the hunting community. Quite often the annual quota allocated to hunting companies was not fully utilised. It would always be sold, but many clients did not shoot everything they paid for. Unused quota would sometimes be re-sold at a discount to company employees at the end of the season and obtaining a pair of medium-sized elephant tusks would substantially boost most people's income. One year Mike, egged on by Mel, bought an elephant licence in September. Neither of them had ever hunted before and so they enlisted the help of Willie Phillips, who was a very experienced private hunter and had lately become a PH, having given up his transport business. Despite my frequent darting escapades and buffalo sampling, I too had never been on an elephant hunt and was easily persuaded to accompany them.

We set off into the hunting concession area behind Khwai River Lodge for a weekend. Three wives and a few children made up the party and we all pitched camp on the river in a pleasant spot. Early on Saturday morning the four men headed northwest on foot into the area to look for elephants, or at least fresh spoor. Willie was an expert tracker, I was a relative novice, but Mike and Mel were real "babes in the wood". We walked pretty much all day, mostly along elephant paths, and saw very little except a few tiny steenbok and a couple of giraffe. A few of the bigger pans in the clay mopane belts still held a little water from the last rains in April, but most were either bone dry or just mud. By late afternoon we were thirsty and unsure of the way back to the cars and camp. Mike and Mel didn't have a clue and Willie and I disagreed. Even if we had seen an elephant it was now too late to shoot it. We had no food or blankets and began to realise that we would be spending a very uncomfortable night in the bush unless we were lucky enough to stumble on a track back to camp. As the light started to dim Willie and I decided we would sleep at the next pan with water in it. Mike and Mel were distinctly unhappy, believing that we might be playing a trick on them.

We found a grove of tall mopane trees, often an indicator of pans. True enough there was a pool with some fairly smelly water, not pleasant to taste, rather flavoured with buffalo urine I thought, but it would keep us alive. It was now dark and the moon had yet to rise. Willie and I drank some of the foetid water and made ourselves as comfortable as possible in the sand a few yards from the pool. Mike and Mel had begun to be concerned, even worried, about our survival. There was some dead wood lying around and they wanted to light a fire. Willie responded by saying he only had two matches left and one was indisputably for his pipe. Mike managed to get a fire going and we settled down for the night. The first of many hyaena howls woke all of us and that was the last sleep that Mike or Mel managed. No amount of reassurance from me or scathing indifference from Willie would persuade them that they were safe. It was a very long, cold, uncomfortable night punctuated with animal sounds that made a mockery of the day's lack of wildlife sightings.

As daylight crept in and the mopane trees became visible again, our two "tenderfeet" slurped greedily at the water on offer, throwing off their revulsion of yesterday. We discussed the way back to camp, but Willie and I still disagreed. Willie was going his way whatever, so I reluctantly yielded and we started along an elephant path towards the light. Mel quietly approached me and tried to hand me his large gold watch, entreating me to make sure his son Kieran received it if he didn't make it back alive. I refused and told him to "get a grip" and that we were only a few hours at most from the Khwai. We walked at a pretty brisk pace in the cold morning before sunup. There was lots of spoor crossing the track: buffalo herds, impala, kudu and other antelopes, as well as hyaena and lion tracks following the path for short spells. We saw nothing alive except for a couple of puff adders that were lying in the path waiting for the sunlight to warm them. These made Willie, who was leading, jump and exclaim. It would have been funny, but Mike and Mel had completely lost any sense of humour. We finally came into sight of our starting point at about noon and were subjected to a justifiable barrage of questions from three very angry but relieved spouses. Willie, the only singleton, remained fairly aloof, maintaining that elephant hunting could not be taken for granted, but that we had never been in any peril. We enjoyed an extensive, very mixed, but delicious Sunday lunch with a few cold beers before packing up and heading back to Maun. Mike refused any offer of further attempts to obtain his trophy in the near future.

One memorable visitor to Maun was a wealthy Californian lady, Jessie Neal, who fell totally in love with the Okavango (as well as a number of its residents) and returned every year for an extended visit, camping fairly luxuriously and enjoying the Delta and Maun social life. Jessie was remarkably attractive for her age, courtesy of some expert plastic surgeons, and she cultivated a series of much younger paramours among the hunting and guiding fraternity. A dark-haired young guide from Francistown, Howard McDonald, escorted Jessie on numerous safaris and became a firm favourite.

Jessie bought a small double-decker houseboat called the *African Queen* and gave it to Howard. After an extensive refit carried out on the bank near Croc Camp, a big relaunch party was organised. The good ship was dragged down to the water's edge by a gang of excited partygoers, filled to the gunnels with cool boxes of all kinds of booze. She floated triumphantly on the calm Thamalakane waters. Everyone climbed aboard for the maiden voyage. Howard, at the wheel, turned the boat upstream and sailed smoothly past Croc Camp and Okavango River Lodge to cheers and waves from shore-based onlookers. The party was well underway as they passed Island Safari Lodge. Howard turned left up the Boro River, a much shallower channel, and the craft slowly came into contact with a submerged sandbank on the starboard side. This was normally not a problem, but amid all the revelry Howard had forgotten to remove the axle and wheels that had been attached to the hull to move it up and down the bank. The starboard wheel just rolled up the sandbank and the *African Queen* rolled over into the river. The passengers jumped or dived overboard and made it safely to the bank. Only one young woman was missing, apparently shut in the boat's toilet cubicle. Cecil Riggs dived back in and managed to open the door to allow the distressed lady to escape and rejoin the party, which just continued on dry land as more volunteers rescued much of the ship's alcoholic cargo.

Across the river and slightly upstream from Riley's Hotel was a small fenced game reserve that had once been a bush golf course. It was intended as an educational facility and a few impala lived there that had been captured in Moremi Game Reserve by some of the young bucks from Maun, using spotlights and Land Rovers. The new game warden in Maun, Peter Morris, wanted to put some more animals into the reserve so Peter, Norbert, Russell Biggs (an MSc student from Joburg), and I set off for the Makgadikgadi and managed to dart half a dozen zebras from our pick-ups. They were firmly tied up and taken back to Maun as quickly as possible before being given an antidote and released in the reserve.

Peter was really keen to get a few giraffes, so we moved to Nxai Pan, where giraffes were abundant and where the flat, short-grass plains made pursuit relatively easy. Peter organised a cattle truck, which we converted to hold young giraffes up to about four years old. Neither Norbert nor I had ever darted a giraffe, so our doses and methods were somewhat experimental. We chased the first animal flat out across the pan and managed to get a dart into it through the clouds of dust and debris thrown up by its hooves. It eventually went down and we got some ropes on it before giving the antidote. It never got up, dead from the drugs or from overexertion or from a combination of factors – we just didn't know. Saddened, but undeterred, we managed to dart and load four young animals without further loss. Looking back now, with years of experience, I know we were just lucky; our methods were woefully unsuited to the safe and successful capture of giraffes. The four were released into the reserve and lived for many years, but they were all females so there was never any increase in numbers. As for the casualty, I informed everyone that the meat should not be eaten because of the M99 in the carcass. We cut it open to make it easier for vultures and jackals, without a thought for the effects of M99 on them, but Russell, true to form and his Boer heritage, couldn't resist taking the fillets and making biltong, which had no reported noticeable effect on any of the consumers.

One of Peter's most difficult problems was lions killing cattle. The Makalamabedi quarantine and livestock development ranch was one of the worst affected areas and their losses were considerable. The Ghanzi cattle-farming block to the south of Maun also had problems with lions, but reports indicated that the farmers shot the culprits themselves. This was technically illegal, although the law changed from time to time to allow farmers to protect their stock.

Peter investigated and was told that Bushmen, many of whom lived and worked on the Ghanzi farms, were adept at hunting lions and could be hired pretty cheaply. He put out the word and very soon we had four Bushman recruits. We made a life-size cut-out silhouette of a male lion and headed off into the game reserve to give the Bushmen some target practice. Peter set up the target, paced out fifty yards and scraped a line in the sand. We had a couple of government-issue .375 calibre rifles and a box of soft-nosed ammunition.

Communication with the little men was sketchy to say the least because neither Peter nor I spoke their click language and only one or two of them spoke a little Afrikaans, the language of the Ghanzi farmers. We managed to explain what was wanted and the first Bushman took the rifle, loaded a bullet and crouched on his haunches on the line. It was an unusual position for shooting, but who were we to interfere. We didn't see where his shot went; it certainly didn't hit the lion silhouette. There was much excited click discussion and not a little laughter. The second volunteer took the gun and loaded it, then crouched and fired, with the same result. Peter commented that he didn't think much of these ostensible lion hunters. All four tried a shot, in the same style and without getting anywhere near the target. Peter was now really exasperated and the Bushmen were quite agitated. They insisted that they had killed lots of lions. We decided to give the one we could communicate best with another chance and told him to show us how he shot lions.

He loaded the gun and crept towards the cut-out. He got to within five yards before crouching down on his haunches and shooting, he could just as well have swung the gun and hit it! Peter and I were incredulous, but the other Bushmen were jumping up and down, laughing and cheering. Peter decided he had to give them a chance and posted them out at Makalamabedi with ammunition and rations for a couple of weeks. They shot seven lions on the ranch.

As the warden responsible for Ngamiland, Peter was technically my boss, whereas I was in the research division with no powers of investigation or arrest. One morning he came to my office and asked if I would dissect a couple of large crocodiles, both over twelve feet in length, that had been shot in Xaxanaka Lagoon in Moremi. A German journalist, camping at the public campsite, had disappeared from the bank of the lagoon early one morning, leaving her washbag and towel on the sand. A staff member reported hearing a splash. Peter called Lloyd Wilmot, a guide and one-time crocodile hunter, who shot and retrieved the two crocs a few nights later. I was to identify the stomach contents, but if I suspected that any of the remains were human that would have to be confirmed by a doctor. The crocs were certainly big enough to take a person, but I didn't find anything suspicious. The journalist's husband supplied a description of jewellery she might have worn but I found nothing. There were several lion claws in one stomach, but everything else was the remains of normal prey.

Veterinary officers were allowed to shoot any animal they suspected might have FMD for investigation; on occasion this was rather freely interpreted and a springbok or impala would be taken for fresh meat during bush trips. In fact, most vets regarded it as a perk of the job. Father Mike liked to throw a big party for St Patrick's Day, traditionally a lunchtime *braai,* and decided to provide a gemsbok for party meat instead of the usual beef from Maun Butchery. He borrowed a rifle from a professional hunter friend, Cecil Riggs, and set off to the Makalamabedi quarantine camp, which was under his jurisdiction. He arrived back in Maun with a dead gemsbok in his Land Rover and was apprehended by Peter Morris, who, taking his job seriously, confiscated the carcass, a decidedly unpopular move. This was a blow for the next day's festivities, but worse was to come. Mike was prosecuted for poaching and was heavily fined as well as having his Land Rover and Cecil's rifle confiscated. The latter was eventually returned to its owner, but Mike was declared a prohibited immigrant and forced to leave the country. It seemed an excessively severe punishment, so maybe there was more to it than met the eye.

Whatever the true circumstances behind his departure, Mike left a void in the town's society that was hard to fill. I once saw him castrate a frisky adult stallion belonging to a Herero herdsman from Sehitwa. He was adamant that in Ireland he had always done these operations with the horse standing and with only an injection of local anaesthetic into the testicles. He asked me to apply a twitch to the horse's upper lip, which was meant to distract it from any pain in the groin and to give some control. With the owner holding the bridle, me hanging on to the twitch and a large group of onlookers congregated in the dusty street outside the vet office, Mike ducked under the stallion's abdomen and injected some lignocaine into each testicle. Even this relatively minor procedure caused an alarming degree of kicking and bucking, but Mike scrambled away unhurt and we just had to wait for the animal to calm down and the anaesthetic to do its work.

Mike was from the old school that believed a really sharp blade caused less pain and distress than more elaborate anaesthetic administration, and after ten minutes he pronounced the horse ready and sloshed an antiseptic solution over the scrotum and groin area. Instructing us to hold tight, Mike took up his position under the abdomen again, grasped one testicle through the scrotum and sliced confidently through the skin with his scalpel into the mass. The horse, with me and the owner attached, almost went into orbit! Mike landed on his back while blood sprayed liberally down the horse's hind legs and onto the dust.

"Bogger it!" yelled Mike as he grabbed the emasculator from a bucket, enjoined us to hang on tighter, and ducked under again to crush and sever the spermatic cord and its blood vessels. Like a demented rodeo horse the stallion bucked and kicked, but Mike, covered in blood, hung on and after what seemed like an age emerged with the testicle and a pleased announcement, "One bogger off – one to go!"

The second testicle was a bit of an anticlimax for the street crowd. The horse must have been exhausted by its earlier frenzy, or maybe the injection into that testicle had worked better. Anyway, Mike removed it with relatively little resistance. Blood was still dripping from the open wounds but Mike assured the owner that it was insignificant and would stop in its own time. He told me later that, in Ireland, a bucket or two of icy water thrown over the animal's back stopped the bleeding very quickly, but that was hardly an option in tropical Ngamiland. The lesson I took away from this performance was always apply ropes and cast the horse first or, better still, use intravenous sodium pentothal anaesthetic to put it down before cutting anything. Unless, like Mike, you had a close connection with the Almighty.

No account of Maun and its hinterland in the 1970s can leave out the tsetse fly and the considerable efforts to eradicate it. Locally, nationally and internationally the fly made significant news for several years. Early travellers in many parts of Africa had been limited by this insect's distribution, in particular the savanna species that inhabited the Okavango and nearby areas, *Glossina morsitans*. Everyone knows that tsetse flies spread sleeping sickness, a severe, often fatal, human disease, but their greatest impact was because of *nagana*, a disease deadly to domestic animals, and resulting in a situation where "tsetse flies keep cattle out of an area of Africa larger than the United States", a claim drummed into us at veterinary school. Wild animals are not susceptible to these trypanosomes, probably because they have evolved with them, and many people held, and still hold, the view that tsetse flies are valuable guardians of wildlife areas. The Botswana Veterinary Department had maintained a Tsetse Fly Control Unit (TFC) in Maun for years, traditionally headed by a veterinarian, perhaps reflecting the potentially huge economic impact of livestock disease compared with the few cases of human sleeping sickness recorded each year.

When I arrived in 1972 the Chief Tsetse Officer was a British vet, John Kendrick, a lively and popular individual whose son returned in the 2000s to run Okavango River Lodge. Early methods employed to limit the spread of tsetse flies had included bush clearing to deprive the fly of its preferred habitat and attempting to shoot out the wildlife hosts that provided blood meals. The inner and outer tsetse fences along the "Maun front" still demarcated the attempted de-stocking area (the outer fence now forms part of the buffalo fence). Hundreds of wild animals had been shot over many years, but with little effect. The practice was abandoned in the late 1960s when it was shown that the vast majority of blood meals were from warthog, a species almost impossible to exterminate. Selected ground spraying with Dieldrin and DDT had also been used in small areas and the fly was limited to the Delta, with Maun and its immediate surroundings kept clear. Vehicles travelling into town from the north were sprayed in the "one-two hut" at Shokamokwa, near Shorobe, where the gate through the buffalo fence is now. These traditional methods had proved reasonably successful for control, but required perpetual financial commitments. The fly also made life painfully unpleasant, especially while travelling in vehicles, and the increasing influx of tourists produced endless complaints. It was reasoned that an expensive, but one-off eradication exercise, if successful, would save money in the long run. New technology, in the form of aerial spraying of ultra-low volumes of insecticides, looked like it might make this possible.

DDT and Dieldrin had been banned on environmental grounds, following Rachel Carson's seminal book *Silent Spring*, published in 1962. A related organochlorine insecticide, Endosulfan, was selected because of its extreme toxicity for tsetse flies and therefore very low doses could be applied with limited, if any, effect on non-target insects. Unfortunately, it was also extremely toxic to fish, but the argument put forward was that the fish population of the Delta was so wildly variable anyway because of the inconsistent flooding regime that it should be relatively resilient and recover from any die-off. Trials proceeded in 1973 with the insecticide being applied in very small aerosol droplets from low-flying aircraft at night during the winter months in doses as low as 6 gm/ha. In the mid-1970s Jeff Bowles, another British vet, took over as

Chief Tsetse Officer. He was an extremely bright and larger than life character who suffered no fools gladly. He took on the obstinate tsetse fly and all-comers, including Greenpeace, some prominent Maun inhabitants, and occasionally his own superiors, but the eventual end result was the almost complete eradication of the fly, with minimal transient environmental effects and no permanent harm to the Delta. Certainly, complaints are not heard today!

Two aircraft flew parallel transects at night across the Delta, just above the trees, using navigation equipment based on the Doppler principle. This was augmented by using parallel cut lines at each end of the transects marked by bonfires or spotlights. We spent several cold nights on the cut lines, moving the beacons up two transect widths every time the planes flew over. The aerosol was directed downwards and held in the vegetation because of the inversion layer effect of the winter climate, otherwise it would have blown away and been ineffective. The effects on non-target insects was assessed by collecting at sites along the transects. These were usually caused by overdoses resulting from inaccurate flying or excess wind drift. By repeating the spraying five times, strategically timed during the winter, it was calculated to kill tsetse flies as they hatched from their pupae in the soil and to prevent any further breeding.

Ground spraying continued to be used in certain localities, and to enhance the accuracy and efficiency of the method it was decided to investigate the fly's resting behaviour more closely. Reg Allsopp, an expert in tsetse control, was recruited and he decided to mark individual flies with a radioactive substance, which could be detected at night with a handheld Geiger counter. The substance could be obtained from the South African nuclear research facility at Pelindaba, near Hartebeestport, but import permits were problematic and would have taken far too long to get. So he and I flew down to Pretoria in the Wildlife Department aircraft and smuggled a flask full of the isotope back to Maun. Captured tsetse flies were marked with a drop on their abdomens and released. It was then a simple matter with hand-held Geiger counters to locate their roosting places at night in the dark. This provided valuable information on targeting the vegetation to be sprayed and also for deciding on droplet sizes for the aerial spraying.

There was a great deal of popular and sometimes near-hysterical opposition to the spraying, but the government, especially Jeff, stuck to its guns. Unfortunately, although very effective, it did not succeed in completely eradicating the fly. Pockets survived, mainly in the dense *Phoenix* palm islands in the permanent swamp, from where the survivors spread again. Attempting to be environmentally friendly, over the years various chemical cocktails were tried, with an emphasis on the relatively benign pyrethroid compounds. But it wasn't until the early 2000s that the technology and methodology improved enough, with better navigation avoiding some of the earlier overdosing mishaps and more advanced microdroplet aerosols being employed, that total eradication was finally achieved using very low dose applications of the synthetic pyrethroid Deltamethrin.

In the 1970s one of the main flying crews was run by a colourful German expat called Dick Hilland. He was an experienced Africa hand who operated in some unusual corners of the continent and carried a small suitcase with dozens of rubber stamps, beloved by all minor African civil servants. He could "validate" a passport with immigration stamps for any number of countries and "authorise" customs, health and veterinary documents, import and export permits, and more. The stamps must have saved him lots of time and money, but it was a very high-risk operating practice.

Dick's crew of young pilots was highly experienced, mainly in crop-spraying, which is a daylight activity, but they quickly adapted to the night-flying techniques and amazed everyone with their skill and daring. Their twin-engined aircraft carried huge tanks that filled the fuselage behind the pilots' seats and were fitted with Micronair spray nozzles under the wings. They flew low, almost touching the treetops, operating powerful spotlights that caused roosting birds to take flight from the trees. This was a serious hazard, so they used reinforced transparent shields to protect them from birds coming through the windscreen. One Australian pilot was heard over the radio exclaiming, "Jeez, I didn't know you guys had kangaroos over here!" at his first sighting of a springhare – a burrow dwelling, rabbit-sized rodent. As an aspiring young pilot, I persuaded Dick to let me go up with them one night. It was exciting, but I didn't ask again.

EIGHT

DELTA DUTIES

In late 1974, when the UN project was truly underway, I planned how to continue and expand the collection of data on buffalo that had begun with the Veterinary Department's buffalo sampling exercise two years earlier. Apart from the FMD aspect, the biological data were limited to basic measurements and a crude age determination of the sampled buffaloes. Some had been tested for pregnancy, but this manual, *per rectum* examination was subjective and a bit hit and miss, depending on the position in which the buffalo was lying and the degree of expertise on the part of the examining vet. In the heat of the moment more than one vet had even been embarrassed by being found up to his armpit in a prone bull! Some vets had plenty of experience of the required technique in cattle, but even these had never tested buffalo. The gestation period in buffalo is eleven months, compared to the nine months in domestic cows, so the findings on rectal palpation had to be adjusted, which was a further subjective judgement. We wondered what our Batswana field assistants, many of whom were new to veterinary matters and had certainly never seen a helicopter, thought of these strange *makgowa* (white people) who went to such enormous trouble to catch a buffalo, then stuck their hands up its backside before letting it go again. More than once I was asked incredulously, "Why don't we eat it?"

The sampled buffalo were fitted with coloured collars and numbered brass ear tags for later identification. The collars were colour-coded depending on the area in which they had been captured: red for Savuti, yellow for Khwai (eastern Okavango) and blue for Matsebe (western Okavango). Unfortunately, the colour differentiation did not last well, although the collars themselves remained highly visible, especially from the air.

While the FMD sampling exercises would continue for a further two years at the same time of year (late dry season), we decided to collect other data on a monthly basis all year round. This entailed shooting a number of buffaloes each month, measuring, weighing and dissecting them and accumulating as much biological information from them as possible.

I set out to obtain data from fifteen animals per month from near the three original study sites. Unfortunately, the Savuti Channel ceased to flow for a number of years and the buffalo moved away, so I was forced to limit my efforts to Khwai and Matsebe, both conveniently part of the Okavango Delta and therefore fully complementing the UN project's work. As a ground-based undertaking I needed to recruit a small team with hunting and tracking skills. Thanks mainly to Safari South, especially Ryland Wallace, I was able to put together a group of four local men who had various levels of bushcraft skills and wished to work year-round rather than only during the six-month safari season. Ryland, a Lancashire lad like me, became one of my closest friends and helped me immeasurably with his local knowledge as an ex-TFC survey officer. Immensely popular and with a sense of humour second to none, he was probably the kingpin of Maun social life as he transformed his office in Safari South into the "Pheasant Pluckers Arms" at 5.00 pm on most nights of the week. As Operations Manager for the largest safari company he was able and willing to help my project in any way he could. Supplies were delivered to camps and spares found for my frequent mechanical problems. I tried to reciprocate when I could by supplying their camp caretakers with fresh meat out of season.

Jonathan Juramo from Malawi became my foreman and two cheerful Batawana men from Okavango villages, both known as Brown (Big Brown and Little Brown) were recruited as skinners, and Little Brown could also drive (a little). Our cook and skivvy was a timid, small, desert dweller, Bahense Baholole. From a minority tribe, he was a Monajwa (eater of mice). Their enthusiasm for the job was boosted considerably when they realised that the meat from fifteen buffalo would be shared among them every month. Batswana are noted for their almost single-minded dedication to acquiring and consuming meat, and buffalo is their absolute favourite. I was astonished at first that they seemed hell-bent on consuming everything we shot. Given that an average female buffalo would provide about 300lbs of prime meat this was a serious challenge. It wasn't long however before the bulk of the harvest was cut and dried into strips, tied together with grass in bundles (*segwapa)* and transported back to Maun for sale. This must have done wonders for their esteem as well as boosting their incomes and sex lives and I was soon inundated with job applications.

Khwai was the location of one of my camps and study areas in the 1970s. A couple of small rondavels just inside the Moremi North Gate, with a shower and long-drop latrine, were provided by DWNP for researchers to use and were home for up to two weeks each month. The camp was situated just to the west of the mopane pole bridge on the south bank of the Khwai River, among a grove of knobthorns or *makoba* trees, and was the only facility within Moremi Wildlife Reserve, apart from four rudimentary public campsites at North and South Gates, Third Bridge and Xaxanaka. However, during the 1970s three upmarket, tented camps were built at the beautiful Xaxanaka Lagoon and provided with an airstrip – the thin end of the wedge.

From this camp we could work on the buffalo herds that inhabited the Khwai and Mababe areas. They used to gather in very large aggregations, often 3,000 to 4,000 strong, towards the end of the dry season in September and October, along the north bank of the Khwai as far west as Xugana lagoon, to take advantage of the green floodplain grasses generated by the receding floodwaters. As soon as the rains began they would splinter into smaller herds averaging about seventy animals and head away from the Delta north and eastwards into Mababe where the grazing was more nutritious and rainwater gathered in pans scattered throughout the bush.

These areas were leased as hunting concessions by KDS, whose managing director, Harry Selby, a famous East African professional hunter, had built the first two luxury lodges in the Okavango Delta: Khwai River Lodge and Xugana. These were initially used by rich clients to relieve the "hardship" of life in hunting camps, but they gradually attracted more and more non-hunting visitors who flew in to view the game from vehicles and boats. The KDS hunters, with the exception of Darryl Dandridge, were rather more formal and less welcoming than the Safari South staff. But our relations were mostly cordial, except for one or two of the older hunters who regarded a young researcher as an intrusive upstart in their exclusive world. I was soon asked to avoid the vicinity of Khwai Lodge when returning to camp with a Land Rover full of buffalo carcasses. I suppose they thought it put them in a bad light especially if their PHs had been struggling to find one for a client, but gradually they realised that I could often provide them with useful recent information on the whereabouts of trophy animals and their attitude softened.

On the western half of the Delta were hunting concessions leased by Safari South, where I usually spent the other two weeks of each month, fly camping. There were countless beautiful spots with access to clean water in the myriad channels of Matsebe, Queenie and Jao – the most wonderful part of the Okavango. The intricate mosaic of different habitats with a spectacular array of wildlife was unbeatable. One evening I climbed on the roof of the Land Rover and counted nine different animal species, from giraffe to impala, in one sunlit vista down the Queenie floodplain.

Those floodplains of the western Delta were hardly visited by anyone other than safari hunters and their clients and they remained beautiful, pristine and unchanged for many years. Poaching was minimal because any signs of ingress from the villages on the western edge would soon be picked up by the professional hunters and their trackers. Colleagues and friends who accompanied me on collecting trips all marvelled at the idyllic environment and the way of life that I was so privileged to enjoy. Those areas are still beautiful, but inevitably now bear the scars of numerous airstrips, networks of bush roads and a significant number of lodges and camps. Hunting was ill-advisedly banned in 2014 and although photographic tourism has expanded, it is limited to the most scenic sections, which leaves the majority of the area at the mercy of poachers.

Darting buffaloes from a helicopter was fun and exciting, but hunting them on foot was something else altogether. I had shot a few animals during FMD exercises, so I had become familiar with rifles and could shoot fairly straight. I chose a .375 Holland & Holland Magnum as my main weapon, mostly because of its versatility. I didn't think I needed the stopping power of the professional hunters' favourite, the .458, because I didn't normally shoot big bulls and hopefully wasn't going to face a close charge. I tried solid and soft point ammunition, but eventually settled on 300 grain "silvertip" bullets as standard; finding the spent, mushroomed bullet under the skin on the far side after a chest shot seemed to me to be optimum performance.

Our normal *modus operandi* was to drive out of camp at daylight and follow the sandy tracks that ran alongside the river channels or along the floodplain edges. Buffalo herds would generally graze on the floodplains during the night and retreat into the shade during the day. When we came across fresh tracks crossing the road we would park the vehicle and Jonathan and I, sometimes with Big Brown, would then follow the tracks on foot. Jonathan carried our other rifle, a 30.06 calibre, as a back up. It could take anything from a few minutes to a couple of hours to locate the herd. We would then commence a careful stalk to get within an effective shooting distance, which I regarded as not more than forty yards. Further than that increased the chances of wounding an animal in the thick bush with the prospect of hours of difficult and possibly dangerous tracking. If the first target dropped instantly or was obviously mortally wounded we would often run after the retreating herd and shoot a second animal. This was easier than shooting the first one because in the dust and mayhem we could usually catch up with the herd. They would normally stop after 300 to 400 yards. Most of the animals shot were females of various ages, but we occasionally wanted calves and adult bulls for our data sets. It became almost routine, thanks mainly to Jonathan's expert tracking skills and bushcraft. Invariably, I waited with the buffalo while Jonathan returned for the vehicle, and the other staff to help load the carcass, and we'd return to camp to process it.

A full set of measurements was taken of each buffalo and then it was weighed, using a very large spring balance and a block and tackle. Next, it was skinned and disembowelled and every organ was examined, weighed and measured. Detailed examinations of the reproductive organs were carried out to determine breeding cycles, seasons and fecundity. Teeth were measured and photographed to develop a fairly accurate ageing technique. Similar studies were being or had been carried out in East Africa, South Africa and Rhodesia, so comparative data were important to establish regional similarities or discrepancies. Finally, as much veterinary information as possible was collected, such as internal and external parasites and blood smears. It was not possible to collect samples for live viruses or antibodies, as we did during the darting exercises, because of the lack of refrigeration, but occasionally Norbert would come along to help and would check fresh blood for the trypanosomes that cause nagana in cattle or sleeping sickness in humans.

Although it was mainly routine, there were occasions when things didn't go according to plan and we had our fair share of excitement. One overcast afternoon in the upper Sandveld Tongue in Matsebe, Jonathan and I were on foot and came across the fairly fresh spoor of a small group of bulls. The tracks led us through the rainy bush for over an hour. The mopane was in full leaf and at its thickest. Jonathan was slightly in front, following the spoor, when we came across our quarry. A bull was head up, watching our approach less than ten yards away. I could only see his head and part of his neck and I took careful aim as Jonathan ducked silently behind me. The direct route into the brain of a buffalo in this position is through the nose. I fired and saw the bull drop instantly, dead before he hit the ground. From my right, and nearer than the first, a second, unseen, bull charged. I couldn't swing my rifle fast enough in that direction, but a shot rang out and that was the last I remember.

I woke up, alone, lying in the sand with two bull buffalo carcasses very close. My head was spinning and I had a pain in my right ear. My rifle was lying next to me, but there was no sign of Jonathan. I had no idea how long I had been out and decided to walk back to the car. In a befuddled state I wandered off and quickly lost our earlier tracks. The overcast sky didn't help, but I tried to walk in as straight a line as possible back to where I thought we'd left the vehicle. I must have walked for three or four miles and, as it started to go dark, I realised I was completely lost. I had no idea where I was or where the Land Rover was. I stumbled across a herd of buffalo and they crashed off through the bush. I became worried, but I had three bullets left in the .375 and thought I should be able to scare off any danger, such as lions, which are often found in the proximity of buffalo. It became very dark because of the cloud cover – no moon or stars. I had no torch or matches, so I couldn't light a fire. I sat down with my back against the bole of a fairly large mopane tree and pondered my survival. I toyed with the idea of climbing the tree for safety, but decided that I would be unable to climb and hold the rifle, so I sat where I was. I must have dozed or even slept for quite a long time because I first heard the Land Rover at almost 11.00 pm. It was quite close and I soon saw a torch coming slowly towards me. I got to my feet and shouted, making my way towards the light and noise. The vehicle's headlights came on and I could see it making its way carefully through the mopane. Jonathan was sitting on the bonnet with a torch and I recognised the driver as one of Safari South's camp staff from Queenie. They were overjoyed to see me and drove back to Queenie hunting camp, regaling me with the story of their search for me.

Jonathan had shot the charging buffalo with his 30.06 and by a miracle had killed it instantly by hitting the spinal cord in the neck. The muzzle of his rifle must have been within an inch or two of my ear and I had collapsed. He was understandably quite shocked at our narrow escape – the buffalo was dead a yard from where I had fallen. He was even more distraught to see blood coming from my ear and thought he had shot me as well. He decided the best thing to do was go for the vehicle. In those early days he didn't know how to drive but had watched me often enough to be able to start it and get back to the buffaloes in first gear.

He expected to find me lying dead next to the buffaloes and was taken aback to find me gone. He found my spoor and followed on foot until it was too dark. He then went back to the Land Rover and managed to drive it to the nearest safari camp – still in first gear! The two-man skeleton staff at the camp included a driver, so they picked up a torch and returned to the buffaloes. From there they tracked my wanderings for several miles with Jonathan walking in front or sitting on the bonnet, following my spoor by torchlight.

At the camp I was given hot soup and a generous measure of whisky before being put to bed in one of the tents at around midnight. I awoke early the next morning, not sure if my headache was due to the shooting incident or to the first aid I had received. I decided to drive back to Maun where the doctor confirmed my burst eardrum and instructed me to rest and refrain from showering or swimming for a few days to give it chance to heal. The two bulls were collected by Jonathan and donated to Queenie Camp.

My roles as a counterpart ecologist to the UNDP project and as a buffalo biologist complemented each other very well and life became extremely enjoyable for me. Sadly though, my life in the bush, with hedonistic interludes in Maun, was taking its toll on our marriage and Jenny grew ever more resentful of my selfish behaviour. She began to regret coming back to Botswana and finally left with Sammy for England in 1977, returning only sporadically to Maun for short periods.

Visitors would ask if I really got paid for my lifestyle and what did I do for leave? The answer to the latter was that I rarely took any, unless compelled to do so. Jeff Bowles, the vet who headed up the TFC, was in a similar position. His deputy director, whom Jeff disliked, eventually called him to Gabs and insisted he took leave for his psychological well-being. Jeff was so enraged that he grabbed him by the shirt-front and shook him saying that he absolutely refused to be "diagnosed" by the likes of him – apparently no one was supposed to live a life of endless enjoyment!

Anyone who has visited northern Botswana will tell you that Savuti, in Chobe National Park, is the best place in Africa to see lions. It's always been that way. The place is alive with them, sometimes in prides of more than twenty, and visitors cannot fail to be impressed. The lions and hyaenas thrived in the early 1970s, when the Savuti Channel flowed consistently and, at its termination, the great marsh teemed with zebra, tsessebe (a large colourful antelope) and, above all, buffalo. We once estimated 6,000 buffalo in a single herd at the end of the dry season. Large prides and packs of predators were the order of the day – every day – and the nights echoed with their roaring, whooping and shrieking. The prey species have now mostly diminished and dispersed with the long periods of drying of the marsh, but the carnivores are still very evident.

It's therefore no surprise that there has been a steady stream of books, videos and films of the area and its rich and spectacular wildlife. I suppose that they started from the series of scientific studies, like our buffalo surveys, which Savuti hosted. Chris McBride's lion study was one of the first. He had made a name for himself by discovering a pride of "white" lions in the, then, Eastern Transvaal. He subsequently received permission to study lions in Botswana and had set up camp on the south bank of the Savuti Channel.

I also used to camp at the channel with a small team of observers at least twice a year to carry out aerial censuses in the Chobe-Okavango region in wet and dry seasons. It was a pleasant spot and central to the survey area. One late afternoon we had landed after a three-hour census flight and parked the Maule Rocket at the side of the sandy airstrip. We pegged it down as we waited for our driver to pick us up – he had driven from Maun with our camping equipment and a supply of avgas for the survey. He told us that there was a group of people camped with Chris who had invited us to visit that evening.

After a refreshing bath in the channel at our campsite – keeping a wary eye out for crocodiles – I picked up a six-pack of Castle lager and, with my foreman Jonathan, drove the two miles to the other camp, downstream. Chris, tall, bearded and gaunt, greeted us profusely and introduced his family. A cheerful little chap came forward who was introduced as the project's sponsor, Rodney Fuhr, a successful young mail-order entrepreneur from Johannesburg with a passion for lions.

We sat round the campfire and had a drink. Chris enthusiastically explained that Rodney had come to see how he was getting along with the latest radio-tracking equipment, which had been sent to him a month or so earlier. He had managed to fit two radio collars on lions in different prides and was thrilled to be able to find and follow them on their nocturnal wanderings. This technology was new and exciting in the 1970s and the lions seemed oblivious to the spotlights he used to observe them and just carried on with their usual hunting activities. He insisted that he would demonstrate to us how easy it all was later in the evening after supper.

We enjoyed a delicious meal, accompanied by some of Rodney's excellent red wine, and swapped stories, listening to the occasional distant roars from some of Savuti's best. Jonathan, a non-drinker, quietly informed me that the lions were calling from the direction of the airstrip.

"Don't worry," I replied. "We can easily find them with Chris's new toy."

We set out to locate the lions at about 9.00 pm, with Chris and Rodney in the leading Land Rover, Jonathan and I following in ours. The lions had stopped calling, but no one seemed concerned as we threaded our way through the camelthorn trees, washed with Chris's spotlight. Every so often Chris would stop and climb on the roof to brandish his radio antenna, then, apparently satisfied, climb back into the driver's seat and continue. We followed expectantly. After about half an hour we were approaching the northern end of the Marsh, the opposite direction from the airstrip. Jonathan was the only one showing any signs of misgivings. We had seen lots of antelope, a few smaller predators – genets and jackals – and a couple of spotted hyaena, but no lions so far. We stopped for further refreshments from the cool box and gathered at the Land Rover.

"We must still be out of range," said Chris, "but I'm sure we'll soon pick them up."

I mentioned that we thought the earlier sounds had come from the direction of the airstrip.

"Yeah, maybe, but they usually stay this side of the channel and they move about a lot at this time of night. We'll find them though – this system never fails."

We continued to criss-cross the bush in a rough grid pattern, but without a bleep from the tracking antenna. We saw elephants and giraffe, a couple of old *kwatale* – buffalo bulls with worn away horns and even shorter tempers – who reluctantly got out of our way, but still no lions. We got the Land Rover stuck in an antbear hole and needed the hi-lift jack on a couple of occasions, but we still had the contents of the cool box to sustain us and we persevered until quite late. In the interests of safe flying the next morning, I called it a day about 11.00 pm and Jonathan and I took our leave, driving back the shortest way to the road and then to our camp. Chris and Rodney were going to try for a little longer.

Jonathan and I were sound asleep in our blankets by the fire shortly after midnight and awake as dawn paled the tree tops. One of the trackers had already blown the embers into life and boiled water for our morning coffee.

We heard the distant grunts of a male lion as we drank and discussed the previous evening's activities. Jonathan was singularly unimpressed with the new technology, but then he could follow a track unerringly where the average "townie" like me could see absolutely nothing. For years he had repeatedly amazed me with his abilities, and had quite certainly saved me from several extremely unpleasant situations.

We left camp as the light grew; there was no reason to be airborne before the light was good enough to see animals clearly from the plane and we didn't have far to fly to the starting point of our census transects. We drove through the channel in about two feet of water and continued. It was quite chilly on the back of our Land Rover as our driver sped along the dusty track to the airstrip. We slowed right down to watch a black and white honey badger scuttling along the edge of the track, nose down, searching for breakfast. He seemed oblivious to us until we got within about five metres, when he picked up his head and, after a brief pause for thought, decided our front tyre was on the menu. The driver accelerated in response to our shouts from the back. Luckily the honey badger gave up without feeling threatened or too upset, otherwise our morning flight might have had to take place with the windows open – these handsome beasts can spray the strongest and foulest odour imaginable.

We turned off and drove along the slip road to the airstrip. Even I could now clearly make out an assortment of pug marks in the sand. We laughed heartily as Jonathan's evening suspicions proved true and pictured Chris, with his antenna waving, struggling through the bush in the dark on the other side of the channel. Then we turned on to the airstrip and our laughter faded. Our aircraft was surrounded by fifteen lions! Several lionesses were lying under the wings and fuselage and a couple of young cubs were chasing each other around the tail. A large male was lying, unconcerned, a few metres away. There was no real problem; we could easily chase them away with the vehicle. But, as we got close enough to do that, we noticed that they had been "playing" with the tail and elevator. The tiny tail wheel had been punctured and the elevator had been chewed and badly torn. This was the point at which I began to agree with Jonathan and wish I'd never seen Chris and his new gadget.

Surveying was now out of the question; the aircraft could not be flown in that state. I had to consider whether to call on the radio and ask for assistance or try to patch it up well enough to at least fly back to Maun. The former course of action was in accordance with the rules, but I knew from experience that the new DCA desk jockeys from ICAO would make more of a meal of the incident than the lions had! We would be instructed to sit and wait until an engineer could be found and dispatched, which could take days. We therefore took a chance and fixed the punctured tail wheel and patched up the worst holes in the fabric of the elevator with masking tape. There didn't seem to be any damage to the frame or control cables and everything seemed to work, at least on the ground. Jonathan was happy to fly with me, so, after a short solo test circuit, we flew nervously back to Maun – and a severe reprimand from the DCA flight safety officer.

Meanwhile, our international project to try to understand how the Okavango Delta functioned rolled on with measurements of water flow, seasonal variations in distribution, rainfall and evapotranspiration. The Deputy Project Manager, Turgut Dincer, eventually produced a mathematical model that took into consideration all these variables plus the results of measurements from a "mini delta", constructed on the Kiri River by the hydrologists and hydraulic engineers.

Apparently, ninety-two per cent of the inflow of the panhandle at Shakawe disappeared into the atmosphere by physical evaporation from the water surface and transpiration through the leaves of plants. A further five per cent soaked into the sand and disappeared underground, leaving the rather insignificant quantity of two to three per cent to arrive in the Thamalakane River in Maun. This rather ruled out the possibility that any tampering with the channels down near Maun would produce a worthwhile increase in outflow and none of the previously proposed augmentation schemes have ever been implemented.

However, these results did not stop another investigative study in the mid-1980s, conducted by the incongruously named (for Botswana) Snowy Mountains Engineering Corporation from Australia. They reached similar conclusions after spending colossal amounts of international "aid" funds. But it wasn't until after yet another expensive multidisciplinary study by the International Union for Conservation of Nature (IUCN) was published in 1993 that the Delta was left to its natural evolution and variation. Maybe they should have just asked Pete Smith and his baNoka friends back in 1974.

A year or so after the lion incident we were en route to Khwai but, as was often the case, leaving Maun to go on safari was taking longer than anticipated. We now had two Land Rovers, having been allocated one by the UN, and Jonathan had obtained his driving licence. We also had two extra field assistants, also courtesy of the UN. The vehicles had been loaded with the essential scientific equipment and camping paraphernalia but Jonathan and I still had to collect the others from their homes. This meant a bewildering (for me) tour of hundreds of similar reed and thatch huts, divided by narrow, sandy alleyways, puddled in the rainy season, and fringed with untidy hedges of rubber plants, poles and broken wire. The bare, sandy yards were littered with similar collections of cooking pots, broken bicycles and buckets and scruffy, scratching fowls. The inhabitants were also variations on a theme: near-naked children laughing and waving, supported by noisy, rib-thin, yellow dogs, all chasing the vehicle driven by the *lekgowa* (white man); women sweeping or sitting chatting around small fires who cheerfully called directions in answer to my carefully rehearsed but wildly inaccurate Setswana enquiries. At each stop an assistant would load his blankets, rations and usually a battered transistor radio, then climb aboard the pick-up.

It took me at least an hour before I met up again with Jonathan outside the old Riley's Hotel to fill up with fuel and allow the men to buy cigarettes. Jonathan obviously had less difficulty finding his way through the maze and was inevitably there before me, with his contingent leaning against the Land Rover smoking and exchanging tales about their days off. Our last requirement was to fill the cool boxes with ice from the bottle store to keep our biological samples fresh until we returned to town – and to keep our perishables cold in the meantime.

We finally left town just before noon and headed northeast across the picturesque old Matlapaneng Bridge over the Thamalakane River and along the sand road through the mopane woodland to Shorobe village. There had been good rains, which had left large pools across the road every few hundred yards through the mopane woodland. These made our progress slower than usual and it took us an hour to get to the "One-Two" hut at Shokamokwa, which, for me, was where the wilderness really began. Getting past the hut never ceased to thrill me. It derived its odd name from the activities of the TFC staff stationed there. Any vehicles inbound to Maun were required to drive into the corrugated iron shed and were sprayed with old-fashioned flit guns containing insecticide. This ritual was directed by the foreman chanting "one-two", each utterance being followed by four squirts from the flit guns as the operators moved slowly down each side of the vehicle. After a few minutes the front doors were opened to the bright sunlight and you were allowed to continue your journey. I wondered about the long-term effects of the insecticide spray on the TFC staff, who wore no masks or protective kit, just standard issue blue overalls. Outbound traffic like us merely had to wait for a mopane pole boom to be lifted to bypass the chamber and continue our journey. We were familiar to the guards and were always the subject of light-hearted banter, mainly in the hope of acquiring meat from us on our way back into town.

Now we began to see game, lots of tracks crossed the road and I was always on the lookout in that area for sable and roan antelope or even eland. We soon branched left and north, leaving the road to Savuti and Chobe, to follow the track towards Moremi Game Reserve. This meandered through attractive, mature mopane woodland, dappled bright green in the summer sunlight, interspersed with sandier patches dominated by large camelthorn or *mogotho* trees, which were covered in crescent-shaped velvety pods in winter. We were still at least an hour from camp, and just outside the southern boundary of the game reserve, when one of the men on the back of the Land Rover tapped sharply on the cab roof and hissed "*Dinare!* [buffalo]".

We stopped and I climbed up to have a look through my binoculars. It was a large herd, maybe 150 animals, about 500 yards away to our left, grazing slowly across a grassy, dry floodplain. Any fortuitous sightings of herds from the vehicles presented a welcome opportunity for a short stalk, but I decided it was too late in the day and that we should proceed to camp. After all, there was no way we could load an animal on the already packed vehicles. This was greeted with such a display of collective disappointment and anguish that I relented and agreed to try to collect a couple. I decreed that someone would have to stay with the animals we shot until we could send back an empty vehicle to collect the carcasses in the evening, but there were plenty of volunteers.

Jonathan and I took our rifles and I instructed Big Brown, the next best tracker after Jonathan, to accompany us. Little Brown, the only other driver, though unlicensed, was to bring a Land Rover to pick us up after he heard our shots. Our strategy was, as usual, to stalk as closely as possible to the herd before running in and choosing our quarry. The point at which we began to run was usually dictated by our being spotted by one of the sentinel buffalo on the fringes and the whole herd stampeding off as if a single organism. True herd animals like buffalo behave rather like shoals of fish or flocks of birds in having nearly simultaneous reactions to stimuli from outside the herd. Running, almost at a sprint, within a fleeing herd for a few hundred yards was an exhilarating experience. By then, or earlier if we were lucky, they would pull up with much bellowing and milling around. There was always thick dust, which seemed to obscure us long enough for us to select and shoot before they took off again. Sometimes we would literally push our way between animals to get a clear shot at our quarry.

On this occasion we wanted to obtain samples from two-year-old females. The wind was perfect for a stalk, blowing gently from the herd directly towards us. We walked briskly across the floodplain, obscured from the buffalo by stooping in the waist-high grass; Brown was in front with Jonathan close behind me. I would shoot first and he would only use his rifle if necessary. The leading buffaloes, on the far side of the herd from us, had entered a narrow band of knobthorn woodland containing a few fan palms. By now we were within seventy-five yards of the stragglers – mainly bulls – so we decided to wait until they'd also crossed the slightly higher woodland. We could now see that the herd was larger than we thought, numbering at least 300. Crouching in the grass we could hear the familiar herd noises, like contented cattle lowing and grunting, with higher pitched calls from calves, as they moved slowly away from us. They had no inkling of our presence.

When the herd had disappeared into the woodland we advanced quite quickly. I was no longer aware of Brown in front of me but gave this no thought and continued after the buffalo – after all I hardly needed a tracker to follow them at this stage. When I entered the woodland I could see the herd standing quite clearly in the floodplain beyond. Their behaviour had changed and I suspected they sensed danger, whispering so to Jonathan who had come up to crouch at my right shoulder. Suddenly the herd swung away to the left at speed and I immediately began to run as fast as possible after them, hoping to cover the fifty or so yards that still separated us. As I closed in on the lumbering tailmarkers, whom I needed to overtake to approach the body of the herd, I became aware of something on a converging course to my right. I clearly remember thinking, quite illogically, that it was a donkey and that it was moving faster than I was. The next thing I knew we collided. I tumbled over the top, realising in the same instant that the donkey was a fully-grown male lion! Somersaulting, I came to rest on all fours thinking, "gun! tree! run!" in that order. I can't be sure what the lion was thinking as, two yards apart, we looked at each other for a couple of milliseconds, but it must have been the feline equivalent, as he grunted once, turned and disappeared into the grass. He had obviously got as big a shock as I had.

I stood up, dusted myself down, picked up my rifle and began walking back the way I had come. Jonathan quickly joined me having seen the fun from a few yards behind. He had noticed the lion chasing the same buffalo as me and shouted a warning that I had not heard. He was astonished by the incident and concerned by the fact that I was limping on my right leg, a fact that had not registered with me. My right knee had made hard contact with the left side of the lion's chest and was beginning to stiffen up. As we walked back towards the vehicles Brown appeared out of the bush laughing uncontrollably. He had been the first to see the lions (three in all) stalking the buffalo away to our right and had sensibly decided to leave the hunt to the two of us with guns. Around the fire that night, as I drank an ice-cold beer or two and nursed my knee, the witnesses told, retold and re-enacted the story with heightened drama and hysterical mirth until their companions were satisfied that it had been the biggest and fiercest lion in the whole Okavango Delta.

It wasn't only the animals that gave us problems. The terrain, with its constantly changing water distribution, made every trip different. The Okavango Delta is unique. Perhaps its most critical and paradoxical condition is that it floods during the dry season when the rainfall in Angola six months previously has reached northwest Botswana via the Okavango River. In mid-dry season, after months without rain, we would struggle to cross floodplains and river courses. TFC and the safari companies had constructed bridges of mopane poles across many of the deepest channels and where this proved impossible they'd placed pontoons. These were usually made from forty-four-gallon drums, securely fixed into a metal frame, with parallel poles or steel channels on top to guide the vehicle's wheels. They were hauled across the channel by cables attached to trees on either side.

In contrast, in the middle of the summer rains, the river courses were mainly shallow or even empty and we would bypass the bridges, driving across a dry riverbed, but would then struggle to cross wet patches of black cotton soil or deep puddles along the sand tracks. Digging and jacking the vehicles out was a frequent chore. Usually a few minutes' work with a hi-lift jack and a few branches under the problem wheel was all that was needed, but it wasn't unheard of to spend a few hours getting out of a particularly bad spot, sometimes even sleeping the night there and completing the job the next morning. I used to get stuck so often that some folk called me "Puddles".

Hi-lift jacks (a wonderful American invention) were essential but temperamental. The springs in the climbing mechanism, if neglected, became highly unreliable and needed assisting with anything at hand, usually a screwdriver, but a knife or even very quick fingers would do, at some personal risk. When operating the jack it was essential to keep a firm hold of the handle, which, if left free, could fly up at speed with considerable force. On one occasion the cook, Bahense, was jacking the Land Rover, a task he wasn't normally asked to perform. The jack handle slipped from his muddy hand and delivered a fierce uppercut, removing his two upper incisors which flew into the grass verge. The crew found them and after I'd washed them I tried to persuade Bahense to let me push them back into the sockets because I thought there was a chance they would heal. He had other ideas though and, howling, grabbed them and flung them into the bush. The rest of the crew showed little sympathy and were making as much noise laughing as he was howling. For the remainder of his time with us Bahense was known as "Jack".

John Counihan, a big redheaded Irishman who had arrived in South Africa as a one-year-old, was visiting Maun on business from Gaborone and asked if he could accompany us into the Delta. I agreed, much to the annoyance of Norbert, who would be collecting blood smears and checking for trypanosomiasis. He knew John vaguely and regarded him as a hard-drinking, unreliable townie, who would prove to be a liability in the bush. After a couple of days camped near the pontoon on the Xudum River in Khurunxaragha we had only managed to shoot and process one buffalo. Norbert and I decided to leave camp very early one morning in his Land Cruiser to search for buffaloes. John wanted to sleep in, so I asked him to deliver the meat from the first buffalo to the nearby camp of Safari South after he got up. We'd loaded about seventy-five per cent of the buffalo carcass into the back of my Land Rover.

We arrived back in camp around midday to find John sitting by the fire, but no sign of the Land Rover with the meat. I asked if he had delivered it as planned.

"No," he said. "I got stuck in the river."

"Whereabouts?" I enquired, scanning the river bank. "I can't see it."

"No," he replied glumly. "It's in the middle."

The Xudum at that point was about thirty yards wide and ten or twelve feet deep in the middle, where the pontoon crossed. The flood was at its highest in June and the water was cold. John had attempted to drive onto the pontoon without securing it properly to the bank. Once on, he had applied brakes, but the momentum of the vehicle caused the pontoon to move into the river. Panicking, he jumped out and the vehicle started to roll off the pontoon, coming to rest on the riverbed in mid-channel. As well as the meat on the back, the cab contained all sort of items that shouldn't get wet: books, maps, permits and personal belongings.

No one was keen to dive into the river. Apart from the cold water, crocodiles were common and the raw buffalo meat was prime bait. John "volunteered", as the one with the most subcutaneous insulation, and stripped down to his underwear to attach a rope to the sunken Land Rover. Sheer good luck had left it on its wheels on the sandy riverbed and we planned to tow it backwards up the bank to dry land. Unfortunately, the driver's door had been left open and acted as a brake, making it almost impossible to pull out with the Land Cruiser. A second dive by John rectified that and we had just begun to make a little progress when a Unimog belonging to Safari South appeared on the opposite bank, planning to cross the pontoon. The driver was a friendly young mechanic who, once we had pulled him across the river, gladly hitched the powerful German vehicle to our submerged one by his winch cable (after another dive by John) and quickly extracted it from the depths. We shared a celebratory beer and the mechanic headed off for Maun.

The recovered Land Rover was opened out to allow maximum drainage and drying. Because we had no spare oils it was left motionless on the bank overnight to allow the water and oils to separate. Early the following morning we carefully removed each drain plug, one at a time, to let water out of the fuel tank, engine sump, gearbox, transfer case and both diffs – quickly reinserting the plugs as soon as the lighter oil appeared. The top of the engine was drained of water by removing the spark plugs and hand cranking. Following this lengthy procedure we pulled it behind the other vehicle and, following a few coughs, it started after about twenty yards.

The data we derived from the shot buffaloes supplemented that obtained from the immobilisation exercise and we built up a picture of the species' life history, including the seasonal movements and home ranges of the herds. During a spell of good years, with more than average rainfall and plenty to eat, they would breed and grow in a manner exceeding that of the local domestic cattle under traditional management, but not compared with improved breeds under intensive husbandry, such as feedlots. They gained weight quite spectacularly during the rainy season when they grazed in the sandy woodlands, using the water in the ephemeral pans, but then lost condition when they were forced back onto the lush-looking, but apparently less nutritious, floodplains during the dry season. They could live for about seventeen years, which is when their teeth wore out, and went on breeding into their final year. They could move vast distances and we found a few Okavango buffalo as far afield as Hwange National Park in western Zimbabwe. Mainly though, their movements were restricted to Ngamiland, ranging more widely in the wet summers in herds averaging sixty to 100 individuals and concentrating near permanent water in the dry winters, when they could aggregate in their thousands.

For a couple of years I often joined forces, and therefore resources, on field trips in Moremi with a South African student from Pretoria University who was working on lechwe in the Delta. He would sometimes stay at my camp at North Gate, while working around South Gate and San-ta-wani when the wide floodplains were seasonally inundated from the Mogoghelo River. This was a regular annual event in the 1970s – strangely, the neighbouring and almost parallel, much deeper channel of the Gomoti River was completely dry for several years, a situation which has now reversed.

Russell Biggs was in his late twenties, tanned and rugged with a thick mat of curly hair. He was extremely bright and as rough and tough as he looked. Although he was of English extraction, following his education and a spell in the South African Defence Force he identified more with Afrikaans culture. He was also a prodigious drinker and inveterate party animal when he emerged from his isolated study area to buy supplies and unwind. After enough brandy and Coke he was often completely uncontrollable.

One evening, at a party at my house, he punched a Swedish visitor for espousing what Russell considered extreme left-wing views (this was in the days of apartheid). After we overpowered him he proclaimed that he was going home for his gun and would be back to "sort us all out". A few minutes later he re-entered the room and asked me to help start his car, his animosity towards me forgotten. I found his keys on the floor and persuaded him to let me drive him home. All the way to his flat he muttered about communists ruining Africa and how, if there were enough bullets, he could put things right. On arrival at his flat he opened the passenger door of his short-wheel-base Land Rover and fell out head first into a forty-four-gallon rubbish drum. Only his frantically kicking legs were protruding from the top accompanied by muffled yells about shooting "every bastard in town". I was laughing so hard I was hardly able to get him out of the drum and through his front door. I left him passed out on the floor and returned to the party in his vehicle, confident that he wouldn't be back. We were due to go on safari together the next morning, but all my attempts to rouse him failed, so I left his car at my house and went on without him.

On another occasion, at his camp on the west side of Chief's Island, he was hunting lechwe in the floodplains near Xaxaba and was bitten on the calf by a snake. His tracker, James, a muscular Yei mokoro poler, assured him that he had seen the snake and that it was a deadly black mamba. Most indigenous people believe that snake incidents always involve black mambas and scarcely ever differentiate species. They walked back to camp and Russell inspected the bite. Whatever snake it had been it must have been a considerable size, judging from the wound, so James could well have been right. There was no vehicle access to Chief's Island in those days and the boat journey down the Boro to Maun was several hours, so if it was a mamba bite he wasn't going to make it. Russell decided there was nothing for it but to get drunk. After a bottle and a half of Klipdrift brandy he fell asleep. He woke up the following day with nothing but a headache and claimed for evermore that Klipdrift cured snakebite.

Russell received a master's degree from Pretoria for an exceptionally good thesis on the ecology of red lechwe. In those days the standards required by this and other top South African universities (notably the veterinary faculty, also at Pretoria) surpassed those of most international seats of learning. It is a sad indictment of modern Africa that this is no longer true. Russell's academic supervisor at Pretoria was the prominent mammalogist Professor Bothma, with whom I had been in contact about buffalo research. He wanted to visit to assess Russell's fieldwork and wrote to me for advice on how feasible it was to travel to the camp in central Okavango. One of the many questions he asked was about the availability of antidotes for Bushman arrow poison. It amazed me that so many well-informed and highly educated South Africans were almost completely ignorant of the rest of Africa.

Another illustration of the remote nature of Maun and the Okavango and our poor communications played out in mid-1977. I applied for two weeks' leave to visit Namibia (then known as South West Africa). I heard nothing from HQ in Gabs so I went anyway with Norbert and Kate, driving via Ghanzi to Windhoek. We had such an enjoyable time touring that fabulous country that we stayed for an extra week. A little after our return I was in Gabs having an aeroplane serviced and I called in to see the Director. In his office I was about to apologise for taking extra leave, when he was called out briefly. I noticed my original leave application in his "in tray", so I quickly picked it up, folded it and put it in my pocket. When he returned, during a short conversation neither of us mentioned leave and he obviously wasn't aware that I had been away from Maun, so I got away with a three-week paid holiday!

There was disagreement about the exact role buffalo played in spreading FMD to domestic stock since it had only been demonstrated once, and that under extreme, artificial conditions – and I was one of the sceptics. However we knew from our samples that the buffalo did harbour all three types of

African FMD virus. Live virus was isolated from a small proportion of younger animals and we demonstrated antibodies in a majority of all ages. Although this information might have been prejudicial to the buffalo, ironically we managed to turn it around and use it for the conservation of its habitat.

One of the great questions of the time in relation to the UN Okavango Project was how to preserve the area's natural integrity. Historically, in the late nineteenth century, pre-rinderpest, there had been cattle posts along the Khwai River on its northern fringes and there was now also pressure from the growing communities on the western edge to move cattle further into the Sandveld Tongue towards the Queenie and Matsebe Rivers. This would eventually have led to the complete destruction of the Delta as a pristine wildlife area. Our UN Project's ecological team of Bill and Alistair, with Pete and me as local counterparts, was striving to come up with a robust wildlife management plan for the Delta to counter the embryonic development ideas of the other project staff. We had little faith in the proclamation and administration of the so-called Wildlife Management Areas that were being touted for large parts of the country.

"We don't want a paper 'plan', we need a bloody brick wall around it!" Alistair remarked at one of our meetings.

"What about a fence?" I proposed. "The veterinary cordon fences around the country work well."

I was fully aware that this was, politically, a highly charged suggestion that bordered on treason for an ecologist – especially following recent international furore about Botswana's "fences of death", but as a vet I was able to see both sides objectively.

"Maybe one fence at least can be environmentally friendly," I continued. "It will be easy to sell the idea on the grounds of disease control, keeping the buffalo away from the cattle, but keeping the cattle and people out of the Delta will be fantastic."

Bill was highly sceptical, arguing that the sociologists on the team would oppose it, "And think of the press reaction overseas; we'd be crucified!"

However, Pete and Alistair agreed it was an approach worth trying, so we co-opted Jeff Bowles, as an exceptionally enterprising civil servant who got things done against the odds (often his own superiors). We put the idea to the Director of Veterinary Services (DVS) who, in those days before environmental impact assessments and extensive consultation became de rigueur, could independently authorise such developments. Jeff's TFC unit had the funds and manpower to begin as soon as we had approval and within weeks he and I flew a survey with Alistair to site the fence. Jeff and I then followed the proposed alignment as closely as possible on the ground, marking trees along the route for his fencing gang to follow.

Almost before construction started protests were heard from several quarters, especially the "greener" elements in Maun and the wider Botswana expatriate community. But, armed with the scientific findings of the buffalo sampling, the DVS stood his ground and the fence was completed, first by beefing up the original outer tsetse fence and then putting one along the western fringes of the Delta. Our wildlife surveys showed a clear annual migration of zebra across the proposed alignment, particularly in the southwest of the Sandveld Tongue near Setateng, but this area already contained a substantial number of cattle and we reluctantly conceded it, compromising the zebra population but calculating that the conservation equation was overwhelmingly favourable. Nowadays, nobody, especially the original green sceptics, would doubt that this "southern buffalo fence" has played a vital role in protecting the Delta's integrity.

When the UNDP/FAO Okavango project ended in 1977 most of the foreign staff departed leaving just the counterparts, Pete and myself, to carry on as Botswana Government staff members. Norbert and Kate left to take on a new German aid project in Ghana on tsetse flies.

Alistair continued to conduct wildlife surveys over most of the rest of Botswana for a few more years. He designed a component of the Countrywide Range Assessment Project (with the apt acronym of CRAP), and carried it out under the auspices of the Dutch environmental and engineering Company DHV, with funds from the EU. Alistair persuaded Aerkavango to buy a Cessna 210 to replace the Helio Courier because, he reasoned, he would have to fly long transects and even longer ferry flights over the Kalahari Desert, so the extra speed would be essential.

Many people considered that the population estimates obtained by these surveys were highly questionable, which caused friction among the observers. Nevertheless, the government accepted them and they've been used often since to make highly speculative statements about wildlife numbers and population trends in the Kalahari. It seems that once data has been published its statistics and conclusions often become set in stone.

The Cessna 210 was fitted with some specialised and very expensive equipment for the project. The now-ubiquitous GPS had not been invented in the late 1970s, but there was an accurate navigation tool known as GNS, which relied on triangulating very low frequency radio transmissions from US military installations around the world. Picking up at least three of these transmissions meant that the on-board instruments could calculate the aircraft's position with exceptional accuracy – but it came at an exceptional price, US$90,000, almost more than the aircraft. Alistair insisted that without this system he would not be able to navigate accurately, let alone fly parallel transects over the almost featureless Kalahari Desert. It was this system that, a year or so later, enabled us to find the scheduled flight that went down on its way to Gabs.

He then bought a huge camera, which had to be mounted in the middle of the cabin and took pictures through the floor of the aircraft. It was operated by a pair of bicycle-like handlebars. This created great difficulty because of the stowage area of the undercarriage and caused Bob Hampshire at the DCA weeks of intense scrutiny before an aircraft with a hole in the floor could be declared serviceable and legal.

I was the lucky crew member who was first to try to operate the thing. Maybe it was an improvement on sitting on the floor with legs dangling below the Helio Courier, but it was fiendishly difficult to aim, focus and shoot. The film magazine could hold 250 exposures, but we discovered that it could only be processed in Canada. The upshot was that only one roll of film was ever used and the camera was abandoned and gathered dust in the storeroom for years. The cost of this can only be imagined, but EU funding for "development projects" was easy meat. When the aerial survey programme was first proposed the budget had been $250,000, but the EU representative informed us that only proposals of $750,000 and more were normally considered. It proved very simple for a man of Alistair's talents to inflate the budget to the required amount, hence the Cessna 210, GNS system and Wilton camera. Imagine this kind of profligacy repeated over many years in many African countries and a very negative but true picture of much international aid emerges.

The populations of blue wildebeest and zebra on the Makgadikgadi Pans were another of our targets. Their numbers were unknown but believed to be substantial. However, because of their extremely clumped distribution, they did not lend themselves to any normal systematic aerial survey method. Ian Parker, a friend of Alistair's from Kenya and an experienced and knowledgeable wildlife researcher, was visiting Francistown for a meeting with Botswana Game Industries. He came to Maun and we asked him for ideas on censusing the animals. At a curry supper in Alistair's house on the river he came up with a novel idea using flight lines in random directions and a very narrow transect width which we agreed might work, although after a few drinks our grasp of the statistical theory was probably not the firmest.

Early the next morning we flew down to the Makgadikgadi Pans and looked for a concentration of zebra and wildebeest. I had been relegated to observer while Ian took the seat next to Alistair. I was a poor aerial observer because, being colour blind, I often couldn't make out the animals in the bush, but this wasn't a serious problem in the flat, open terrain of the Makgadikgadi. As the flight progressed into the third hour of skimming over the ground and making tight turns I started to feel queasy. This was a new sensation for me; as far back as I could remember I had never been sick for any reason. I tried to fight the rising nausea, praying for an end to the survey, or at least a period of straight and level flight. Eventually I quite suddenly and explosively vomited, hitting the back of Ian's neck with the bulk of my supper! Needless to say, I was very unpopular and the flight back to Maun with the windows open was extremely unpleasant for everyone involved, especially Ian. This was an extremely rare occurrence for me, and months afterwards Jane, Alistair's zany wife, admitted to me that she had added a tin of cat food to the curry because she thought there wouldn't be enough for the extra dinner guests. My unfortunate behaviour couldn't have ruined Ian's day completely though, because he later told us that in his opinion the spectacle of the zebra and wildebeest matched the famous sights in the Serengeti and the only difference between the two was "a good PR person".

I stayed on in Maun until the end of 1981 as the senior ecologist responsible for the Okavango and Chobe and continued to fly surveys in the north and feed the results into a new national database. Along with the "scientific" quota allocation, the Game Department adopted new rules, proposed by Alistair, for regulating hunting based on single licences, rather than the old system of "packages". Hunting returns were, in theory, now much easier to obtain and record, and for some key species, such as elephant and lion, trophy size and quality were monitored. This allowed a degree of management far superior to the old system. Fears that adult male lions were being shot excessively, leaving only immature animals, were quashed when for the next year every lion trophy obtained in northern Botswana was aged and measured. Results showed that these were all fully mature animals, indicating that the population was healthy.

During the late 1970s more and more, mainly citizen, hunters were returning with smaller elephant tusks. Safari companies however appeared to maintain trophy weights even though very large tusks remained scarce. Several theories were advanced to explain this, with one argument being that big tuskers had mostly been shot out and the remaining population was left only with young bulls. The age of an elephant can be determined by examining their molar teeth; the animals have six sets, but only one set at a time. The largest, sixth, set wears out at between sixty and seventy years of age and the animal, unable to eat properly, then dies. It was therefore decreed that all hunters must bring in the lower jaw as well as the tusks for registration. The age of the elephant and the weight of its tusks were then recorded. After the odd anomaly had been ironed out (rocks and other heavy objects were sometimes hidden in the nerve cavity to try to avoid confiscation) it transpired that large numbers of young animals were being shot. This tied in well with the new aerial census results showing a fast-growing population and the expectation that many citizen hunters would not spend the time required to find an older animal if lots of younger ones were available more quickly and therefore more cheaply. It was made illegal to hunt elephants with tusks of less than twenty pounds each. To me the logic of the new rules seemed awry. I argued that shooting younger animals was preferable if the requirement was that more middle-aged bulls should survive to old age and replenish the numbers of large trophy bulls.

NINE

ELEPHANT AFFAIRS

Botswana is justly famous for its large elephant population that now accounts for about half of the remaining elephants in Africa, but this majestic beast is being relentlessly exterminated from most of its natural range on the continent and there are signs that Botswana's animals are now being targeted. I've been lucky to spend many years working with these wonderful beasts.

The enormous old bull elephants that habitually hung around on the Chobe floodplains near Kasane were pretty docile and normally allowed vehicles to approach close by. One morning we darted an enormous old fellow and he quietly fell over on his side after a few minutes. It was more in the way of a demonstration than for any specific project (my boss Wolfgang and a few other senior people were in attendance). After everyone had poked and posed and taken photos I injected him with antidote and we all backed off to a safe distance to watch him recover. Nothing happened in the usual two or three minutes so I walked back to him to investigate. All his vital signs appeared normal and he just lay there breathing noisily but normally through his trunk. After about ten minutes and another injection of antidote, to no avail, I suggested that if we rolled him over he might wake up. It was a trick I had seen and used in many animals and it nearly always stimulated them. However, rolling a six-ton elephant over was not as easy as rolling a cat on an operating table.

I had a long hemp rope that came with the capstan winch on the front of my Land Rover. As a good Boy Scout I knew a few knots and explained to my colleagues that we could tie the rope to his lower tusk using a highwayman's hitch, a quick-release knot. We could then pass the rope under a front leg and over his back and pull it with the Land Rover. They were a bit sceptical, but I persuaded Wolfgang to let me try. Because I would be holding the free end of the rope ready to pull and detach it from the tusk, Wolfgang would have to drive the vehicle. Practical tasks were not his forte, but he reluctantly agreed and decided to use his own Land Rover. I tied the knot around the thick tusk and passed the rope around a leg without any reaction from the bull, who was apparently sleeping soundly. After attaching the end firmly to the tow-hitch on the vehicle we got in position, ready to give it a try.

Wolfgang drove slowly in low range 4x4 to tension the rope. The vehicle was about ten yards from the elephant and I was holding the other end of the rope standing about half that distance at a right angle to his head. On my signal Wolfgang began to pull, the vehicle strained, the rope stretched alarmingly, but the great beast slowly rolled over on his back. As he settled on his other side he began to rock in the way elephants do and then slowly got to his feet. Success! I heaved on the rope to release it from the tusk, but it was stuck – so much for the Boy Scouts. The bull stood absolutely still, as if he hadn't noticed us. I pulled again for all I was worth, but it wouldn't budge. I left the rope and backed off. Wolfgang jumped out of his vehicle and ran to join us. We now had a very large, six-ton bull elephant firmly attached to a two-ton Land Rover by a very short length of strong rope. He continued to stand immobile, as if asleep on his feet, and we hoped he would stay like that, imagining the wreckage if he took off with the vehicle attached or if he decided to get angry with it.

As it had been my idea and I was the junior, Wolfgang decided that I would have to "make a plan" and quickly. Giving more immobilising drug was not an option because of the antidote still circulating in his body. I decided to try to pull the rope off by driving the Land Rover away. Its engine was still running and in low range I gingerly drove forward hoping the elephant wouldn't take exception. The rope stretched and stretched, but didn't come off or snap. I pushed in the clutch and the elasticity of the rope pulled me back towards the bull. I just managed to brake before I hit him on the nose. Now I was in a fluster and instinctively drove forward at high revs to get away. This time, as I reached high tension on the rope, it slipped down the taper of the tusk and dropped free. Panic over, we regrouped and watched for several more minutes until, with a flap of his great ears he walked slowly away, apparently oblivious of the whole episode.

Unusual reactions to M99 immobilisation are thankfully rare, but every animal is an individual and the drugs are administered under less than perfect conditions, with only a remote assessment possible of the animal's condition, age and body weight. A year or so later, in almost the same spot on the Chobe, Norbert Drager and I darted a large bull for a demonstration for some visiting VIPs, the local District Commissioner, other local dignitaries and a class of about thirty youngsters from the local school on the back of a large truck, all eager to see the event.

The bull went down in a textbook manner and I examined him with all the onlookers stationed about 100 yards away. Anthony Ziegler, our game warden colleague, asked if the observers could approach more closely.

"Sure!" I replied. "They can come and touch him, it's quite safe."

Lots of posing and photographing took place and I was chatting to the visitors about the drugs we used and how they worked. After about ten minutes, with a swarm of small boys and girls clambering all over the huge bull, he suddenly moved and then began to rock. The kids all made it back into the truck in one bounce and under a second! Everyone else retreated to their vehicles as he slowly rose and stood quietly, not even moving his ears or trunk. After about twenty seconds he went down again in the same spot. I walked up and checked him and everything seemed absolutely normal. I indicated to the kids that they could approach again, but not a single volunteer got off the truck. After I administered the antidote he rocked and rose again and moved off sedately, across the floodplain away from the gathering of people. I did wonder if it was the same elephant.

As more attention was paid to elephants, research workers had to be able to recognise animals for their studies. This often meant that individuals needed to be fitted with collars, although other madcap ideas were tried, such as throwing eggs filled with different coloured paint at them. One young American hero was convinced he could outrun an elephant (allegedly he had made the US 1968 Olympic squad) and volunteered to mark some study elephants. A cow with a bright blue bum gave him a twenty-yard start and caught him in fifty. He was incredibly lucky to be thrown into a shallow muddy pool, whereupon the elephant quickly lost interest in him. Those of us not quite so athletic decided that drug darts were probably the way to go.

Malte, based in Kasane, was one of the first to request veterinary assistance for tagging and Norbert agreed to help. As I had darted elephants before in Uganda he asked me along. We drove for two days through the bush from

Maun to the game warden's house on the banks of the Chobe River, in the Park just west of the village. Mike Slogrove, the warden, was sceptical to say the least, but we needed his knowledge and skills in the bush and as a marksman for safety. He agreed to accompany us and help to locate suitable herds.

The next morning we inspected all the equipment and ensured that everyone in the team knew their jobs before we set off to find elephants. Only the bulls habitually hung around on the floodplains and for Malte's study we were forced to seek out breeding herds in the bush. They were far more skittish and harder to approach than the bulls and we often had to stalk them on foot, with Mike's expert assistance.

On one occasion Norbert managed to dart a female from the back of Mike's Land Rover and, as usual, the herd disappeared in a pandemonium of dust and noise. We were able to follow slowly along a rough track in the general direction of their flight, checking periodically by climbing trees to gain a vantage point. Experience showed that they often settled down quickly and would next only be disturbed when the darted individual displayed signs of being affected by the drug, usually after about eight minutes. We usually couldn't see this but would hear the distinctive vocalisations as the affected cow became distressed.

This herd was about thirty-strong and seemed to be very cohesive. The subject was an older cow who was well placed in the family hierarchy. Approximately fifteen minutes after darting, our progress along the track was barred by three aggressive elephants. They seemed unusually determined to prevent the vehicle from going further. The usual shouting, banging and engine revving had only slight, transient effects and the three turned and advanced on us repeatedly. There seemed no way we could pass, short of shooting, which was not an option. I climbed high up a jackalberry tree to try to see the darted cow. What I saw and what followed truly amazed me.

About 200 yards further along the track there was a frenzy of activity, with elephants milling about, trashing the bush. Then it became apparent that some were breaking down branches and uprooting shrubs and taking them to a spot just off to the left of the track. All the time the three guards below me continued to prevent our car from moving forward. Then, in response to a distinctly audible and urgent vocal rumble, the herd abruptly moved away to the right of the road and disappeared into the bush towards the Chobe River. The three guards simultaneously wheeled away and followed at speed.

I quickly descended and climbed on the vehicle telling my colleagues what I had seen. We drove forward until we reached the area trashed by the elephants. Just to the left of the track was the immobilised cow, lying on her side and almost completely covered by broken branches and other vegetation. It was a striking display of coordinated and organised elephant behaviour to hide their stricken companion from us, and they had kept us at bay while they did so.

We brought the vehicle up close and Mike kept a lookout from the roof while we cleared the branches and started to fit the collar on the cow. Twice we were forced to make a swift retreat from aggressive approaches by other elephant cows, but we were able nervously to continue our work. Eventually things calmed down and we completed our tasks: fastening the collar; taking measurements and biological data; and ensuring the wellbeing of our patient. My job was monitoring her heart rate, breathing and temperature while Norbert supervised fitting the collar. All seemed normal and our procedures were completed routinely. When everyone was safely on the vehicle Norbert injected the calculated dose of M285, at that time the recommended antidote to M99, into an ear vein to wake her up. This normally takes only a minute or so, but in this case nothing happened, she continued to lie on her side, breathing regularly and resonantly through her trunk.

I joined Norbert at the elephant and a few minutes later we injected a dose of Nalorphine, an alternative antidote, but this also had no discernible effect. We tried again with more M285, but still nothing happened. She just lay there, her vital signs unchanging. In such situations unorthodox procedures often come into play. We tried noise – shouting, banging, revving engines, hooting – but to no avail. We tried cold water in the ear canal; we tried acrid exhaust fumes. Still no change. Throughout it all I monitored her breathing and heart rate and they remained constant. It was probably thirty minutes since the initial injection of antidote and almost an hour since she was darted.

We had run out of ideas. Malte and his assistant sat on the back of the Land Rover and Mike was behind the wheel. Norbert was standing downcast near the head of the elephant and I was sitting on her chest reading my notes, at a loss what to try next. There was an alarming pause in breathing for a few seconds, followed by a deep inspiration and Norbert and I looked at each other. The elephant awoke very suddenly, quite unlike the normal recovery following an injection of antidote. We ran for the vehicle. Mike had the engine running and as Norbert, who was just ahead of me, cleared the already moving tailgate I reached up to grasp Malte's hand but, encumbered by my clipboard and other paraphernalia, I missed my footing on the rear bumper and was deposited on my back in the sand behind the accelerating vehicle.

I instinctively curled up and closed my eyes as the high-revving Land Rover and yelling voices receded. When I next looked up, the elephant had passed me and was closing on the vehicle, which then stopped suddenly as it hit a stump about 100 yards from where I was picking myself up. Luckily, this unnerved her and she veered away to the left, missing the back of the truck by a foot or two at most, and crashed away through the trees. The elephant had either not seen me or ignored me to pursue the offending vehicle. Her spoor indicated that she had passed almost directly over where I lay, but she had not touched me.

I remember walking slowly towards the back of the truck, dusting myself down, feeling very lucky and relieved to be unhurt. I don't remember my semi-coherent, defamatory outburst aimed at my colleagues on the truck for "leaving me behind". Later that evening, when I was transcribing the tape I had been carrying, I realised it had been switched on throughout and had recorded the whole episode. The microphone had been clipped to the collar of my shirt and had picked up everything in fascinating detail: the pandemonium of our hasty retreat; the thump of my hitting the ground; the clear footsteps of the charging elephant passing me; the bang of the truck's impact; the elephant crashing away through the bush; all the yelling and revving; then almost silence, followed by my voice, in a very high falsetto and mainly fluent Anglo-Saxon, describing my colleagues and their closest immediate ancestors in less than flattering terms. This created great amusement at supper, but I mostly remember being unable to use my knife and fork because my hands suddenly began to shake.

That was the only really close call I had working with elephants, but an almost eerie experience a couple of years later gave me cause to marvel again at their intelligence. In the northern Tuli Block in the Limpopo Valley there was a small elephant population that had gained a reputation for being "difficult". This was, of course, from the point of view of people like us who wanted to interfere with their way of life. Unlike their larger and more benevolent-minded cousins in Chobe, who were placidly becoming accustomed to the hassles of vehicles, people and the associated noises, smells and sights of a tourist park, the Tuli elephants were chased, harried and frequently shot for conflicting with the farming enterprises in the three countries which came together in their Limpopo Valley territory. Hostile and cantankerous, they were not to be taken lightly. A few pioneering tourist guides treated them with the greatest respect and kept both a safe distance and their engine running.

As a separate, or relict, population they had attracted scientific interest and researchers from Pretoria University wanted to fit several animals with radio-tracking collars. It was considered desirable to know their movement patterns, particularly any trans-frontier wanderings, in order to understand the requirements for future management. Malte was asked to assist the South African researcher in Tuli, Bruce Paige, to put on some collars. Since Norbert and I had helped him with several elephants in Chobe by then, he asked if we would meet him in Tuli to handle the darting.

It quickly became apparent that we were not going to be able to dart the animals from the comparative safety of a vehicle, which was the typical East African savanna method and usually worked well in Chobe. The rugged Tuli terrain, almost devoid of motorable tracks, coupled with the elephants' demeanour, made this approach impossible. Each small group of elephants that we saw quickly disappeared in the bush, crossing deep dongas and melting through thickets that were impassable to a vehicle. We were going to have to do it on foot, since there were no funds available for a helicopter.

Our "hunting" party consisted of two trackers, two biologists carrying the equipment, an allegedly experienced elephant hunter with a heavy rifle in case of emergencies, and two vets with a dart gun. The hunter we recruited was an old friend (Jack Chase from Mahalapye) who, before the War, had been in the precursor of the Wildlife Department as an elephant control officer. His eyes gleamed with the prospect of honing his past skills. He assured me that a good elephant hunter never fired at more than twenty-five yards from his quarry and showed me a little cloth bag of wood ash that he silently sprinkled to ascertain the exact direction of any slight movements of air. I confess wondering which element of our imminent situation was likely to pose the most risk. The trackers' main task was to follow the darted animals and find them as quickly as possible. In thick bush and broken country there are much higher risks to an immobilised elephant; it may fall on its trunk and suffocate, or merely go down in an awkward position, which can compromise its breathing quite quickly. We might have to get everyone there swiftly to push the drugged animal over onto its side.

Finding elephants proved easy; darting one not so. We were able to approach several groups to within 100 yards, but either the wind was wrong or some other clue to our presence warned the animals and they would disappear before we could get close enough to fire a dart. The bush was very thick and a clear shot was going to be difficult. Their favourite resting places seemed to be in clumps of fan palms, forming thickets with plenty of cover and impossible to walk through silently. Occasionally we were on the receiving end of a charge; either a young male's half-hearted attempt at bravado, or, once or twice, a more determined seeing-off by an enraged female. Distinguishing between a mock charge and the real thing has always seemed to me to be much easier in bar discussions than in the field. In practice I am all for discretion and giving the benefit of doubt to the elephant. Our hunter-guardian, Jack, was apparently of the same persuasion and on more than one occasion I caught sight of his back disappearing at surprising speed before I had made second gear. At the end of the first day the upper hand was definitely with the elephants and we returned to camp still carrying our collars.

The next day we set out early. There was a fairly brisk easterly breeze that boded well for us. The elephant groups we saw were moving deceptively quickly, apparently feeding at a leisurely amble, but covering the ground apace. We left the vehicle on the edge of a steep, almost vertical bank of a dry river channel about ten feet deep, crossed on foot and made our way through the bush. We had to jog to catch up, using the cover provided by the terrain. Jack began to show his age as it warmed up and we decided to continue ahead of him. After half an hour or so we were within striking distance of a target group of three adult females, two small calves and three or four subadult teenagers.

The senior tracker, a Bushman known as Sixpence, and I stalked carefully forward to within darting distance, about forty yards. The others remained about fifty yards behind us. The elephants appeared calm and unaware of our presence, moving slowly through a mixture of sickle bush and umbrella thorn shrubs. Suddenly, one of the cows shrieked and came towards us at speed, crashing through the vegetation in a straight line – something we couldn't emulate. I turned and fled, no thought of a dart, and kept going way past the empty spot where our companions had been.

We gathered breathlessly a few hundred yards back, everyone very relieved and agreeing that it had been a close thing. We had no idea what had caused her reaction; it had been so sudden and completely without warning. The wind had not changed and it was unlikely that she would have seen us. We were perplexed, but agreed that she had certainly meant it. A few joking remarks were exchanged nervously – comments on our relative speeds of flight, lack of bravery and so on.

Then, belatedly, someone asked about Sixpence. Where was he? We assumed that he had fled like the rest of us, but no one recollected seeing him –

it had definitely been a case of every man for himself. Well, no doubt he would turn up. We headed back towards the car, joking and chatting. We arrived at the dry river a little downstream of where we had left the car, clambered down the steep bank into the sand and crossed diagonally before climbing up the opposite side and gathering at the vehicle. Jack had been dozing. We related our tale, with the permitted degree of embellishment and personal interpretation. Everyone laughed at Sixpence, still running, "all the way back to the Kalahari". Just then his head appeared above the edge of the riverbank, which stimulated more good-natured banter at his expense. In his halting English he told us his story.

He had made himself scarce when the elephant charged. He hid behind a termite mound and watched her pursue the rest of us through the bush. When he considered it safe to do so, he had followed. To his consternation the elephant stopped running but continued to follow our retreat towards the car. She seemed to be stalking us. He followed her the whole way back to the riverbank where she had moved upstream and downstream, apparently looking for a place to cross and continue following us. She had finally given up and returned to the herd. We were incredulous, it seemed too far-fetched.

But Sixpence was adamant. "That elephant, she knows you – she will get you next time boss."

We laughed at him and he challenged us to look at the spoor, so we re-crossed the dry river and made our way along the edge of the high bank. We saw our tracks coming out of the bush in single file to the edge and where we had slithered down into the riverbed. With a communal shudder we noted the unmistakable, huge prints superimposed on our own fresh tracks. They also followed the lip of the riverbank for some twenty-five yards or so in both directions, apparently looking for a place to descend, before peeling away. Here and there were Sixpence's tiny footprints on top of the elephant's – proof, if any more were needed, that his story was accurate. To this day I have no better explanation than that of Sixpence for what the elephant had in mind or why she had followed us closely for over a mile. I have had numerous experiences that bear evidence to these animals' seemingly exceptional powers of reasoning and intelligence, several have amazed me, but none have disturbed me quite so much.

In normal years it doesn't rain much in Botswana. You can usually rely on clear skies from early April until at least October and in June and July the mid-winter temperatures can fall several degrees below zero Celsius during the night. Fieldwork frequently meant sleeping under the stars in a bedroll and you quickly learn that it can be several degrees warmer under even a sparse tree canopy than in the open.

I was on my way from Maun to Chobe again to dart elephants for a research project with two young Aussie students who had asked to come along. I parked my Land Rover under an old camelthorn tree at Savuti and spread my bedroll on the ground with my head close to the side of the vehicle. The students pitched their pup tent on the other side of the vehicle.

I was awakened by a curious metallic pinging sound. Something was falling on the metal canopy of the Land Rover. Surely it couldn't be rain or hail – in June the skies were always cloudless and I looked up expecting to see stars through the branches, but all was dark. It then became startlingly obvious that I was looking at the underside of a very large elephant. He was standing with his forefeet at the bottom of my bedroll, reaching over me and feeding contentedly from the pod-laden branches of the camelthorn. When he pulled a chosen morsel from a branch there was some fallout, which clattered onto the vehicle. He knew I was there, but had obviously decided he could reach what he wanted without the extra inches that stepping on me would have afforded. I was grateful for that, and for a few moments I lay very still, gathering my wits and deciding on the best course of action, in case he changed his mind. Obviously I could not stand up without the possibility of annoying him, and rolling away to the side was equally risky. I therefore decided to squirm, head first, out of my blankets and under the vehicle in a caterpillar-like fashion. This I accomplished with difficulty but without dignity, as I was naked, and on the other side of the vehicle were two wide-eyed female students peering out of their tent in amazement.

The following night I pitched a small dome tent and felt certain I would sleep soundly and undisturbed. But I awoke again in the small hours, alarmed by a furious racket, apparently inside the tent. It was pitch dark and thoughts of leopards and other forms of my possible demise flashed through my mind as I reached for my torch. The beam fell on an enraged honey badger who had wriggled in under the door flap where I had neglected to close the zipper completely. The attraction was my small plastic cool box containing meat and fruit. He had it firmly in his grip and was attempting to drag it out of the tent. It would not fit under the door flap, hence his intense irritation. The growls and snarls intensified as my torch beam illuminated the scene. Anything else would have given up and run away at that point, but not the honey badger; he just redoubled his efforts and noise levels.

I reached out with the torch, still in my bedroll, and hit him on the head as hard as I could. He let go of the cool box and snapped at the torch, which I dropped and retreated within my blankets in alarm. There was enough light from the torch on the floor for me to see him transfer his attention back to the cool box. He was reversing under the door flap and I plucked up the courage to grab the other side of the box and pull. The badger's side of the box broke off and he disappeared outside with it, leaving me with three-quarters of the box and all its contents. I zipped up the flap completely and tried to get back to sleep.

On a later job in Tuli, the elephant collaring had been going smoothly and without incident. We had put collars on three elephants from different herds. One morning a darted cow went down normally, although we had taken a while to get to her because of the terrain. The rest of the group was easily chased away – except one. No matter what we tried she would just not leave her stricken companion. It was impossible to get the vehicle closer than about 100 yards because of the thick bush, littered with fallen trees. We approached on foot, but the guardian forced us to retreat several times. Eventually it was decided that we would have to dart her as well, which was accomplished without too much trouble and a few minutes later we could approach safely. The second elephant was swaying unsteadily next to where the first was lying, but was no longer a threat as the drug became effective.

Imagine our astonishment when we found a tiny newborn baby next to the two elephants, just clambering to its feet for the very first time, still wet and covered in soft hairs. The second female had not been protecting the first one we had darted, but had just given birth and was not going to leave without her offspring.

We worked quickly and put collars on both elephants to take advantage of a rarely observed event and to collect as many data as possible on the calf. The little one was duly measured and fully recorded. It was so "friendly" that one of us had to divert its attention while the rest of us worked, and it seemed not to have any interest in either of the sleeping adults. When it was time to administer the antidote to the two cows we carried the equipment and retreated to the vehicle, followed by the infant. This posed a problem because we obviously did not want to separate mother and calf. There was a risk of disrupting their bond, with possibly fatal results for the calf. A volunteer would have to hold the baby until the mother was sufficiently revived to take an interest. This volunteer would have to be fleet of foot… and more than slightly crazy!

The two vets immediately declared themselves dedicated family men with immense responsibilities and short fat legs, leaving the lean, long-legged, young and single biologist with no choice. I injected antidote into both cows' ear veins and retreated to the getaway car, assuring a very nervous biologist, whose hands were extremely full, that I would signal as soon as possible when he could follow. It had not occurred to me that it would have been sensible and safer to give the mother the antidote a minute earlier than the first darted female, but luck was with us and it was she who stirred first. As she rocked back and forth to get her feet on the ground, a couple of yards from the biologist, he glanced repeatedly towards us, imploring us to give the signal for him to abandon the calf and run. When we eventually did, he broke all hurdles records, clearing fallen tree trunks like Ed Moses in his prime until we pulled him over an accelerating tailgate. The mother did chase him for a while and I saw enough to convince me that an angry elephant can also clear surprisingly high obstacles at speed. She did not follow the vehicle for long however and soon turned back to her baby.

A short time later we were able to stalk back and ensure that mother and baby were safely reunited and on their way home. At first there were only the three sets of spoor, tiny footprints occasionally visible among those of the giant sisters. Then the trail left the woodland and descended the valley, where we could clearly see the trio making their way towards the distant herd taking a morning bath in the Limpopo River.

In the late seventies and eighties I was kept pretty busy flying wildlife surveys over much of Botswana, either for the Wildlife Department or often through the Kalahari Conservation Society (KCS) founded in 1983, which had taken on a serious role in the country and raised significant funds internationally to address some of the important issues of the day. Foremost in most people's opinion was the steadily increasing and expanding elephant population, which became a favourite target for research and speculation. The usual meetings and workshops were held with a plethora of stakeholders. Lots of money was spent and a decision was made to draw up a national elephant management plan. KCS was charged with producing it and I was hired to write it in consultation with other conservationists and with input from sections of the Wildlife Department.

The aerial censuses described a population of elephants that was growing at close to the biological or intrinsic maximum rate. Photographs of elephant herds were taken from above to ascertain their age structure and, together with information on breeding performance, they provided a picture of a young, fecund population. There were relatively very few older bulls carrying large ivory, another indication that we were witnessing a young, swiftly growing population of animals. Additional research by a series of independent workers showed that in certain areas, particularly along the Chobe and Linyanti Rivers, there was an overabundance of elephants (at least in the dry season), which was having a detrimental effect on the riverine vegetation and the other animal species in that habitat, such as the endemic Chobe bushbuck. Work in other areas of Africa, most notably the Kruger National Park in South Africa, indicated that elephant densities of over one animal per square kilometre could affect woodland composition. In Linyanti we were recording densities as high as fifteen per square kilometre in October – the height of the dry season. In terms of management of the population, reducing numbers had to be one option considered and I was asked to investigate culling methods.

I knew a little about the technique used in Zimbabwe, where experienced teams had removed up to 4,000 elephants a year by culling whole herds; leaving survivors was considered inhumane because of the social structure and behaviour of elephants. The animals were driven by aircraft towards the shooting teams and very efficiently culled. The ivory was recovered by the government, the skins (at that time the most valuable item) were sold for leather and the meat was cut into strips, sun-dried and supplied to the local communities. It was a massive undertaking and required high levels of expertise and lots of labour.

The South Africans were also culling whole herds in Kruger NP and I went to observe their operations. Their objective was to keep the Park's elephant population close to 8,000 individuals, which was regarded by the authorities as suitable for the area, and above which unacceptable habitat change would occur. Their method was to locate a suitable herd and then to dart the older cows, especially the matriarch, from a helicopter. When they were immobilised the waiting ground teams would move in and finish the job. They caught young calves that could be reared in captivity and taken to selected game ranches or other reserves. Calves too small to survive without their mothers were shot with the other animals. The meat was processed in a specially constructed processing plant and cannery in a very efficient operation.

The drug used to immobilise the herd elders was Scoline (succinylcholine), a paralysing agent related to curare used by South American native tribes in their blowpipes. Darted animals suffocated when the muscles used in breathing became paralysed. It was effective but, together with the shooting of small calves that had no commercial value, it attracted a lot of criticism, mainly because the drugged animals were aware of their situation until they became unconscious through suffocation. On humane grounds, we eventually recommended that if Botswana were to undertake a cull the Zimbabwe method should be used.

Our aerial censuses in the mid-eighties indicated an elephant population in Botswana of around 80,000, about double what had existed a decade or so earlier. Various committees and consultants arrived at a figure of 60,000 as the recommended maximum population for Botswana's wildlife areas. Above this number habitat changes would be likely to occur that would be particularly drastic in the northern riverine woodlands to the detriment of other animal populations and biodiversity in general. Political correctness was becoming prevalent and we were encouraged to use the expression "habitat change" rather than "damage". My view was that it depended on the desired situation, which was a management choice or value judgement. If "pristine" riverine woodland and its associated animal species, such as bushbuck and kudu, was what you wanted then elephants had to be managed in a way that protected this habitat. On the other hand, if you were happy that tourists could see more elephants in Botswana than anywhere else, you might want to let them dominate the environment. As is often the case, a laissez-faire situation ensued that has led to the elephant population multiplying over the long-term due to a number of factors, including immigration from neighbouring states as well as intrinsic increases.

The Botswana Government, like any other, is sensitive to international pressure driven by animal rights activists, but we also concluded that the logistics of, first, reducing the population to the target figure of 60,000 and then holding it there by annual culls were beyond our capabilities. It would have been a far greater project than either the Zimbabwe or Kruger exercises and we certainly didn't have the skills or resources to undertake it. So, one more management plan was researched, written, agreed and signed off by the authorities, only to gather dust on a departmental shelf. There have since been at least two "ten-year revisions", but no implementation, and the population is now around 130,000. It should be said that this continuous growth of the elephant population over half a century has taken place with an almost uninterrupted hunting policy.

Maybe things are changing; Botswana's President Masisi, under quite intense pressure from many rural communities, instigated a nationwide series of public consultations in July 2018. It is widely believed that this will lead to the reintroduction of some form of controlled general hunting, as well as measures to contain the elephant population and to reduce the scale of human–elephant conflict. These might involve limited culling exercises in targeted areas if a way can be found to make them practical, sustainable and, most importantly, widely acceptable. However, entrenched opinions are rarely swayed by accurate factual analysis; human emotions often override rational thought processes and celebrity opinions on social media nearly always attract more support than the conclusions of experienced scientists.

TEN

BACK INTO PRACTICE

By late 1980 the Game Department was vastly different from when I had joined seven years earlier. Alec Campbell had retired as Director and taken up a post as curator of the National Museum in Gaborone. He had been replaced in 1977 by Chucks Matenge, the first indigenous citizen Director. Chucks was an affable man who, although a competent administrator, had no background in wildlife or natural resources conservation. The Deputy Director, or Chief Game Warden as he was known, Lindsay Birch, had retired to run Crocodile Camp in Maun a couple of years earlier (and became responsible for most of the town's hangovers). My original boss, Wolfgang von Richter, had left the UN and returned to Germany. Alistair Graham and Jane had moved to Gaborone as contracted consultants and then left for a new career in Australia. External funds for research projects seem to have dried up and the departmental research team had all but disappeared.

Over the years I had resisted offers of promotion, because it would have taken me out of the field and into a mainly administrative post in headquarters, so I remained as Senior Wildlife Biologist in Maun. Two young Batswana, with degrees from the University of Botswana, were vying for the position of Principal Wildlife Biologist, technically my immediate boss. Neither had much experience and their qualifications were minimal. Neo Moroka had worked briefly for me as a research assistant. He was bright and pleasant but showed no aptitude or real enthusiasm for wildlife research. He had once refused to join us carrying out plant transects on Chief's Island, claiming he was a zoologist not a botanist. He eventually joined a bank and became a very senior executive before becoming a government minister, which I think bears out my assessment of him. Mushanana Nchunga, a critically shy man from the Chobe enclave, eventually became Director but wasn't an unqualified success.

Their rivalry made my life quite difficult and in December I reluctantly handed in three-months' notice – my dream job in a state of terminal collapse. I was asked to train my replacement, Derek Melton, in flying aerial censuses before I left, using the unsuitable Cessna Centurion that we had inherited from Alistair's project. Derek was a biologist from Natal, where he had studied waterbuck, and he soon got the hang of things – but apparently did not stay long.

I was owed slightly more than three months' leave and therefore decided to take a complete break and visit Australia and New Zealand over Christmas. Bluey Carmichael was going home to see his family and he was happy for Piet Jacobs, a friend from Pretoria, and me to accompany him. We landed in Sydney and spent a few weeks travelling around New South Wales, Victoria and Tasmania before heading north to Cairns and joining his uncle on his prawn trawler near the Great Barrier Reef. As far as I could see the trawler was basically a floating freezer that we gradually filled with prawns and other delicious seafood before returning to port. We visited the beautiful Atherton Tablelands and experienced some of the social schemes supporting the local Aboriginal population, reminiscent of the situation back home with Bushmen, or Remote Area Dwellers (RADs) as we were now expected to call them.

Next was a month travelling around New Zealand in a camper van. The scenery was unbelievably spectacular and I was able to spend a thrilling few days in Te Anau with a helicopter team capturing red deer in the mountains. Never again would I consider that flying and darting animals in sunny, flat Botswana was anything special. These guys fired nets over their quarry from helicopters just feet away from rock faces and precipices and then jumped out to grab them!

I returned to Gabs in March to wind things up and leave Botswana for good. I was due a sizeable payout of 30 per cent of my last three years' salary as a tax-free gratuity which was held back by the government, but when I received the cheque it was for considerably more than I expected. Questioning this it was pointed out to me that it also included three months' leave pay. Apparently no one had recorded that I had just been away on leave for three months! This time honesty got the better of me and I requested a smaller amount. By the end of March I was on my way to England and a projected future back in veterinary practice. I reasoned that after ten years I hardly knew which end of the dog did the biting, so maybe it was time for some professional revision.

I got a job in Leamington Spa at a mixed veterinary practice owned by Sandy Lyons. Sandy provided a flat above the surgery and a small Ford Firefly. The work was mainly small animals (dogs and cats) with some cattle and horse work thrown in. Although I had been qualified for almost eleven years, at the age of thirty-four I still had very little clinical experience, but Sandy was quick to brush the rust off me and I enjoyed a busy life as one of his two assistants, commuting between Leamington and a branch surgery in Rugby. Very little outside of the ordinary happened in my time there and it was an acute contrast to my life in the Okavango. Not surprisingly, I particularly enjoyed the cattle and horse cases that got me out and about in a pleasingly bucolic part of England that I didn't know. The proximity to cultural gems such as Warwick and Stratford allowed a variety of enjoyable excursions and I have only agreeable, but rather vague, memories of the period.

One vivid exception was an accident with my practice car. Even this wouldn't have been remarkable except that I hit Sandy's Volvo quite hard with the nippy little Firefly. I had driven into the practice forecourt many, many times and on this occasion I was too quick and drove into the boss's car, which was parked outside the front door. I went inside and asked the receptionist where Mr Lyons was, to be told he was operating in the theatre. I plucked up courage and walked in to where Sandy, with his reading spectacles perched on the end of his nose, was deep inside a large dog's abdomen, intent on removing something. After the normal greetings had been exchanged I confessed that I'd had an accident.

"Only a matter of time," he observed in an almost distracted manner. "All you young fellows drive far too fast. Much damage? What did you hit? Nobody hurt, I hope?"

"No," I replied. "In fact I crashed into your Volvo outside."

"Whaaat?" he yelled, and his specs flew off his nose and landed in the dog's belly.

I fished them out, taking care not to touch anything sterile, wiped them and replaced them on his nose. I think I was quite lucky that his sterile, gloved hands were quite full at the time.

Another incident that caused some temporary damage to my reputation involved the practice's biggest dairy client. The farmer owned an enormous

Friesian bull that needed his feet trimming. Left alone this condition would have badly impaired his ability to work. The problem was that no one could get near the beast. He was over a ton in weight and about six feet at the shoulder, with tiny, bloodshot eyes and a murderous disposition – just like the cartoons. Around that time the super-potent drug, etorphine hydrochloride, the M99 that we used to immobilise elephants and other wildlife became available in the UK to veterinarians. It was marketed ready combined with the tranquiliser acetyl promazine as Immobilon. Sandy was aware that I had used the drug often in Africa and asked me if it would work on the bull. I confirmed that it would be very effective as long as we could get an injection into the beast. Sandy telephoned the farmer to say we were on our way and could he somehow confine or restrain the animal before we got there. We arrived to find the monster in a loosebox filled with clean straw inside the cowshed. He seemed quite placid, but no one had tried to interfere with him yet. While I prepared our kit, a farmhand put some tasty concentrated feed in the small trough outside the loosebox which could be accessed by animals putting their heads through a steel yoke that could be fastened to secure the animal. In the bull's case this wasn't possible, his neck was just too wide to allow any adjustment. However, I did manage to inject the calculated dose into his neck as he hoovered up the cake. He then backed off into the loosebox and we all waited for the drug to take effect.

I explained that before animals became immobilised they often went through a short, mild excitatory phase, most noticeable through a high-stepping gait. After about five minutes the bull started to move about slowly on "tippy toes" just as predicted. In this condition they become unaware of their surroundings and soon succumb completely and lie down. Unfortunately for us, the bull danced towards the external brick wall and disappeared straight through it, coming to rest in the field about twenty-five yards beyond. We quickly followed suit through the door before the roof caved in! With the bull now at our mercy, Sandy and I cut his "toenails" without fuss, before I gave him the antidote and we all retreated through a nearby gate to watch him recover and stand up. The farmer seemed pleased with the result, but I was not party to the negotiation about our fee and the cost of building repairs.

I had been in the south Midlands for about six months when one Sunday morning in July I was on call and had to visit a mare that had foaled during the night. When I got back to the surgery around 10.00 am the duty nurse informed me that someone had called from Africa and would call again at lunchtime. I couldn't think who this might be or why they might be calling. At 12.00 sharp the phone rang and the nurse handed me the receiver. The voice introduced himself as Mike Dommisse, a vet from Durban, on the east coast of South Africa. He said he'd heard that I was keen to return to Africa and he needed an assistant for his small-animal practice in the beach suburb of Glen Ashley. I had never been to Durban, nor had I heard of Mike Dommisse. I also had never thought of working in South Africa and had no idea where he got my number. But he was very persuasive, comparing the English environment with the sun, sand and surf that he claimed could be seen from his clinic. He would pay my airfare as long as I registered with the South African board and agreed to spend a year working with him. I told him I would think about it for a day or so before making up my mind but, in all honesty, the thought of returning to Africa was very appealing.

So, after working a month's notice I caught a plane to Johannesburg and spent a couple of weeks with my old friend and colleague Bluey Carmichael at his smallholding in Pretoria North, near the Onderstepoort Veterinary College. As usual with Bluey it was a time of unfettered hedonism, making it very difficult to understand how he regularly walked away with academic achievement prizes from one of the world's leading veterinary research establishments. We spent many evenings carousing at Adelaar Sports Federasie, where the bar was occupied by an eclectic congregation of older sportsmen and Afrikaner professional men, including: former world heavyweight boxing contender Kallie Knoetze, *"die Bek van Boomstraat"*, who had just retired; a senior physicist from the nearby Pelindaba nuclear facility; and a medical technician who maintained and operated heart bypass machines and had assisted Dr Chris Barnard at the world's first heart transplant operation in Cape Town. After innumerable glasses of brandy and Coke they melded extremely well and the atmosphere was convivial, although, as the sole *Engelsman*, I was often dependent on Bluey's Australian-accented translations from Afrikaans. During this time I was at least able to register as a veterinary surgeon at the board's head office in Pretoria, with Bluey's contacts and reputation oiling the wheels, and by the end of September I had the necessary professional certificate and a work permit for South Africa.

I took an evening flight to Durban and checked in at a small self-catering hotel where Mike Dommisse had booked me a room. He arrived early the following morning, driving a fairly old, brown Toyota Corolla station wagon, which was to be for my use. We drove to his clinic at the Glen Ashley shopping centre, next door to a doggy beauty parlour. I remember thinking that perhaps this wasn't my scene, but at least it wasn't Ramsbottom, and the proximity of sand and surf, along with excellent weather, held some promise. Inside was the usual reception desk in a waiting room and behind it was a small consulting room, through which another door allowed access to a staff common room and an operating theatre off to one side. It was very much a single-vet practice that had grown too busy for Mike to handle on his own.

There were two lady receptionists and two nurses in blue uniforms. I was welcomed in a friendly but slightly reserved manner and the practice routine was explained in detail. I was given a white coat (something we never had in England) and spent the morning in the consulting room with Mike, getting to know how he liked things done. The next morning I had to deal with consultations on my own while Mike was busy in the operating theatre. I spent the first few afternoons looking for more permanent accommodation and eventually found a small second-floor apartment in a block of flats in nearby Durban North.

The routine of a busy, 100 per cent small-animal practice took some getting used to. We were very occupied indeed, mainly with cat and dog consultations for three to four hours every morning, followed by as many operations as we could handle before seeing clients again from 4.00 pm until about 7.00 pm. Saturday mornings were filled with consultations and the rest of the weekend we shared a duty roster for emergencies. I soon became a quick and competent surgeon, at least on routine procedures such as spays, often sterilising eight bitches in a day, plus a number of cats and dealing with the odd exotic, such as a pet snake or a rabbit. It was enjoyable in its way, challenging and satisfying, except that I never left the building, unless there was time for a run around the beachside Virginia Airport at midday. One day I heard the head receptionist describing how her son, on leave from the army in Angola, had been swimming with a basking shark just off the beach and had even "hitched a ride" for a few hundred yards!

I was given Wednesday afternoons off and I joined Durban Collegians soccer club. I also negotiated later to have Saturday afternoons off in exchange for working every Sunday. This arrangement kept me sane; the club was a lively social centre, as well as enjoying a fairly high standard of amateur soccer. I had just worked my way up to the 1st XI when I succumbed to what the physiotherapist called "Peter Pan Syndrome", with a badly torn thigh muscle from trying in vain to keep up with the teens and twenty-somethings in the squad. After recovering I was relegated to a social team, where the consumption of beer was the main mode of training.

Shopping for groceries was interesting and I soon learnt to leave the Toyota's engine running if I had any foodstuff in the car. The smell of fresh bread in particular aroused a multitude of resident cockroaches that would swarm over the shopping and soon make inroads into the food. With the engine running they would remain hidden in corners and crevices and the food would be safe from their depredations, even if there was a significant chance of the car being stolen. From time to time I tried fumigating the vehicle, but a few always survived and quickly multiplied back to the ecological carrying capacity of their mobile environment. Durban was renowned for its cockroaches and these were only the smaller, brown *Blattella* species; most buildings were infested with the much larger *Periplaneta* variety and many clients facetiously assured me that their Jack Russell Terriers were kept to control these pests.

My flat was fairly new and didn't seem to be overrun with cockroaches, but there were other pests… my immediate neighbour downstairs was a night-owl. A young guy of about twenty with fashionably shoulder-length hair, he would regularly arrive home after midnight and play very loud rock music that would make it impossible to sleep. Late one night, after I'd been living there for a couple of weeks he played Foreigner's latest hit 'Urgent', over and over again. It was so bad that I took a long-handled brush and, reaching down precariously over the balcony, banged on his window. This had no effect; even between numbers he apparently didn't hear the knocking. I eventually banged so hard that his lounge window shattered, still without response. It was about 2 am and I went downstairs to investigate and maybe apologise for the damage. The front door of the flat was ajar and the noise of the hi-fi was deafening. I yelled and yelled into the flat to no avail and then slowly entered through the kitchen and on into the lounge. My neighbour was lying on his back on the floor with his head in between two of the largest speakers I'd ever seen, surrounded by shards of broken glass from the window. I yelled at him from a foot away and nudged his shoulder, to no effect. I pulled out the hi-fi plug from the wall socket and attempted to wake him. Although he was breathing I failed to rouse him. At a loss, I just left him and closed the door on my way out. The following morning I left for work as usual and didn't see him for a couple of days, until we passed on the stairs. We greeted each other briefly, but neither he nor I mentioned anything about the incident and I've always wondered what he made of the broken window and his disconnected stereo.

I stuck at the humdrum routine of small dogs with smelly ears and blocked anal glands for about ten months, and although I learnt a lot and was occasionally stimulated by an unusual or difficult case, I knew that small-animal practice, even in a tropical paradise, was not for me. I missed the bush, but wasn't at all sure how to begin to forge a life or career there. In August 1982 I was due a couple of weeks' holiday and I asked Mike if I could leave at the end of August, with the two weeks' leave due to me fulfilling my year's commitment to him. To his credit he must have realised that I had severely itchy feet and he allowed me to go a couple of weeks early with no hard feelings. So I headed up-country back to Botswana, to stay with friends in Gaborone and explore the possibilities of private employment.

Gabs was hardly the bush, but it was a lot closer than Durban. The town was growing fast and modern infrastructure needed building, but there were almost no local companies to implement the required development projects. An expatriate workforce, mainly South Africans and Zimbabweans, was rapidly increasing and with the new families came pets, especially dogs. I knew all the vets in the country very well; there were less than a dozen, and all working for the Ministry of Agriculture (MoA). There wasn't a single private veterinary surgeon in the country. Pets were seen after hours by some of the government veterinary officers, with a couple of the keener ones doing consultations on Saturday mornings for a bit of beer money. I sensed an opportunity and, although a couple of the busier vets (Roger Windsor and Mike Brown) said there wasn't likely to be enough business to sustain a full-time practice, I decided to seek permission to start one. I figured that if I were to have lots of spare time I might also find something to do in the wildlife sector. Armed with a letter of recommendation and "no objection" from the Permanent Secretary in the MoA, David Finlay, I applied for work and residence permits.

According to the rules I had to be outside the country while these were being processed. I thus found myself once more at the mercy of Bluey's exceptional hospitality in Pretoria and put my liver to its sternest test yet. I made the mistake of signing up for a trip to Cape Town with the Adelaar club to watch the Currie Cup Final, South Africa's premier rugby competition. It was to be contested between Western Province (now the Stormers, from Cape Town) and Northern Transvaal (now the Bulls, from Pretoria). I had never seen a live rugby match and was very much a novice in all things about the game. All the Adelaar members were fanatical supporters of Northern Transvaal, whereas I had a slight preference (private of course) for Western Province, believing them to be more "English".

The Adelaar travelling fans were to meet at Johannesburg railway station on Thursday morning to catch the Trans Karoo Express to Cape Town, a twenty-four-hour, 1,000-mile journey. There were about twenty of us and we occupied several compartments close to the bar and dining car. Two stalwarts lugged a very large, heavy case onto the train and opened it in their compartment to reveal enough booze to keep an average bar going for a week. When I enquired naïvely if the train's refreshment car would not be open, they replied, "*Jaa Mynheer*, but not all night." I have never been involved in, or even seen, alcohol consumption like it; they partied non-stop from getting on the train at 10.00 am until it arrived in Cape Town the next morning. One unfortunate soul with a less robust constitution was taken off the train late at night in Kimberley, the famous diamond-mining town, and taken to hospital, but the others kept it up for twenty-four hours. I escaped to find a compartment where I could get a couple of hours' sleep.

The train passed through some of the finest scenery in the world just after daylight, descending the Hex River Valley into the Cape Winelands, but maybe our party had seen it all before because they certainly didn't pay it any attention. In Cape Town at least half of them had to be transported by baggage trolley from the train to a waiting bus to be taken to our hotel. Incredibly, there were a few takers for lunch and one of the main party animals telephoned a couple of local nurses' residences to arrange a party for that night. I was severely under strain but, after a few hours' sleep, I managed to join in and enjoy the evening's party in the hotel.

The next morning – the day of the match – we climbed aboard the bus and headed down to the fish market to buy some fresh *snoek*, a delicious, very tasty, but bony, South African fish. We had filled a few cool boxes with ice and booze and we headed up Chapman's Peak, a spectacular coastal road and beauty spot, for a fish *braai*. A slight drizzle spoilt the view, but not the enjoyment. I was beginning to wonder just how these Afrikaners could keep it up, but around midday we were back on the bus to go into the city to Newlands Rugby Stadium, where we joined about 50,000 other hysterical fans to watch the match.

I tried hard, but slept through most of it, despite the deafening noise. Western Province won 24-9, I think, giving our Pretoria contingent an excuse to drown their sorrows in another marathon drinking session. I couldn't take any more and certainly not another twenty-four-hour train journey back to Johannesburg on Sunday morning. Back at the hotel I picked up my bag and caught a taxi to the airport and a Saturday evening flight to Johannesburg. Bluey thoroughly derided me, but I don't think any of the Adelaar Club stalwarts missed me in the slightest.

When Bluey arrived back he was able to introduce me to a number of companies that supplied veterinary drugs and equipment. He seemed to know just about everyone and the managers and reps all greeted him like a long-lost friend. As a red-haired Australian I suppose he did stand out, but I'm sure it was his phenomenal lifestyle and personality that made him unforgettable. It was useful for me to spend time with him at the Onderstepoort Veterinary Research Institute and at large in the Afrikaner business and scientific community, even if his social life took its toll. I was able to garner enough promises of free credit for the supply of everything I would need to start a clinic once my Botswana permits came through. For a break I visited my old Maun companions Kate and Norbert Drager who, after a fairly trying couple of years working with tsetse flies in Ghana, were in Swellendam in the Western Cape. Norbert was also struggling with life choices. He was not particularly keen on clinical veterinary work and it wasn't too long before he left the Swellendam practice, moved to the Eastern Cape and bought a small farm near Grahamstown.

My Botswana permits came through in mid-September and I returned to Gabs very excited about my new venture. At first I stayed with John and Joyce Counihan, friends since the early days in Mahalapye. I had almost no money and, apart from the kit I'd been promised from Johannesburg, I needed premises and a vehicle to begin work. Andy Saunders, the friend of plane crash fame and frequent visitor to Maun, had just finished building a large warehouse next to the Notwane River, on the Tlokweng Road. It was still empty and there were a couple of offices in one corner near the gate that he said I should use. Generous to a tee as always, Andy insisted that we would work out the rent once I had made some money. He regularly arrived at about 6.00 pm on Friday with a six-pack of cold beer and we used to sit on the concrete steps outside the front door and watch the dusk close in.

I scraped together a deposit of P250 for a new Toyota Hilux 4x4 pick-up from Satar Dada's Motor Centre, located on the Old Lobatse Road. After a trip to Johannesburg to acquire some drugs and equipment on three months' free credit from Dave Goldkorn and Norman Fisher at Fishervet wholesalers, I was ready to start my first business venture and even had some business cards printed. In early November 1982 Gaborone Veterinary Clinic, the first private veterinary practice in Botswana was up, if not yet running.

Advice from the Director of Veterinary Services was that I should follow the British Royal College of Veterinary Surgeons practice guidelines and code of conduct because Botswana, never having had a private veterinarian, obviously did not have its own. That meant that I was not allowed to advertise and could only "put up my plate" and wait for clients to turn up. Undeterred, I hired a local lady, Florence Maribeng, as a secretary/receptionist and a young man, Edward Molome, to clean up and help with the animals. We waited for most of the first week until an expat lady arrived with her Alsatian dog wanting annual booster vaccinations. That amounted to fifty per cent of the first week's business, but in the second week we trebled our turnover – six clients! I was beginning to think my government colleagues had been right and that there would not be enough business to sustain a private clinic. However, word got around that there was a full-time veterinarian available and work quickly picked up, far too fast for my liking.

My idea had been to service the growing capital's dog and cat population for my bread and butter, while having ample opportunity to get out among Botswana's incomparable wildlife by offering a wildlife consulting service. No chance. I soon found myself working flat out, seven days a week, without ever leaving the confines of the clinic. By mid-1983 my sanity was under severe threat. With Botswana in the grip of a severe drought there had not even been much cattle work to get me out and relieve the tedium of vaccinations, spays, ears and anal glands, so imagine my relief when I was at last able to hire an assistant, a young Zimbabwean called Richard Hoare, and take my dart gun out of mothballs.

One day an attractive young blonde woman came to the surgery without an animal. In a voice unmistakably well-to-do English she introduced herself as Eleanor Warr. She asked me if I was able to catch wild animals. I was immediately interested and when I affirmed that I could, she explained that she was a wildlife biologist working for Debswana, the country's diamond-mining conglomerate. I was puzzled; why would a huge diamond-mining organisation employ a biologist? It turned out that they were planning to establish game sanctuaries in the sizeable secure areas around their mines in the Kalahari Desert at Jwaneng and Orapa. She was responsible for coordinating this project and wanted to translocate some wildlife species from the Makgadikgadi Pans Game Reserve into a newly fenced area at Orapa. I knew that Debswana, under their local managing director, Louis Nchindo, were keen to project a greener image and guessed that there would be no shortage of funds to mount a capture exercise.

Elephant stuck in floodplain well in Chobe, Botswana

"Saying thank you…?"

Paint marked elephant ready to be followed in Queen Elizabeth NP, Uganda

Later the same day – not a very successful project!

Cattle for vaccination in a Botswana handling crush

Busy day at Maun airport, 1974

Darting buffalo at Savuti with pilot Cor Beek, 1972

Sometimes animals were underdosed and had to be roped

Collared buffalo cow with calf at Savuti

Pregnancy testing an immobilised buffalo cow

Vets bathing in Savuti Channel, 1972

Okavango Delta – working in paradise

Closing in to dart buffalo in the Okavango

Not so easy without a helicopter

Brand new collar for a BBC documentary

Norbert and foal waiting for mother to recover

Game capture team camp at dawn in the Kalahari

Typical capture boma with black plastic sheets

Gemsbok in boma with pipes ready for loading

Wildebeest entering capture boma

Shooting wildebeest in the capture crush

Kalahari Game Services' culling team

Giraffe cross-loaded from capture chariot to transport truck

Delivery next morning

Attempting to blindfold a white rhino

Ready to walk to the transport crate

Collaring wildebeest in Central Kalahari Game Reserve

Darted bull about to go down

Elephants Without Borders fitting collar in cramped conditions

Removing snare in Chobe NP. Elephant subsequently recovered fully

"Golden gnu", the animal that sparked a gold rush!

An unusual hazard at Chobe Golf Club

I put together a small team of friends who were keen to help and could take some time off from their day jobs. They included Mark Murray, an American biologist from DWNP, and Robert Riggs, a local citizen who spoke fluent Setswana and had a lot of bush experience. A young Yorkshireman called Brian Downs was a new neighbour, who became a very close friend, and he persuaded me to let him come along as "official photographer". He had almost no bush experience, but was practical, enthusiastic and great company. Eleanor obtained the necessary permits and I acquired the drugs and darts. Brian organised some camping kit and stores and we left Gabs on a cold mid-June morning, driving 300 miles north to the vast game reserve.

We pitched camp at a prearranged site and met up with other volunteers from the Orapa community. Eleanor arrived with Hymie Ebedes, a well-known wildlife veterinarian from Pretoria, who was working as a consultant for De Beers. He and I had met briefly before at a conference. He was a short, bespectacled man of about fifty and was well known for his valuable work on wild animal tranquillisers, but I had heard mixed reports of his work in the field in Namibia. He was obviously Jewish and none too pleased that Eleanor innocently presented him with pork sausages for supper that first evening!

The first morning we dispatched Brian and another friend, Nick Mather, to Orapa mine, about sixty miles away, for supplies of groceries and fuel. They went in one of the Land Cruiser pick-ups while the rest of us prepared for chasing animals. Eleanor gave them a Debswana credit card that could be used at the mine store to charge the goods to the company account. After dark we were preparing the evening meal and relaxing with a drink around the campfire, discussing the day's work. The shopping party had not returned and we were starting to wonder about sending another vehicle to look for them in case they had broken down or got lost. However, before we decided on a course of action someone spotted the faint beam of vehicle headlights some way off in the direction of the mine. A few minutes later the Land Cruiser drove into camp and out fell Brian and Nick, both drunk as lords. They told a giggly, semi-coherent story, explaining that they had discovered that the company card was also good for credit at the mine's bar and bottle store. The back of the Land Cruiser was stacked full of crates and crates of beer, there were very few groceries and they had forgotten the fuel altogether.

Zebra were our first priority. We had two dart guns and decided to use two 4x4 pick-ups as chase vehicles. Hymie was the marksman in one and I took my place in the back of Robert Riggs' new Toyota Hilux. Each vehicle was accompanied by a recovery vehicle with enough people to load the immobilised animals. Orapa mine had built four sturdy crates in which we transported the animals to the mine. The two "hunting" parties took off early in the morning, in the bitter cold.

It was easy to find herds of zebra grazing on the open, flat grasslands between Ntwetwe Pan and the Boteti River; there were literally thousands. Our strategy was to approach the herds at a tangent, slowly, trying not to alarm them. When they started to move off at a canter, still out of darting range, we accelerated and chased as fast as possible hoping to get a shot at a fast-moving rump. It was a lot more difficult than we had anticipated. The ground was nowhere near as smooth as it appeared and the rough ride was made worse by the clouds of dust and clods of earth that the galloping zebra threw up in our faces as we got close. Trying to aim a gun accurately was close to impossible. Robert's driving was exceptional, given the circumstances, and we managed to dart two zebras and load them into crates. A few darts were sprayed around that were never recovered – thank goodness Debswana had a deep purse. Hymie, on the Land Cruiser, had not fared so well and his team returned empty-handed.

Delivering the animals meant a sixty-mile trek, first across the grasslands and then through an area of overgrazed bush outside the game reserve to the south. A myriad rutted cattle tracks branching and reconnecting meant driving was an unpleasant experience and the talcum-like dust, whipped up by the strong wind, was unbearable. The journey took at least three hours and it was a great relief to arrive at Orapa and release the animals at an offloading ramp in the northwestern section of the new sanctuary. There was a large welcome delegation at the release site, in high spirits and providing generous refreshment. The rough journey back, partly in the dark, didn't seem as bad and we enjoyed a lively barbecue around the campfire, with more than enough drink and stories before we climbed into our bedrolls under the stars.

This routine continued for three or four days and, although strenuous, it was a great adventure. The only one who didn't seem to be enjoying himself was Hymie. He was still finding it very difficult to dart successfully and clearly didn't enjoy being tied to the rails of a pick-up truck hurtling across rough terrain. He'd only managed to get two zebra, but had hit another two in the abdomen. One of these had died during the chase, probably not directly because of the dart, but it was very distressing all the same. On the third evening, after another mortality, one of the African labourers approached me and said conspiratorially, "Sir, I think the old doctor's medicine is too strong."

Hymie announced that he needed to fly back to South Africa the next day and Eleanor drove him to Orapa early in the morning. Over the next few days we caught a further dozen zebra, including a massive stallion who kicked through the crate on the way to the mine. Brian, Eleanor and I managed to get a rope around the frame of the crate and secure it before he could demolish it completely and escape. Brian and I then sat on the back of the vehicle holding the rope and watching for more damage while Eleanor drove the remainder of the journey.

Bouncing around in the back of the darting vehicle was decidedly uncomfortable and my ribs were getting severely bruised by banging against the rails. I didn't want to think what might happen if Robert rolled the Hilux. Mark Murray wanted to try his hand at darting, and although this wasn't strictly legal because he wasn't a vet, I agreed to let him have a go. He was much lighter and less well-padded than me and after his first sortie he came back to camp in serious pain. We took him to hospital in Orapa where the X-ray revealed broken ribs; especially worrying was that one had actually penetrated his pericardium and affected his heart, another half inch could have proved fatal. Luckily the mine hospital was of a much higher standard than any of the government hospitals of the time and they were able to stabilise him and evacuate him by air to Johannesburg.

After a week or so we had caught our quota of zebra and a few gemsbok – or so we thought. After delivering the latest animals and releasing them at the ramp, one of the Orapa wildlife committee told us that they hadn't seen much evidence of the animals we had been delivering. She assumed they must be very shy and hiding in patches of dense bush in the 20,000-acre sanctuary. This didn't seem likely to me, so we decided to follow the spoor leading away from the ramp. Nearly all the animals ran off in the same direction when released, so the tracks were quite distinct. It didn't take long to arrive at the northwest corner of the sanctuary's game fence, where we discovered a sizeable hole through which tracks disappeared into the surrounding bush. We didn't know how long this "back door" had been open, but it was a serious blow and someone sardonically chirped that we could have a job for life.

Robert Riggs had a reputation as a "cowboy" and took pleasure in driving like a maniac. But he wasn't without skill, which was one of the reasons we had asked him to assist. If anyone could get a pick-up on the tail of a galloping zebra or gemsbok it was Robert. It wasn't just Mark's ribs, and mine, that suffered though; Robert's new Hilux was taking a battering. In the course of a week or so it began to look like it had spent years in the bush; wing mirrors were lost and the windscreen was badly cracked. The final straw was when he drove through a small island of dry woodland at full speed and hit an antbear hole. There was a deafening bang and we took off and flew through yards of what most people would describe as impenetrable thicket. After coming to a stop and confirming that we were all there and relatively unhurt, Robert discovered his gearbox had been ripped clean out of the chassis. The vehicle was going nowhere under its own steam and we had to radio for assistance from the other team. We then towed the Hilux slowly back to camp. The vehicle was less than three months old and Robert, unfazed and with a skin thicker than a buffalo, contacted the dealer in Gabs to complain. Amazingly, he was given a temporary replacement while the first one was sent to Japan for assessment. Toyota could not believe how one of their ultra-tough pick-ups could have been wrecked in such a short time of off-road work. We backed him up when Robert had to give an assurance that he hadn't done anything worse than the company's latest promotional advert showed. He eventually received an apology from Toyota, with thanks for "demonstrating some shortcomings and weaknesses of the model", and a brand new Hilux!

ELEVEN

DROUGHT AND TRAGEDY

My clinic at Tlokweng was still a little out of the way then, and in August 1983 I heard of some premises in the town centre that were becoming available. The owner, a local builder called Bruce Berger, had been bringing his dog for treatment and he offered me the building, near the President Hotel, for a very reasonable rent, with an option to purchase after a year if things went well. On inspection it seemed like an ideal site and I told Andy Saunders that I would be moving out. I still hadn't paid any rent and Andy absolutely refused to take anything from me, but I suppose he might have been happy to see me go so that he could carry on with the development of the warehouse. Indeed, as Gaborone expanded and developed, the site of my old clinic morphed gradually into the country's first modern shopping mall, River Walk.

Our new premises on Khwai Road quickly became known and we became extremely busy. Richard had arrived in Botswana hoping to find some wildlife work, but unfortunately for him that was my main interest, so anything in the line of wildlife or darting animals was usually done by me and he was left to watch the shop. He left after six months to study at Reading University for a master's degree and was replaced by a succession of, mainly, young veterinarians that we recruited from places as diverse as Cambridge, Cork, Lusaka and the Channel Islands.

In the early 1980s Botswana experienced one of the most prolonged and devastating droughts on record. It is a dry country anyway and rain can only be expected between November and March, even in good years. This is the time that most wildlife species give birth. Even the so-called non-seasonal breeders such as zebra and gemsbok tend to conform in an effort to give their offspring at least a fighting chance. In the terrible 1980s it was counted as fortunate if there was any rain at all before January and grass production was limited at most to three months.

The stress on both farmed and free-living animals was enormous. Meagre grazing resources were regularly depleted by the end of June and by September the animals were in dire straits, wandering in a dusty wilderness of shadeless, superheated, bare ground. Cattle were mere ribs and skin, standing around sullenly as if resigned to their fate. Survivors from the wildlife calving season were few by then and the only species that seemed to be coping with the atrocious conditions, at least to some degree, were those like impala and giraffe that could derive some benefit from the dry browse on bushes and trees, but even these hardy survivors were gaunt. In the Kalahari Desert conditions were ferocious and cruel, but at least most of its resident species had evolved in a harsh environment. Even so, thousands died. Well-meaning, but naïve environmentalists around the world blamed the country's infamous veterinary cordon fences for the calamity, but these were just one factor exacerbating the exceptionally dry situation.

The Kalahari was bad enough, but in the Limpopo Valley, along the eastern border with South Africa, the rains failed almost totally and repeatedly. The animals here had not been conditioned to extremes in the same way, also they could not range so widely because of the farm fences, and the suffering was intense and unremittingly brutal. Those farmers who could, moved their cattle west to the communal sandveld areas, where they were slightly better off, but many could not and they had to buy feed or watch their animals die. Wild animals were ownerless and thus no one's responsibility – they had to survive on their own. Even though efforts were made to feed a few pods of hippos stranded in the Limpopo River's dwindling pools, the majority of the resident wildlife – wildebeest, kudu and even impala – suffered terribly.

In the northeast at Tuli the celebrated, relict elephant population of between 500 and 800 individuals was pretty much confined to a small area where Botswana, South Africa and Zimbabwe meet at the confluence of the Limpopo and Shashe Rivers, Botswana's lowest point at about 2,000 feet above sea level. These elephants, uniquely famous as the largest surviving population on private land, had devastated much of their available range in an attempt to satisfy their hunger, leading to impossible conditions for the survival of other species. Wildebeest and zebra all but disappeared through starvation, while eland, kudu and others hung on in much reduced herds. This haunting cameo, for those who experienced it, was a prophetic snapshot of the catastrophic prospects that could face one of the world's greatest wildlife areas, further north in Chobe, where over 100,000 elephants can be expected to concentrate should Botswana experience those climatic conditions again.

A call came one Friday morning in mid-October, about the hottest and driest time of all. In the Tuli area there were apparently two elephants and a lioness with snares attached to them. Could I please help? They were in a tourist area (now much more developed and famous) and should be easy to find. I agreed enthusiastically to drive down over the weekend and see what could be done. It was a six-hour drive on gravel roads down through the ranches making up the Tuli Block in the Limpopo Valley. I left before daylight on Saturday and arrived at the Pont Drift border post close to lunchtime. Jan, the manager of one of the dozen or so farms making up the wildlife area, was there to meet me. The farms covered about 200,000 acres, all devoted to wildlife and unfenced. The owners, mainly white South Africans, were co-operating with each other on the big issues, while pursuing their own ideas from luxury tourism to safari hunting or just private recreation on their individual properties.

Radio messages were broadcast and we soon had a small team of owners, managers and workers to begin our task. It was decided that the lioness would best be left until dark, when we could try to entice her pride to a bait using sound recordings. We would therefore start by trying to locate the elephants. They were apparently in separate herds; one was a large subadult female and the other a calf that was about two years old. Each had a wire snare around a leg. The decision was made when one of the farmers said he had seen the herd with the calf on his property that morning. We drove north in a small convoy of three vehicles, away from the oasis of riverine bush dominated by magnificent mashatu trees, across a landscape that resembled the barren surface of an asteroid. Patches of stunted mopane trees showed the only meagre signs of life, their dry, dusty branches chewed and twisted by elephants. We crossed dry, sandy streambeds and gravel plains and began to rise slowly away from the Limpopo. After a few miles, more trees appeared in fringes along the dry watercourses and occasional thickets, mostly without leaves. As we reached the targeted property we increased our vigilance and began to search for fresh elephant spoor. The trackers in the lead vehicle soon sighted a group of about fifteen elephants in the distance. They were standing in the "shade" of a clump of leafless trees, immobile except for the slow regular fanning of giant ears. The trackers assured the landowner that this was the group with the snared youngster, although at that range we could not confirm it.

Tuli elephants were known for their relatively small stature and acute lack of benevolence towards mankind, and I knew from experience that our subjects were unlikely to make things easy for us. I decided to make up two darts, each with enough drug for a young elephant – my first mistake. Then we approached slowly with one vehicle, hoping to get a clear sighting (and, if possible, a shot). The other vehicles remained about 300 yards away. We looped around to approach upwind. We were in the open, but it isn't usually the elephants' eyesight that gives concern. We quite quickly spotted the calf with the wire around his left foreleg, just above the foot. He was younger than I had anticipated and through binoculars the foot appeared very swollen. The vehicle approached to within 100 yards, the elephants had to be aware of our presence, but were surprisingly calm about it. The youngster was clearly unwilling to put much weight on the leg. The herd was so quiet that we approached another ten or so yards, to where I could get out and stalk to within darting range. This was accomplished with ease and I felt reasonably sure that Jan, still in the vehicle, who was my armed backup, would be able to provide adequate protection.

When I first realised how small the calf was, we had discussed maybe darting the mother first. But, having made up the darts for a young animal, I persuaded myself that the herd was so docile we might get away with a dart into the calf without causing too much consternation among the others – my second mistake. Under cover of a termite mound I was able to get into a good position, about thirty-five yards from the nearest animal. All was deceptively calm and with some patience, waiting for a clear view unobstructed by giant legs, I eventually managed to plant a dart squarely into the young elephant's backside. I don't know whether or not it was the baby who screeched first, but pandemonium ensued and amid a dust cloud of nuclear proportions the herd vanished.

I walked back to Jan's vehicle and got there just as the others joined us. They'd had a clear view of the direction the elephants had taken and the consensus was that they would not go far in the few minutes the drug needed to do its work. We followed the unmistakable spoor slowly, until we could see in the distance a thicket of perhaps fifty yards in circumference with elephants in among it. This was undoubtedly the same herd – there was no other cover nearby. We halted to give the drug time to work without chasing the elephants any further in the heat.

Normally the behaviour of the other elephants in the group will signal the onset of ataxia, or staggering, in a darted individual, but in this case there were no obvious signs of such disturbance. Ten minutes after darting we approached the thicket with the three vehicles. The animals were agitated but did not move away. We could only see about six of the larger elephants, the others were obscured by the bush. I was convinced that the young elephant must be immobilised by this time and we decided to try to drive the elephants out of the thicket. This was eventually achieved with some difficulty and lots of shouting, hooting and revving of engines. I was quite concerned by now and ran into the thicket to try to locate the youngster. I came to an abrupt stop some twenty yards in. There, in the centre of the thicket, was a muddy quagmire. Right in the middle were two adult female elephants up to their abdomens in muddy water trying to hide the darted calf and they were obviously not going to leave it just because I was shouting at them.

In a panic now, I ran back to the car and grabbed a rifle, yelling at the others to stay there, since it could have been very dangerous if the cows had been aggressive. I returned to the edge of the mud and from a distance of less than twenty yards fired over the heads of the cows. One, probably an aunt, turned and climbed, slithering, out of the mud and fled. To my horror, the distraught mother began to push the calf deeper into the mud. I could see that it was completely immobilised and needed immediate attention, but the cow was not going to leave it. I tried another shot, but to no avail. Jan had joined me but we were powerless to make her leave. I raced back to the car and frantically made up a dart with enough M99 to immobilise the mother. Darting her in the mud was fraught with risks, but we were desperate. I went ahead and gave her the drug. Minutes passed like days while we anxiously watched the cow and calf, not daring to approach any closer. Gradually she became affected and in four minutes Jan and I were in the mud furiously trying to extricate the calf from under the mother before she fell on it. The mud hole was about four feet deep and although we raised the little trunk clear of the surface we could not pull the calf out. Our shouts brought help and with the aid of a rope and half a dozen people pulling we finally got the little beast to the edge. At that precise moment the cow collapsed and I had to ensure that her trunk did not sink below the sloppy surface. Then with two waist-deep volunteers helping her I was able to turn my attention back to the calf.

Too late… the little elephant had drowned. The well-meant, but inept and misguided efforts of a vet and the desperate attention of a frantic mother had conspired to cause its death. Now was not the time for prolonged heart searching though; we had to get the mother out safely. There was no guarantee that she would be able to get to her feet in the deep mud. I administered the antidote to the M99 into an ear vein. She was sitting on her chest in sternal recumbency – not recommended for elephants, as it can inhibit breathing. But in the circumstances it probably saved her life. If she had gone over on her side, in the approved position, I am sure she would never have regained her footing. As it was she struggled to her feet in a couple of minutes, managed to get out of the mud and, her calf momentarily forgotten because of the drugs, followed the direction her sister had taken back towards the herd, a great relief to the very sad band of human observers.

As we made our way back we were all equally incredulous, despite having seen it with our own eyes. How could there be a deep pool of mud in the depths of a severe drought? How could it be unknown to all the human inhabitants, yet obviously familiar to the elephants? In one of the driest places on earth, how could I have drowned an elephant? The answer was made apparent later that day. An old underground pipe had carried water from under the sand in the bed of the Limpopo for about eight miles to an artificial waterhole near one of the tourist camps. No one present had been aware of the pipe's exact path. The elephants had found it, possibly through scenting a small leak and had created a small oasis from the drought, but it had cost one of them dear. It was a sombre evening and we left the lioness for the next night, spreading our bedrolls on Glen's verandah.

The following day we were up early and quickly located the other herd of twenty or so with the snared female. It was straightforward to dart her from the vehicle with minimum disturbance and the herd only moved a short distance, quite calmly for Tuli elephants. Even though we couldn't see her it was easy to make out when she fell down because of the reaction of the other elephants. We approached as fast as we could, making lots of noise, and nearly all the herd moved off, leaving one older female and another youngster fussing about the fallen elephant, but even they were eventually chased away and we were able to quickly cut off the snare, which hadn't done much damage, and revive her. A couple of minutes after I gave the antidote into an ear vein she got to her feet and headed towards the herd, rejoining them safely.

The lioness remained. I needed to get back to Gabs so I wanted to get things over with as quickly as possible. I suggested that we would have a far greater chance of finding the pride if we dragged a bait around the area and laid some scent trails towards where we would locate our calling station. When I remarked that we had the perfect bait in the dead baby elephant it was received as if I'd proposed murdering Bambi. Only the game ranger and one of the farmers were in favour. It was a hard sell, but we eventually persuaded the rest that the baby elephant could at least help to alleviate another animal's suffering. We therefore skinned one side of the tiny carcass and punctured the abdomen to allow some of the liquid intestinal contents to leak out. It was then dragged behind a Land Cruiser in a wide arc of a half-mile radius and then towards a central point like three spokes of a wheel. We sited our calling station in a clearing where the spokes came together, a large loudspeaker on the back of the Land Cruiser, powered by the car battery and connected to a cassette tape recorder.

Three of us sat in the open vehicle: Glen Divine, the ranger; a farmer with a rifle; and me with my dart gun. Glen had a powerful spotlight and repeatedly swept the clearing and surrounding bush. We had assorted tapes to try to attract the pride, varying from the hysteria of feeding hyaenas to roaring male lions. The hyaenas often worked best, proving that the King of Beasts is a sucker for a free lunch. The roaring males only attract other males looking for a territorial scuffle. The tapes are so beguiling that lions will sometimes come and cock an ear right up to the speakers like the celebrated HMV dog of old.

On this occasion the pride homed in on the sounds of a hyaena feeding frenzy and settled down on the baby elephant carcass. There were three females and two younger males, still sporting faint spots. Darting our target was easy and she lay where she ate, having merely swatted a companion when the dart struck her rump. She became comatose in about six minutes. Revving the car and changing the tape to the roaring males seemed to be enough to move the other four far enough away to allow me to quickly remove the snare. It only took seconds because it was pretty loose around her neck and we could retire to leave them to their meal. Her companions quickly rejoined her and energetically devoured the elephant without any apparent concern that the female slumbered on among them. As soon as she stirred, an hour or so later, we were able to leave the scene knowing she would be safe from any marauding hyaenas.

We returned to Glen's house and chatted for a while over a light supper before retiring early. On Monday morning I began the drive south just as the sun breached the low hills across the Limpopo River. I had mixed feelings about the results of our weekend activities, but we had tried. Sometimes man's best efforts are just not enough. It is extremely upsetting to think how cruel and indiscriminate wire snares can be; neither the elephants nor the lion would have been eaten by the poachers. They had been set to catch antelopes like impala or kudu. There would have been no gain for anyone, just excruciating suffering for the victims, perhaps lasting several days – a real horror. Perhaps the pets that formed the basis of our practice in Gabs (indulged with love, an unhealthy diet and lack of exercise) were better off, but as I listened to Richard's case histories the following morning my old misgivings about the justification for small-animal practice resurfaced.

About this time, there developed an international fad for ostrich meat; it has qualities of both red and white meats and gained a reputation as a healthy dietary option. Botswana has hosts of wild ostriches and efforts were made to develop an ostrich farming industry. Many were captured in order to stock farms in several parts of the country. Inevitably, the boom in Botswana was short lived, for a combination of economic, political and veterinary reasons. The value of an ostrich largely depends on the price obtained for its skin, which is in great demand as a specialist leather for luxury items. The skins of wild and of badly managed domestic birds are often damaged and inferior and do not sell. Also, an export-approved abattoir only became available late in the day, after many farmers had lost money and given up. By the time we had our "ducks in order" there were plenty of ostrich farms in other parts of the world, notably the United States, and the market was satiated.

Early on I was summoned to the Office of the President to see Sir Ketumile Masire, the second president, who had taken over on the death of Sir Seretse Khama in 1980. He wanted to ask me about farming ostriches. "Quett" knew me from my days as a veterinary officer, when I'd had cause to visit his cattle farm in Ghanzi. In his private office he explained that he wanted to start farming ostriches at a new farm he owned near Lobatse and could I advise him on the best way forward. The discussion came around to water supplies, as is often the case in Botswana's arid environment. We worked out how much water he would need for the proposed ostrich stocks and I recommended that he sink a borehole on the farm to guarantee adequate supplies.

"Ah, that's a problem, Larry," he said.

"Why?" I asked, knowing that there was almost certainly sufficient groundwater on the site and cost would be no obstacle.

"Well you see, I applied to the Director of Water Affairs for permission to drill and he refused me."

I was flabbergasted! This modest man, a most untypical African president, did not even think of overruling a mid-level civil servant and, perhaps even more amazing, the mere Director of a government department had the presumption to turn him down. Where else on the continent could that happen? Certainly not in the Uganda of Idi Amin where I had started my African career.

Some years after his retirement from office I encountered Sir Ketumile in the Livestock Advisory Centre in Gabs (a government subsidised agricultural supplies store). Now in his late seventies, he was actually queuing for service behind a line of other farmers. We immediately recognised each other and after the usual formalities I asked why he didn't go straight to the front as his advanced years allowed, let alone his status as a former head of state.

"I have time, I'm not in a hurry," was his gentle reply.

Another true story was when, as President, he was at a function in the Holiday Inn chatting with a small group. A visitor from South Africa, part of the group, asked him, "And what do you do around here?"

This merely elicited a softly spoken, "Not a great deal." Whereupon he excused himself to allow his identity to be explained to the mortified visitor.

One of my earliest meetings with Quett had been in strange circumstances, when he was still Vice President. I had been staying with John Counihan in Gabs on one of my frequent working visits from Maun. John's American wife, Joyce, was in Johannesburg awaiting her first baby. Jan, one of John's bosses from their head office in Vryburg in the Northern Cape, arrived on a business trip. He obviously outranked me and I was given a mattress on the lounge floor, while John gave up the main bedroom and moved into the guest room; the remaining bedroom was being converted into a nursery.

John and I went out to a party but his boss declined to come with us, citing a previous engagement. We arrived home very late and quite drunk and I quickly fell asleep in the lounge. At some time during the night Jan woke me to ask if I had any antacid tablets because he was suffering from indigestion. I was unable to help and he went back to the main bedroom. The next morning John woke me in a worried state and said he couldn't wake Jan. I wasn't feeling too bright, but got up and followed John to the open door of the main bedroom. I could see at a glance that Jan was dead, lying on his back with his eyes open. I approached the bed and confirmed this to John.

"Jesus! How can that be?" he said, shocked. "What are we going to do?"

"I don't know," I replied. "Is there an undertaker in town?"

There wasn't, so we had to make our own arrangements. We drove to the Princess Marina Hospital, very close to John's house. John was very upset, I less so because I hadn't known Jan. We were in the hospital's reception area rather fruitlessly trying to get some help, when Quett walked in accompanied by an Egyptian staff doctor. He knew John, and taking in his distressed state, asked what was the matter. John explained the situation and Quett immediately asked the doctor to assist us. The involvement of the Vice President made a huge difference and we were taken to the small mortuary room where an attendant showed us the single unoccupied drawer in a cabinet of three. We were welcome to bring the body to the hospital and use this facility.

Unfortunately there was no ambulance available and all we could obtain was a stretcher. We returned to John's house and placed it on the floor next to the bed. John did not want to help, but his gardener, who had now arrived for work, flatly refused to go near the corpse and, seeing as I couldn't do it alone, John had to help me put Jan's body on the stretcher. We picked it up with John at the foot and me at the head and started to carry it out of the bedroom and into the corridor to the kitchen because the back door was closer. Attempting to negotiate the doorway into the kitchen the stretcher tipped and the body fell onto the floor. That was too much for John and he walked out to the garden, exclaiming that he couldn't help further. The only way I could move the body through the door and kitchen to the outside was by hooking the feet under my arms and dragging it – undignified, but effective on the smooth tiles. Going back in and retrieving the stretcher, I forced John to help to load Jan again and we carried him to his own Toyota Cressida, a large saloon car. It was easier to load him on the back seat than to put him in the boot and we drove back to the hospital like that. At least there the mortuary assistant arranged some help to put the body into the cold drawer at the bottom of the cabinet.

The next problem was the paperwork. We needed a death certificate and a permit to repatriate the body to South Africa. John knew of a doctor's surgery very close to his house, so I went across and told him the story. He agreed to write out a death certificate and asked me the name, age and cause of death. I gave him the name, and said I thought he was about fifty and had probably died from a heart attack. This satisfied the doctor and he duly handed me the completed certificate. Later we found Jan's passport and ascertained that he was in fact only thirty-nine! John had notified the company's Vryburg HQ and they had contacted the bereaved family. Armed with the passport and the death certificate they were able to leave Botswana with the body in a coffin they brought up with them and return home. I confess I was a little surprised that the official procedures were so easily satisfied by the briefest examination of a mere vet. But that's Africa.

My alternative qualification, a master's degree in conservation, was beginning to pay dividends and I was recruited as a consultant to head up various teams producing management plans for a number of protected areas. These short-term projects varied widely, from national parks to private concessions in so-called wildlife management areas. I also became chairman of the technical sub-committee of the Kalahari Conservation Society. I'd been persuaded, against my usual instincts, to join the organisation by Jeannie Davis, the wife of my bank manager and one of the more spirited clients at the surgery. Eleanor Warr was by then the KCS Conservation Officer and we got to know each other better after the rather rocky start at Orapa. The future president, Ian Khama, then only a Brigadier in the Defence Force and not involved in politics, was also a member of the committee and we had many disagreements based on his profound dislike of hunting, in contrast with my view that it had an important role in conservation.

One consequence of all this was that I was away in remote areas of the country more and more, which left the management of the clinic to a succession of vets, some of whom were better than others. Sid, an Irishman from County Cork, was extremely likeable and a competent vet, but having previously worked for a number of charities he habitually charged fees below cost, which was obviously unsustainable.

Dave, a Scot who had qualified in Zambia (with two excellent vet schools in Scotland, should that have given me cause for concern?), was accident prone and caused no end of embarrassing situations. He operated on the wrong leg of a dog after turning the X-ray round in the viewer and he crashed a practice vehicle badly. But the last straw was losing the favourite cat of my lawyer's wife!

Ingrid had brought the Persian cat (the only one in Botswana) into the surgery one morning when he was busy doing routine operations. The animal was apparently comatose and she suspected poisoning. He told her that the prognosis wasn't very good but he would do all he could. As soon as she left he merely put the cat in one of the first row of cages, thinking it was beyond help and would soon be dead and went back to his operating schedule. The cage he chose was designed for dogs and when he went to check later the cat was gone. It had obviously come round, squeezed through the bars and disappeared. To compound his felony he then telephoned the client and told her he was very sorry, but the cat had died. I arrived back the following day and the staff told me the truth about the incident. I called David in and told him that I could condone his mistakes, but a lazy incompetent action was much worse, and that blatantly lying to the client was completely unforgivable. I further pointed out that in most cases a cat will find its way home. In a strange twist the lawyer himself, Peter Collins, later a judge, called me and expressed his delight that the cat had died. He hated the animal and his wife's doting on it drove him mad. We were now in a real fix, either way. I explained the truth of the situation to Peter and he remarked that the cat had better not survive. Of course, it turned up at their house a couple of days later, apparently none the worse for its experience and, while Ingrid was delighted, Peter threatened to sue us and was only placated by his wife and a bottle of expensive whisky from me.

But it was not only inexperienced young vets who made disastrous mistakes. During a prolonged and hectic, single-handed, Saturday morning session, one of my most difficult clients, Mrs Schoeman, arrived with her cat for a routine annual booster vaccination. I was pretty fraught and distracted and quite unjustifiably annoyed that she had chosen such a busy time to come to the clinic. She placed the cat on the table and after a hurried examination, with the usual small talk, I reached into the fridge for a dose of vaccine. Inadvertently I took out the bottle of Euthatal, a concentrated barbiturate anaesthetic that is used for humane destruction of animals, and drew a single millilitre into the syringe. Without a thought I then injected the cat under the loose skin at the back of the neck as in a normal vaccination. I immediately woke up to the calamity and was horrified at what I'd done.

I couldn't think of anything that I could do immediately to remedy the situation and somehow kept calm ushering the lady and her cat out of the consulting room, without alerting her to my dreadful mistake. Filling out the vaccination certificate and charging for a normal vaccination compounded the felony many-fold, but I was at a loss as to what else to do. The subcutaneous injection would take some time to have any effect and I hoped it wouldn't be fatal, so I waited for the inevitable phone call. A couple of hours later, just as I was leaving the clinic after dealing with the remaining cases, the phone rang. Mrs Schoeman reported that her cat had gone to sleep in the car on the way home and now wouldn't wake up. Could it be a reaction to the vaccination? I replied that it was a possibility, that this was a new batch of vaccine and perhaps her cat was particularly sensitive to it in some way. I told her to leave the animal in a quiet place and call me in the evening. I had no idea how long the cat would be out, so I would have to play it by ear. In the early evening Mrs Schoeman rang to say that the cat was still sleeping soundly. I reassured her and told her to bring it to the clinic in the morning if all was not well. She arrived at 8.00 am with a still comatose cat and I could think of nothing that I had that would make any difference. I did give it a dose of the correct vaccine, under the guise of a revival treatment. More reassurances and the charade continued. The cat finally stirred on Monday morning, to the delight of Mrs Schoeman and to the great relief of a stressed-out vet.

In the mid-1980s a second international project was aimed at the Okavango Delta to try to ascertain if there was potential for improving outflows and storage of water to benefit local agriculture, tourism and possibly even increasing supply to the diamond mines downstream at Orapa and Letlhakane. The lead consultant was the Snowy Mountains Engineering Company (SMEC) from New South Wales in Australia. Some of us who had been involved in the 1970s UN project were sceptical from the beginning, but found ourselves once again investigating the Delta's complex physical and biological systems. This time my role was more focused, flying surveys of a smaller area with a tighter grid in the lower section of the Delta. The aim was to quantify correlations between game species and habitat types in an effort to predict what might happen to the wildlife populations if the proposed engineering works were actually carried out.

One weekend in 1986 the SMEC boss, a fairly elderly Dutch immigrant to Australia by the name of Schelte Raadsma, asked me if I would fly him and his wife Connie on a sightseeing trip to Chobe. Early one morning we took off from Maun in a Cessna 206 that had been hired from Northern Air for the census flights and headed northeast towards Savuti and Chobe. About twenty minutes out I noticed a thin black line on the engine cowling that was getting progressively longer and wider. I realised that I hadn't checked that the filler cap had been replaced after topping up with oil and refuelling in Maun. The oil reached the base of the windscreen and began to rise. I thought of trying to fly back to Maun, but it occurred to me that the airstrip at San-ta-Wani was nearer. I knew the camp and the staff well, so I turned left and headed towards it.

I explained our situation to Schelte and assured him that it was nothing to worry about, but he became quite agitated as the oil spread up and across the windscreen obscuring his, and my, forward vision. It didn't take me long to find the strip by looking out of the side window and I flew a fairly normal circuit for approach and landing, but on the final approach my forward vision was completely obscured, so I was quite nervous, but perhaps not as much as the Raadsmas. I approached blind and side-slipped from quite a high altitude to a position I hoped was over the threshold and kicked the rudder violently to line up on the runway just as I flared to land.

The camp manager and his wife were very kind and took the older couple to the lodge for refreshments while I spent an hour or so cleaning up the mess with the help of some camp staff. I was amazed by the mess a small volume of oil could make, rather like blood in equivalent circumstances I suppose. By the time I had made sure there was still enough oil in the engine for safety and we were ready to continue on to Chobe, the Raadsmas decided they would rather go back to Maun, which was understandable.

The Botswana Government accepted most of SMEC's recommendations but, in the face of opposition at home and abroad, agreed to an independent review by IUCN in the early 1990s before any implementation took place. This report came out against their proposals on environmental and sociological grounds, but the real bottom line was that the proposed interventions probably would not deliver the desired outcomes – pretty much a re-hash of the 1970s conclusions.

Eleanor, in the meantime, had qualified for her pilot's licence and was keen to get more experience. She began to participate in some of the aerial surveys and as we spent more and more time together professionally we found we had much in common, despite our widely different social backgrounds. An affair developed, we shared more and more friends, and things progressed to where we moved in together and she started to take an interest in the vet clinic as well.

We married in 1990, the same day Nelson Mandela was released from prison, in a small private wedding, kindly hosted by my good, barefoot friend Peter Sandenbergh and his wife Mandy at Delta Camp. We flew in a few friends and the District Commissioner from Maun married us under an ebony tree on the banks of the Boro River. I stayed sober to fly the District Commissioner back to Maun after the ceremony and returned to camp to join the others in a fun-filled weekend with good friends and great hospitality. A few years later, while travelling, we saw an article in a glossy magazine, *Harpers Bazaar* I think, that listed the ten most romantic places in the world for a wedding. Delta Camp was at number five – we had started a trend!

In the mid-1980s my younger sister Lynne came to visit. She had been living in New Zealand and working as a hairdresser. She spent a few weeks with us and inevitably found herself cutting friends' hair. Word spread among the European community that there was a skilled stylist in town and she soon realised that there was a niche for an experienced hairdresser. A local lawyer, Julia Helfer, offered to arrange the necessary permits and employ her if she would agree to stay. Lynne had no ties elsewhere and soon became a popular figure with the Gabs ladies, her business grew and she was enjoying life in Botswana.

Then, between Christmas 1988 and New Year, we were headed to Port Alfred in the Eastern Cape for a holiday. I had just bought a new car and Lynne, Eleanor and I set off in style, picking up Caroline Kendrick and her eleven-year-old daughter Geraldine in Lobatse. The journey was going to take about twelve hours and I drove the first six-hour leg across country to Bloemfontein, in the Free State, the geographical centre of South Africa. We then headed for Aliwal North on the Eastern Cape border.

As we approached Smithfield, a small Free State village, I noticed that there were thunderstorms far ahead over the mountains of the Cape. I pulled up for fuel and refreshments in the village and suggested that someone else might drive for an hour or so to give me a break and then I would take over again to drive through the mountains. I came out of the shop with cold drinks for everyone, paid for the fuel and climbed into the front passenger seat. Caroline was sitting behind the wheel and she pulled out and continued down the highway.

Six miles further, on a straight, downhill section she touched the dirt on the nearside of the tar and quickly pulled back toward the centre of the road, over-correcting. She then swerved back and two wheels left the tar again, causing her to lose control completely. The event seemed to play out in slow motion. The car swerved again, then rolled several times, coming to rest on the tar on the opposite side of the road, the right way up but minus wheels and utterly wrecked.

Caroline was unconscious, slumped over the steering wheel, bleeding from a head wound, but breathing. There was nobody in the back seat where Lynne, Eleanor and Geraldine had been. They had been thrown out. I was miraculously unhurt and able to climb out and run to Eleanor. She was lying in the road ahead, also unconscious but breathing. I moved her to the side of the road then heard a scream and ran behind the car to find Geraldine, who had obviously broken both legs. I lifted her to the roadside and ran further uphill to look for Lynne. I found her lying behind some rocks about five feet above the road, but she had succumbed to head injuries. I took off my shirt and covered her.

The road had been deserted except for a Mercedes heading in the opposite direction, which we had luckily avoided, but then a couple of cars arrived and people started gathering. First on the scene was a couple who, incredibly, we knew from Gabs and who were travelling back from the Cape. An ambulance and police car soon arrived from Smithfield and we were all taken to its tiny cottage hospital, where there was some disbelief at my unharmed state.

Although Caroline and Geraldine were able to be treated in Smithfield, Eleanor was critically injured and was despatched to Bloemfontein in a high-speed paramedic ambulance. After some first aid, we followed in another ambulance and arrived about an hour and a half later at Universitas Hospital, a large teaching establishment with an excellent reputation. I was very alarmed when the receptionist told me that there had been no ambulance from Smithfield, but just then it screeched into the entrance bay and two paramedics wheeled Eleanor in at high speed. Apparently, they had diverted to a doctor's clinic in Reddersburg, an even smaller village en route, because they thought she wasn't going to make it. The doctor had stabilised her again and told them to get to Bloemfontein with all haste. I was asked to sign forms authorising surgery, which I did at once, but explaining that we were not legally related – luckily they didn't seem to mind. After six hours in theatre followed by a week in ICU and ten more days in a general ward she was allowed to be moved to a hospital in Johannesburg, nearer home. Meanwhile I had the desperately painful duty of flying back to our parents in England with Lynne's ashes.

Despite the enormously sad circumstances and my worries about Eleanor, I came to appreciate what a fine, friendly and pleasant place South Africa's central city is. I had lots of time on my hands in between visits to the hospital and explored many of Bloemfontein's varying cultural attractions, such as JRR Tolkien's house, the Free State Botanical Garden and Naval Hill. Prior to this I had thought of "Bloem" as a hardline, dour, Calvinistic, Afrikaner stronghold with little sympathy or time for an Englishman – how wrong I was. The hospital staff, without exception, were unfailingly kind and helpful, and the medical specialists highly trained and experienced. Although, they were all unbelievably ignorant of Africa north of the Limpopo; Botswana might as well have been Conrad's *Heart of Darkness*, rather than an adjoining neighbour.

Eleanor was obviously made of tough stuff. Despite her horrific injuries and predictions of a childless future plagued by severe arthritis caused by dislocated hips, she was soon back at work running the KCS and walking as if nothing had happened. Years later she taught our two children how to ski and accompanied them down the black diamond slopes at Vail, while I crept down the green runs.

TWELVE

BIG GAME HUNTER

I gradually acquired more wildlife consulting work through the mid-1980s, in particular flying many hours of game surveys, as the Department outsourced ever more of its wildlife population monitoring function. This was in an effort to produce scientifically based hunting quotas throughout the country and specifically to try to keep tabs on the increasing elephant population.

I was in England on holiday in January 1986 when I received a call from Kukes Ngwamatsoko, who was then Acting Director of Wildlife. He asked me to assist with an aerial census of wildlife in the southern Kalahari Desert, based out of the village of Hukuntsi. It was to provide data for his master's thesis for an Australian university. I was surprised because we had frequently had our differences, but I agreed to help out and flew back to Gabs.

He described what it was he wanted to do and stressed that I was to be merely the pilot and wasn't to be involved in the "science", which would be his personal responsibility. He also said that two young departmental staff had just been trained as pilots and they would come along for additional survey training in a field situation. As I was not a flight instructor I had a few reservations about this: would they want to take the controls during the survey? Would they want to be in the left-hand (i.e. pilot's) seat? It is the norm for instructors to take the right-hand (co-pilot's) seat, but I had almost no experience of flying from the right-hand seat. Census flying involves flying low and slow, with maximum permitted all-up weight and it is inherently a high-risk undertaking; if anything goes wrong there is very little time to sort things out before hitting the ground.

I therefore went to the new Sir Seretse Khama International Airport to discuss all this with the flight instructor at the Gabs flight school who had been responsible for checking them out on the Cessna. He was a red-haired expatriate South African, whose main job was flying more sophisticated aircraft for the Debswana diamond mining company. He did some flight training in his spare time and, although highly qualified, I thought he might not be fully aware of some of the demands of bush flying. I asked him how he'd assessed the two Wildlife Department rookies.

"Oh, they'll probably be OK following the railway line to Francistown, but if they go off into the boondocks they might struggle a bit," was his flippant reply.

I told him we were going into the desert to fly a census and he laughed, "I hope you've got good insurance!"

I was now quite annoyed and asked him how he could have signed them out if they weren't competent for the type of flying he knew they would be expected to do.

"They managed a few circuits and manoeuvres OK, I only checked them out on the Cessna 210, I didn't do their basic training," he replied. "Look mate, I don't want to lose my work permit for failing them."

I walked away, unsurprised. White expats who are reliant on work and residence permits for their livelihoods have always had feelings of insecurity. The underlying consideration of race has always coloured working relationships – it's too easy to make accusations from either side – and is almost never discussed overtly, such is its taboo status. Consequently it detracts severely from productivity and standards in many situations. Botswana is better than most African countries, but the feelings are there.

We flew six-up to Hukuntsi about 300 miles into the southern desert: Kukes, me, the two pilots and two game scouts who would be observers (i.e. do the counting). We stayed in a couple of empty government houses near the airstrip. I made it clear that I would always fly from the left-hand seat during surveys, but that the other guys could fly on occasional ferry flights. They were keen to do more, but I was extremely cautious, knowing full well the pitfalls of overconfidence.

Flying at 300 feet above the bush of the Kalahari at eighty knots we were able to see a great deal of the terrain and its inhabitants. The frequent pans were often dotted with springbok, sometimes accompanied by a few gemsbok and ostrich, with the occasional lone wildebeest bull. Where the human impact of wells and domestic stock was apparent because of the overgrazed patches, the wildlife had obviously retreated and the dominant herbivores were goats and cattle.

Out of sight of human intrusion it was still a pristine paradise. In the dunes there were many herds of red hartebeest, wildebeest, small groups of gemsbok and occasional kudu. Occasionally we would fly over herds of massive eland, more than 100 strong, trotting distinctively away at pace, disturbed by the aircraft. The huge "blue" bulls, almost a ton in weight, sometimes struggled to keep up with the more svelte cows and youngsters and straggled at the rear. I realised that the two game scouts weren't calling out the eland to Kukes, who was recording all the observations as well as regularly noting the aircraft's height and speed. After a couple of days I reluctantly mentioned this to Kukes, at the risk of being told to mind my own business. He questioned the scouts, who admitted to seeing the eland herds but they had thought they were Brahman cattle and therefore hadn't counted them – neither of them had ever seen an eland before!

I'd been in this situation before. A few years earlier I had been flying a training census, also in the southern Kalahari with a team of four young game scouts. As I explained what they were to count they looked sheepish and unsettled. It turned out that none of them had ever seen any significant wildlife and didn't know what the various species looked like. So I showed them pictures of all the animals we would see in my copy of Mark and Delia Owens' new book *Cry of the Kalahari*. It was a stark illustration of the facts of life in many African countries where the vast proportion of the population, mainly living in new urban environments, had little, if any, experience or knowledge of the spectacular wildlife resources in their countries. Another problem in Botswana was that rural dwellers usually didn't have the educational qualifications to be hired by government as game scouts, even though they had a much better knowledge of the natural resources to be managed and protected. For instance, none of my team of expert bush operatives from Maun had been taken on by the Wildlife Department when the UNDP project ended. Only through my friendship with Ryland Wallace had I managed to find a job with Safari South for my outstanding foreman, Jonathan Juramo.

After five days of surveys we were due to fly back to Gabs and I suggested that one of the two rookies might like to fly, with the other as co-pilot. I sat nervously in the back with the two scouts and Kukes stayed behind in Hukuntsi to visit relatives. The two-hour flight was uneventful, but I confess I kept a watch on the heading and engine gauges more than a passenger normally would. I had no headphones so could not hear the radio exchanges with the Gabs controllers, but noticed that we had descended exceptionally low as we got close. In essence we flew a very, very, long final approach to the airfield, perhaps twenty miles, with the last five or so very low indeed – extremely unorthodox. We eventually landed safely and proceeded to the apron. We were taxiing far too fast and I shouted to remind the pilot quite forcefully that he was at the controls of an aircraft, not a BMW! He ignored me and continued at speed before attempting to turn into a parking space. The inevitable happened and we crumpled the tail of a parked aeroplane with our starboard wingtip – quite an expensive blunder. After coming to a halt I said nothing but my goodbyes, grabbed my bag and was heading across the tarmac towards the terminal building, leaving the rest of them to gaze at the damage and yell at each other. My attention was caught by one of the air traffic controllers who had raced down from the tower and was running across the apron towards the aircraft.

"Dr Larry!" he yelled. "Where are you going? You must report this incident!"

I pointed back at the aircraft and said, "Sorry, talk to the pilot. I was a only a passenger." And continued on my way, relieved to be safely back on the ground.

I put in a written report to Kukes about the survey, including my opinion of the flying abilities of his two young pilots. I said that I thought they needed much more experience before attempting any survey flying on their own and concluded by describing the taxiing mishap. I copied the report to the Chief Flight Safety Officer at the DCA. Kukes did not reply directly but I heard that he thought I was being "typically racist" and wanted to monopolise the survey flying for myself. As far as he was concerned the pilots had performed perfectly adequately.

Less than a month later the "BMW" pilot flew Kukes from Gabs to Kasane, via Francistown to pick up another staff member. The youngster could not get the Cessna's engine to restart in Francistown (they are temperamental when hot) and they had to spend the night there. The next morning the cool engine started easily and they all took off for Kasane. The old Kasane airstrip was not for novices; it was situated on a bend in the Chobe River, where the Mowana Lodge golf course is now, and it was necessary to approach quite steeply over the river on finals, avoid a power line and then touch down quickly to use the length of the whole airstrip in order to prevent running off the far end into the Chobe River's only rapids. On this day, as the Wildlife Department aircraft approached, Lloyd Wilmot, a very experienced bush pilot, was sitting in his aeroplane waiting to take off. He described the Cessna's approach as far too high, touching down almost halfway along the strip and, shortly after, turning abruptly into the thick bush at high speed, apparently in an attempt to avoid careering into the rapids. The plane was wrecked and it was lucky no one was seriously hurt. The worst thing was that the young pilot gave up flying afterwards – a great waste. Who was to blame? I think the expat flight instructor had a lot to answer for, but maybe the prevailing sub-climate of enmity that made him fear for his job was responsible, exemplified by Kukes' dismissal of my report.

One of the ways I found to spend more time with wildlife in the bush was to persuade Kukes, as Director of Wildlife, to issue me with a professional hunter's licence. For my part, I thought I would gain first-hand experience that would enable me to advocate safari hunting as a valid and valuable land use for conservation. I had seen quite a bit of safari life through meeting hunters with clients in the field. Although I couldn't quite see myself as a full-time professional hunter I thought I could learn more about the industry and enjoy myself at the same time if I could be on the inside. Thanks to my close working relationship in the Okavango with the safari companies, and Safari South in particular, I was sure I would be employed if I had a licence. Kukes was satisfied that I had enough experience working with dangerous game and saw the advantage of having someone with genuine conservation credentials in the industry, so he went along with the idea.

In 1988 I joined my first safari in the Okavango as a professional hunter with Safari South. Although very much a novice, with a little help from the real professionals – seasoned hunters like Harry Selby, Lionel Palmer, and Soren Lindstrom – I got by. I had never hunted on my own account, not even birds or fish, so I didn't even have a gun, but Ryland Wallace made sure I was issued with a reliable, company-owned .375 rifle and I made my old diesel Land Cruiser just about good enough for safari work, by fitting a seat on the back behind the cab. I had no experience of shooting anything other than buffaloes and the odd antelope for scientific samples. I quickly learnt how much reliance is placed on the trackers and again Ryland helped out, ensuring that I was allocated Mmusi, an experienced and trustworthy man to work with.

My first safari was based out of Cement camp, on the western side of the Sandveld Tongue. It got its name originally from a concrete survey beacon, which was a well-known landmark. It was a beautiful area that I knew well from my buffalo research and was blessed with a great variety of game. There were two hunting clients from California, with their wives. The clients were friends of Lionel Palmer, the senior hunter in camp. Palmer was guiding the older man, who had hunted with him previously. He and his wife were there just to enjoy bush life with a little birdshooting and were not too serious about hunting. My client, Joe, was in his forties and on his first African hunt. He wanted to get as many animals as was allowed and was particularly keen to shoot a lion, which I had no experience of – but I couldn't let him know that. I had darted a few lions, but this was a whole new ball game.

We collected most of the plains game that he wanted in the first few days and he was pleased with the kudu, lechwe and impala he shot. He seemed to be a good shot, but shooting antelope at long range is very different to confronting dangerous game close-up. Palmer's team was also keeping a lookout for signs of lion for us. We had a full twenty-one-day safari, so there was no rush. Joe managed to shoot a quite respectable trophy buffalo bull, nothing for the record book, but he was happy. The bull had been in a fairly large herd of about 120 animals and we'd had to stalk carefully to get a clear and fairly close shot. Buffalo herds are difficult to approach on foot because there are always some animals on the lookout and the whole herd disappears in a cloud of dust at the first hint of danger. One well-placed bullet behind the shoulder penetrated his lungs and heart and he fell within 100 yards. We ran up as the herd disappeared and Joe made sure with a killing shot in the back of the head. The obligatory posed photographs were taken, before Mmusi and his sidekick removed the stomach and other internal organs so we could load the carcass into the back of the vehicle. We dug the back wheels into the sand to make it lower, but it was still quite an effort to lever almost half a ton of buffalo on board. I was beginning to think that safari hunting was no big deal, but we still had a lion to get.

Early one morning, in the dark before we were up, we heard the tell-tale descending roar of a lion not far away to the west, repeated several times. I dressed quickly and grabbed a quick coffee with rusks, South African biscuits that traditionally get dunked. Joe arrived at the campfire very excited.

"What do you think? How far away do you think he is?"

"Not far," I replied. "Maybe a mile or so across the floodplain."

Mmusi and his crew arrived with my car and we headed out of camp with the first morning light behind us. We bumped slowly across the dry uneven floodplain towards the woodland on the far side and joined a motorable track along the edge. Mmusi advised that we should turn north and continue with the woodland close on our left. After quite a short distance we came across fresh buffalo spoor, maybe fifty animals, crossing from the floodplain and entering the woodland. This was a good sign that the lion might be somewhere close. Shortly further on Mmusi indicated that we should turn left into the woodland. We picked our way through the bush following his directions, which he communicated with a stick over the cab from his seat on the back.

The woodland was fairly open, but skirting around the thickets and avoiding antbear holes and fallen trees was slow going. From time to time we saw evidence of where the buffalo had passed, fresh dung and disturbed sand. We came out of the woodland into a pleasant grassy glade with a dry depression in the middle. About 150 yards ahead of us, we saw a large male lion disappearing into the woodland opposite. It was only a glimpse, but it appeared to have a good, blond mane and Joe said it would be a great trophy.

As we drove around the clearing Mmusi picked up three more lion tracks, so we knew he wasn't alone. Mmusi said there were at least two females and he wasn't sure about the third spoor. At the spot where we had seen the big male disappear we got out of the vehicle and looked around for more signs. We found another female spoor and the prints of two juveniles. It was still quite early and Mmusi said following the lions through the woodland would be pointless, but they would find a place to rest when it got warmer, probably not too far away if we didn't push them.

We found a vehicle track that seemed to head north and might take us around the thick woodland and give us access to the next river, the Matlhabanelo, a western distributary of the Queenie molapo. We did indeed find the river and then stopped for coffee. There was a herd of zebra and a few blue wildebeest, but obviously we couldn't shoot one for fear of driving the lions further away. After about half an hour we continued along the edge of the woodland until we saw clear tracks of half a dozen lions coming out of the woodland and crossing the river, where we were unable to follow. We returned to camp with a mixture of disappointment and excitement and planned to try and locate the lions the following day. Palmer advised us to leave camp later in the morning and try to pick up fresh tracks on the far side of the Matlhabanelo molapo, suggesting it was a waste of time to set out at dawn. He discussed with

Mmusi how we could get across the water by going north where we could find a deep but negotiable sandy crossing.

After breakfast the next day we drove out and followed the molapo upstream to find the crossing. The water splashed over the bonnet as we followed the line Mmusi showed us through the narrow river. The trick is to keep moving steadily, creating a bow wave and not allowing the water to back up into the engine compartment. Loosening the fan belt prevents damage to the radiator. Once on the other side, we headed south. We drove for almost an hour without seeing any signs of the lions except yesterday's tracks; there were no fresh buffalo signs either. We had lunch under a large jackalberry tree, grateful for the shade, and I called the office on the HF radio to report our progress (or lack of it). Advice was forthcoming from Dougie Wright and Tony Henley, who were hunting in the other end of the concession, some thirty-odd miles away. Tony reckoned he knew the lion we were looking for from an earlier safari and he'd been unsuccessful then. We spent the afternoon driving slowly around the area but saw no more signs.

The next day, our third in pursuit of this particular cat, we picked up fresh tracks at about noon, quite close to where we had sighted the male two days earlier. This time he seemed to be moving alone. We left the car and, with Mmusi and the other tracker in the lead, Joe and I followed the lion's trail. It was easy following the big pug marks in the sand and we continued parallel to the molapo for about a quarter of a mile before turning into the woodland and following more slowly under tall acacias and around thickets of bushes, picking up the spoor again on the far side. We followed in single file and in silence for about two hours until we came out abruptly on the bank of the river again and saw the lion on the other bank, looking back at us before disappearing again into the woodland. He was indeed a very fine specimen, but seemed well aware of our intentions. Mmusi thought we would be wasting our time to follow him further and we turned back a little crestfallen to walk back to where we'd left the hunting car.

On the fourth day we had almost given up hope of success and were now in the final week of the safari, so I was feeling a little pressure. We knew the lion was still likely to be in the area, but were beginning to think he was playing games with us. Just before midday again we found tracks of several lions on the road, not far from camp. It had to be the same pride, but Mmusi could not confirm that the big male was with them. The spoor was from early morning, at least five hours old. The four of us left the vehicle and began following on foot, with Mmusi in front as usual. We walked for over two hours, mostly through deep sand and fairly dense Kalahari apple bush; Mmusi signalled that we should be extra quiet and vigilant, moving forward slowly through the thick bush and trying hard not to step on any dry twigs or crispy leaves.

Shortly afterwards, he signalled for me to move up a few steps and join him. He pointed out the shape of a lion lying in the shade about thirty yards in front, its flanks moving up and down as it breathed, but showing no sign of a mane. I shrugged questioningly and Mmusi pointed out three more lions, of which I could only make out various body parts. He whispered that he thought there was a big male lying on the far side of the group, maybe forty yards from us. I looked carefully for some time through my small pocket binoculars and finally agreed with him. The bush was quite thick and we needed to get a better look. The only movements from the lions we could see were the odd ear twitches and flicks of a tail to drive away flies. There was no apparent sign of a kill. Mmusi led me, with Joe following silently, in a crouch to the right until we could see the male clearly. He was definitely the one we were after. Mmusi silently set up the shooting sticks, a makeshift tripod of small branches, on which to rest the muzzle of Joe's rifle.

Feeling very nervous, I instructed Joe to fire at the chest, halfway down and just behind the front leg.

Joe whispered, "I can't shoot him while he's asleep!"

To which I replied sharply that I wasn't going to kick him awake. Joe fired and all hell broke loose. There were lions grunting and running in all directions, all around us, several we hadn't seen that were even closer to us. The male jumped and spun around to make off, but before Joe or I could shoot again he fell in the sand growling and quickly lay still. Silence ensued and Mmusi told Joe to shoot at the lion again to make sure he was dead. The second bullet had no effect and hadn't been needed. We approached, still cautious and I had my rifle ready. The lion was a huge male with a full, red-blond mane. The trackers were ecstatic, pumping Joe's hand and slapping him on the back. He seemed almost in shock and spent a couple of minutes quietly examining his prize before putting his gun down and taking out his camera to record the moment. My own excitement quickly subsided and I felt strangely sad.

I took part in two big safaris with Harry Selby, the most internationally famous hunter of his day. On one trip out of Splash Camp on the Khwai River I had been told that the clients were an American ranching family from Montana, husband and wife and two sons, aged about seventeen and twelve.

Mom and Dad had hunted several times before and were escorted by Harry (along with the younger boy as an observer only). I had to look after the older boy and occasionally Mom would come with us.

This boy was the best shot I ever saw, but he didn't seem to be even slightly interested in the safari, or his surroundings, and spent his whole day reading paperbacks. None of the family wanted to shoot an elephant, but otherwise a full package, including lion and buffalo had been booked for him. We would drive around every day with him reading in the front of the car. Whenever a respectable trophy animal was spotted by the trackers he would put down his book, pick up his rifle and we would stalk the required distance from the vehicle, whereupon he would shoot the animal through the neck, killing it instantly, and then walk back to the car and pick up his book again. The only two hunts that differed were a buffalo, for which he stalked about 400 yards, and a leopard that streaked out of the bush over 100 metres in front of us heading for a reedbed. He raised his rifle and killed it with a bullet through the neck. It would have been a fluke for almost anyone else. The trackers at first thought he'd shot a cheetah, but it was the largest male leopard shot for years. The skin in the trophy shed was viewed with disbelief by safaris that followed us into Splash.

The food in camp was delicious, as usual, especially the soups, which got better as they "matured", with new ingredients added daily to the stock pot. However, the younger boy was very fussy and was loath to try anything different. One evening, I remonstrated light-heartedly with him, telling him the homemade camp soup was great, "much better than any of that rubbish in tins." There was an awkward silence, but it quickly passed and the meal and chatter resumed. Early the following morning, as I was preparing the hunting car to leave camp, Mom approached me and asked what I had meant by my comment at supper about tinned soup. Slightly bewildered, I said that I had merely been trying to get her son to eat. She then declared, "You do know that we own Campbell's Soup, don't you?" Their name certainly wasn't Campbell and the office had told me that they were cattle ranchers, apparently because they wanted some privacy – and they probably did own a ranch in Montana anyway.

On another safari I excelled myself by getting the Land Cruiser stuck in the middle of an inundated floodplain in the dark. My clients were an American man and wife who badly wanted to shoot a big buffalo and we had been delayed far from camp. The vehicle was well and truly stuck and despite our best efforts was not going to come out without help. The water was almost waist deep and the bottom was muddy. There was nothing for it, we had to disembark and wade about 300 yards to a small island with nothing but *Hyphaene* palms and prickly *Sporobolus* grass.

The Americans were very nervous and wouldn't let me leave them, so Mmusi and his assistant had to make several trips to the car for camp chairs and the lunchbox (which had a few leftovers in it). I managed to get a fire of sorts lit and had to build it up with palm fronds because the island was completely devoid of wood. The two wet, cold clients sat in the chairs, as close to the fire as possible, while the three of us collected palm fronds throughout the very long night. They blazed brightly, if only for a very short time. We had to keep the fire bright to reassure the clients that they wouldn't fall prey to some marauding animal. I nodded off in the sand a couple of times, only to be awakened by the lady when she heard a distant hyaena. In the dawn light we managed to find some wood on a nearby island and improved the fire. I waded to the vehicle at 7.30 am to radio the office in Maun and thankfully Soren Lindstrom was also on the radio at camp, so he and his staff came out to us. When they found us we jacked up the vehicle, winched it out of the hole and managed to get back to camp by late morning for a welcome hot shower and brunch. Clients paying thousands of dollars a day did not expect to have to put up with such discomforts, but the whingeing gradually abated over the remaining days of the safari, especially after they obtained an impressive buffalo trophy. But I did hear later from Ryland that before they left there had been discussions about a discount at the office.

The "old hands" like Selby and Palmer seemed to be blessed with good fortune and never seemed to struggle like me. Perhaps the old adage "the more I practise, the luckier I get" holds true in any endeavour. On one safari Palmer and I were sharing a tent and we each needed to get a leopard. He heard me getting up before daylight and enquired why.

"Relax, go out after breakfast, the damn cat won't be going anywhere," was his drowsily growled advice. I left anyway and spent the morning scouring many square miles of territory looking for leopard tracks. Eating lunch with the client in the shade of a mangosteen tree I called camp on the radio schedule.

"61 – 66; 61 – 66 come in!"

Palmer's gravelly voice answered "66 – 61; reading you 5. How're you doing?"

I described my fruitless morning briefly then added "And you?"

"Got a big pussy cat near the airstrip about ten o'clock. We're partying back at camp."

I was sceptical – Palmer had a sense of humour. But when we returned to camp empty-handed around 5 pm Palmer's very happy and merry client took us to the trophy shed to see his leopard, a big, old male. They had left camp after a leisurely breakfast and found the cat resting in a large sausage tree about fifteen minutes later!

On another safari Harry Selby's client shot a large elephant and they returned to camp celebrating. On returning to the carcass the next day they came across an impressive male lion feeding on it – two for the price of one!

From my observations and experience safari clients are a thoroughly misunderstood and unfairly demonised lot. Character assassination of hunters and criticism of the incentive and attraction of hunting is usually unjustified. They obviously vary enormously, but most of them have certain things in common. First they have to be rich and consequently they are usually spoiled and used to getting their own way, after all most are, or have been, very successful business people. Maybe this creates some resentment, rather like the English fox-hunters who are mainly vilified for seeming to be "toffs". Most are not unpleasant though and they can be lively and entertaining company. Second, they do not appear to have a blood lust, as many opponents of hunting claim. Nor do most of them just want to prove their virility, after all shooting an impala or steenbok can hardly be called dangerous. The majority can best be described as collectors and want some mementoes of an exotic adventure, and the many returning clients seem to just want to "chill" in a conducive environment, content to shoot very little.

While many clients, especially older Americans, will happily settle for an easy hunt with as little exertion as possible, others relish the hard work and risk that can be required in pursuit of the quarry. Sure, it rarely needs heroic courage or exceptional skill because the guide and trackers look after the client's safety – but this is not a bullet-proof guarantee and anyone who claims it is not thrilling to stalk dangerous game like lion and buffalo on foot has simply never done it. There are undoubtedly elements of competition and boasting involved, trophy size for example, but that can only be expected of the majority of successful alpha-male clients and is hardly grounds for fanatical opposition.

THIRTEEN

CAPITAL GROWTH

Meanwhile, work at the clinic in Gabs carried on, mainly dogs, with a bias towards large breeds, reflecting their role as guard dogs. There were also large numbers of Maltese terriers (Maltese poodles in the UK), little, white, fluffy things that seemed to live forever. I spent many hours suturing them back into shape after they had been savaged by bigger dogs – maybe mistaken for rabbits – but they always seemed to survive and go on until they were around fifteen years old. Other popular breeds were Staffordshire bull terriers – "great with kids" but death to anything on four legs – and basset hounds, a breed designed by a drunken committee. One of my best friends, a pilot called Mark Sampson, had a basset called Randy who used to sit on the front of his windsurfer with his long ears streaming. Mark represented Botswana in the Goodwill Games in Russia, but Randy didn't quite make the team.

There were exceptional cases, like the eighteen-foot python that was brought in by soldiers from the Botswana Defence Force. It had been caught in a noose and badly wounded with a panga by an irate farmer after raiding his chickens. The lead soldier, a corporal, walked into the waiting room holding tightly to the huge head, followed by five other soldiers, stationed at intervals along the rest of the snake. Luckily, the room was empty or there would have been chaos. As it was, Florence, the receptionist, made herself scarce and my lay assistants also disappeared. I had no idea how to anaesthetise the beast but, with the soldiers holding on tight, we managed to clean and stitch the wounds and apply antiseptic powder. They took it back to their base in Mogoditshane, where they had a snake collection, and it healed well.

Gabs was growing fast, expanding westwards and north by acquiring farms on the perimeter of the old town. Andy Saunders' farm, Bonnington, towards Mogoditshane, was bought and developed as new suburbs, and in the north, Broadhurst farm became another large new suburb. It was claimed that the City, declared in 1986, was the fastest growing population centre in the southern hemisphere and it was exciting to be a part of it. Admittedly it had started small – merely 4,000 people in 1964. Central Gaborone had new shopping centres and the Mall, next to the new government enclave, was upgraded with many new stores, mainly branches of South African retail chains. The Mall also became a pedestrian precinct, full of small hawkers' stalls down the centre. This led to the creation of a one-way traffic system around it in a clockwise direction.

There was more and more traffic and inevitably controls had to be introduced. Traffic lights, or robots as they are called throughout Southern Africa, were unknown in Botswana before 1984, when the Gaborone Town Council decided to introduce them at the road junctions on the four corners of the Mall. For weeks beforehand the authorities mounted an intensive education campaign aimed at motorists and pedestrians, explaining how these new devices would function. Radio programmes, posters and even policemen dressed as traffic lights were employed to get the message across. It was eventually announced that the new system would be turned on at 6.00 am on a Monday morning in April. Traffic builds up early in Gabs because schools and government offices start at 7.00 am or shortly after. The first collision came at about 6.15 am outside the Anglican church, a driver turning right on a green light into the path of an oncoming vehicle. No one was hurt, but the ensuing chaos following accidents at each of the four junctions provided more entertainment than the capital had ever seen. The staff from the clinic could not be restrained and rushed out to watch. Crowds gathered on the four street corners where the new lights had been installed. Many drivers had come in from rural areas and had not experienced traffic lights before; they had not understood that turning right on a green signal was dangerous if a car was coming from the opposite direction. For hours there were the sounds of brakes screeching, followed by a bang and loud cheers from the assembled spectators.

1984 also saw the opening of the town's first "pub" – The Bull and Bush. This was a resounding success and major boost to all our social lives. The proprietors were three strangely assorted individuals: Peter Collins, Irwin Tellis and Charlie Sheldon; lawyer, chartered accountant and property developer respectively.

Charlie was the best-known, larger than life, character in the town, if not the country, and stories abound. Many may be at least partly apocryphal – no one could have survived them all, but most are true and Charlie's exploits and longevity belie his dedication to alcoholic and other chemical recreation. My favourites relate to his many adventures as an unorthodox pilot. One morning, at the old Gabs airport, hungover as usual, he taxied several hundred yards to the threshold of runway 08 and asked for take-off clearance. The controller knew him well and asked "Charlie, have you performed a pre-flight check?"

"Yes sir."

"Well please get out of your aircraft and walk around it again."

Charlie did as requested to discover he had taxied all the way with a "tie-down", a heavy drum of concrete, still attached to the tail of his plane!

In October 1979, a world boxing championship bout took place at Loftus Versfeld, the rugby stadium in Pretoria. Gerrie Coetzee, the local champion was up against Big John Tate from America. Quite a few groups of Botswana fans made the journey. Five farmers from Ghanzi decided to fly down to South Africa with Charlie as their pilot. Almost before they were airborne from Ghanzi a bottle of Johnny Walker whisky was produced and passed around. It didn't last long. On crossing the border into South African airspace the air traffic controller in Johannesburg asked the routine question:

"Please state your point of origin, present position and destination," which elicited the response,

"Ag well, we're coming from Ghanzi, eh, we're not sure where we are now, but we're going to the boxing."

Also memorable from Gabs of the mid-1980s were the two raids by the South African Defence Force to eliminate cells of Umkhonto we Sizwe, the military wing of the ANC. The first one took place mainly in central Gabs and we were awakened by explosions about 2 am. Several houses, some used as offices, were damaged and Gabs residents were warned by megaphone to stay indoors and not get involved. Several people, mainly South Africans, were reported killed. The second one was airborne and apparently focused on keeping the Botswana Defence Force confined to their Mogoditsane barracks while a small number of plain-clothes troops attacked targets in town. Even though it was a "front line state" against the apartheid regime, Botswana had tactfully avoided any hostilities and was unused to such reprisals, which caused much consternation at the time.

There was a "lion park" just south of Gabs, on the Lobatse road. It didn't really amount to much, but the owner, Jimmy Kannemeyer, a former government auditor, tried for years to make it a success. There were half a dozen lions and the best-looking one was a totally blind, large male. The enclosures were fairly small, untidy and contained by rather poor quality, wire-mesh fencing. There were occasional escapes and my dart gun came in handy. Like lions nearly everywhere, they were fairly prolific and Jimmy used to sell most of the progeny to South Africa. One of the younger males developed a limp in its hind leg and Jimmy called me to investigate. I suspected that a mineral deficiency from feeding a meat-rich diet, without any calcium or phosphorus supplementation, had resulted in weak bones and a fracture of some kind. I darted the cat with Sernylan, our drug of choice in those days. Its chemical name was phencyclidine, and it acquired notoriety as Angel Dust, a popular recreational drug that produced hallucinations, sometimes with a fatal outcome when the user thought he or she could fly. It was subsequently banned and became unavailable, even to vets.

We loaded the lion into the back of my Hilux pick-up, drove the few miles back into town and carried it into a consulting room at the clinic. The room was quite small, but it was crowded with curious onlookers. I was manipulating the lion's limbs when, without any warning, the beast raised its head from the table and grunted loudly (roar would have been an exaggeration). In a split second I was the only person left in the room. There was only one door, but at least a dozen people had got through it in a flash. The lion then lowered its head again, its hallucination over, and continued to be completely tractable, but it took some persuasion to get my staff back to assist. An X-ray confirmed my theory and we persuaded Jimmy to offer the cats whole chickens and animal entrails as well as the donkey meat he used as a staple diet. The fracture in that particular animal's thigh was of the greenstick variety, which required no other treatment besides a sustained, increased mineral intake.

Another occasion when I used Sernylan on lions was in unusual circumstances. One Saturday morning a lady burst into the clinic and implored me to go at once to the National Showgrounds, where two lions were in great distress. The annual Agricultural Show was in full swing and there was a host of exhibits. A couple of Afrikaner brothers who farmed in Ghanzi, the de Graafs, had somehow caught two subadult male lions that had allegedly been killing their cattle and had managed to put homemade leather collars on them. They had then fastened them together and put them on the back of a Wildlife Department pick-up, chaining them to the rails. The poor animals had then been driven 500 miles across the Kalahari to be put on show. When I got there a small crowd of mostly young people were crowding around the vehicle, very excited at their first sight of lions. It looked as if one of the lions was already dead and its companion was in a frenzy, much to the noisy delight of the crowd. With my assistant, Edward, we managed to clear a way through and I squirted some Sernylan into the mouth of the snarling lion. It began licking its lips and was quite quickly sedated and lay down next to its companion. We then climbed on the truck, released the animal and transferred it to my own Hilux. I confirmed that the second lion had indeed died, in dreadful circumstances.

We drove the survivor away from the crowd and took it to Jimmy's lion park, where we dressed its wounds, injected some long-acting antibiotic and multivitamins and waited until it came round. Several of us complained to the Wildlife Department about the cruel treatment meted out to the animals, but nothing ever came of it. A year or two later the same brothers were involved in an infamous hunting safari with the famous heart surgeon Chris Barnard, where lions were shot in appalling circumstances. Despite media involvement and a court case the perpetrators escaped suitable punishment, although Barnard was at least declared *persona non grata* in Botswana. It's always been a source of despondency for me that people like these bring hunting into such disrepute and cause incalculable harm to the safari industry, making it extremely difficult to endorse what is a really valuable form of conservation.

The mid-1980s in Gaborone saw the advent of parvovirus, a distressing and deadly gastroenteritis that struck mainly puppies, but also older dogs and especially certain breeds such as the popular Rottweiler. Repeated vaccination of puppies at an early age provided some immunity, but it was expensive and out of the reach of many Batswana dog owners. The mortality rate in infected animals was over eighty per cent and the disease became firmly entrenched in the canine community. We saw so much of it that we were able to diagnose the illness by sense of smell. The bloody diarrhoea was unmistakable and we struggled to keep our premises clean and free of disease. Lots of cleaning with chlorine disinfectants helped and we were able to pull through some of the sick animals by keeping them on intravenous fluids and other supportive treatment, although most didn't make it.

The cost of parvovirus treatment was a major problem for many local dog owners and we became almost a charity organisation, with payments being made almost exclusively by expatriate clients. One exception was Charles Tibone, a prominent and well-connected government minister. He had pedigree Alsatian dogs that were well cared for. He bought an expensive new puppy from South Africa that had received its first vaccination, but became sick a few weeks later. It was obviously parvo and we admitted the pup and spared no effort in trying to keep it alive. There were several other dogs in our ward at the time and one of them was an almost identical Alsatian pup belonging to an expatriate. Unfortunately, one of the pups died and David, my accident-prone assistant, called Charles and gave him the bad news. A couple of days later the other owner duly collected the survivor, but after a day or so called me and asked if the illness might have changed the dog's personality; it wasn't very friendly and behaved differently. I realised at once what must have happened and asked him to bring the pup into the surgery. I also called Charles and asked him to come at the same time. Charles arrived with his small identical twin sons and when the surviving pup saw them it greeted them with great tail-wagging excitement. It was a potentially awkward situation, but luckily Charles and the other owner accepted it as a genuine mistake. Mistake or not, it should never have happened and was another of David's "last straws".

Andrew, a fairly new veterinary graduate from Cambridge took David's place. Tall, athletic and good-looking, he seemed to fit in well at first. He was a little slow at surgery and the nursing staff found that odd, complaining that they could do better themselves, especially after he requested two assistants to spay a bitch. I reasoned that he could only get better with experience and practice; everyone has to start somewhere. It was outside the surgery where things began to happen that made me question my latest choice of recruit.

Andrew joined the local rugby club where his enthusiasm was remarkable but somewhat exceeded his skill level. At first this was viewed with mild amusement by the rugby club stalwarts, many of whom were more inclined to excel in the bar than on the field. A little while later I began to hear stories of "Psychovet"; apparently Andrew's play had become even more aggressive, with the odd excessive reaction. He also began dating a young Canadian aid worker and this relationship seemed to follow the same pattern. He went to extremes, such as completely filling her apartment with flowers while she was away and putting up welcome banners at the airport on her return. Clearly this was over the top and the poor woman had to resort to acquiring a restraining order from the court. After a few months, as more and more outlandish behaviour traits became apparent, this troubled young man handed me his resignation and disappeared to Australia.

An English couple in late middle age brought their ancient cat to the clinic more and more frequently. They obviously doted on the animal and as it became more infirm they spent immense amounts of time and money on looking after it. They would not listen to my recommendations, bordering on pleas, to have it put to sleep. Among other ailments, the cat suffered from chronic kidney failure and during severe episodes it needed to have copious amounts of intravenous fluids, as a poor substitute for dialysis. These drips, together with multivitamins and a low protein diet, somehow kept it going. When it reached the age of twenty-five (almost unheard of in cats) there was a cake and birthday cards, and an announcement in the local press thanking our clinic for our ministrations! By now the couple were devoting their lives almost completely to caring for the cat. The husband would sit up with it from midnight until he went to work at 7.00 am, when the wife would take over. At four he would come home and look after the cat until six so that his wife could get out for some shopping and then he would go to bed until midnight. They never went away on holiday or had any other kind of break – it was crazy.

I had given standing orders to my assistants that, since the old folk wouldn't listen to me, they should somehow persuade the couple to have the cat put down on their next visit to the clinic. Eventually, the day came when the animal was brought in suffering another kidney failure episode. I was away for the morning, but Andrew somehow convinced the couple to let him put the old cat to sleep. They went away broken-hearted, but reassured that they had done the best thing. I returned to the clinic just before lunch to be told the news and I was delighted. After lunch, still happy with the news, I had to visit the golf club, which had a problem with large numbers of stray cats and we were baiting cages and catching them for euthanasia. The club's manageress, Anne Simpkins, greeted me from a table she was sharing with another woman who had her back to me. I replied breezily that "it was a good day for killing cats." I have never felt so terrible, ever, as when the lady at the table turned around and I recognised her tearful face.

FOURTEEN

CATCHING TO CONSERVE

A good friend of mine, Gavin Richards, was a partner in a fairly successful building company in Gabs called Wharic Construction. His partner, a huge rugby prop, Keith Whatley, supplied the "Wha", Gavin the "Ric". Gavin was also a colossal man, close to six and a half feet tall. He had married Vicky, one of the Vickerman family, who were prominent cattle farmers in Ghanzi. The Vickerman brothers, Henry and Theuns, had married identical twin sisters called Ada and Ivy, and had built up an empire of cattle ranches, almost a quarter of a million acres in extent in a single block of land. They all lived together in a single, large house in the middle of their ranch, rather like Southfork in *Dallas*. Their beef operation was probably the finest in the country and I occasionally visited the ranch to pregnancy-test cows or fertility-test bulls.

In the late 1980s Gavin began to spend more time in Ghanzi. As an Englishman in a very Afrikaans community, he was rather like the proverbial fish out of water and he speculated on how he might get more involved. He knew next to nothing about cattle farming, but he was a great ideas man. He persuaded the family to divide part of their land and create a game ranch. There was a great deal of wildlife on the ranch anyway, and they decided that about 75,000 acres should be fenced off with an eight-foot-high game-proof fence and that the internal paddock fences should be removed. With this agreed, it was only necessary to add to the existing stock of wild animals. Being a successful ideas man requires enhanced skills of persuasion and delegation, and Gavin excelled in both.

He didn't know anything about animals, but I did. So in 1988 he and I formed a company called Kalahari Game Services (KGS), to capture wild animals and stock the new game ranch, now called Kanana (Setswana for paradise). We would also supply other wildlife ranching pioneers, of which there were half a dozen at most in the country. Game ranching was taking off in South Africa, Namibia and Zimbabwe and Gavin was convinced it had a bright future in Botswana. The government was happy to issue permits for live capture of animals in parallel to the quotas issued for hunting in the controlled hunting areas into which the whole country was divided. Fees were payable, but other than that there were few rules.

Hardly anyone had tried to capture large numbers of wild animals before; a few museum collectors had supplied the odd individual for export, but no one, apart from a company exporting birds, had caught animals on a commercial scale. We didn't know how to go about it and didn't possess any of the necessary equipment. But no problem… in the days before cell phones and the Internet, Gavin soon got in touch with a Zimbabwean, Speedy Holden, who apparently operated four game-capture teams with great success. Very soon Gavin and I, accompanied by his father-in-law Henry, were in Zimbabwe discussing partnerships and mutually beneficial arrangements with Speedy and his business partners. Only some of them though, because Speedy had more businesses than we could imagine. He was a human dynamo and the greatest huckster I have ever met, having survived and thrived under the successive antagonistic governments of Ian Smith and Robert Mugabe. He had been an active sanctions buster under the former regime and had morphed into one of the country's most successful entrepreneurs under the latter. By recruiting experienced former National Parks staff he had created a very successful wildlife management business. He habitually rose very early, and once in my house at 4.00 am I heard him negotiating with a Mexican company (on my telephone!) to buy a machine that could imprint an elephant-skin pattern on hippo hide. He later explained that he had a contract to cull a large number of hippos, but no buyers for the skin. Gavin was an early riser too and they soon had an agreement whereby we owned a small stake in Speedy's white-water rafting business at Victoria Falls and he had a share of KGS. As a start and a gesture of good faith he dispatched one of his capture teams to us in the Kalahari to show us how it was done.

Clem Coetsee was a true legend in conservation circles, the most dedicated wildlife man I ever knew, but he had found acute disfavour with the "cocktail conservationists" from Kenya, who condemned him for having taken part in the culling of elephants in Hwange National Park, part of the Zimbabwe Government's conservation programme. It is true that he killed a lot of elephants with frightening efficiency, but, although controversial, it was part of an approved policy that had received the backing of most leading wildlife scientists in southern Africa and was also taking place in Kruger National Park. The flip side was he also spent countless nights awake, nursing young elephants and other animals back to health, as well as many years pursuing poachers under extremely harsh and hazardous conditions, something the champagne set would not be able to imagine. He arrived in Francistown one midday in early July with a team of a dozen bush-hardened Matabele labourers in an old 4x4 truck and two Land Rovers that had seen better days. His right-hand man was Doug Evans, another National Parks veteran, younger and powerfully built.

Our crew of motley farm labourers and a few curious, "social" assistants were waiting on the Boteti River, near Motopi, some 200 miles up the Maun road. The first section, as far as Nata, had recently been tarred, but from there it was still fairly rough dirt or gravel across the northern edge of the Makgadikgadi Pans and we arrived in camp in the early evening. The Zimbabweans had brought a heavy-duty crush that Clem had built as an almost exact replica of the one he used back home. It consisted of welded, steel-framed sections, ten feet high and fifteen feet long, which were clad with mine conveyor belting. Explaining these and all his other equipment to the Botswana Customs had caused some delay. Each panel could be lifted by two men, just, but it took four to manipulate them and assemble the crush. They formed a passageway about a yard wide and twenty yards long, which culminated in an even heavier loading ramp. It had been designed to cope with buffalo and obviously wasn't going to wear out any time soon.

Early the next morning, which for Clem was well before daylight, we were roused unceremoniously from our bedrolls in the cold and managed only a quick mug of coffee before leaving camp. We were going to try to catch zebra for delivery to Ghanzi and we were all very excited, anticipating the task ahead.

First we had to select a site for the capture boma. The loading ramp and crush obviously had to be accessible, preferably on a road or track. The boma's wide mouth had to be upwind of the crush so that the zebra would not scent it or hear anything as they approached. Equally, they must not be able to see it or the helicopter would never be able to herd them into it. These basic requirements, common to all capture bomas, are not always easy to fulfil; the triangular or cone-shaped boma can be 500 yards long with a 300-yard wide mouth, and at eight or more feet high is pretty hard to hide. We had bought a number of long, ten-foot wide rolls of plastic curtains for the walls that we had cut into useable lengths of thirty and fifty yards.

With Clem's guidance we quite quickly found a suitable site and his staff commenced to cut the lines through the bush for the cables and support poles. Others were employed erecting the crush and loading ramp. Our men watched fascinated and helped where they could by carrying folded curtains and other items when they were needed. The whole boma, with three or four cross-curtains, utilised almost half a mile of the black, woven, plastic curtains. I think our inexperienced labourers were actually more fascinated by the Matabele men who did everything on the double, while singing or chanting. They scoffed at our men wanting a tea-break and a cooked lunch while they merely drank water and ate boiled *kapenta* – small, dried, freshwater sardines from Lake Kariba, that they had brought in large plastic sacks, another puzzle for the Botswana Customs staff. After a long hard day Clem declared the boma ready just before dark, but not before we had tested the boma curtains by running at top speed, pulling them closed a couple of times. Then everyone returned to camp for a well-earned meal, a few beers – except for Clem who didn't drink – and an early bed.

Again, reveille was before daylight and our coffee was drunk a little more slowly while we discussed how the day's work should pan out. People were allocated stations where they would hide until the signal for them to run as fast as they could, pulling the cross-curtains to close the boma sections. The fastest were posted on the longest curtains at the boma mouth and the bravest down at the narrow business end where they might come face to face with the zebras.

When the light was good enough the helicopter took off, with Clem, to find some zebras. There were hundreds fairly close to the river at that time of year because the water in the pans further east had dried up. We made our way to the boma and took up our positions. I was with Doug, supervising the crush and the loading ramp. There were three sliding doors dividing the crush into compartments. They were painted successively green, orange and blue and needed to be operated swiftly to separate animals into manageable groups as they came into the crush. A modified cattle truck from Ghanzi was stationed at the top of the loading ramp with the driver and an assistant ready to close its rear doors on command.

Everyone waited eagerly. After a short while the handheld radio crackled; they had found some zebras and were herding them towards the boma. ETA was approximately ten minutes away. The stations were quickly inspected again to make sure the runners and curtains were well hidden, then everyone waited silently. The helicopter was soon heard, with the characteristic clatter of blades as it swooped and circled, keeping the zebras moving towards us. Next we could hear the alarmed "barking" of a few of the animals as they tried to avoid the helicopter. When they were quite close we could clearly hear the animals running through the bush and make out the helicopter above a cloud of dust. Clem was hanging out of the passenger side and signalled, by firing his revolver, for the first curtains to be closed. Shortly after, he fired again to close the second curtain and then again at the third. Now the noise and dust caused by the chopper and the animals created pandemonium. Far more animals than expected careened into the last section of the boma. They stampeded on into the crush and piled up against the closed blue door at the foot of the loading ramp, with those following making it impossible to close any of the sliding doors. Total, terrifying chaos!

How the crush walls held I'll never know, a tribute to Clem's welding skills, but there were so many zebras charging in that they quickly started to come over the sides by clambering on the lead animals. They must have been four or five deep in the front section of the crush. Most of the men ran for their lives and it was a miracle that no one was seriously hurt or killed. Literally dozens of zebras went over our heads as we cowered next to the crush walls praying that it wouldn't burst. Eventually things calmed down a little and Doug climbed up the crush and began trying to move back some of the top layers of zebra to release those trapped below, which were in serious danger of being crushed and suffocated. A few of us followed his lead and, armed with cattle prodders, we managed to get most of the top zebras back out of the crush towards the boma where a gaping hole torn in the plastic sheeting allowed them to escape. Although many animals appeared shocked and traumatised, there were almost no obvious physical injuries as they regained their feet and separated.

Only three zebras, trapped at the bottom by the blue door, had died of asphyxiation – but it could have been much worse. Later we estimated that over 200 zebras had been through the boma. Obviously the *modus operandi* had to change to ensure that many fewer animals were chased into the boma, preferably at a slower pace. Zebras live in family groups averaging eight up to twelve or so, whatever the dominant stallion can control. The migration from the pans to the Boteti River brought together hundreds of such groups in huge aggregations and it would be up to the helicopter pilot to try to separate a manageable number for each capture. Mixing families was problematic, especially if more than one stallion was involved. They would fight and also attack females and young foals that they did not recognise as their own. A dominant stallion would grab a foal by the neck, shaking it like a dog with a rat. In due course we managed to catch several truckloads of animals and keep them mostly in their family groups. They were dispatched to three or four Ghanzi farms and a couple in Tuli Block, where they settled successfully and seeded significant new populations in regions where no zebras had occurred for over 100 years.

From the Boteti River we moved to the southern Kalahari and caught a number of blue wildebeest, red hartebeest and eland, which were sent to game farms in Ghanzi, and, in the case of the latter two species, to Tuli Block in the Limpopo Valley. Clem and his Matebele stayed with us for three weeks in the freezing Kalahari, until he decided that we could probably cope by ourselves, albeit with a steep learning curve ahead of us. He left us with the crush and loading ramp, which are still in use thirty years later. KGS bought a couple of old Bedford 4x4 J-series trucks, some more plastic sheeting and cables and continued through the rest of the winter of 1988 and the following year. Unfortunately, the number of game farmers investing in new stock was limited to a few in Ghanzi and two or three in Tuli Block. Most of these had significant existing wildlife numbers anyway and after two seasons most of the capture work dried up. The game ranching industry in Botswana was stalled almost before it began, even though it was rapidly expanding in neighbouring countries.

Our salvation, if merely temporary, was ostriches. Around the world ostrich meat was in demand. Lots of hype about health-giving properties and low cholesterol fuelled the growth of ostrich farms. These had long been out of fashion, since the early twentieth-century craze for feathers. Even the South African industry, once booming, was just a relic in the Karoo, reliant on tourists and ostrich races. When we were asked if we could catch ostriches to provide breeding stock on Botswana farms we replied, "Of course!"

There were lots of wild ostriches in the Kalahari and the government had always issued permits for the collection of eggs and the capture of a limited number of live birds, usually chicks. Driven by demand and the prospect of exports, they increased the capture quota in most areas and the permits were quickly acquired by a number of prospective farmers. We modified the boma capture method to deal with ostriches, the main problems being their extraordinary eyesight and their preference for open country. But they weren't very intelligent and we quite quickly learned to outsmart them. We caught and delivered hundreds of birds all across the country. We had a few casualties at first, usually in the trucks, where they would squash into a corner and occasionally trample on the neck of a companion, but we managed to solve the problem by closing off the corners with bales of straw and loading fewer birds in each compartment.

We did have one major emergency, when a full load was almost lost on the Makgadikgadi Pans. A very large rig, driven by Piet Lewis (pronounced Leveece), a Ghanzi farmer, was filled and dispatched to Tuli Block on an overnight journey. There were over 100 birds, mostly fully adult, in the two trailers pulled behind a powerful Mercedes "horse". They had been caught on the edge of Ntwetwe Pan, near where we were camped by a sweetwater spring. Piet left in the late afternoon and was escorted by Gavin and me in my Land Cruiser along the way northeast to Zoroga village, where we hoped we could replenish the camp's beer stocks. Piet was ahead of us, following the narrow track across the salty, dry grassland. He was an extremely competent driver and very capable in sandy conditions where many others struggled. After about half an hour he stopped at the edge of the salt pan. He said he thought he could save over an hour by crossing the pan surface to the next grassland, about two miles away, rather than following the edge all round. It seemed quite dry and firm and Piet had already reduced the pressure in his tyres to improve his traction and provide a greater surface area for contact with the sand. Gavin and I had a few misgivings, but agreed and duly followed him onto the pan's white surface.

He made good speed across the firm, flat surface and I began to relax. I was watching the spoor his rig was making on the salt surface and suddenly noticed that it was becoming more evident – slightly deeper. I pulled out, accelerated and caught up abreast of Piet's cab. Shouting, I told him what I'd seen.

"Ja, it's a little harder going here, but I'm OK," he replied.

I took up my position behind him again. The spoor was now getting deeper and Piet was slowing considerably as he engaged lower gears to pull harder. The tracks were now seriously deep and even though I could see "land" about half a mile ahead I knew he wasn't going to make it. When he was just crawling and the engine was screaming, I drove up alongside again and pleaded with him to stop before he was completely stuck. I knew it would be impossible to dig out the wheels if the rig went down to its axles and diffs. Smaller vehicles had been stuck for days after going through the surface crust on the pans.

Gavin and I drove back to camp, arriving just as the sun sank below the flat horizon. We mustered our complete team with the two 4x4 Bedfords and two other Land Cruisers. Collecting as many spades and shovels as we could find and taking chains and some unused boma cables, we returned across the pan to the Mercedes. It was now dark, but the headlights of the assembled vehicles reflecting off the white salt pan made it easy to work. Gavin took one wing and I the other, harnessing each Bedford some ten yards diagonally in front of the stricken Mercedes. We then hooked up one Land Cruiser in front of one Bedford and two diagonally in front of the other. With all vehicles in four-wheel drive and diff-locks applied we slowly and carefully crawled forward like a gigantic, mechanical dog sled. At the first sign of any wheel sinking we all stopped. One of the Land Cruisers was sent to the nearest "island" to get a load of sand, which was shovelled in front of any suspect wheel. We thought seriously about letting all the ostrich go to lighten the load on the Merc, but decided it wouldn't make a significant difference and would cost us a hell of a lot of money. We inched forward and had made 200 yards, almost halfway, by midnight. It then became a little drier and easier nearer the edge of the salt pan and we finally got onto dry, firm sand just after 2.00 am. From there Piet went on easily by himself and delivered the ostriches in good shape near Martins Drift just before noon. The rest of us returned across the salt to camp, very relieved, and went to bed exhausted.

The 1980s drew to a close and Gaborone Veterinary Clinic became a busy practice that kept three vets employed, although I was away in the bush a fair amount of the time. No one had opened a practice in opposition and after eight years it remained the only private clinic in the country. Eleanor was gradually growing more annoyed with having to field complaints and deal with the everyday dramas of the practice while I was away; after all, she wasn't even a vet. After a trip to the Central Kalahari Game Reserve, I returned to an ultimatum – either stay in town and run the clinic or sell it.

Gaborone had expanded remarkably during the eighties on the back of the diamond mining industry and was hailed as the fastest growing city in the southern hemisphere. My latest assistant, St Clair (Saint) was a sharp, young South African with big ambitions. Extremely competent and energetic, he made it known from the start that he craved financial success and saw huge potential in Botswana. He was more than able to manage the practice in my absence and made a success of it, but he swiftly became dissatisfied with merely managing the business. A partnership was discussed, but things moved too slowly for Saint and when I returned from one consultancy in the Moremi Game Reserve he announced that he was opening his own clinic in Tlokweng, a developing village next to Gabs and in effect a suburb of the capital.

From my point of view the problem was that, although he hadn't said so, I knew he was being backed financially by my biggest cattle client and was therefore taking a significant portion of the business with him. After a short legal skirmish we parted company on less than friendly grounds and he went on to develop his new clinic. This episode made me think seriously about my future; I'd never really committed to domestic animals, after all I'd only gone to vet school as a way into wildlife work, and during the last few years I had been able to spend quite a lot of time on conservation projects. I decided it was time to pursue wildlife conservation as a full-time career. With Saint branching out doing his own thing, I sold Gaborone Veterinary Clinic to Ignatius Ndzingi, a Motswana friend who had qualified in New Zealand and had been in charge of the National Veterinary Laboratory. He had therefore fulfilled his commitment to the government and was keen to try his hand in the private sector. The sale went through almost exactly ten years from when I had first put up my plate in Tlokweng – a significant chapter in my professional life was over.

I kept busy with a number of short-term environmental consultancies in Botswana, writing management plans for wildlife areas and flying surveys, and was eventually approached by IUCN to go to Ghana and head up a project to rehabilitate their national parks, which had suffered through years of political and economic turmoil. I agreed to check out the feasibility of the project and in early 1992 headed off to Accra, my first look at West Africa.

The flight via Harare in Zimbabwe went smoothly, giving no clue to the chaos at the crowded airport in Accra that was my first taste of the frenzy of that part of the continent. I was engulfed in a noisy, and physically daunting, tumult of exotic Africa, completely unlike anything I had experienced in either the eastern or southern regions of the same continent. Everyone, it seemed, wanted a piece of me. Health, immigration and customs officials appeared to play only minor roles in the process of entering the country, I was completely swamped by hordes of competing baggage porters, hotel agents, money changers and taxi drivers. I had no idea where I should be going, other than the name of my hotel, and after a lengthy scrum I ended up in a car I assumed was a taxi and headed downtown.

The Novotel in central Accra seemed fairly well organised when we finally arrived and I was pleasantly surprised to find my booking in order and a completely acceptable room available. The late evening drive from the airport had been an eye-opener, ever busier traffic as we hit the city centre, bright lights, music and crowds of people walking, dancing, eating and drinking at roadside stalls. It was far livelier and more exhilarating than anything I'd ever experienced in any city from Kampala to Cape Town.

I went straight to bed and got up early the following morning to start my exploration of this new and exciting environment. An IUCN driver took me to their small office in town where I met two expatriate staff members who briefed me about conservation in the country, the proposed project and its relationship with the local wildlife authority. The Department of Game and Wildlife seemed to be in a niche somewhere between the Ministry of Forestry and the Ministry of Lands and Mineral Resources. That was the first confusing fact and I quickly realised that things in Ghana were not run the same way as in southern Africa. I was taken to meetings with senior officials of the Department and the Ministry. Everyone was enthusiastically welcoming and hospitable and spoke with great passion about the planned project. I was wined and dined over a couple of days and nights. The lavish generosity and warmth of the Ghanaians seemed far too much and I became a little curious, if not sceptical, as I started to find my feet and started to speak to drivers and other ordinary citizens.

On the third evening I managed to meet up with a couple of acquaintances from Botswana. Joe Gadek was an American sanitary engineer working for USAID with a Tanzanian wife, Mmonye, whom I knew well from her previous employment in the National Veterinary Laboratory in Gaborone, where she was an outstanding microbiologist. They were enjoying a very different spell in Accra after finishing contracts in Botswana a year or so earlier. They were able to fill in a lot of useful detail on how the various ministries and NGOs functioned in the environmental sector. This information was priceless for me to begin to understand the intricacies of the situation I was faced with. It gave me excellent pointers on what questions to ask of whom and what to look out for.

Over the next few days I also began to realise that the IUCN people were somewhat naïve in their enthusiasm to get their project up and running. I was taken to wildlife reserves and forestry projects and even on a luxury cruise on Lake Volta, claimed as the largest reservoir in the world. My earlier doubts gradually firmed up as I met more officials and ordinary Ghanaians. I was able to establish well enough in my own mind that the project as planned could not be satisfactorily carried out. The wildlife officials were very keen to get their hands on the hardware and funds that came with it, but it became obvious that, as a mere wildlife technician, I was not going to get the job done. I reported my observations to IUCN locally and HQ in Switzerland. Their reaction more than confirmed my misgivings; I was obviously not the first candidate that had backed out. They offered a much bigger salary and increased benefits, but I had to refuse their offer and advise them that the project as it stood was a non-starter and needed wholesale revision, with much tighter controls from them.

I had certainly enjoyed my West African experience, with the unforgettable "highlife", in every sense. The colour, music, dress, food and all the rest of Ghanaian culture made my home part of Africa seem drab and dreary by comparison, but at least back home we still had the space and the wildlife. I spent the last evening with the Gadeks, sampling more highlife in downtown Accra. As it was getting dark we took a walk through main streets alive with revellers, even though the only "event" was that the day's work had ended. An unforgettable experience was eating roast fruit bat from a roadside charcoal brazier. The stallholder explained that he shot them out of their roosts in the huge trees that lined the main road.

The next morning I fought my way through the airport's mayhem in the departure direction to board my Air Zimbabwe flight to Harare. I don't know for sure, but it might have been the roast fruit bat that made me sicker than I could ever remember being. I checked into Meikle's excellent hotel in Harare and spent the next eighteen hours between the bed and the bathroom, barely making the Air Botswana flight to Gaborone the following day.

Eleanor met me at the airport with an exciting proposition, and even in my weakened state I could summon up some enthusiasm for it. She had seen an advert for a post with Tanzania National Parks (TANAPA), which she observed "could have been written specially for you". The job was to head a small team to rehabilitate and develop Ruaha National Park, the second largest park in the country, in the relatively remote and neglected southwest. Almost all tourists visited the world-famous Serengeti and Ngorongoro areas in the north, but Ruaha, a spectacular and scientifically fascinating ecosystem, attracted fewer than 200 visitors a year.

The job description certainly appealed: a remote wilderness, vast numbers and variety of wildlife, integration with surrounding safari-hunting areas and communities, my own aeroplane – what more could I want? The British Government was funding the project through their Overseas Development Administration (ODA, a precursor of the current DfID) and interviews were to be held in London the following week. We managed to persuade the ODA to accept my late application and I booked my flight to London for the interview. It signalled the end of almost exactly twenty years of hard work, excitement, frustration and fun in Botswana, fulfilling a dream inspired by black and white television safaris on rainy nights in 1950s Lancashire. Now I wondered, could Tanzania measure up to the Okavango?

FIFTEEN

RUAHA NATIONAL PARK

After a holiday in the USA and some preparations in London we took up residence in Ruaha National Park, Tanzania in September 1992. The British Government was undertaking a major project to rehabilitate and develop the Park, which had been neglected for many years. In the new conservation spirit of the times we were to integrate the Park's management with the surrounding areas and communities. These varied from game reserves used for safari hunting to communal village areas with subsistence farming, as well as a large-scale, ongoing influx of pastoral people from the north, bringing thousands of cattle. I had been recruited to lead the project, known as the Ruaha Ecosystem Wildlife Management Project (REWMP), and been given a crash course in kiSwahili at SOAS in London, followed by a practical course in off-road driving in a Land Rover. After spending the previous twenty years doing just that I thought that the latter might be a waste of time, but who was I to argue with ODA. As it turned out I was able to demonstrate, partially unwittingly, to the instructor how to bog the vehicle and prove that the winch could not extricate it. This entailed my jogging a mile or so to beg a farmer to help us with his tractor – the instructor was too wet, muddy and depressed by then to function at all. It was a Friday afternoon and he was finally reduced to tears when the short-wheel-base "pride of England" slid off the trailer as he negotiated a roundabout on the busy A3 in his Volvo.

Tanzania had just spent the previous three decades under President Julius Nyerere's brand of socialism and his party, CCM (The Party of the Revolution), was still firmly in charge but beginning to liberalise policy in an effort to kick-start the economy. The main policy of enforced villagisation had broken down and large numbers of people were migrating and threatening to overrun protected areas. On the positive side, banks were beginning to function again, the laws against "hoarding" were not enforced and a South African stamp in a passport no longer meant instant deportation. The administration of wildlife and the environment in Tanzania fell under several departments, most of them in the Ministry of Natural Resources and Tourism. Ruaha came under the Tanzania National Parks Authority (TANAPA) based in Arusha, just like the famous Serengeti further north, but although it was just as big and worthy it had received very little attention. The adjoining game reserves, Rungwa and Kizigo, were administered by the Tanzania Department of Wildlife (Game Department) based in Dar es Salaam, but the communal areas were mainly the responsibility of local government departments in Iringa and Mbeya. With no telephones and poor radio communications I would be doing a lot of travelling on very bad roads.

I was happy to concentrate on the Park, at least to begin with, and the first priority was to arrange somewhere to live and then build an office in the park headquarters complex at Msembe. Construction of our accommodation had begun before we arrived, under the supervision of Park Warden Ole Moirana. He must have seen films of English villages and, upon hearing that there would be two staff, had built two semi-detached houses, close to his own rather larger one. Each of ours had three bedrooms, with a lounge, bathroom and kitchen – almost suburban in a rural African way – but perfectly adequate if pretty basic. It was only a matter of a few weeks to complete the building and we could move in. My co-worker had not yet been recruited, but would be a very close neighbour on a wide, gently sloping plain, dotted with baobab trees, overlooking the Great Ruaha River.

Moirana (or Baba Moi as he was universally known) was a Masai and therefore almost as far from home as I was. Unlike the typical Masai warrior of countless images, he was fairly short and overweight, drank lots of beer, smoked heavily, and could never be imagined in a red cloak standing on one leg holding a spear. He was nevertheless an exceptionally clever and very effective individual. He was my "counterpart" and as I got to know him I came to respect his exceptional abilities and ambition. He was also extremely wily and manipulative, so it was necessary to work very closely with him. He had been assigned to this remote, "failing" park a couple of years previously as a kind of punishment posting. Details of his transgressions were never specified, but allusions to the tribal nature of the civil service hierarchy and TANAPA were frequent. My assumption was that he had probably become "too big for his boots" and had to be exiled. He was certainly far more capable than any of the TANAPA "top brass" that I met.

When Baba Moi had arrived in Ruaha the only way into the park from Iringa via the "neverending road" was by ferry at Ibuguziwa. Tourists numbered only a few hundred a year, poaching was rife and the rangers and game scouts were dispirited. There was very little infrastructure or equipment. He set about improving staff morale, working alongside the local Friends of Ruaha Society (FORS), and through his persuasive personality gradually turned things round. Lyambangari (the local name for the river) Social Hall was built, with a bar, fresh produce kiosk and even television, and became the busy heart of community life in Msembe. A small clinic was also built to cater for the 250 or so staff and their families. A major project had been the opening of a road bridge, high above the river at Ibuguziwa. The bridge had previously been situated almost 100 miles downstream, but with the completion of the Mtera Dam it had become redundant. Moving it upstream and reconstructing it at Ibuguziwa in 1991 had transformed the park, making it much more accessible to tourists.

I quickly learned that the Tanzanians had been very influential in the project design. They believed that TANAPA already had the required management skills, but they were very keen to obtain equipment and funds for operations. Our project was therefore heavily skewed towards the development of infrastructure and the provision of equipment, with ecological considerations and resource management a lesser priority. I therefore divided my efforts between generating a medium-term management plan for the park and enabling the procurement and delivery of the hardware including an 80 KVa electricity generator for Msembe, a stonecrusher for road and bridge construction and twelve Land Rovers. Moirana's practical skills and exceptional man-management meant that, while keeping a watchful eye, I could mostly leave the construction projects to him and his staff.

During the first few weeks it was necessary to visit Dar and Arusha more than once; although TANAPA headquarters were in Arusha, I needed more contact with the Ministry and Game Department in Dar, which was a full ten-hour drive from Ruaha. The journey was on tar after passing Iringa, through striking, dramatic landscapes of steep river valleys, then the plains of

Mikumi NP and finally 100 miles or so of green shambas as Dar got nearer. I occasionally stayed over at a Baptist mission boarding house in Iringa on the way back and it was always a round trip of several days, mainly because senior civil servants in Dar seemed to keep their own schedules, not the government's, and were difficult to pin down. I learned that arriving in an office early and putting a coat over the back of a chair was the sole contribution to work of many civil servants. This was not really surprising when government salaries were often inadequate and irregularly paid, leading many to pursue alternative, but coincident employment.

FORS had provided a Cessna 182 aircraft to the Park, mainly through funds donated by the Belgian chocolate company Cote D'Or, whose logo is an elephant. At that time Ruaha was thought to hold the largest concentration of elephants remaining in East Africa. Peter Fox, the owner of Ruaha River Lodge upstream from Msembe, was a commercial pilot and prominent member of FORS and had been flying the aircraft on their behalf. In order to start survey work in the park I would have to obtain a Tanzanian pilot's licence as soon as possible and Peter introduced me to the Civil Aviation Authority personnel in Dar who could assist me.

Early in December Peter and I flew down to Dar together in 5H-FOR. It was quite an eye-opener for a pilot like me who was used to the level ground and clear blue skies of Botswana. Ruaha lies in the Great Rift Valley at about 2,000 feet above sea level. The route to Dar took us over mountains near Iringa at over 9,000 feet and then dropped to almost sea level for an hour across the famous Selous Game Reserve and coastal plain. With mountains come clouds and rain. We flew the last thirty minutes in thick cloud and occasional torrential rain. Peter seemed very calm and matter-of-factly explained that if we missed Dar airport we could just go out to sea, descend and come back to find it. It sounded like a recipe for suicide to me, but in the event Peter managed an instrument approach with only the VOR, instructing me to watch the dial and tell him immediately the needle flipped. At this signal Peter banked sharp left, descended and broke cloud about 150 feet above the runway threshold. I was very impressed and equally relieved to be safely on the ground. I made a promise to myself to be extra careful flying in East Africa and never take chances with the weather. One I wouldn't keep!

It was necessary to take an exam in Tanzanian Air Law and have a medical to obtain my licence; my Botswana licence and experience covered everything else. Peter was staying in Dar on business for a few days, but I wanted to return the following day if possible. I was directed to a very dilapidated house in a run-down suburb near the airport. Affixed to the wall was a large sign saying: *"Dr A. Mogolo, Specialist in Space and Aviation Medicine"*. I knocked on the open door and called "Hello". Inside was equally scruffy, with broken furnishings, filthy curtains and no sign of any staff. A middle-aged man in a white coat appeared from a back room and greeted me politely. We chatted briefly and he claimed that he had spent several years at Cape Canaveral practising medicine before returning to Tanzania. Unlikely as this seemed, he was apparently certified to carry out aviation medicals for the CAA. He checked my blood pressure and asked about my eyesight and then explained that I would need a blood test. This was highly unusual, but it became bizarre when he said it would cost ten dollars extra if I wanted him to use a new, i.e. sterile, needle and syringe. In the event I paid, at which he decided the test was unnecessary after all and wrote out my medical certificate!

My appointment with the CAA examiner was later in the afternoon. I produced my new medical certificate and my Botswana pilot's licence. He pleasantly explained that for him to mark my test paper he would miss his bus home and therefore could not process my application that day. Of course, if I were to supply ten dollars for a taxi he would happily stay and complete the formalities. I received my licence ten minutes later, without any examination, and was able to fly back alone to Ruaha early the following morning – the best time for weather. I soon became very familiar with the Tanzanian system of petty bribery that was endemic throughout the civil service. Officials of every kind existed on these unofficial payments, apparently in lieu of regular salary cheques, something completely unknown in Botswana.

Eleanor had flown back to England in November because she was expecting a baby in January. With the usual, generous allowances of ODA she flew Club Class, the same as our flights from the UK two months earlier. I flew back to London a few days before Christmas, but wasn't entitled to a free ticket so Eleanor booked me on Gulf Air. This was very cheap, but the flight was very long and indirect via Muscat and Bahrain. It was also "dry", very sweet tea or coffee seemed to be the only refreshments for the few passengers. That was until Bahrain, where the plane filled up with expats from the oilfields returning to the UK for Christmas. There was a large contingent of very drunken, celebratory Scots, mostly in Santa Claus garb, varying from just red hats to full outfits with white beards. All of them appeared to have bottles of whisky from the Bahrain duty-free shop and these were opened and generously passed around amid much singing and revelry. It was a good start to the festive season, which culminated for us three weeks later with the birth of Katharine at St Thomas' Hospital across the river from Westminster.

I left mum and baby and flew back to Tanzania in late January. They would follow after Katharine's check and vaccination at six weeks. My first job back in Ruaha was to carry out a wet season game census. This involved flying and counting the animals in the Ruaha/Rungwa/Kizigo complex, about 17,000 square miles. From reports and my limited observations it did not appear worthwhile to extend the survey into the communal lands to the east of Ruaha, where a large human population existed and only relict fragments of previous wildlife populations remained.

It was my first real opportunity to get an overview of the Park's location in the greater ecological scheme of things. Ruaha occupies a position that straddles the juxtaposition of the Southern African miombo woodlands and the East African mixed acacia savannas. These two huge biomes come together in the Great Rift Valley in Tanzania, and Ruaha contains elements of them both, making it scenically as well as scientifically very interesting. Basically, the valley of the Great Ruaha River and the northeastern park fall into the latter, while above the escarpment and to the west the woodlands approximate those further south in the continent. Ruaha also has a climate more akin to Southern Africa, with a single wet season from November to March as opposed to the East African pattern of two wet seasons separated by a dry period in the early months of the year.

When it comes to wildlife there are many species that occur in both these types of savanna, but a few are restricted to one or the other. In Ruaha, for instance, elephant and buffalo are distributed throughout, while lesser kudu and Grant's gazelle occur only in the Acacia savanna, with sable and roan antelope and Lichtenstein's hartebeest limited to the miombo. This wide variety of habitats and species makes Ruaha a special and fascinating place.

We conducted one wet season and one dry season aerial census each year for three consecutive years. Elephant numbers, our main target, seemed stable at between 16,000 and 18,000, but since then have fluctuated wildly and, having peaked in excess of 30,000 in the early years of this century, they have since been drastically reduced by poaching.

No useful map of the Park or its surroundings existed, so one of my main tasks was to produce one. This meant setting up a GIS system. We bought the necessary computers and software and I began digitising the main geographical features from aerial photographs and ground-based information obtained by driving the Park's network of roads and tracks recording data on hand-held GPS devices. I had some experience of GIS from my Botswana days, but a specialist was needed to do the job properly. We therefore hired Emma Hunter, a GIS consultant, who spent several weeks over two years polishing my amateurish efforts and advising us how to proceed. We eventually produced a useful and fairly accurate topographical map of Ruaha, with a detailed digital database.

We mapped some of the larger features by air. This involved flying as accurately as possible, while an assistant operated a laptop computer programmed to record our position every few seconds. This mass of data was then loaded into the GIS back in our office at Msembe. Halfway through the project I was assigned an Associate Expert from ODA. He was a young Welshman, Simon Jennings, who had previously worked on a project in Kenya. Keen and bright, he was something of a mixed blessing. One day we were mapping Mtera Dam, a large reservoir about fifty miles downstream where the Great Ruaha River was impounded. A major hydroelectric station that provided most of Tanzania's power was situated there. I flew the little aircraft on a very tight course around the perimeter of the reservoir. This involved a great many steep turns and changes in direction – great fun! Unfortunately Simon, in charge of the laptop, became quite airsick and after a couple of hours was greatly relieved to land again at Msembe. I plugged the laptop into our GIS in the office, to find that there were no datapoints at all from the morning's flight. Simon had somehow contrived either not to record anything or had deleted all the data. I was furious and insisted that we go back and repeat the flight immediately. Simon suffered through another two hours, this time with increased turbulence through the heat of the day.

Simon had a series of "ups and downs" during his eighteen months at Ruaha, some personal and some professional. He was on course to be fired about halfway through his contract when one of life's serendipitous events intervened on his behalf. Our project was subject to mid-term assessment by senior ODA and High Commission staff. One of the project's biggest infrastructure undertakings was to build a causeway across the Mzombe River, that formed the northern boundary of the Park, in order to provide year-round access between Ruaha and the adjoining game reserves and ultimately to the main road north from Mbeya. The assessment team wanted to pay a visit to the site. This entailed a three-hour drive through the Park or a thirty-minute flight. I could only take three passengers in 5H-FOR and the other three would have to travel by Land Rover with Simon. On the way back they would swap around. Back home that evening we waited for hours for Simon and his party only to get a message that they had suffered an accident. Simon had rolled the Land Rover and we had to mount a rescue. Luckily no one was very seriously hurt, except for our project administrator who suffered a broken arm. This was the man who was threatening to fire Simon, but now had to reconsider unless it appeared he was acting out of personal retribution. Simon made it to the end of our project, but then joined WWF in Uganda with even more catastrophic consequences.

Around this time, while we were away from Msembe camping in the Park, our hi-fi set, radio and cassette deck disappeared from our house. Obviously we asked our maid, Mwanaidi, if she knew anything about it, but she said she had no idea what might have happened to it because she had kept the house locked the whole time we were away. Somehow we learned that a boyfriend of hers had visited her from Iringa and it seemed likely that he was the culprit. After some police investigations in Iringa, the set turned up and I went to identify it. The suspect was duly charged with theft and eventually the day of his trial came along. In court he maintained his innocence and stated that our house merely had mosquito netting at some windows and that baboons could tear it and enter. This had actually happened once some months previously and Eleanor and Mwanaidi had chased them away. The suspect claimed that baboons had probably stolen the hi-fi set and cassettes. I was dumbfounded when the magistrate judged that this could indeed have happened and that there was no proof that Mwanaidi's friend had anything to do with it. He was duly acquitted – strange justice – but at least we got our property back.

Baby Katharine thrived in Msembe, spending many hours wrapped in a blanket on the back of Mwanaidi. She survived bathing in briefly boiled river water when the pools just upstream were full of carcasses – casualties of an anthrax outbreak – at the end of her first dry season. Then there was an invasion of large *Parabuthus* scorpions in the house as soon as the rains broke. Luckily none got into her cot, but I killed several in the room in one night. After two or three days they were gone until the beginning of the next year's rains. In fact I was actually the closest to an early demise when one day an elephant took offence at my hanging her nappies on the washing line in the back yard. His fairly committed charge ended in a cloud of dust less than five yards from me as I dived behind a low wall – not quite a red rag to a bull, but the same effect.

We enjoyed having animals and birds close to our house and noting the changes with the seasons. Elephants, buffalo and impala were constantly in view between us and the river. Dwarf mongoose occupied an old termite mound a few yards from our porch and entertained us, while their larger cousins, banded mongoose, appeared every now and then in large foraging troops that cleared just about every living thing from the area before departing. Giraffe were frequent visitors, but never came very close, unlike the elephants and buffalo. Best of all were the packs of wild dogs that came through occasionally. Totally unafraid and relaxed they would lounge around close to the house. These visits motivated Eleanor to record the occurrence of different species on a short driving circuit around Msembe every day. Surprisingly, she saw wild dogs very often and encouraged the game scouts to report their sightings to her. The apparent numbers and frequency of sightings certainly indicated that there was a healthy population of wild dogs in the Park which taken together with those in the Selous Game Reserve suggested that Tanzania was a stronghold for this species though they were reportedly in decline in most other countries.

The river itself teemed with hippos and crocodiles. Just upstream of Ibuguziwa Bridge was a large pool that held dozens of big crocodiles. When the flow and water levels dropped during the dry season they were crowded together like sardines, waiting patiently for the new flow from Usangu when the rains started. Even in the early 1990s the Ruaha River seldom lived up to its full name, "Great". It dried to a trickle during the middle of the year and in 1994 was reduced to pools. The main reason for this was not climatic, but the extraction of water upstream in the Usangu swamps for rice farming conducted by the Chinese. It was a serious threat to the future of the Park and as a project we attempted to address it.

The Usangu wetlands upstream near Mbeya were a gigantic sponge fed by a number of rivers flowing from the Southern Highlands. This was the source of the Great Ruaha River on which the Park as well as Mtera Hydroelectric Plant depended. Sadly the Usangu was in decline and severely threatened on three fronts: reduced inflows stemming from increased settlement and subsistence agriculture in southern highlands; the new Chinese rice schemes; and a huge influx of pastoralists, mainly Wasukuma from the north, bringing thousands of cattle. We surveyed Usangu from the air to establish the extent of the rice schemes on the east and the influx of cattle mainly on the northwest. The project, through the British High Commission, brought the looming threats to the attention of the Tanzanian Government but I had little confidence in any meaningful action being taken. Although we only documented the situation over three years, it was apparent that serious declines in inflow to the Great Ruaha River were likely to continue and that it was unlikely to survive as a perennial river.

I had been accustomed to writing management plans for parks and other protected areas as part of a team of specialists: soil scientists; hydrologists; botanists; wildlife specialists; tourism experts etc. The inputs from these various disciplines would be brought together by the team leader and shaped into a draft management plan. But times were changing apparently; a centralised planning unit had been established in TANAPA HQ under the direction of a tall, cowboy-booted Texan, Bart E. Young III, from USAID. A process had been adopted that involved team consultations, consensus building, and priority allocation. I was invited to attend a planning workshop for Lake Manyara NP, close to the world-famous Ngorongoro Crater.

The Great North Road from Iringa only scored one out of three; it was hardly a road and certainly not "Great", but it did head north. Eleanor came with me, hoping that we'd have time to visit Ngorongoro as well as experience Lake Manyara. The drive as far as Dodoma was uneventful and our new Land Rover Discovery made it bearably comfortable. We stayed overnight in the Railway Hotel at Dodoma, the country's new administrative capital, a seemingly sleepy place, with almost no activity and very few resident civil servants, but maybe that would change. The hotel was basic, but fairly clean, and the plumbing functioned – a distinct advantage over most provincial Tanzanian hotels. There was a loud band playing popular, Zairean, dance music into the small hours, but we eventually managed some sleep. There was also a Railway Hotel in Iringa. This puzzled me because there was no railway line to Iringa. It was explained to me that there were several hotels throughout Tanzania with the same name and in colonial days they were served by buses from the towns that actually were on the railway line.

The following morning we left early and continued north towards Arusha. The road was marginally better but still slow going and it was lunchtime before we turned off left after 200 miles, at Makuyuni, to head along the road towards Lake Manyara, Ngorongoro and Serengeti. The Park's headquarters were situated in the village of Mto wa Mbu (Mosquito Creek) just outside the Park itself. We were met by a Mr Kajuni, Bart's counterpart, who was earmarked to take over as Chief Planning Officer when the USAID-funded planning project terminated. He took us over to the small guesthouse where we would be staying and introduced us to the Park Warden and Bart.

Early the next day we all met in the small conference room of the Park HQ. The gathering numbered about thirty people, mainly park staff with a few individuals from TANAPA in Arusha and some local people, including the village headman from Mto wa Mbu. Eleanor was invited to participate as well. We thought this was strange because no one was aware that she was a qualified ecologist and obviously she had no knowledge of the park. Perhaps it was just more typical African politeness. The workshop process was explained by Bart in English and by Kajuni in kiSwahili. Essentially anyone who thought they had useful information on the Park was given a chance to speak. It was extremely inclusive, with sometimes quite long-winded contributions, even from people who clearly did not understand the proceedings and had little or no knowledge of the Park. Kajuni, acting as bilingual *rapporteur,* wrote everything down in English on large white paper sheets. The outcome was a long list of the Park's ecological "assets", ranging from landscape features to wild animals, including some that I thought rather pointless, most notably the Park's famous tree-climbing lions. These no longer existed. The Park Warden told me that the prides with that proclivity had died out years earlier – but they remained on the list.

The following morning everyone voted on each of the listed assets and they were then put in descending order of merit. I was perplexed when the non-existent, tree-climbing lions were ranked number one! The next step was to highlight the top seven assets; all others were discarded. Apparently the "magical" number seven was an indispensable factor in the process leading to consensus. I privately questioned this with Kajuni and Bart to no avail; the process was paramount, even with its serious flaws. The participants were then divided randomly into small groups to discuss the seven assets. Reconvening at a plenary session after lunch a representative of each group related the conclusions of its discussions and the main points were duly recorded, again by Kajuni. The outcome was a series of lists of opinions with little or no factual analysis, completely devoid of scientific scrutiny. These were taken by the Planning Unit to be drafted into a provisional management plan to be modified and confirmed at a second workshop. I was dumbfounded. What was the point of expertise and experience if a random, numerical process in which untrained people under obvious misapprehensions had as much say as trained specialists. In the event a draft management plan for Lake Manyara NP was produced that claimed non-existent lions were its number one feature! I determined that nothing of the sort would happen in Ruaha, even if it meant open hostilities between USAID and ODA. Before we left I was handed an envelope containing a substantial amount of Tanzanian Shillings. When I queried this I was told it was a "sitting allowance" for the meeting and all participants received it. I tried to refuse it on the grounds that I was already being paid by ODA, but Kajuni insisted, pointing out that even NGOs like Frankfurt Zoological Society (FZS) representatives accepted it. Markus Borner, the head of FZS, who was very influential, explained that the allowances were necessary to ensure the participation of Tanzanian civil servants and any differentiation was frowned upon. This was very different to how we did things in Botswana, but I thought it best not to rock the boat. Eleanor and I then spent a couple of days exploring Lake Manyara NP and the neighbouring, astounding Ngorongoro Conservation Area and vowed to return when we had more time. We drove home to Ruaha enchanted by the Tanzanian environment, but more than a little concerned at its future management.

Having the aircraft at my disposal was invaluable for fieldwork in Ruaha and for commuting on business to Dar and Arusha. It also provided the means to visit many of the parks and protected areas in the country, often when I was drafted as a wildlife veterinarian to advise and participate in various activities. I was lucky enough to visit other national parks and conservation areas: places such as Mikumi; Tarangire and Tony Fitzjohn's brilliantly successful project at Mkomazi. Occasionally it meant flying to Seronera, Serengeti NP HQ, where there were many researchers working on a wide range of projects. Most memorable was in October 1994 darting buffaloes on the grasslands, a vastly different proposition from our difficult terrain in Botswana. It was part of a survey of rinderpest in wildlife and was fairly easily achieved from the back of 4-wd pick-ups. But after hanging on to the tail of a stubborn young bull that was only partially drugged, something I'd done many times years before in Botswana, I realised for the first time that I wasn't twenty-something anymore. The following morning I had to roll out of bed and struggle to my feet, I was so stiff.

Back home in Ruaha the mapping and building projects continued steadily. We finished an elevated causeway across the seasonal Mwagusi River, quite close to Msembe, that allowed for much better access to the scenic, game-rich, downstream valley area, as well as all-year-round access to tracks up the escarpment and north to Rungwa and Kizigo. I had to admit that supervising the stone crusher to produce aggregates of various sizes for concrete and bridge foundations was a little outside my skill set, but together with Baba Moi we succeeded in bridging the Mwagusi before the rains made work impossible.

My co-worker had finally been recruited by February 1993, but because she had no driving licence her arrival in Tanzania was delayed until she had passed her driving test. She was a young Englishwoman named Dawn Hartley. She had previously worked as a sociologist in Sierra Leone and her terms of reference were to build a sense of ownership of the national park among the villagers living close to its boundaries, notably in the Iringa District across the river. It was hoped that this would have positive effects on the villagers' attitudes to Ruaha and reduce conflict. One of the Park's main problems was poaching by the neighbouring villagers. This took various forms, from illegally collecting firewood and thatching grass, to setting wire snares for bushmeat and a limited amount of commercial poaching of elephants for ivory. Dawn arrived in March and quickly made herself at home next door to us. She formed a special bond with baby Katharine.

Dawn and I flew several hours for her to get an idea of the distribution and number of people in her study area. She then spent several weeks with a local guide and interpreter visiting as many villages as possible in an effort to design the parameters of her study. I remained sceptical about this sociological initiative, particularly as it appeared that at least 30,000 people were neighbours of the Park and for them to receive any tangible benefits in the way of employment, natural resources or other advantages seemed unlikely. It seemed to me that it was akin to the biblical "loaves and fishes" challenge. Nevertheless, this was part of the agreed project plan, so I would have to bury my reactionary views and assist Dawn wherever possible.

My crash course in kiSwahili in London had been in the company of a slightly older man, Roger Westbrook, a career diplomat, who was about to take up the position of British High Commissioner to Tanzania. As the only two students we became quite friendly and subsequently got to know each other well in Tanzania. He visited Ruaha at least twice officially. Once was to hand over the twelve Land Rovers that the Project supplied to the Park and on another occasion, to inspect the causeway or "Irish bridge" as it was known across the Mzombe River. We in turn were lucky enough to stay at the High Commissioner's residence on the odd visit to Dar. On one occasion I arrived in Dar by myself in the little Cessna and I was staying at the Kilimanjaro Hotel. Roger heard that I was in town and called to ask if I would be able to fly him to

Zanzibar the following day. I had never been to the island and also had never flown across the sea, so I enthusiastically agreed. The next morning the two of us flew across to Zanzibar Island and landed at the quiet airport at Stonetown. Roger had arranged for a car to meet us and we drove to the old house just outside Stonetown that had been the Governor's residence in times gone by and was still owned by the British Government. It was sadly pretty dilapidated and Roger said he would try to find funds to do some restoration. Relating this to Eleanor later she informed me that one of her uncles, Sir William Addis had, in fact, been resident in the house during the war.

We were given a brief but fascinating tour of Stonetown and its environs, followed by lunch with Mike Liebst, one of the founder members of FORS. When we were dropped back at the airport we found that word had got out that the British High Commissioner was visiting the island. We were ushered to the VIP lounge, seated on plush red velour sofas and served tea while someone rounded up a guard of honour. The coffee table on which our tea was served had a sign that read "Reserved for Heads Of State". Roger surreptitiously told me to pocket this while he distracted our host. When I asked later why he wanted it he replied, "It will look fabulous on the loo in my flat in Westminster".

The rains brought great relief all round after a long, hot dry season. But they also brought a variety of problems, including difficult communications. The Mdonya River, just across the airstrip next to Msembe, periodically came down in a deep, unruly torrent making it impossible to drive to Ibuguziwa Bridge and therefore cutting us off from Iringa. Luckily this was never for very long, usually only a couple of days. It also made it impossible to get to Ruaha River Lodge, the only tourist facility in the Park a few miles upstream. This comfortable and well-appointed lodge was a credit to the Fox family who had pioneered tourism in Ruaha and was a popular destination for us at weekends for excellent meals and company. We became firm friends with Peter and Sarah Fox who lived there and managed the facility. They also had a baby son who was a great companion for Katharine.

The stone and thatch bungalows were perched on huge rocks overlooking a spectacular series of deep pools and rapids in the Great Ruaha River. Depending upon the time of year the view from the open dining room was either a white-water cascade or hippos and crocodiles basking in the still pools. We would also occasionally escape the heat, by flying up to Mufindi, where the Foxes had a guest house at their family base in the tea estates. It was possible to drive there via Iringa, but that took several hours; flying was a nearly vertical climb out of the valley up 5,000 feet and down twenty-five degrees Celsius to a different world of green vegetation, running streams and log fires in the bungalows of the Brooke-Bond sports club. After a refreshing weekend, the trip home was a fifteen-minute drop off the end of the runway down the escarpment to the baobabs and dry bush of the rift valley and the throbbing heat of Msembe.

Except for occasional "goodies" from Dar that I could fly in, basic provisions were obtained in Iringa, which was quite a large town about fifty miles away. The road was just a bush track and took three or four hours to negotiate, with a long, dead-straight stretch that earned it the name "the neverending road". The town had no supermarkets (neither had Dar), but there were a few small shops owned by Baluchi traders that stocked a limited choice of tinned goods, and a thriving market for agricultural produce like eggs, flour, beans, tomatoes etc. There was one butcher, but no refrigeration, so meat was not always reliable. We struck up a friendship with the Phillips family who had been dairy farmers on the outskirts of Iringa for thirty years. Richard and Victoria Phillips were carrying on the tradition started by his parents David and Elizabeth and the farm was uniquely successful and a joy to visit. They had a small daughter, Rebecca, so a social occasion for Katharine was an added bonus. David had developed a technique of pasteurising milk in pressurised churns. The sealed churns were heated in a large vat of boiling water for a few minutes and the milk so treated could be kept fresh for up to a month without refrigeration by only taking out enough for immediate consumption through a valve. This was ideal for our purposes, especially catering for a young baby. The bulk of their production was sent to Dar es Salaam on the bus.

Once or twice there were mishaps on the so-called "neverending road". Coming home late one evening in the dark I saw a hippo in the track a couple of hundred yards ahead. I slowed down a little and dimmed my headlights to allow him to find his way into the bush. He seemed to have gone as we approached closer so I accelerated again only to hit him squarely in the behind as he reversed back into the track. He then made good his escape at speed leaving us with a badly dented front wing and a few small bloodstains. Eleanor was quite concerned at the blood, but I'm afraid that my reaction was not that of a caring veterinarian and I cursed the creature quite irrationally. With a bit of effort I managed to straighten the bodywork sufficiently to allow the wheels to turn and we limped back to Msembe. The vehicle was an almost brand new Land Rover Discovery and the incident took quite a lot of explaining to the insurance company in London before they would pay for the repairs, which of course could only be carried out in Dar, ten hours' drive away.

A few months later the "Disco" was substantially re-modelled by Eleanor on the same stretch of road. On the way back from a shopping trip she rolled the vehicle on to its roof and back on to its wheels. Very luckily baby Katharine had been left in Msembe with me for the day and the only passengers were Peter Fox and Simon, my Welsh assistant. Nobody was hurt, but Simon, seated in the back, had been "nursing" four-dozen eggs on his lap that were liberally scattered and smashed, mostly over him! Peter managed to drive the car back to Msembe with a smashed windscreen and the roof considerably lower than before. This time the insurers wrote off the wreck though we drove it for a while around Msembe as a rather atypical drophead coupe.

One of the hazards of the rainy season was malaria. This was extremely common amongst the Park's staff and the little clinic was kept busy dispensing chloroquine tablets, which seemed to relieve the symptoms if not provide a definitive cure. Eleanor and I decided not to take prophylactic tablets, reasoning that we would recognise the symptoms and treat the disease if we got it, but one of our problems was how to keep baby Katharine safe. She was under a mosquito net in the evenings and we knew that the malaria mosquitos were not normally active until later, but we couldn't take any chances. At first we managed to get her to take a syrup containing chloroquine, but before long we had to resort to tablets which we coated in melted chocolate and stored in the fridge. In the three years spent in Msembe she didn't contract the disease, but both her parents did.

I was first to succumb. In late February 1995 a couple of days of headaches for no apparent reason heralded the onset of a fever. I visited the clinic and the nurse gave me some chloroquine tablets. A couple of days later I felt quite a lot worse. Baba Moi assured me that this was normal and meant that the pills were doing their job. Two days later still I was really ill and obviously needed urgent medical attention. Unfortunately it was a holiday, both Baba Moi and Peter Fox were away and nobody else could fly. Eleanor resorted to our HF radio, but the offices in Dar and Arusha were closed. In a panic she drove to a tented tourist camp at Mwagusi but found no one there. The frequency and call sign of the AMREF Flying Doctor service was on a list by their radio and she called in desperation. By an astonishing stroke of luck her transmission was picked up by one of their pilots who was flying in southern Kenya. He said he would divert to Msembe as long as she was ready and waiting at our airstrip because he would arrive almost at dark. Helped by Mwanaidi, our maid, she bundled the baby's stuff together, packed passports and a few things and drove a semiconscious husband the couple of hundred yards to the airstrip just as the plane was landing. I was loaded on a stretcher into the back of the aircraft and she and Katharine climbed in front with the pilot. Taking off just as darkness fell we flew to Nairobi, the last half hour of the flight through some very stormy weather, and landed at Wilson Airport after 9 pm. I obviously don't remember, but the pilot later told me it had been touch and go whether or not we had made it through the weather. Luckily for me we had, because I was rushed to hospital where I received excellent life-saving treatment. The Italian doctor who worked on me told us that two hours later I would have been beyond saving! He gave me a new experimental drug from China, artemisinin, now the basis of a widely used routine treatment, which killed the parasites in hours. In three days I was cured and discharged, fairly weak and a lot lighter and very grateful to all concerned.

A week's convalescence in Nairobi visiting friends and erstwhile colleagues was a pleasant interlude before we chartered a small aircraft and were flown back to Msembe. Six weeks later it was Eleanor's turn. This time diagnosis was easy, but the doctor at the tea estate's clinic in Mufindi told us that treatment would be complicated because she was pregnant. She would have to go to Nairobi. I therefore loaded her and Katharine into the Cessna and headed north. Just beyond Dodoma the weather closed in over the mountains and I had to turn back and land at Dodoma. The air traffic controller made a call to the Nairobi headquarters of the Flying Doctor, who immediately despatched a twin-engined, fully equipped aircraft to Dodoma. The expert crew were able to take Eleanor on to Nairobi while I flew back to Msembe with a fretful little girl. A few days later we were able to fly to Nairobi in good weather and rejoin Eleanor who had been gently treated with intravenous quinidine drips without damaging her pregnancy. Simon wanted a lift to Nairobi to attend a job interview with WWF, so he looked after Katharine as I flew. She was very sick all over him, poor guy. First eggs, then baby vomit – he was truly jinxed! Mother and daughter were reunited only for us to be told that Eleanor must not return to a malaria area until the third trimester of her pregnancy, so Eleanor and Katharine were flown back to London for three months until it was deemed safe for her to return to Ruaha in July. What a boon to work for a generous government agency!

In the meantime I spent some time in the neighbouring Rungwa and Kizigo Game Reserves. Rungwa was leased at the time to a French safari company and I visited one of their hunting camps near the Mzombe River. It was their first season in Rungwa. With my past experience of the safari hunting industry in Botswana the visit and discussion proved very interesting. I was impressed with the apparent professionalism of the company and with the quality of most of their clients' trophies. I mentioned the reported corruption in the Ministry that I was gradually coming to terms with, saying how different it was from Botswana. The two Frenchmen laughed at this comment and said they thought Tanzania was a paragon of virtue! Noting my perplexity they explained that they had previously operated in the Central African Republic where things were infinitely worse.

About a year later I came across the leading professional hunter in East Africa, Robin Hurt. I was in the Director of Wildlife's waiting room at the Dar HQ. Robin was extremely upset. Apparently his company had won the tender to hunt in Rungwa for that season. His employees had travelled to Rungwa to put up a hunting camp, only to find the French company already building. They showed Robin's manager a copy of a lease entitling them to hunt in the concession. When the Director was confronted with this "mistake" he nonchalantly suggested that Rungwa was a big place and surely both companies could operate there. What's more he assured them both that they could each have identical hunting quotas for the year, effectively doubling the offtake calculated and recommended by us and his own departmental scientists! Later I learned that Robin Hurt had actually been awarded the tender first, but the French company had arranged for a free trip to the soccer World Cup in the USA for the Director. I was also told that his local nickname translated as "Richer than God". I had wondered how a middle-ranking civil servant on a monthly salary in the region of 200 US dollars could wear a succession of very smart suits and expensive jewellery, but I was learning.

As is usual, a proportion of the project's funds had been earmarked for "training". I was under great pressure from the High Commission to arrange excursions for members of Ruaha's staff to other conservation areas to give them exposure to what was being done regionally. Most of the senior staff had visited Kenya, to the north, so we decided to go south and take a look at Zambia. I arranged with Zambia's Department of National Parks and Wildlife to visit South Luangwa National Park and we eventually left Ruaha in two Land Rovers. We numbered eight; six Ruaha staff plus Dawn and me. Our first night was spent in Mbeya and the next day we crossed the border and drove down to Mpika, where Mark and Delia Owens, from the Kalahari, were based with a new project in North Luangwa. Leaving Mpika was where the fun started as we branched off the Great North Road and headed down the steep

Muchinga escarpment into the Luangwa Valley. At first the track wasn't too bad, but as it got steeper, with more tight bends, it became rougher, with lots of rocks to negotiate. This was outside Dawn's comfort zone but fortunately Baba Moi took over her vehicle and we made it in one piece down to the valley floor. From there it was a fairly easy drive to the pontoon crossing the Luangwa River between the North and South Parks. After being pulled across on a platform of 44-gallon drums we headed southwest through the park towards Mfuwe. The similarities between Ruaha and South Luangwa were striking. Baba Moi and the other staff members discussed all manner of management issues, mainly anti-poaching, with their Zambian counterparts and we were treated to some wonderful, scenic game drives. The ubiquitous puku antelope was something new to the Tanzanians – there was no equivalent in Ruaha – but all the other species were familiar, with the exception of the endemic Thorneycroft's giraffe, a subspecies found nowhere else.

Another training event was a trip to Hwange NP in Zimbabwe in March 1994. This time we flew so participants were limited to three, apart from me as the pilot. We flew from Msembe, cleared customs and immigration at Mbeya and flew to Lusaka, the Zambian capital, where we refuelled before continuing to Victoria Falls in Zimbabwe. The three Tanzanians were overawed by flying over the amazing Falls and I'm sure they remembered the experience long after forgetting the details of the workshops held at Hwange Main Camp. Something else that astonished them was the state of the road from Lusaka International Airport to the city. We decided to spend the night there on the way back. It was probably a mistake because immigration formalities were tortuous, but we couldn't be sure of getting home in daylight. The road into the city had obviously been recently resurfaced and the lack of potholes was a source of wonder to the Tanzanians. I assured them that most of the Zambian roads were actually no better than those in Tanzania, but they were still very impressed. Months later Eleanor and I were having lunch in the Kilimanjaro Hotel in Dar. Three glamorous, young Tanzanian women were seated near us. One of them had just returned from a visit to South Africa and was regaling her companions with descriptions of the California-style shopping malls. Very few Tanzanians had ever been to South Africa by then because it was forbidden during the apartheid era, and of course there were no supermarkets, let alone shopping malls, in Tanzania. We were most amused by her assertion that the most extraordinary feature of South Africa was not the shopping facilities, but the absence of potholes!

By mid-1994 Dawn had concentrated her efforts on a selected sample of village communities, mostly based around Idodi, the main village, situated about twenty miles from Msembe on the road to Iringa. Her life seemed to be a never-ending series of interviews with headmen and community leaders. A number of consultant sociologists, mostly from the UK, visited the project and assisted her to design and distribute meaningful questionnaires intended to reveal the attitudes of the people towards the Park. Emma's GIS expertise and Simon's statistical skills were employed to identify and quantify the relationships between the Park and its neighbouring communities. My inputs were limited to practical support such as facilitating transport and other logistics for the surveys and meetings. Both Baba Moi and I remained fairly sceptical, preferring an old-fashioned custodianship arrangement and unable to see any substantial long-term benefits flowing from an integrationist approach. We saw the project's primary goal as conserving the Park directly, whereas the modern sociological view was that the Park should benefit the communities and therefore contribute to its own long-term security.

In the next eighteen months Dawn had some success in the Idodi and Pawaga areas, forming village wildlife committees and allocating hunting quotas to the communities. There was some opposition from resident hunters (mostly relatively wealthy citizens in Iringa) who lost out on cheap hunting opportunities, but Dawn advised the villagers to sell some of the hunting quotas to the residents, thereby increasing income to their communities. Her schemes persisted for a few years after the end of the Project but I believe they, like the initiatives to secure water flow out of Usangu down the Great Ruaha, stalled owing to bureaucratic squabbling and inertia and the relentless demands of an increasing population. Twenty-five years later I still haven't seen any significant successes of "community conservation" except where the consumptive use of resources brings significant benefits to communities. This inevitably means high-end exclusive safari hunting as in the CAMPFIRE initiative in Zimbabwe or some of the USAID-funded community schemes in Botswana and even these have foundered in recent times. The universal, critical weakness is failing to ensure that the rural community has a capacity to deal with the substantial funds when they receive them. A strong element of benign, experienced supervision is necessary.

Preparation of a park management plan for Ruaha proceeded alongside all the other project activities inside and adjacent to the Park. The TANAPA Planning Unit, keen not to allow us too much autonomy, ensured that we followed their systematic model as much as possible. They would schedule occasional planning meetings in Msembe and invite various representatives of the Game Department and other government agencies as well as NGOs like Frankfurt Zoological Society. As in Lake Manyara many of the participants knew little about the Park and even less about the surrounding areas, but we faithfully followed the USAID planning process, even paying sitting allowances to everyone, including some expats who had generous, tax-free salaries. Somehow, first a Park Zoning Concept Plan was produced which divided Ruaha into various zones from wilderness to high-density tourism. With more local effort and field work we eventually produced a draft General Management Plan (GMP) that was accepted by TANAPA in early 1995.

Also by mid-1995 most of what I termed the tangible elements of the project had been achieved. We had a detailed and accurate working map of the Park, a widespread road network with all-year access to most areas, two major causeways crossing the Mwagusi and Mzombe Rivers, and almost complete boundary demarcation. A fleet of 4-wd vehicles with basic spares and maintenance facilities enabled regular patrols of scouts in all sectors. From aerial surveys we had fairly reliable population estimates of the major wildlife species and their seasonal trends and we had developed a fire-management strategy as part of the management plan.

The development of tourism became a major priority. There was still only Ruaha River Lodge and a tented camp on the Mwagusi, also developed by the Fox family. Apart from these there was a small public campsite on the river at Msembe. Great interest was being shown in developing more lodges and facilities in an effort to diversify the tourist product beyond the northern circuit based around Arusha and the Serengeti. The improved access to the Park was also a positive factor. The General Management Plan had identified a number of sites for lodges and camps in accordance with the zoning plan. These were clearly defined by us and approved by the planning unit in Arusha HQ. Also well defined were specific areas where there would be no development of any kind. This was for either scientific reasons or, more often, they were localities with exceptional tourist appeal that we judged should be available for all visitors to access equally, without exclusivity. Companies expressing an interest in developing a tourist facility in Ruaha were given a list of approved sites with geographical coordinates. In mid-1995 we began to see representatives of these companies visiting the Park and requesting to be shown the sites. Because I was busy finalising other aspects of the GMP I usually delegated this responsibility to Baba Moi or one of his senior wardens. This was a mistake. Over a few weeks it became apparent that the Tanzanian staff had a very lax attitude to the requirements of the GMP, especially with regard to the development of tourist facilities. I met one or two businessmen, usually those based in Iringa who had some knowledge of the Park and acquaintance with Baba Moi, who claimed to have been offered access to sites that were certainly not designated in the GMP. I had no proof that any unorthodox payments or favours were involved, but after spending three years exposed to the goings on in all sectors of the Tanzanian civil service I had strong suspicions.

After ministerial approval of the GMP my last few weeks were spent mostly flying on routine park management duties. Moirana was away on leave so I flew a mixture of staff deployments to the various outposts and other anti-poaching duties, fire reconnaissance and even several hours one day looking for clients of Mwagusi Camp who had gone missing. It was a pleasant, stress-free, winding down period and I enjoyed observing corners of the Park that I had seldom visited previously. I flew again to see the despoliation of the Usangu wetlands and wrote a report pleading for remedial intervention, but although there were some changes in the status of the area later, the damage continued, with desperately sad consequences for the Great Ruaha River and the Park.

My years in East Africa were thrilling, eye-opening, instructive and mostly very enjoyable, but underlying most of it was a sense of despair. This was born of the inexorable increase of humanity, something that had not yet impacted Botswana. The environmental consequences of the growth in human population conflicted with the natural world, mostly through exploitation of resources – loss of habitats, water shortages, land degradation, poaching, overfishing, badly planned infrastructure and an almost complete lack of responsibility towards the natural environment. Only a tiny educated and enlightened few cared and even fewer tried to do anything about it. Every FORS member was outnumbered by hundreds of thousands of people whose existence depended on degrading the environment through farming, mining, building and a host of other activities. Even the efforts of apparently well-meaning NGOs like FZS and WWF, as well as a host of international aid organisations such as USAID, FAO and ODA, seemed to me to be more about the careers and lifestyles of their expatriate employees. Time spent on meetings about "terms of service" – allowances (I had three different types of expenses for time spent away from home), leave allocation, transport etc – seemed to be a priority. These attitudes were inevitably reflected in the behaviour of local civil servants at all levels and had evolved further into a quagmire of corruption.

I'm afraid that I left Tanzania at the end of October 1995 with very mixed feelings and little optimism for the future of its amazing landscapes and incomparable wildlife.

SIXTEEN

ZAMBIAN INTERLUDE

We were in London over Christmas 1995 because Eleanor was expecting a baby boy on Christmas Day. The obstetrician discovered that the baby was an unusual breech presentation and after failing to correct this declared that a caesarian section would be required. He was quite a flamboyant character who performed his private work at the famous Lindo Wing at St Mary's Hospital, Paddington, where the celebrated princes, William and Harry, had made their debuts. Our health insurance classified a "caesar" as an emergency and therefore covered the associated costs of "going private" so that's what we did. The consultant suggested, "We don't want to work on Christmas Day, do we? I think we can fit it in tomorrow if that's OK with you." Michael was therefore delivered a week early on the eighteenth.

I was approached at that time by an Italian company, ARCA Consulting, that was bidding for an EU project in Zambia. The project was to oversee the formation of a Zambia Wildlife Authority (ZAWA) to replace the current Department of National Parks and Wildlife (DNPW) that was seen as corrupt and dysfunctional. The team of consultants was to include a Protected Area Planning Officer. The Italian company's bid mentioned a list of well-known African wildlife scientists who appeared to be taking part, including elephant and predator experts, wildlife census specialists etc and I was excited to be part of the team. In the event none of them materialised and I eventually learned that they had merely been "window dressing" to make the bid more competitive. It was a first lesson for me in the dark arts of international consultancy. I gradually came to realise that the EU's tendering system almost guaranteed the worst job at the highest price for the client. Previously I had operated in a sheltered world where an organisation like ODA or USAID provided the funds, hired the required expertise and administered the project. It wasn't very efficient, but at least it was an honest attempt to deliver the goods. Now I was a freelance individual working for a private company that knew how to exploit the system for their own maximum benefit. Still, all I knew at the beginning was that the job sounded exciting and the rewards seemed generous. We would start in March.

Escaping the British winter as soon as baby Michael could travel, we headed down to South Africa's Eastern Cape where we owned a small 1820s settler's cottage in the small village of Bathurst, a bohemian community just eight miles from the sea and surrounded by pineapple farms. The cottage didn't amount to much, but it was a relaxing place to spend a couple of months with two small children. We became friends with a few of the local farmers who lived in a state of constant, mild bewilderment at the dress, hairstyles and behaviour of some of their neighbours. Nearby was Port Alfred with miles of beautiful, empty beaches that we made the most of, and Grahamstown, South Africa's mini-Oxford, just an hour's drive inland.

Of course, the project did not start on schedule in March – this was Africa after all – but we eventually made it to Lusaka in July. The Zambian capital was a pretty large, shambolic city with bad roads and worse traffic. Not as big or bad as Dar had been, but it didn't have the benefits of a coastline. We were booked into the Pamodzi, one of three large, modern hotels in the city centre. The project manager, Vanni Puccioni, was based in Firenze in Italy and arrived about the same time as us. He looked and sounded Italian, a sharp dresser and sharp operator and I started to have second thoughts about the project despite his assurances. The proposed "stellar" team now seemed to have dwindled to four and I had met two of the others previously. The Project Leader was John Boshe, a Tanzanian whom I'd met a few times when he was WWF's man in Dar. There was a Scots financial manager, Russell Clark, who had worked in Zambia and Zimbabwe for many years and finally my old adversarial colleague from TANAPA, Asukile Kajuni, who would share the planning duties with me.

We had the usual introductory meetings with the ministerial and DNPW staff and discussed the approach we would take to perform the terms of reference. Kajuni and I were expected to visit all nineteen Zambian national parks and draw up thumb-nail sketches of each one – conservation value, condition, potential for revenue generation etc, while Russell and John would start evaluating the structure and function of DNPW at their headquarters at Chilanga, just south of the city. Our first progress report would be due after three months.

Two weeks in the Pamodzi Hotel with two very small children was taxing, especially for Eleanor, and we were very relieved to meet the son of Mike Woodford, my old "boss" from Uganda, who offered to let us stay in his house while he was on leave. Shortly afterwards we found an acceptable house for ourselves and after some heated discussions eventually persuaded Vanni to provide the rent. We were quite shocked to see the security measures that seemed to be the norm for expatriate houses in the suburbs. The outgoing American tenants had constructed high concrete walls around the garden and installed floodlighting. There were also substantial steel burglar bars on the inside and outside of all the windows, but we supposed we would get used to it all. The Americans also left us two very large dogs that were confined to a small fenced area during the day, but roamed the garden at night. They were quite friendly, but looked very intimidating. This was a problem for young Katharine who was terrified of all dogs, having been constantly warned as a toddler in Ruaha to avoid monkeys, baboons and other potentially dangerous animals.

Visiting people with pet dogs was always a problem, especially embarrassing for a veterinarian. Nevertheless, with intensive supervised contact she became used to them fairly quickly, particularly when the female rottweiler produced eight puppies soon after we moved in. The *piece de resistance* was a "Dirty Harry"-style .44 Magnum revolver that the American insisted I take over from him. I could hardly point it, let alone shoot it and thankfully never had to use it! It was all a bit over the top really and I think reflected more on the Americans than Lusaka.

In fact we found Lusaka a very pleasant place to live in. It was obviously a lot more hectic than our previous few years in Ruaha, but there were compensations in the wonderful climate and far more social opportunities. We found Zambia much less exotic than the Arab and Muslim influenced Tanzania; it was far more like the southern Africa we had been used to for many years. Eleanor became quite busy and found a good nursery school for Katharine. The Zambian people were happy and agreeable and we quickly found help with baby Michael, the house and garden. With most of a very large country to cover I was away in the bush much of the time, but Eleanor seemed to cope in town with a busy social life and working with the Wildlife Producers Association, a pro-active subsidiary of the National Farmers' Union.

Kajuni and I divided our responsibilities between the distant and remote parks and those that were more easily accessible from Lusaka. Because I could fly it made sense for me to deal with the former, so I arranged to acquire a Zambian pilot's licence. The process followed a similar pattern to that in Tanzania; I needed to pass a medical and an examination in Zambian air law, after which my previously logged experience would qualify me for a licence. The medical was slightly more orthodox, in that the doctor checked my blood pressure and my eyesight, but the air law exam was more demanding. This time there was no taxi fare involved but the CAA official "recommended" that I take a course of lessons without which I was unlikely to pass. He thought six lessons would suffice and he was happy to teach me in the evenings for twenty dollars a lesson. After a few minutes, a total "tuition fee" of fifty dollars was agreed and the licence was duly issued on the spot. I then arranged with Proflight, a local air-charter company to hire an aircraft at a reasonable rate. After a brief flight test, the owner, Tony Irwin, was happy to let me have first call on a six-seater Cessna 206 for our work and by early October we were ready to go. In the meantime, I had discovered that ARCA Consulting had arranged that my salary and other administrative matters would be handled through their partners in the project, a leading Swedish consultancy company, Carl Bro, a great source of relief.

My first real project was to conduct an aerial game census in two national parks, Sioma Ngwezi and Liuwa Plains, situated west of the Zambezi River in Barotseland. We started with Sioma Ngwezi, down in the southwestern corner of the country against the Angolan and Namibian borders. I therefore arranged a delivery of avgas in drums to an airfield at Senanga on the Zambezi River. There was a fairly run-down fishing camp there where we could base our crew. After six days of survey flying, first a recce and then systematic transects, it became clear that Sioma Ngwezi was very depleted of large wild animals. We counted 200 elephants, a few sable and some small groups of impala. Driving on the few tracks in the Park revealed little in the way of wildlife and there were no infrastructural developments. I was surprised to find that beacons marking the international boundary with Angola were some distance from the Kwando River. This meant that the river and most of its floodplains were not Zambian territory as we had assumed. We found several settlements along the river on both sides and all were technically in Angola, an unusual situation that made it impossible for the Zambian DNPW staff to effectively police the area and left any wildlife using the river extremely vulnerable. Park staff had no vehicles and were restricted to patrolling locally on foot. They had even created a few fields for growing food and lived more as subsistence farmers than park managers.

We turned our attention to Liuwa Plains, further north, before the imminent rains started. Basing ourselves out of Kalabo, a large village on the west bank of the Zambezi, we covered the vast short grass plains between the Luambimba and Luanginga Rivers quite quickly. Even though the wet season influx hadn't really started we were pleasantly surprised to see large numbers of blue wildebeest, with some zebra and tsessebe, as well as plenty of oribi scattered throughout. There was definitely some potential in this unusual place, in contrast to the disappointing Sioma. In fact a tour operator, Robin Pope, was already making a limited number of fly-camping visits during the time of year when access was possible across the floodplains via the town of Mongu on the opposite bank of the Zambezi.

We stayed in a small guesthouse in Kalabo and crossed into the Park via a small pontoon on the Luanginga River. It was interesting to see quite substantial villages with domestic stock inside the Park. These originated from previous times before the Park was proclaimed, when it was a royal preserve under the King of Barotseland and the resident villagers were charged with protecting various species of wildlife. The airport at Kalabo had obviously seen much better days. The surface was tar, although grass and forbs had grown through it over most of the runway and apron, so there was obviously very little traffic. There was a fairly substantial but derelict terminal building with a small passenger lounge, toilets and various offices, all long-since abandoned. Apparently the national carrier, Zambia Airways, had previously flown regular schedule flights from Lusaka, but that was several years ago.

My Cessna parked on the apron attracted attention. One evening while we were enjoying a pre-dinner cold beer at the guesthouse the lady proprietor called me to the door to meet a man who wished to talk to the pilot. From his accent I judged him to be Angolan. After very little small-talk he asked me if I was interested in buying some elephant tusks. He assured me that they were small enough to fit in the Cessna. He was only slightly taken aback when I told him that I was working for the Wildlife Department, but realising that there was no chance of a sale he changed tack and offered me some contraband diamonds. Kalabo had more to it than met the eye!

Next was to visit West Lunga NP. No one had any useful information about this remote, densely forested Park in North-West Province, even at DNPW headquarters in Chilanga. There was reportedly an airstrip at Jivundu in the southern end of the Park next to the river, where I was told the park headquarters were located. I took off one morning from Lusaka and headed northwest across the Kafue NP towards West Lunga. With me was a lady biologist from Chilanga who professed an interest in seeing the area. Weather and visibility were good and we easily located the airstrip on the West Lunga River. On landing I was surprised by the excellent, newly cut grass surface of the airstrip and the white painted stone markers spelling out the camp's name. Two rangers approached the aircraft when I parked and saluted smartly as we got out. They appeared delighted to see us and explained that visitors from Chilanga were very rare. The senior of the two proffered a battered notebook that served as a register of visiting aircraft. The last flight had been over two years ago! These neglected employees maintained the airstrip, regularly cutting it by hand and keeping it in excellent condition on the off chance that someone would fly in. I was astounded! We then walked down to their dilapidated office by the river bank. The roof had mostly caved in and the walls seemed to be held up by termite mounds. There was a powerful smell of bat guano. All the furniture and fittings apart from one steel filing cabinet had succumbed to termites, but the senior ranger produced an occurrence book for me to read and sign. I was truly flabbergasted to see that the last entry was signed by my old boss, the retired Chief Game Warden in Botswana, Lindsay Birch. He had been Chief Warden in Zambia until about 1980, so the entry was truly historic!

They explained that there were eight staff in all, but four were away in Solwezi collecting salaries and buying rations. They farmed a tiny patch of land next to the river and grew some cassava, vegetables and melons for subsistence. We were shown a boat with a small outboard engine that was meant for crossing the deep river into the Park proper. From the other bank a short network of paths penetrated a little way into the park, but there was no road. In the following year I returned by road to the northern park boundary at Ntambu village and tried to penetrate south towards Jivundu, some forty miles away. Even reaching the park boundary along a rough, overgrown track was hard enough, but inside the track soon became almost impossible to follow. After a very short distance we came across a human skull attached high in a tree over the track. Below it was a kind of notice adorned with feathers and bits of animal skin. The driver and game scouts abruptly refused to go any further.

They were very animated and obviously worried. Eventually one of them explained to me that this was very bad witchcraft and protected the park from unwelcome visitors. Later I learned that a small-scale rebellion had taken place in that area a few years previously and the ringleaders had sheltered inside the Park to avoid arrest. Some people thought they were still in there and as there had been no DNPW patrols or tourists there was no evidence to the contrary. That was the end of our expedition, but I had seen enough to provide me with material for a situation report at our next project meeting. The park had little potential for tourism, very few large mammals and virtually no infrastructure. It had been proclaimed many years before to protect the yellow-backed duiker and although I hadn't actually seen one, there were reported sightings and nothing to suggest that it was not thriving in the thick forest.

The so-called "northern parks" were next to be assessed, but very briefly. These were about 750 miles from Lusaka, close to the Congo and Tanzanian borders in the vicinity of Lake Tanganyika. After transporting fuel drums to Kasama airstrip, Lusenga Plains and Mweru Wantipa were quickly scanned from the air and found to be heavily settled by people with very little wildlife remaining. Although there were some scenic features in the region, most notably spectacular waterfalls, it was decided that little could be done to rehabilitate the parks during the lifespan of the project. Sumbu on Lake Tanganyika had more potential for tourism, especially fishing for the celebrated Goliath tiger fish. This park also had some remarkable scenery and some wildlife, but was simply too remote and lacking in infrastructure to be a high priority for us. I did not survey Isangano or Lavushi Manda NPs, relying on local opinion that they were almost completely degraded and invaded by very large numbers of illegal settlements. In this area, however, we did survey the Bangweulu wetlands and noted the spectacular concentrations of endemic black lechwe antelope. Clearly some sort of conservation initiative was justified there. The nearby Kasanka NP was a special place, the first privately managed park in Zambia, under the auspices of the Kasanka Trust. It had tourism potential and scientific importance if for nothing more than the massive migration of straw-coloured fruit bats that it hosted in November and was later celebrated on television by David Attenborough as the largest mammalian migration in the world – a degree of hyperbole that I'll allow my hero!

In the eastern part of the country the two large parks in the Luangwa Valley dominated. The world famous South Luangwa NP attracted most of Zambia's tourists and had consequently received most attention from the authorities, so we spent very little effort on it initially. There was also an ongoing community conservation project, the Luangwa Integrated Rural Development Program (LIRDP) in the game management areas in the valley. This was very similar to the ODA initiative we had started adjacent to Ruaha in Tanzania and I was familiar with it from my Tanzanian staff field trip. The North Luangwa NP, by contrast, was heavily poached and was closed to visitors. By coincidence it was the subject of a major initiative by Frankfurt Zoological Society, with a large project based out of Mpika, managed by Mark and Delia Owens whom I knew well from Botswana a decade earlier. We concluded that this specialised project was best left to be independent, at least for the time being. The smaller Luambe and Lukusuzi NPs were not surveyed either and again we relied on local opinion that they were heavily degraded and poached, with little immediate chance of rehabilitation.

I used to play tennis on Sunday mornings at the US Ambassador's residence. During one match he was called away for an important telephone call. He returned to the court after some time, clearly disturbed. Mark and Delia Owens had been placed under house arrest in Mpika and the Minister who had telephoned explained that they might be charged with murder. Allegedly Mark had ordered one of his anti-poaching guards to shoot a suspect that they had been interrogating. I knew that it could be a brutal conflict in North Luangwa and according to reports Mark had been becoming more obsessive and irrational, but this seemed too unlikely to be true. The Ambassador was aware that I had known the Owens well in Botswana, so I think he was happy to talk to me about the incident. I told him that eventually they had been thrown out of Botswana by presidential directive after some strange behaviour on their part and recent stories seemed to describe a similar tendency in Zambia. The Ambassador informed me that they had been given forty-eight hours to leave the country before any charges or arrests were made. The saga continued back in America, where they were quite high-profile celebrities, but eventually died down. FZS brought in a South African couple to take over as head of the North Luangwa Project and it continued with some success.

I visited the tiny parks of Blue Lagoon and Lochinvar to the west of Lusaka on either bank of the Kafue River. They had both been private ranches in colonial times and were notable for their floodplain concentrations of Kafue lechwe, another endemic subspecies. Each year the DNPW authorities culled a large number of these antelope and distributed the meat from Chilanga. It was interesting to note a high incidence of bovine tuberculosis among the lechwe herds, but this seemed to be no deterrent to the annual cull – oh the power of meat in Africa!

We surveyed the spectacular Lower Zambezi NP situated in the floodplain below an escarpment to the east of Lusaka. The escarpment seemed to confine the large herds of game, notably buffalo and elephant, to the Zambezi Valley where they were contiguous with populations in Mana Pools in Zimbabwe. There was some tourist development beginning in the area, though road communications were difficult seasonally, and the revenue generating potential was thought to be enormous.

Kafue NP in the south-central part of the country is an enormous protected area, about the size of Wales. It was beyond our means to accomplish anything really meaningful here and we took the temporary position that it was "too big to fail", a principle that must be used with extreme caution in conservation. However, in the project's early days we did have a look at the elephant population mainly in the southern sector, leaving the spectacular Busangu Plains in the north for a later day. We took the opportunity to build a training component into the elephant surveys and camped at Ngoma for a week in June 1997 with some DNPW staff and an experienced aerial census consultant from Namibia, Colin Craig. We decided that I would fly the aircraft and Colin would deal with the training of the observers, both ground schooling and in the air. We flew six up for training with four observers in the rear seats. To demarcate the transects that the observers would use we tied strings to the aeroplane's wing struts at calculated intervals. These indicated 250 yard-wide strips on the ground if we flew at 250 feet above the ground. The strings were positioned by means of small plastic funnels that trailed behind the wing.

On one occasion, luckily on the last day, the observer sitting right behind me tapped me on the shoulder just after take-off. I turned and he pointed out that one of the strings on our side had become tangled around a wheel. I indicated to Colin that he should take over the aircraft's controls and fly slowly. I opened the window to reach out and rectify the situation, but my new, very expensive, superlight spectacles immediately blew off and disappeared. This was a problem. Although Colin could see the aircraft's instruments with his reading glasses, I couldn't. Conversely, he could not see out to fly the aircraft safely, but I had reasonable distance vision without glasses. We abandoned the final training flight and managed to land back at Ngoma with a joint effort. Flying back to Lusaka International Airport the following day was more challenging, but we somehow managed it safely.

Of course, the jewel in the crown of Zambian natural resources is its share of Victoria Falls, an iconic tourist asset on the Zambezi River. Zambia, like Zimbabwe, had created a very small national park called Mosi oa Tunya ("the smoke that thunders"), the original local name of the huge cataract, and we were obliged to include it in our project. Livingstone, the adjacent small town, had been very run-down but was beginning to revive with an increase in tourism revenue.

In May 1997 we presented the results of our whistle-stop assessment of the country's national parks estate to a large workshop in Lusaka in which participants deliberated over our findings and recommendations before drawing up a list of priorities for more detailed management planning. In true participatory and autonomous fashion the plenary decided its highest concerns were the potential cash cows of Lower Zambezi and Victoria Falls, though the project's technical team suspected some political pressure had been applied from the Ministry or even higher. Nonetheless, we embarked on the production of general management plans for these two national parks as part of the second phase of our project.

Meanwhile the analysis and appraisal of the structure and function of DNPW continued in parallel. It was more or less agreed that the national parks estate and its responsibilities for conservation and wildlife management should be removed from direct government control. The Kenya Wildlife Service (KWS), with its charismatic chairman Richard Leakey, formed in 1989, had been very much in the limelight. He had raised millions of dollars, mainly from the World Bank, to finance the fight against elephant poaching and corruption. Although KWS and Leakey were experiencing problems in the mid-1990s the Zambian Government and ARCA Consulting decided that the model was worth emulating. Consequently the project undertook to create Zambia Wildlife Authority (ZAWA) by 1999.

This was a mammoth task and involved our management team and a host of specialist, short-term consultants in intensive negotiations and discussions with all levels of government, NGOs, communities, labour unions and aid donors. One of the main obstacles was finding a person of equivalent ability and principle as Richard Leakey to head the organisation. Obviously it needed to be a Zambian national and unfortunately there was no stand-out candidate. Luckily, as field technicians Kajuni and I were able to avoid most of this often unpleasant job and concentrate on park planning. While the project in Lusaka set about firing the whole DNPW work force I spent most of my time in

Livingstone developing a detailed management plan for Mosi oa Tunya NP. Kajuni had chosen to deal with Lower Zambezi, so I had to concentrate on tourists and Victoria Falls – not really my forte.

It took the rest of 1997 to come up with an acceptable management plan for the Park. Six months of meetings, workshops, and brainstorming in Livingstone culminated in a draft plan that was agreed by all the participating interest groups, or stakeholders, as we were advised to call them. They were an extremely disparate assemblage, including local politicians, biologists, physical and social geographers, hoteliers and traders, traditional chiefs and tourism operators. I found I had a surprising talent as a moderator, far removed from my previous technical roles. Balancing the sometimes conflicting interests of local tribesmen, "Kiwi" bungee jumpers and hard-core ornithologists was taxing but interesting. It was good to get back to Lusaka for short family breaks and progress reports with Russell and John Boshe, even occasionally touching base with Vanni, who made brief visits from Europe to liaise with the higher echelons of government and present our main reports on which ARCA's payments depended.

In late October on one such short visit to Lusaka I got out of bed and drove through the city to the office at Chilanga. I habitually listened to the BBC African News on the radio by my bed at 6.30 but for some reason had missed it on this particular morning. The traffic was much lighter than usual in the city centre, but I didn't give it much thought, I was just grateful for the easier journey. Arriving at Chilanga just before 7.30, I found the gates to the compound still locked. I was puzzled, but not alarmed, until I asked the security guard to open up. He was very reluctant to help and appeared agitated. He didn't speak very much English and I could not understand any of his Chibemba, but something was amiss. I waited for almost half an hour but nobody else showed up so I turned around and drove home again. There was very little traffic but nothing else of note. When I arrived home Eleanor told me excitedly that the BBC had reported a coup attempt in Zambia and that there had been explosions and gunshots heard in the capital – everyone was advised to stay indoors. I had seen and heard nothing! The following day I drove back down to Livingstone and all appeared normal, with President Frederick Chiluba still in charge and a "state of emergency" declared – perhaps the Romans should have said *"ex Africa* ***numquam*** *aliquid novi"*!

Another remarkable car ride across Lusaka happened just before that. Eleanor and I were driving home from dinner with Russell and Naomi Clarke, probably about 10 pm. Ahead, across the brightly lit highway, was a police roadblock. My heart sank because I had drunk a few beers and a couple of glasses of wine; I knew it could mean a hefty fine (probably unofficial and unreceipted) and, worse, maybe a few hours at the nearest police station. One of the officers waved me down and as I stopped he flung open the Land Rover door behind me and jumped in. "Follow that car!" he ordered, pointing at the back of a Mercedes disappearing into the city. I did as I was told and he shouted, "Faster, faster – catch him!" The Merc wasn't speeding so even my Land Rover caught up quite quickly and the policeman yelled, "Pass him and make him stop!" This was fun! I duly passed the unsuspecting driver and quickly pulled over in front of him, giving him no choice but to stop abruptly. I remember the startled look on the driver's face as the policeman shouted, "Thank you sir!" and jumped out before I had actually stopped. I never found out what the motorist had done wrong and just carried on driving home, relieved and very amused.

My relations with John Boshe and more so Vanni Puccioni had been growing more fraught for several months. I believed that John was too "lightweight" and unlikely to make much progress with the more intransigent Zambians who resented our intrusion and revolutionary approach. John's main qualification, I judged, was that he was an African, an important factor in ARCA's bid to win the job in Brussels. He was honest and hard working, but was nowhere near forceful enough. Vanni, the ambitious, consummate businessman, knew the EU setup in Brussels well and tacitly admitted so. Things came to a head between us at a staff meeting where he quite openly stated that we could get the lucrative project extended for several more years if we "played our cards right". This was not something that sat well with me and I made it clear that I disagreed strongly with that sentiment. Something had to give, and in September the decisive event leading to my resignation occurred.

The draft management plan for Mosi oa Tunya was agreed by all the stakeholders and presented to senior government. The ecological component of the fieldwork had identified a single small site of great biological diversity in the tiny Park. All the stakeholders had agreed that this unique site should be fully protected and kept free from any infrastructural development. This was highlighted very clearly in the management plan. On my next visit to Livingstone I was shocked to hear a story that a large hotel chain had secured that very site for development of a luxury lodge. Nothing could be confirmed in Livingstone so I drove back to Lusaka and cornered John Boshe, who feigned ignorance, but hinted that the Vice President might have become involved, despite the fact that the responsible Minister of Natural Resources had signed-off on the plan. The word was that a "consideration" of $50,000 had sealed the deal. It was so blatant, even if there was no tangible proof. I confronted Vanni with my tale, but he shrugged it off too casually – it was their country after all. He must have known all along, but was willing to let it go in the interests of extending the project. It was too much for me – I said I wasn't going to waste my life producing expensive and elaborate plans just so some corrupt official could undo months of effort for personal gain. ARCA would have to find someone else to undertake the next plan that was scheduled for Kafue. Three months later, between Christmas and New Year, after serving my notice period, we were back in the Eastern Cape considering our family future. I knew only that the international consulting scene was not for me, no matter how lucrative. I would have to find some way of getting back to a "hands-on" role with wild animals.

SEVENTEEN

BACK TO BOTS

We no longer owned our settler cottage in the curious pineapple-farming and hipster community of Bathurst in the Eastern Cape, so for a few weeks we rented a holiday house in Kleinemonde, a tiny coastal hamlet a few miles to the east of Port Alfred. Gavin and his family owned a house there and entertained lots of visitors so we were instantly back among friends from Botswana. We had quickly determined to return to Botswana as the sensible place to re-start our domestic and professional lives. Alone among African countries (at least those with wildlife opportunities), it had a stable government and a relatively prosperous economy with freedom of movement of assets. The recently proclaimed city of Gaborone boasted a buoyant housing market, good private primary schools and, most important, a network of old friends and colleagues.

We arrived back in Gaborone in mid-January 1998 and stayed with Brian Downs, who had become a very close friend and Katharine's godfather following the game capture adventure for Orapa Mine fifteen years earlier. Katharine duly started at Thornhill Primary School and clearly enjoyed every minute, Eleanor searched for somewhere permanent to live and I explored different possibilities to earn a living. Good accommodation was scarce, but Sandy Matthews, the wife of Bob, my first accountant at Gaborone Veterinary Clinic, informed us that there was a vacancy at a modern block of flats that she administered. It was centrally situated, with three bedrooms and perfect for our immediate needs. We were very lucky and moved in as soon as we could. The flat was in an upmarket complex of four blocks around a large, well-kept garden with a swimming pool. Its actual name was Mopane Court, but our kids immediately took to calling it "Red Railings" after its most obvious external feature.

Gavin, as enthusiastic as ever, had ideas of revitalising our mothballed game capture business, claiming that there were now more Botswana farmers experimenting with wildlife production, following the exponential growth of the industry in South Africa and growing interest in Zimbabwe and Namibia; surely Botswana would follow suit with its innate advantages of space, relatively cheap, undeveloped farmland and an underexploited, huge wildlife resource. But Gavin was busy with a number of new business ventures and could only offer limited time and support. His ideas were worth considering though and I started to make enquiries through my contacts in the cattle ranching industry and wildlife scene. Still nobody had started a game ranch from scratch, but since I left in 1992 there were more rich, mainly European farmers beginning to utilise their existing wildlife stocks and one or two had even dedicated portions of their cattle ranches to wildlife production by removing cattle and improving their fencing infrastructure. These "pioneers" were mainly situated in cattle-farming blocks on opposite sides of the country in Ghanzi and the Limpopo Valley, separated by the Kalahari Desert. It seemed promising but there were no guarantees of a living, so other avenues had to be explored as well.

My registration as a vet was still valid and in May I also renewed my professional hunter's licence. In July I was checked out again as a pilot and had my licence revalidated. Surely now I was good to go. Gavin lent me an old Land Cruiser station wagon and I looked around in earnest. The obvious choices were veterinary work and safari hunting, with short-term ecological consultancies as a backup. The latter were available, but after my recent experience with the EU, I was not very keen. Gavin, brimming with business acumen and enthusiasm, suggested starting a company that would import veterinary medicines and equipment. I still had a number of contacts from my days in practice, so I called Harry Mahieu, a Belgian working in Johannesburg, whose company exported veterinary products to Botswana. Harry mainly supplied the Ministry of Agriculture with stocks for its countrywide chain of outlets known as Veterinary Vaccine Stores. These sold veterinary and farming supplies direct to the public in all the towns. Volumes of many products they sold were quite large and could be quite profitable, so there was keen competition to supply – even my dentist used to bid on some tenders!

Being a registered vet was an advantage and so we started a company with Harry which we called Kestrel Consultants and entered the field. We won tenders to supply various items from injectable antibiotics to syringes, needles and even burdizzos. The problem was I hated it; I had not an iota of business sense and even less enthusiasm. I just could not understand how people such as Harry and Gavin could generate a passion for such a "dry" activity, even when it made money, but since I was the nominated company veterinarian I had to stay involved, I couldn't let the others down.

On one of Harry's frequent visits to Gaborone we had a "business meeting" at Mike's Kitchen, a restaurant/bar that was another of Gavin's new ventures and run by a very popular mutual friend, Peter Malcomess. Naturally, this involved a few of the local St Louis lagers. I left before 5 pm to beat the traffic and headed home. I decided to cut through a fairly run-down central district of the city that I remembered to avoid the busiest roads. The place had changed a lot in the six years we had been away and the route I was taking was also very busy. Unknown to me one of the road junctions had changed priorities and although I noticed a *"Stop"* sign it seemed to be pointing at the road on my left as it used to (it was actually at about forty-five degrees to the traffic, so open to interpretation I suppose). Whatever, I sailed across the junction and collided with a kombi that I had assumed would stop at the sign in question. My station wagon then bounced off a deep concrete culvert and ended on its side in a ditch. I was very shaken and, not wearing a seat belt, had damaged my ribs and sternum on the steering wheel. Before I could react much a policeman kicked out the damaged windscreen, hauled me out and into his car and we sped off to the nearby Princess Marina Hospital.

A doctor in A&E established that I was not going to die imminently and had me moved to a waiting room at the X-ray department. Somehow Brian Downs appeared quite shortly afterwards and suggested that as I had medical insurance, I move to the new Gaborone Private Hospital, where facilities were much better. Discussing this with the doctor, he was pleased because he'd just been informed that a bus crash had occurred and a number of casualties were expected very soon. Brian drove me across the city to the GPH in Broadhurst and I registered at A&E again. I was immediately taken to the X-ray department. Gavin duly arrived and joined Brian in the waiting room. While I was being X-rayed a policeman arrived to interview me about the crash. Luckily he was intercepted by my friends in the waiting room. The officer explained that he needed to breathalyse me and that the kombi driver had tested negative. Brian quickly turned to Gavin and said with a wink, "Dr Patterson might be a while, but he doesn't drink, does he?" to which Gavin replied, "No, he's always been teetotal". This satisfied the policeman, who politely thanked them, saying he would come back later to take a statement, and departed. I don't think I would have tested positive after just a couple of St Louis, but you never know!

The X-rays showed three fractured ribs, so I was admitted overnight for observation. Gavin and Brian went over to the "Red Railings" to report to Eleanor who collected me the next morning. A friendly police sergeant visited me and took a statement. He advised me to accept an admission of guilt for careless driving and pay a small fine to settle the matter. He explained that contesting it would be a bad option because three policemen sitting on the *stoep* of a sub-district police station, 100 yards away, had witnessed the accident. Gavin's station wagon was a write-off, but it was insured and he didn't seem to mind too much. Ironically, a few years earlier his teenage daughter Brit had turned over my Land Cruiser on his farm's airstrip while "giving driving lessons" to my daughter Samantha. So I suppose we were kind of quits!

I started to get requests for game counts, mostly from private ranchers but also from the diamond mines at Orapa and Jwaneng. Both of these had fairly large fenced game reserves surrounding the actual mines. These had been established in the mid-1980s based on the work done by Eleanor for the mining conglomerate Debswana, a partnership between the Government of Botswana and De Beers. As closed ecological systems with almost no harvesting, the wildlife populations in these reserves had multiplied over more than fifteen years. The mine management suspected that they were overstocked, but had no figures to work with.

So in early August, Kalahari Game Services carried out its first wildlife census/game count at Jwaneng. I had obtained the use of a six-seater Cessna-206 aeroplane that belonged to a Gaborone businessman, Gerald Peinke. Unusually, it was registered in the USA, but under the arcane civil aviation regulations I could fly it legally using my Botswana licence as long as I remained within our borders. The census, with four observers, took three hours to fly and produced acceptable results. The reserve was not generally overstocked, but certain species were imbalanced and I recommended some adjustments – selling a number of animals and using those funds to obtain new blood and a couple of different species.

Conveniently, at the same time we were also engaged to count the game on the nearby farm of Sir Quett Masire at Sekoma. This made the ferry flights from and to Gaborone more economical. Quett had retired from the Presidency in March and been succeeded by Festus Mogae as Botswana's third President. His Sekoma ranch had been neglected while he was dealing with more important matters, but it still held good numbers of some species, such as zebra and gemsbok, so there was something for him to work with.

The same year saw the introduction of so-called "green hunts" on game ranches in South Africa. Clients were allowed to dart certain animals (usually rhinos) under the supervision of a veterinarian and a professional hunter. Usually the animal would undergo some procedure such as tagging or collaring to justify the activity and the paying client would get some unique photos as well as the satisfaction of contributing to a worthwhile process. A leading Botswana safari company, Rann Safaris, approached me and asked if we could start a similar activity in Botswana targeting elephants. A number of researchers had proposed to put radiotelemetry collars on selected elephants and I thought it would be a good opportunity to cover some of the costs of the procedures and help the researchers. However, true to form, the Wildlife Department procrastinated for months and when pressed further decided not to allow it. Some years later we learned that some less scrupulous operators in South Africa had been abusing the practice and it was subsequently banned. It was a pity because with the correct management and ethical behaviour it could have been very useful to some of our research projects.

About a year earlier a man called Braam Coetsee had begun catching and exporting game to South Africa. He operated mainly in the Tuli Block along the South African border, and being one of the Afrikaner community there, he kept pretty busy in a "one-man band" fashion and seemed reasonably successful. An odd character, his last venture had been running a sweet factory in a small Transvaal town, he struggled to get his wildlife export health certificates endorsed by a government vet. There were only two in the area and neither was readily available or really familiar with wild animals and their health conditions. Being held up waiting for a government official to arrive and certify the captured animals as fit for import into South Africa was a major frustration for him. He approached me and I was able to get approval from the Director of Animal Health to examine and certify wild animals for export. The South African authorities were no problem either because I was also registered there. I began flying to wherever Braam was catching and inspecting his animals, mainly impala, wildebeest and kudu, as they were loaded. Of his ilk, Braam was an unusually gentle operator and his animals were only minimally stressed, consequently his survival rates were good. This was in stark contrast to many operators in South Africa and Namibia at the time who sometimes killed about ten per cent of their animals, and a lot more in the case of sensitive, fragile species like impala. This led to pressure from the public and authorities for capture companies to employ veterinarians.

Braam unfortunately got himself into financial difficulties. As good as he was with animals, he was equally bad at managing his accounts. Some bills just have to be paid, such as helicopter hire, fuel and labour. But others, like the purchase price of animals, he found could be delayed, especially as most of his farmer clients were his friends. As payments became more problematic he started bartering; he would take say, 200 impala from a farmer and promise him forty zebra from a future job in exchange. But maybe the weather changed, or for some other reason he wouldn't catch the zebra and his problems multiplied and became more complicated. One or two of his larger clients, like the diamond mines, threatened him with legal action as their invoices piled up, but he still struggled on somehow and I continued certifying his export shipments.

Family life at the "Red Railings" was enjoyable. Eleanor and the kids settled into a busy social life centred on small children, school galas, birthday parties etc and we rekindled many old friendships. Brian and a few other close friends had made the effort to visit us in Ruaha and Lusaka, so we had been kept abreast of some of the major changes to Gaborone's infrastructure like the Western Bypass and the explosive development of adjoining areas like Mogoditshane and Tlokweng. Gabs had become a small, modern city as opposed to the big, sprawling and untidy village it had been when we left. It had come a long way in thirty years.

We were looking for somewhere more permanent to live, and our main search criterion was that it should be within walking distance of Thornhill School; the thought of running the gauntlet of Gabs' ever-increasing traffic at up to four rush hours a day was just too grim. This limited, central area was the first to have been established, close to parliament and the headquarters of most government ministries. Many embassies and foreign missions were also situated there and these factors combined to make it very expensive. Luckily we had some funds in England and the pula to sterling exchange rate was extremely favourable. In July we found a fairly run-down house on a large plot on Khama Crescent. It was owned by the Bank of Botswana. We thought we could just afford it and the magnificent mopipi tree in the otherwise empty garden convinced us, despite Brian, a trained architect, advising us not to slam the door too hard in case the termites "stopped holding hands"! Eleanor organised a transfer of funds from our UK bank and I flew off into the Central Kalahari Game Reserve (CKGR) for a few days to put radio-collars on eland and wildebeest as part of a EU-sponsored research project.

Unknown to me there were dramatic developments... Eleanor found a better house! While I was happily flying around in a helicopter enjoying myself, Gavin's wife, Vicky, told Eleanor that the Flying Mission was selling a property in a quiet cul-de-sac very close to the gate of Thornhill. It suited our needs perfectly, and what's more it came with a separate suite of offices in the back garden. Eleanor immediately offered to buy it and that evening excitedly called me in camp by radio to give me the news. I didn't know what to say – I hadn't seen the place after all, but I knew we didn't have any more money. I could only plead with her somewhat forcefully to re-sell the first house very quickly! Luckily, the first sale was being handled on behalf of the bank by an old friend and he managed to stall for a few days, though we were under severe pressure to find another buyer with minimum delay.

Eleanor went into overdrive; she had the brilliant idea that, as the house adjoined the Vice President's official residence, he should buy it in the interests of security and more space. Ian Khama had been Vice President since March and Eleanor knew him well, mainly from her days as CEO of the Kalahari Conservation Society where he was a committee member. She called him and suggested the idea. He was in favour in principle but since he was preparing for his investiture later that day he couldn't do much about it immediately. He anyway doubted that even he could turn the wheels of government fast enough to release any funds in the required time. Eleanor told him she would have to seek another cash buyer.

On my return from the CKGR I too looked frantically for a buyer and we discovered that John Bennett, a Scots electrician we knew, was urgently looking for a property for his family joining him from Australia. He had the money and the wherewithal to fix the place up quickly and its central situation suited him; it was a great relief. So within a week we had owned two properties in one of Gabs' most exclusive suburbs. We moved into the Flying Mission's house in August and Eleanor, particularly, was kept very busy making it comfortable and functional. The main house had been used as bachelor quarters for some of the Mission's young pilots so needed some attention and decorating. The offices in the back had been used by the boss, Dr Malcom McArthur, so were in pretty good condition. Some of the walls in the offices were at unusual angles and he explained that years previously the Mission had used the building as a recording studio and the strange angles were to reduce echoes.

The main house was soon made perfectly habitable by Brian's best friend, Alan Rice. Alan was, and still is, one of the country's characters. A "Scouser", from Birkenhead, he arrived in the 1970s as a bricklayer and became a top building foreman in a very busy sector. Everybody knew him, but his main claim to fame was being the only white man ever to play for the national soccer team, the Zebras – Everton never knew what they had missed!

An old friend, Chris Collins, called me and asked if I could help him with a couple of hunting safaris in the Okavango. He had branched out on his own after years of working for older established companies and his freelance ventures seemed to be bearing fruit. I was available and cheap, so my relative inexperience didn't worry him too much. Sometime in June I headed up to Maun and joined Chris at his base on the Thamalakane River just south of the town. He had two serviceable hunting vehicles and several rifles, so I was quickly kitted out. I heard that my old tracker Mmusi had left Safari South and I set about locating him. It didn't take long to find him and establish that he was at a loose end, though that seldom bothered most of the seasonal safari workers. He agreed to join up with me again and we left for Chris's hunting camp in the lower Delta on the beautiful Santantadibe River.

Chris had formed a relationship with an absurdly rich Californian real estate mogul who had a thing about collecting big elephant trophies. Every year he would hunt in northern Mozambique and shoot two elephants and then come to Botswana for a more relaxed safari with Chris. Because there were very few big trophy elephants in Botswana he often bought a licence but didn't use it. Chris told me that at his colossal ranch house in California he had a "trophy room" with over a dozen full mounts of elephants – his own still-life herd! He also had a collection of hundreds of exceptionally rare and valuable motor cars, though he didn't drive. Like many extremely wealthy individuals he was thoroughly spoiled and selfish and made camp life quite unpleasant, despite all the rare delicacies and vintage Chateau Lafitte wine he had flown into Maun in his own jet.

On this occasion he had with him a Spanish banker and his son-in-law who he was entertaining in anticipation of a big marina development project. I would look after the Spaniards while Chris escorted the American. It meant I was busy because the banker had never been on an African safari before and he and his son-in-law wanted to shoot as many trophies as possible, but not lion or leopard. Over two or three days we worked through their licences, collecting specimens of the common species like impala, kudu and lechwe. The banker proved to be an excellent shot and never used more than one bullet on any animal. Each evening in camp the American host would complain about the lack of trophy elephants in the area – he didn't want to shoot anything else.

On the fourth morning he and Chris left camp early and the rest of us headed off in the opposite direction, through a non-hunting area along the river and then into another section of the hunting concession. The Spaniard shot a buffalo with his customary expertise and while it was being skinned and butchered for loading I went on the radio to see how Chris was getting along. He calmly announced that they had shot a 100-pounder and were back in camp. I laughed, thinking he was joking; there had only been five or six 100-pound elephants shot in Botswana in the last thirty years. "Really!" he insisted. "One tusk is worn and maybe a bit less, but the other is definitely over 100 pounds." This we had to see, so as soon as we could load the buffalo we headed back to camp. Vintage champagne was flowing when we arrived and the American was ecstatic. We drove out to the dead elephant and examined the impressive tusks. They were fairly short, unlike those in East Africa, but like most Botswana bulls, they were really thick. Chris recounted how they had been crossing the river at a ford when their tracker spotted the animal in the non-hunting zone on the far side. They crossed back and waited, hoping that the elephant would also cross the river into the hunting concession. They drove upstream for about half a mile to where they thought the old tusker might cross and waited. Sure enough he slowly approached and crossed the river. They followed on foot the legally required distance away from the river into the hunting concession and the Californian killed him with a shot to the chest that went clean through the heart.

Back in camp the party went on late in the evening. Everyone was pretty drunk, when the Californian, in keeping with his capricious nature, abruptly announced that they would be leaving the next day. The Spaniards implored him to stay on until they too had shot an elephant. A maximum four-day extension was reluctantly granted, even though the safari had been paid for and scheduled for another two weeks. I would have my work cut out; the 100-pounder was a hard act to follow.

Over the following two days we saw dozens of elephants in the concession area, it seemed to be prime bull habitat. Nothing came close to the Californian's trophy size though and the banker became reconciled to collecting a more modest trophy. Then on the next to last day we came across a group of three old bulls. They all appeared to be at least fifty pounders, with the biggest one perhaps sixty-five. He was the biggest we had seen in the week so far and I suggested that we might not see anything bigger. Most of the elephant tusks shot on safari in Botswana weighed between fifty and sixty pounds, anything bigger was exceptional. The Spaniard and I stalked carefully upwind and when we were within thirty yards, with the three bulls unaware, I whispered that he should shoot the biggest when he had a clear shot to the chest. He did so and all three wheeled away. I then also fired, again into the bull's chest. We didn't have to run after them because it was immediately obvious that the biggest bull was not keeping up with the other two and within 100 yards he fell over.

By the time I reached him he was already dead, no need for a *coup de grace*. The banker arrived beside me and was hyper-excited, like many clients with their first major prize. He and his son-in-law exchanged congratulations in Spanish and asked me to take a number of photos. A few minutes later he asked me why I had fired. I explained that it was official policy if there was any chance of a wounded animal escaping. This went for all the "dangerous" game. He accepted this, but was obviously disappointed. "But you know I shoot very well and would not make a mistake," he exclaimed. "Yes, that's true," I conceded, "but I can't take any chances". He calmed down as his son-in-law approached with a satellite phone and proceeded to place a call on the big, unwieldy gadget, something I'd never seen. After some excited exchanges in Spanish, he called me over and gave me the receiver saying "The King wants to speak to you"! Then I heard a clear voice say in perfect English "This is Juan Carlos, I'm very pleased that you managed to secure a nice elephant for my friend. I really hope that I can come to Botswana myself soon and make a safari." Slightly taken aback, I just replied "Yes, I hope so too, thank you," and handed the receiver back to the banker who continued his animated dialogue with royalty. Later, I was able to show that his first bullet had been lethal and that my back-up shot had not been necessary, much to his satisfaction.

Shorty after this King Juan Carlos was told that Botswana could not properly guarantee his security if he were to go on safari, so the idea was shelved. But in 2012 he did visit Botswana for a hunting trip under a strict news blackout. This ended in a PR disaster when the King fell and was injured, curtailing the safari and hitting the news headlines. Ultimately, the negative publicity from the anti-hunting lobby contributed to his abdication in 2014.

After this safari I concluded that professional safari hunting was not for me. I had had enough of babysitting the super-rich, and although some clients were entirely pleasant and even entertaining, for the most they were too egocentric and philosophically alien to my principles of conservation for me to feel comfortable with them. Almost exclusively their motives were based on recreation; only rarely did I meet someone who shared my beliefs and never my passion. Not that I was against enjoying and using natural resources in a consumptive manner, I considered that ethical hunting operators had no detrimental effects on the environment and were infinitely preferable to the damage and desecration caused by the photographic or so-called "non-consumptive" tourist industry. In later years, witnessing its increasingly destructive effects on every tourist destination from Venice to the Galapagos, this belief has been strengthened exponentially.

Another venture started by Chris was to build a luxury camp near Tubu Island in the western Delta. The site he had chosen was just outside the Buffalo Fence, so of no particular interest to the big safari companies who were bidding at that time for long-term leases in the Delta. The closest prime area was Jao, inside the fence, which Chris had been interested in but where he had been outbid by greater financial muscle despite tendering a competitive, practical management plan. Tubu was a much smaller enterprise in partnership with the village community and based on a combination of bird shooting and mokoro tourism. He had painstakingly set up a development trust in the village, where he knew several residents who had worked for him for years as trackers or mokoro polers. The village headman was well known to him and was appointed as chairman of the trust. Chris asked me if I would be interested in becoming a partner in a new company, Tubu Safaris, with the headman and Chris as co-directors. He was quite persuasive, extolling the finer qualities of the area and how he had lots of potential bird shooting clients lined up. The local Subordinate Land Board, based in Gumare, had approved the scheme and Chris was waiting for a lease from the main Land Board in Maun. It sounded cut and almost dried and was an attractive and interesting proposition. My role, apart from providing some funds, was to prepare the required management proposal documents, something I had a lot of experience with. I agreed to join them and I became a director of Tubu Safaris (Pty) Ltd.

Chris and I bought some luxury tents, a generator, water pump and various items of camp hardware and set to work. I spent a couple of months on-site, bush clearing, building decks and pitching tents, plumbing and wiring etc.

It was an enjoyable hands-on experience in a beautiful spot. The labourers from the village were keen and cheerful, if a bit raw. By July we had something approaching a mid-level luxury camp ready for use. I went to Johannesburg and bought six fibreglass mekoro – part of our commitment to the village and in line with the latest "green" effort to conserve the Okavango's big trees. We supervised the clearing and basic construction of a community campsite about a mile away from the camp on a lagoon nearer to Tubu village. The idea was for the trust to manage the campsite and take visitors on mokoro trips while the main camp, run by Chris, would be mainly for foreign bird-shooting tourists.

At that time, in mid-year, we had two problems: there was no water in the lagoons and nearby channels; and the Land Board was dragging its feet. The former eventually resolved itself and the area was transformed into an idyllic wilderness, more so because the water prevented the village cattle from getting anywhere near the camp. We were extremely upbeat and enthusiastic. Unfortunately the lease continued to be elusive. From previous experience and reputation we concluded that the Land Board in Maun must be holding out for a bribe. I returned to Gabs leaving Chris to sort things out. We were adamant that we would not pay any inducement to the Maun "fat cats" and instead Chris engaged a lawyer to try to move things along. This was the wrong move. Discussions with other operators confirmed our suspicions and we were advised to try things in the "time-honoured" fashion. We refused and there was an expensive year-long stand-off at the end of which we pulled out as much equipment as we could and sold it unused, but second-hand. Tubu never operated and the trust and village were denied a golden opportunity.

The following year continued with a series of aerial game censuses for a mixed bag of clients – farmers, mines and even the Wildlife Department. I also continued to assist Braam with his exports, but he seemed to get ever deeper into financial difficulties. I arranged a couple of game capture operations at Jwaneng mine on behalf of Specialist Game Services of South Africa. This was a well-funded and equipped company managed by a young "whizz kid", Kester Vickery, whose many talents included being a brilliant salesman. These operations were very successful and enhanced our reputation with Jwaneng and the fledgling industry generally. As I was the local front man, as well as responsible for the exports, it raised my profile and put KGS in an advantageous position. I was however still dependent on personal income from the occasional short-term consultancy. I wrote one or two management plans for concession areas in and around the Okavango, mainly based on the work I had done in the 1980s with Australia's Snowy Mountains Engineering Corporation. I even returned to Zambia for a few days to write an Environmental Impact Assessment for a scheme to improve the main road from Kapiri Mposhe to Mpika, an exercise in "painting by numbers". Slightly more interesting was a scouting expedition up the west bank of the Zambezi from Senyanga to Kalabo to try to find a route for heavy engineering equipment to be used on the planned Mongu to Kalabo causeway across the Zambezi floodplains.

There was one remarkable experience in early October. I was shaving at about 6 am preparing for an early flight to Mashatu in northeastern Tuli Block for a game survey. Our new house in Sebina Close was less than 100 yards from the perimeter wall of State House, the President's residence. I heard an aircraft circling quite low. This puzzled me because the centre of town was restricted airspace and no flying was permitted. I drove out to the airport, arriving about 6.30. On my way to the pilots' briefing room to file a flight plan I met an official called Selwyn Lloyd, the Chief Safety Officer. He was rushing to the control tower and shouted to me that the airport was closed, "We have a crazy up there!" I immediately drove around to the eastern side of the airport where my aircraft was parked and climbed aboard, switching on the radio, just in time to hear the tower instructing the "crazy" to switch to a private channel. Of course I did the same and eavesdropped on an amazing dialogue between the tower and the circling pilot. I was the only other pilot at the airport so had exclusive access to the transmissions.

Chris Phatswe, the pilot, had recently been grounded for medical reasons he claimed were unreasonable and harboured a serious grudge against his employers, Air Botswana. He had entered the airport before dawn using his security pass and taken one of the three ATR-42 aircraft that made up Air Botswana's fleet and were parked in a row on the apron in front of the passenger terminal. He proceeded to fly around Gaborone until someone arrived at the control tower, when he explained his intention to commit suicide and crash the aircraft into State House! This alarmed me so I called Eleanor and told her to take the kids to school early. As I listened, he recited a list of grudges and demanded to speak to the President. On being told he was out of the country he asked to speak to Ian Khama, the Vice President. He too was said to be unavailable, but General Masire of the Defence Force arrived in the tower and took the microphone. He tried to persuade Phatswe to land and discuss things, but the latter refused saying he knew they would shoot him. He then said he would crash into the new Air Botswana building adjacent to the passenger terminal, but was dissuaded because people were turning up for work. His girlfriend took the microphone but was rebuffed and failed to persuade him to land. His next demand was that they move the other two ATR-42s and position them on the runway where he could crash into them. The controller told him there were no crews available, but he said he knew from experience that they were preparing the aircraft for early morning flights and that passengers would be in the departure lounge. Saying he would crash into them where they were on the apron if they were not moved, he abruptly announced that he was running low on fuel and he didn't want to waste more time talking. With that he told them to clear people from the two aircraft and switched off his radio.

Just then my friend Mark Sampson ran up to my aircraft, accompanied by a local man. I told him what I'd heard but said I was sure he was bluffing. "No, he means it!" said Mark. "I know him well! This is his brother," he added, pointing to his companion. "Yes he does!" confirmed the brother. "Let's go!" and all three of us started to run down the taxiway towards the parked Air Botswana aircraft about 250 yards away. We saw the aircraft on base leg turn left on to its final approach, but lined up on the apron not the runway! The aircraft descended towards us and flew into the first of the parked aircraft, shunting it into the second. There was a huge, spectacular explosion that generated a big mushroom cloud of smoke and all three aircraft, Air Botswana's entire fleet, went up in flames. I always wondered what the passengers waiting to board thought when this inferno erupted just in front of the departure lounge windows – they had merely been informed that their flight was delayed due to technical problems! We watched from the tarmac a safe 150 yards away. No one took any footage or stills – we were all too shocked and there were no phones with cameras then anyway. The airport remained closed for a few days while they cleared up the mess and investigated and I never got to fly to Tuli.

I was able to fly out of Botswana a few days later. Air Botswana chartered a couple of aircraft to fulfil their commitments and I went to spend six weeks in Uganda as a consultant evaluating an EU wildlife development project. I was keen to revisit my old haunts where my career in Africa had started almost thirty years earlier. Like many others, including ones I had been involved with, the project had not been a resounding success, but I really enjoyed seeing Murchison Falls, Kidepo and the other protected areas, especially the site of my MSc studies in Queen Elizabeth NP. The country still struck me as extremely beautiful, and despite Idi Amin's havoc the natural resources appeared to have largely recovered. However I was reminded of the insecure status of that part of the world when visiting the fortified villages in Kidepo near the Sudanese border and, more alarmingly, when we learned that a tourist bus that left Queen Elizabeth NP just after our own vehicle was attacked by a group of rebels causing the death of a foreign tourist. This was only six months after eight tourists were slain in the same area by rebels probably from the Democratic Republic of the Congo. It seemed that in matters of security, economic stability and general living conditions Botswana was still swimming against the African tide.

EIGHTEEN

KGS REVIVED

Towards the end of 1999 it became obvious that I needed more work than the odd piecemeal wildlife job. Aerial surveys and export certification were well and good, but the highly competitive commerce of government agricultural supplies was not really my scene. Gavin (who else?) persuaded me that we could do a better job than Braam and make game capture profitable if we got KGS up and running again for the 2000 season. I knew from experience that Gavin's "we" seldom involved much direct effort from the big man himself, so I hired a young man called Bruce Riggs, the brother of Robert, of Makgadikgadi Hilux fame fifteen years previously, and we started to get things organised. First we drove the 500 miles up to Ghanzi to ascertain the condition of the capture kit that we had stored on Gavin's family's farm ten years earlier. Most of it was, unsurprisingly, pretty dilapidated and beyond repair, but the heavy-duty loading crush built by Clem Coetzee in Zimbabwe was easily reconditioned and some of the steel cables and plastic curtains were serviceable. Unfortunately the two old Bedford 4x4 trucks were unsalvageable, so our first requirement was for some vehicles that could transport the crush and other equipment.

The game capture season in Southern Africa started in mid-March and continued until the end of September, basically six months. The rains normally finish in March and the roads and track become passable. Most of the species breed during the summer rains so no capture permits are issued then anyway. Botswana has the most extreme climate in the region and after getting freezing temperatures on June mornings it becomes too hot for capture in early September, whether or not the rains have arrived again by then. The brutal heat building up means that animals can only be pursued in the first few hours of daylight and helicopter flying conditions at Kalahari altitudes and temperatures are too dangerous later in the day anyway.

In February, with limited funds, Bruce and I headed for Johannesburg and its hundreds of acres of scrapyards and used truck outlets. We found an eight-ton Isuzu flat-bed truck that seemed in reasonable mechanical condition and which we could fit with a twenty-foot shipping container. This would carry most of our kit and we modified the container with sliding doors so it could be used as a game delivery vehicle. In what would become our greatest stroke of luck we came across a South African ex-military 4x4 truck, called a Samil 50 that was sitting in a scrapyard. We realised that this indestructible and powerful beast would be ideal for our purposes in the vast areas of Botswana where there were no roads. It had no batteries, but after obtaining two we were able to start it amid clouds of diesel smoke. The owner of the scrapyard seemed grateful to be rid of the monster and gave us a discounted price. Bruce managed to make the thing move, but neither of us had much idea about the various gear levers and diff locks in the cab. None of the buttons, switches and controls had any legible signs, so it took a while driving up and down through the puddles in the scrapyard to work out what were the indicators and light switches and what the various dials and warning lights signified; most of them didn't work anyway. Eventually Bruce declared himself competent to drive through the city and out onto the 300 miles of open road back to Botswana. I wasn't as confident as Bruce seemed to be, but I had my own trials to worry about following him through the busy traffic in the big Isuzu. I had never had a heavy-duty vehicle licence, but managed to acquire one through a friendly official who postulated that if I could drive a car and fly a plane I must be able to drive a truck!

With the Samil leading the way and me following the cloud of black diesel smoke behind it, we made it across Johannesburg, through Krugersdorp and the small town of Magaliesburg, before setting off across the highveld towards Zeerust, the nearest town in South Africa to the Botswana border. The roadside verges were a full palette of purple and white cosmos flowers, and behind were swathes of tall green maize stretching for miles, much more impressive from the high vantage point of the big truck. We spent the night on the outskirts of Zeerust at the old-fashioned Abjaterskop Hotel and were at the border when it opened at six the next morning.

We headed for Mark and Sue Sampson's Pangolin Farm at Notwane, just south of Gabs. Mark was an old friend and Chief Flying Instructor for the BDF, while Sue, a Canadian, ran a stables and taught most of Gabs' kids to ride. They kindly allowed me to keep the two trucks, the crush and some other kit on the farm. At first we stored things in two shipping containers, but eventually built a large open shed that functioned as our company workshop, garage and stores.

Bruce was fairly practical in a scruffy, disorganised way, and with a couple of Batswana labourers he gradually made things workable. It was mainly rough welding and painting, but we were ready to try things out by April, when the weather had cooled down sufficiently and the rains had definitely stopped. I bought half a mile of ten-foot wide, black, reinforced plastic sheeting to supplement that left over from years previously and made a range of curtains, from twenty to fifty yards long. More cables, winches, shackles and clips and we were about ready to go. We just had to buy camping equipment and catering items for our staff, six labourers who didn't know what they were letting themselves in for. I bought an old Land Cruiser pick-up and a slightly newer 4x4 Toyota Hilux for the "executives".

The quintessential item of equipment to catch wild animals is a helicopter with a suitably skilled and experienced pilot. There were none in Botswana and only very few in South Africa – machines were scarce, but good capture pilots were extremely rare. The old maxim that there are old pilots and bold pilots, but no old, bold pilots is particularly appropriate to game capture. Fortunately, I had got to know a couple of competent pilots while doing Braam's export certification the previous year and I managed to book a machine for a couple of weeks in May. KGS had won the tender to buy a package of animals from Jwaneng mine. It mainly consisted of red hartebeest, gemsbok and eland. I had arranged buyers in Tuli Block for most of the animals, but hoped to export the hartebeest, which were mainly surplus males, to South African buyers.

In the second week of May 2000 our first commercial game capture job got under way. We left Notwane at 5 am and drove in a small convoy into the cold Kalahari, taking the best part of three hours to arrive without mishap at the main gate of Jwaneng mine. Unlike its sister mine, further north at Orapa, Jwaneng mine is separated from the township and very securely fenced. It is divided into zones: white for administration; green for the game reserve; and red for the mine itself; all of which are separately fenced inside the perimeter fence. After a cursory inspection of our permits we were shown to a campsite inside the green zone. It consisted of "A"-frame thatched shelters with picnic areas and a communal shower block. Mine employees and their families used it at weekends for recreational camping and game viewing, but the reserve had been closed to everyone for the duration of our activities.

We unpacked before proceeding to a compulsory "health and safety" induction meeting at 10 am in the white zone. This boring lecture, warning us against proscribed activities and describing many regulations (most of which we were compelled to ignore by the very nature of our activities), took up the rest of the morning, after which we all signed compliance guarantees and were issued with gate passes for the white and green zones. We were strictly forbidden from entering the red zone where the actual diamond extraction took place. In fact, anything entering the red zone was destined to remain in there forever and we saw from the air acres of impounded, rusting vehicles and equipment, worth hundreds of thousands of dollars.

After lunch we proceeded to start building our crush and capture boma. We had selected a site earlier when flying the game census. The boma had to be hidden by vegetation with the wide entrance to the "funnel" facing northeast, the direction of the prevailing wind. The loading ramp, positioned at the narrow end obviously had to be accessible by large trucks for loading animals. Our team numbered Bruce and me, our six Batswana labourers from Gabs and ten casual labourers hired from Jwaneng township. In addition we had a cheerful, young Australian volunteer called Cameron, who had tagged along for the fun. I estimated that it would take our inexperienced team that afternoon and the whole of the following day to build and camouflage the boma and crush, so we had scheduled the arrival of the helicopter for the next evening. We just hoped that the wind direction wouldn't change before we got started. Also the next day, a farmer from Ghanzi, Piet Lewis, was due to arrive with his cattle-truck and trailer that he had modified to carry wild animals. Piet was an old Kalahari "hand" and could drive his rig in sand that would be impassable to most mortals. We had hired him to do most of our deliveries and Bruce would also assist with the Isuzu truck and a trailer we had acquired. But first we had to catch something…

The helicopter, a Robinson R-22, arrived from South Africa on time and we met Fritz Leitner, the owner of the company Gamework Helicopters based in Pretoria. Fritz was very experienced and came with an excellent reputation. We explained our requirements and agreed to start early the next morning. It was very cold at dawn, but our excitement sustained us through coffee and rusks and we were at the capture boma by 7 am, when the light was suited to spotting game. Fritz took off alone and after a twenty-minute recce announced over the VHF radio that he was bringing a herd of twenty hartebeest to the boma. Bruce and I checked that the men at the running-curtain stations were all in place and ready and then waited by the crush. The hartebeest cantered in through the first curtain and hardly noticed it closing behind them. They continued through the boma and the second and third curtains were closed. I was responsible for closing the swing door at the entrance to the crush and this too didn't seem to unnerve them. They merely stood in a group breathing quite heavily, but not distressed. The men arrived running from the curtain stations and were excited to see the animals in the crush – this was going to be easy! Without causing undue stress we put two men waving flags in with the hartebeest and persuaded them to move forward into the next two smaller compartments where they were confined by closing sliding doors on the crush. Now we could reach them from over the crush wall with pole syringes and we gave all the adults a shot of haloperidol, a tranquiliser. Ten minutes later we were able to go inside with them quite safely and fix short lengths of plastic pipes to their horns so that they would not harm each other during transport when the drug wore off. The hartebeest were then herded up the loading ramp into compartments on the truck and trailer. By 10 am Piet was on his way to a game ranch in Tuli Block with a full load of thirty-six hartebeest. He would offload before dark and be back with us to sleep for a few hours before the next day's capture.

After Piet left we asked Fritz to try to bring some gemsbok to the boma. From experience I knew this was likely to be more of a challenge for the helicopter and the ground team at the boma. Without a doubt this Southern African variety of oryx is the most difficult and dangerous of the many species routinely caught and transported in the game ranching industry. It is a strikingly handsome, large antelope, which inhabits the drier areas of western Botswana, Namibia and the northern Cape Province. Probably for nutritional or other environmental reasons, the Botswana specimens are the biggest, weighing up to 500lbs. It is a sought-after trophy and its meat is excellent, so it is a popular game ranch species with many herds on ranches far outside its natural range. They may not have the damaging power of eland, kudu and waterbuck bulls, but with their rapier-sharp, forty-inch horns and stubborn belligerence they must be accorded due respect. A gemsbok is uncannily aware of the tips of its horns and will hit any small object, such as a coin, that is tossed towards it. I once had my shorts torn and was only saved from serious injury by the Swiss Army knife I always carried in my pocket.

Although they can be found in sizeable mixed herds, they are more often encountered in small groups of between two and eight individuals. Bigger herds also tend to splinter when herded by helicopter resulting in higher costs per animal brought into the capture boma. Once in the tapering loading funnel they refuse to move. They stand and "growl" alarmingly while lengths of plastic water pipes are heated and hammered over their deadly horns. This is an essential safeguard, preventing serious injury or worse to them and the capture operators. Loading can now begin, but with difficulty. They will not respond positively to any form of physical stimuli, cattle prods merely elicit kicks and intensified growling. They must be forced towards and up the ramp by pushboards, strong, steel shields with handles allowing two operators to shelter behind them. Even then it can be a risky business.

Whereas a herd of fifty eland can be loaded into trucks often with less than thirty minutes flying time and ten minutes in the boma, a similar number of gemsbok are likely to take much more flying and a longer time in the boma. Fritz had experience with this most difficult species and in the fairly open terrain of Jwaneng he quickly found a small herd of a dozen individuals. Bringing them to the mouth of the boma proved challenging and he arrived with seven animals galloping through the first curtain and on at speed right into the crush where I closed them in with the swing door before they could double back. They immediately stood still and growled alarmingly. Our four wranglers entered with their pushboards and immediately realised the value of these protective shields when the gemsbok went into a kneeling position and lunged at the steel with their horns. It took quite a while just to get the seven through into the next narrower compartment and secured behind a sliding door. We all had to scramble then as Fritz was arriving with another group. This time it was eight animals and we managed to hold them inside the back compartment. Fifteen gemsbok was an economic load, so Fritz stood down while we continued the loading process.

We had modified one wall of the crush so that it could swing down and form a platform for us to stand on. From here we could hammer lengths of plastic pipe onto the dangerous horns of the gemsbok. One end of the pipes was first heated in a fire next to the crush to soften them so they would fit tightly over the ridges at the base of the horns. When the animals in one compartment of the crush were done, a man with a narrower pushboard got behind them and tried to move them forward towards the ramp. They growled even louder and kicked back at the board, but unlike most species they never tried to jump. Further persuasion with battery prodders was also necessary before the stubborn animals were moved as far as the loading ramp. Then the eight at the back were moved forward in two groups of four and the process repeated. Eventually all fifteen were secured in two compartments of the Isuzu truck and Bruce, after suffering a severe kick to the stomach, was on his way, accompanied by two assistants. It was almost dark and Bruce planned to offload at first light in the Tuli Block. He took prodders, rope and a couple of pushboards to help with offloading.

Once inside the truck they usually travelled well, even over long distances and casualties were rare. Offloading however, was often more difficult and perilous than loading was. Gemsbok are as reluctant to leave the truck as they are to board it! First it is necessary to take the pipes off the horns. They are firmly stuck and require cutting at the base. This is done for two or three animals with great care from behind a pushboard and then they are propelled, usually backwards, growling down the ramp to freedom. Many will then stand at the bottom of the ramp stubbornly fighting with the next few coming down. Why they don't jump out and run away like any other species is a mystery. Tales abound of injuries and worse catastrophes during gemsbok deliveries. One unfortunate driver tried to smoke some gemsbok out of his truck by throwing in smouldering elephant dung, only to set fire to the straw bedding and burn his trailer. A load of twenty-five animals that we once despatched with a commercial transporter were offloaded with their pipes still in place. They were seen for over two years running on the recipient's farm. The only remedy would have been to dart them individually to remove them and we decided it was cheaper not to charge the farmer for the animals at all.

We never resorted to fire, but tried many ways to persuade them to leave the truck. We left sliding doors open overnight to no avail and we sometimes roped an especially difficult animal and dragged it down the ramp. Flashing lights, noises, spraying with water all had no effect whatsoever. One of our strongest Afrikaner foremen once left a rope attached round the neck of a particularly stubborn gemsbok bull halfway down the ramp, while he had a cigarette break after being brutally kicked, only for the animal to suddenly disappear into the gloom, rope and all.

The following morning we were missing Bruce and his two men, so we elected to catch eland. These were generally the easiest species to catch and load. They are large cattle-like antelope and the fully adult bulls can weigh a ton and be six feet at the shoulder. These individuals luckily tend to be lazy and can usually be left behind by a skilful helicopter pilot, otherwise they can cause havoc in the crush, fighting and killing each other. Eland live in large herds and need to be separated into smaller groups for loading purposes. Piet's truck and trailer could accommodate up to fifty eland in four compartments. Fritz was despatched and asked to bring no more than that, and without any older bulls. Our staff were briefed to move very swiftly to close off compartments with sliding doors, separating the eland into small manageable groups in the crush. Further back in the boma the animals would have more room and were unlikely to harm each other. The only problem there was that they might try to jump over the plastic side-curtains which, although nearly ten feet high, would be no obstacle if they were spooked.

Fritz rounded up a herd of about thirty animals, mostly cows with yearling calves. They trotted through the boma in a fairly relaxed state and we let them straight up the ramp onto Piet's truck, separating them on the truck into two compartments. They appeared unfazed and stood calmly. Fritz called to say he had another herd of about the same size so we were going to have to let some animals go. Eighteen animals entered the crush and I managed to stop the rest with the swing door. This group of a dozen or so circled in the final and smallest section of the plastic boma. When they got close to the corner where one of our staff was holding the third curtain closed, he panicked and ran away. The leading eland spotted the small gap and made for it, closely followed by the others. They burst through and headed back towards the second and longer curtain, where our staff also ran away at their approach. The group repeated their escape and made off into the bush because the first curtain had already been opened and tied back. Lessons were going to have to be learned before we caught more animals. We loaded the eighteen without incident and Piet left before noon with forty-eight eland and headed back towards Tuli Block, this time to tycoon Derek Brink's game ranch, Saas Post, on the Tropic of Capricorn.

Without any trucks remaining we spent the afternoon repairing the boma and augmenting the camouflage for the following day. Fritz was a little upset at having nothing to do for the rest of the day; he wanted to get the job done and be off to the next one as soon as possible because his helicopters were in demand. I told him that if we successfully caught another load of hartebeest and one of gemsbok we would be finished. He could possibly return to South Africa the next day. Meanwhile I had to give the staff a pep talk to try to instil some understanding of wild animal behaviour and try to avoid any future escapes.

Modern Africans are predominantly urban people who no longer have any daily experiences of living alongside wild animals. Very few have spent holidays in game reserves and national parks even in their own countries; most cannot afford it. Equally, there is almost no culture of watching the likes of David Attenborough's television programs. The result is that most of them are terrified by their first close encounter with wild animals and they cannot differentiate between a fairly harmless hartebeest and a potentially dangerous gemsbok. This is a slight oversimplification and generalisation, but it is nonetheless an accurate practical observation. Our staff were inevitably drawn mainly from Gaborone and its satellite communities. Many of their parents had grown up in the bush on cattle posts, but they had not. No matter what I said they would feign agreement, but when it came down to facing unconstrained animals they ran away. Only months of experience would change them and we had a high turnover of staff. All in all however, on our first job we caught and delivered forty-eight eland, thirty gemsbok and seventy-five hartebeest from Jwaneng – 153 animals with no losses. I handed over a cheque for almost a quarter of a million pula, Jwaneng mine was delighted, and I hoped KGS would be paid promptly by the farmers in Tuli Block. None were exported which simplified things because I would not have been allowed to issue my own export permits, something that caused us many delays over the years to come. After paying Fritz for his helicopter services and Piet for the transport we still came out with a healthy profit, albeit only for one week. We would have to see how things worked out over a full season.

Flushed with success we pursued other capture work for the rest of the season. There was plenty to do back at Pangolin in terms of maintenance to the equipment and vehicles. We did not have a mechanic, so Bruce and I did what we could with our unskilled labour force. We found out how quickly we could learn when circumstances demanded and we managed to keep the Isuzu and Samil running. Our labourers became adept at stitching curtains and we bought additional material. Our capture jobs varied from the small and convenient to the large and ambitious. In amongst all this I was kept busy with aerial counts, some of which inevitably led to capture jobs. I even squeezed in two brief consultancies with community-owned wildlife initiatives in Ghanzi and Tuli Block. The former was advising a Basarwa (Bushman) community at D'kar on the management of a ranch that they had acquired through a Dutch development agency and the second was producing a development plan for another ranch, Winteroord, in the northern Tuli Block, that had been repossessed by the government from a long-term absentee owner and donated to the residents of three local villages.

When it became too hot in late September, we suspended operations until the following March. We had proved Gavin right and had a sound basis for continuing. With my simple business logic I had only one rule: never owe money to anyone except the bank. It made for easy book-keeping and happy clients. By the end of September KGS had captured and delivered just over 1,100 animals with a casualty rate of two per cent. This was better than we had dared hope for, particularly as twenty of the mortalities had been in two loads of 100 impala each that were delivered to Salambala Conservancy in Namibia.

This ill-fated project was blighted from start to finish. Even allowing for a degree of ineptness on our part, the problems were mainly an example of bureaucratic incompetence. WWF was assisting the local community of Salambala in Eastern Caprivi, Namibia to set up a conservancy. The villagers supplied the land and there was some wildlife already on it, at least transiently. WWF funds were to provide more wildlife stocks to make the area viable for hunting and photographic tourism. The conservancy was a few miles from the Ngoma Bridge across the Chobe River and walking distance from the game-rich Chobe National Park on the Botswana side that teemed with thousands of impala.

Someone in authority in Namibia decided that more impala should be bought and supplied to the conservancy. With some goodwill and a degree of bureaucratic flexibility and common sense, the required impala could have been supplied from Chobe at an insignificant cost. But it was decided that the impala must come from an FMD disease-free zone of Botswana. Chobe District is not free of FMD – but neither is Salambala, it is also in an FMD active area! The nearest "clean" impala were in southern Tuli Block and we were given a contract to supply 200 animals in June. After a great deal of pleading the Veterinary Departments of the two countries allowed us, under special restrictions, to transport the animals through Chobe District in sealed trucks without stopping. Although this was a journey of over 500 miles it was by far the shortest route. The alternative was to travel through the Kalahari Desert and the length of Namibia – over 1,500 miles! However, the Botswana Wildlife Department stipulated that the animals must not travel on the transit route through Chobe NP at night, so the trucks were held up for twelve hours in Kasane. Unsurprisingly, when the animals were offloaded in Salambala, over twenty-four hours after capture, they were not in good shape, and they had cost taxpayers about three times the going price – a tiny, undocumented waste of international aid money in Africa.

KGS continued in the new century with a mixture of capture work – bigger jobs from the mines, with quite a lot of exports to South Africa, and more modest work from individual farmers. Botswana still had only a handful of functioning game ranches, but the industry was exploding in South Africa and Namibia. Many of the ranches in Limpopo Province (the old Transvaal), the hub of activities in South Africa, were quite small, just a few thousand acres and most of them depended on hunting in one form or another for their main income. As the business grew they could not breed and grow enough of their own stock on such small units and needed to import extra adult bulls for hunting trophies. The ranches that catered mainly to weekend biltong hunters also could not meet demand, so needed more stock. Botswana was ideally placed to meet these demands and to develop a fairly lucrative export trade in live wild animals. Remember that these were species that we had in excess, even in the cattle ranches of the Tuli Block and, in truth, many wandered freely across the border via the mainly dry Limpopo riverbed at will.

KGS concentrated its efforts in the Tuli Block and supplied quite a lot of wildebeest, impala and kudu to farmers and game dealers in South Africa. It paid quite well and kept us busy throughout the season. The Botswana Government produced a Game Ranching Policy that seemed to support the use of wildlife for commercial use, though the regulations were still being discussed. More cattle farmers became interested in their residual wildlife populations and applied to become registered game ranches. Mainly this entailed enclosing a farm with a game-proof fence, to ensure that farmers did not sell their game and "suck in" replacement stock from their neighbours. They were then subject to a cursory inspection by the Wildlife Department before being given permission to trade their wild animals. This increased interest in wildlife led to a few ranchers wanting to acquire other species to diversify their stocks and we were asked to obtain giraffe, zebra, gemsbok and springbok.

We made one or two forays into Namibia to obtain gemsbok and springbok, but quickly learned that it was easier and more profitable to order them through Namibian and South African based companies. KGS merely obtained the necessary wildlife and veterinary permits on behalf of the farmers and supervised the border crossings and deliveries. There were a few hiccups when foreign companies underestimated the difficulties of some of Botswana's roads or the distances involved and overestimated the availability of refuelling facilities. We occasionally had to mount late-night rescue missions, carrying drums of fuel to stranded trucks or extricating them from deep sand. Overall, this embryonic two-way commerce augured well for the wildlife utilisation industry and the diversification of ranching.

In 2001 the export of over 100 roan antelope was allowed from Pandamatenga to South Africa. This was controversial for a number of reasons: roan were a protected species and they were thought to be in limited numbers; they were extremely valuable commercially in South Africa; they were allegedly to be exchanged for a number of white rhino from South Africa; and finally, Pandamatenga was in the active FMD zone from which animals and their fresh products could not be moved. Although KGS was not involved, I was hired to assist with the capture, quarantining and export of the antelopes. It was a quasi-government deal, but the funding came from a private source in South Africa. A number of very experienced wildlife veterinarians from the Government of South Africa were involved, but for reasons of protocol they could not legally operate in Botswana or import the drugs necessary for darting the animals. This led to some embarrassing moments and the rather farcical solution was for me, as a Botswana veterinarian, to be attached to the exercise to validate it.

The antelope were caught individually by darting from helicopters and transported slung in nets to temporary quarantine pens at Pandamatenga. After three weeks in quarantine they were loaded into trucks and driven to South Africa to spend another three weeks in quarantine there. Altogether the project was only a qualified success and several animals succumbed in quarantine, particularly in South Africa. I also heard that some of the animals were diverted to private game reserves. I also have no recollection of Botswana receiving the promised rhino.

In the third year of the century Gavin (again) was the leading light in re-instigating an association of game farmers to promote the fledgling industry and liaise with government in an orderly fashion, so the moribund Botswana Game Farmers Association was reborn as the more positively named Botswana Wildlife Producers Association (BWPA). There were very few members at first, but it eventually grew to slightly over 100 farmers, of whom maybe one-third were active in investing time and money in game farming. The main protagonists were the original rich, white, cattle farmers who owned extensive landholdings in Ghanzi and Tuli Block and had been dabbling in hunting for years. To motivate this block of conservative, mainly Afrikaners, Gavin's main proposition was to pursue a change in the law that would make wildlife on a game ranch the property of the legally registered landowner, as opposed to remaining state property like the free-ranging animals in the national parks and reserves. This revolutionary reform would have been a game changer. To pursue this end a new BWPA Committee was formed with Derek Moore, the recently retired mine manager from Jwaneng, as chairman. Derek was seen as being scrupulously honest and a proven administrator who did not bring to the post any of the "baggage" of some of the other key members.

The upsurge in activity brought with it a number of South African capture operators attracted by Botswana's relatively cheap and plentiful game. Unfortunately the booming industry in South Africa, with over 10,000 game ranches, compared with less than 100 in Botswana, had spawned a glut of capture companies with mixed abilities and credentials. Naturally, some of the worst thought Botswana would be an easier and less competitive option. Stories of poorly performing capture companies in Botswana emerged, particularly in the border areas like Tuli Block where the Afrikaner farmers had connections across the border. While KGS maintained a low casualty rate over the range of species of one to two per cent, some of the South African operators were much higher. At one stage KGS was abruptly ordered to cease operations during a large job at Orapa mine because there had been reports of poor operating standards and mortalities in the Tuli Block. The Director of Wildlife and National Parks had assumed that KGS must be responsible despite our not having operated in Tuli Block for several weeks. Unfortunately for us we were the only registered capture company in Botswana at the time. Luckily I was able to prove that more than one unregistered South African capture company was operating unofficially in Botswana and produce documents which clearly showed that KGS was not involved. BWPA lobbied government to apply strict controls on foreign companies entering Botswana and the problem soon dissipated.

NINETEEN

HELP FROM AUSTRALIA

In 2002, my friend John Counihan converted his small cattle ranch at Dovedale in Tuli Block to a game ranch. He had an Australian friend who asked him to take his son as a volunteer for the season. There was lots of fencing, as well as other tasks requiring hard practical work, so John was happy to oblige and Kyle Chute Houston Smith, aged twenty, arrived on the scene. According to John he came with a reputation for independence, hard work and hard drinking. Dovedale was no challenge and within a few weeks he had transformed the place almost single-handedly. With very little left for him to do, John offered Kyle to KGS and I agreed. I should have paid heed to John's throwaway remark that though Kyle came salary-free, his beer bill merited consideration.

Kyle was of average size and build with thick black hair and bright, disconcerting, green eyes. He was everything John had said, and quite bit more. After arriving by air in Gabs he had caught a bus to Mahalapye and then hitch-hiked to Machaneng, a small village situated in the central Tuli Block with one basic store and one bar. Other than these the village's main feature is the District Prison. Opting for the bar in the late afternoon, Kyle ended up spending the night in a prison cell! He befriended one of the prison staff in Prince's bar and with nowhere else to go and a skinful of beer was invited to sleep across the road in a cell. The following morning he was given directions to Dovedale, walked to the nearby road junction and managed to get a lift taking him the required forty miles of dirt road south. He arrived at Dovedale Trading Post, also John's property, on the edge of the village, and introduced himself.

Kyle's first job with KGS was near Machaneng on a ranch that belonged to Leon Grobler, a wholesale butcher in Gabs and prominent member of the BWPA. We were catching impala to take to a startup ranch in what was known as the Western Sandveld between Serowe and Orapa. This was owned by one of the first black game farmers and everyone wanted it to get off to a good start. The first thing after ascertaining the predicted wind direction was to build the boma accordingly. In June 2002 this was still taking our fairly green crew almost two days. The helicopter was booked for day three. Bruce and the field staff had sited the boma and begun to clear the lines through the bush for the cables when I arrived with Kyle from Gabs. I introduced him to the whole crew including the dozen or so casual labourers recruited from the nearby villages of Makwate and Dovedale. I had business elsewhere and left everyone to it, returning just after midday the following day. The men had eaten and were relaxing, lying about in whatever bits of shade they could find. Bruce was back at camp, a mile away, also relaxing, but there was no sign of Kyle. Bruce said he was on site with the staff and we returned to the boma. One of the men said that Kyle had taken the Samil truck and gone to cut bush to camouflage the boma. This was the last job for everyone just as the boma was almost ready. The bush was placed strategically to hide the plastic curtains near the front, especially at the running stations, where they were folded and ready to be deployed when the animals passed. The men were rather sheepish and avoiding telling me everything. Even Bruce who was fluent in Setswana could not get to the bottom of it.

As we were talking the Samil appeared in a noisy cloud of smoke. Kyle killed the engine and jumped out. The back of the huge truck was full of green bushes. "Did you cut that all on your own?" I inquired sceptically. "Yeah," Kyle replied, "these lazy f… ing bastards didn't want to help because it was lunchtime." I was astounded! The whole team would normally have taken longer to collect the same amount. Now they were a little embarrassed, but Kyle's insulting language gave them the excuse they needed to turn on him. "We can't work with this man!" a spokesman shouted, to everyone's apparent agreement. "He insults us black people and calls us names!" It took most of the rest of the afternoon in the best "trade union" fashion to calm everyone down and meanwhile Kyle offloaded all the camouflage near the mouth of the boma on his own. We were still arguing when the helicopter arrived and I left to collect the pilot. That evening back at camp I tried to explain to Kyle about the sensitivities of the local people and how he would have to control his language, particularly by not using "bastard", "stupid", "nonsense" and one or two other locally offensive terms. He seemed to understand and we enjoyed some *braaied boerevors* with *mielie pap*, together with a few beers before turning in. The young Afrikaner helicopter pilot who had been sent by Fritz seemed to find the colourful discussions very amusing.

The next morning the boma was finished and the camouflage was strategically applied to hide the boma mouth. There was a light breeze blowing into the mouth and conditions were perfect. Impala are the most difficult species to drive into a boma. They have extremely keen eyesight, hearing and sense of smell, so everything needs to be right. They usually don't drive directly, but need to be herded slowly from one favoured spot to another, gradually getting closer to the front of the boma where they can be pushed a bit harder for the final thirty or so yards. The curtains must be closed very quickly and just at the right time or they will turn back and disappear, after which they cannot be driven again. I was a bit nervous about the rookie pilot's ability, but he managed to get most of a large herd into the boma quite expertly. There were over 100 animals moving through the boma and we needed to split them into manageable groups of thirty to forty with minimum disturbance. This was achieved using the curtains and we were left with three groups in separate boma compartments. We needed to work quickly on the first group nearest the crush. These were in the smallest space and therefore under the most stress. In these circumstances the big rams start to fight between themselves and, even worse, stab any females that get too close to them. We needed to remove these dominant animals as quickly as possible. Our options were to shoot them in the head using a .22 rifle or attempt to catch them by hand and put pipes on their horns to render them safe. Obviously the latter was our preferred option, because we were catching to deliver live breeding herds and the males were necessary. Sometimes, in later years, if we were combining a live capture with a cull for venison we would take the first and easier option.

There were two or three problematic males in each group and two of our best handlers would grab them one by one by the horns as they were driven past them into the metal crush. This was quite hazardous and as soon as one was grabbed another man had to assist to overpower the ram. Pieces of heated plastic pipe were forced over the horns and the ram was then released to join the others in the truck. We soon had four compartments full and the load in the Isuzu and trailer was ready to go. This was the first boma capture experience for Kyle, but he made himself more than useful in the style we were to become accustomed to.

The pilot said he thought we needed to move the boma site in order to catch more impala, so he and I flew in the R-22 to find somewhere suitable. When this was done I headed off back to Gabs and some administrative chores, leaving Bruce and the team to pull down the boma and rebuild it in the new site. Our head driver, Wathuto, would be away at least twenty-four hours on the delivery, so the truck and the boma should have been ready to go the day after next. I happened to be delayed and only returned to the farm in the late evening after they had caught and loaded the second time. The truck and trailer, with 120 impala, had already been gone several hours and I was dumbfounded to learn that Kyle was driving it and that he was alone! Apart from having no valid driving licence, he only had the vaguest idea of the destination and even less notion of how bad the sand was in that part of the Kalahari. Apparently, none of the men would agree to go with Kyle and Bruce lacked the necessary authority to either prevent Kyle going or force someone to accompany him. Kyle had typically driven off with a tirade of bad language directed at the rest of the workers. I thought there was no chance that Kyle could get there alone and I was pretty angry at the more senior men, especially Bruce.

There was only one route and it was pretty straightforward, so I told Wathuto and three other men to take our old Land Cruiser first thing in the morning, before daylight. They were to take spades, chains and anything else they might need to get the Isuzu out of any bad situation in the desert. They left on their rescue mission and the rest of us pulled down the boma again and prepared to move farms to the next job.

The rescue team arrived back just after dark and reported that they had not seen Kyle or the truck. They had been to the farm but found no one there, so they retraced their path and came back. This was now serious; a young, inexperienced foreigner with a large truck and trailer gone missing in the Kalahari Desert – a very small needle in a very large haystack! The welfare of the impala also exercised my mind, but I was at a loss as we ate supper around the campfire and endlessly pursued improbable possibilities.

At about 9 pm we heard the unmistakeable sound of the Isuzu truck. It got louder and nearer and we raced down to the old boma site to see it grind along the track leading from the farm gate and pull to a stop next to the other vehicles. The labourers too started to arrive from their camp and we all watched Kyle jump down from the cab with a casual "G'day". He had been gone about thirty-six hours with no food or water but had survived and arrived back apparently unscathed.

We were obviously very eager to hear his story and while he ate supper back at camp he described his adventure. He had followed the tar road from Serowe for 100 miles, as far as the veterinary cordon gate approaching the village of Letlhakane. Turning southwest along the cordon fence he began to struggle as the sand spoor got deeper. Eventually, about forty miles from the tar road he could not go any further. He had never been in that part of the world before, but undeterred, he disconnected the trailer and managed to continue slowly with just the Isuzu into the early evening deepening gloom. He calculated from the previous evening's discussion that the farm he was aiming for could only be another twenty or so miles ahead, so he pressed on through the deep sand, making slow progress.

Arriving at the farm in total darkness he found a solitary labourer cum watchman who directed him to where he could offload his animals. There was no ramp, but luckily impala are excellent jumpers. He then asked if there was a tractor available to go back and collect the trailer. There was, but in typical fashion it had no battery and he and the watchman failed to start it. He then drove back alone to the trailer with the empty Isuzu, positioned it alongside and somehow managed to crossload the fifty or so impala from the trailer into the truck. This was something we frequently did, but never single-handed! Also Kyle had never seen it done. He then hitched the empty trailer onto the truck and managed to pull it to the farm. All this was done in the darkness alone. The last impala were offloaded and Kyle then asked the watchman if there was another road he could take back towards Serowe, 100 miles away, that wasn't as sandy. The watchman indicated a track through a gate that headed southeast and gave him vague directions, so he set off, still without food or refreshment or sleep.

With the empty rig not such an impediment, he eventually made it through to a large graded cutline just on daylight. All night he had seen no dwellings, vehicles or people. Turning left along the cutline he continued for two hours until he came across a small group of huts with some women who described how to reach the main road to the town of Serowe. He made it finally in the late afternoon and this is probably where the rescue team missed him, because they took the by-pass road to Palapye while he was in the centre of Serowe. After that, unknown to either of them, he had followed the rescue truck back to the farm. How Wathuto and his men had failed to see the Isuzu's tracks leaving the farm I couldn't work out. I concluded that they probably weren't really that interested in finding and helping this offensive young newcomer. It was an incredible tale of ill-founded determination and stubbornness. The following morning I read the riot act to Kyle and told him that if he was so irresponsible again he would have to leave, but at the same time I bore a grudging admiration for a young kid fresh from Australia who could do what he did. When I said he was mad to venture though the remote Kalahari sandveld like that, he replied that they had sand in Australia too. I had to have the last word by observing that theirs came without lions!

We moved up and down Tuli Block for the rest of the season catching the usual common species and distributing them to new as well as established game ranches. Unfortunately, our export trade was banned because of an outbreak of FMD in the northeast near Francistown. Stringent controls on the movement of live animals and their fresh products, mainly meat and hides, were introduced and our business was severely curtailed. The portion of Tuli Block in the far northeast beyond Baines Drift contained lots of wildlife but it was now out of bounds to us. A new veterinary cordon fence was built and our activities were limited to the south of it.

The off-season was spent much like the previous year in repairing equipment and maintenance of transport. We bought another big truck and trailer, this time an old Nissan, and modified it for our purposes with separate compartments and sliding doors. This increase in our loading and delivery capacity was spurred mainly to transport ostriches, which was becoming a year-round activity. I mentioned in previous chapters that Botswana tried to become a significant player in the fad for ostrich meat and skins. Eventually, after years of frustration, the Botswana Ostrich Company obtained (largely through Gavin's efforts) a grant to build a state-of-the-art abattoir close to the international airport at Gaborone. This opened in 2002 and required ostriches to be delivered from the handful of productive farms situated mostly in the east of the country. KGS was perfectly placed to take on this work, which neatly complemented our game capture business. Ostriches are nothing if not stupid and we quickly got the hang of loading our trucks and trailers, usually with a few labourers to escort the blindfolded birds up the loading ramps. At first we stationed a man in each compartment to ensure that if a bird sat down (or worse, fell) it would not be trampled by its companions. Later, as the birds gradually became more domesticated, this wasn't necessary. The ostrich sideline sustained us through some hard times for about four years when FMD outbreaks limited our game work.

In 2003 Gavin had yet another bright idea. We had attended and sometimes participated in live game auctions that were regular occurrences in

South Africa. He thought that a similar sale could be successful in Botswana, though FMD meant that it would only attract local buyers and hopefully a few from Namibia because South Africa had banned imports from Botswana. The animals on sale would likewise have to be from "clean" areas of Botswana. This meant that his farm, Kanana Ranch, in Ghanzi would be an ideal site for the event. This was the birth of the Ghanzi Game Fair!

KGS spent a few weeks building temporary holding pens close to Gavin's farmhouse and then filling them with suitable Kalahari animals for sale, many of which were caught on Kanana. Species on offer were eland, zebra, hartebeest and wildebeest, with a few gemsbok imported from Namibia. The sale took place over a weekend in late August. Gavin, who claimed to have completed a course in auctioneering, officiated. A "band" from Gaborone was engaged to provide entertainment on the Saturday evening at a dance to be held in the huge barn on the farm. The name of the band was "The Two of Us", but only one arrived! A refrigerated truck full of beer and other drinks was ordered through a wholesaler friend of Gavin's in Gaborone. This arrived on the Friday night so a few of the thirstier workers sampled the contents in a sort of dress rehearsal. Without anyone being aware, the driver decided that his allocated accommodation was not up to scratch and disappeared with the truck in the middle of the night. At first light on Saturday there was mild panic in the hungover ranks when the booze truck was discovered missing. Grand larceny was suspected!

Gavin chartered the game capture helicopter to try to spot the fugitive and Brampie DeGraaff, the Minister of Agriculture and a local farmer, arranged for the police to station road blocks on the only three roads leaving Ghanzi. The truck was eventually traced to a house in Ghanzi township, some twenty-five miles away and a rescue team was dispatched to retrieve it. The truck was back in place on the farm by lunchtime as the first people arrived.

The remote Ghanzi farming community, overwhelmingly Afrikaners, love an event of any kind so we were assured of a good social, if not necessarily commercial success. Many of the ladies turned up with plates of food: salads and vegetables as well as their cultural specialities of sweet pastries such as *koeksisters* and *melktert*. The farmers made sure that there was no shortage of meat for the *braais* and steaks, *boerevors*, lamb chops and even chicken (the Afrikaners' concession to vegetarians) were in abundance.

The actual auction took place on Saturday afternoon and disappointingly few buyers registered. One or two lots went to a buyer from Namibia and the rest were taken by three local game farmers, most notably Mark Kyriacou from Seribe, the old Vickerman family ranch adjoining Kanana. A couple of loads of wildebeest were bought by a farmer in the Hainaveld to the north of Ghanzi. This poor result in no way put a damper on the evening's festivities. The "band", now dubbed "the One of Him", bravely performed in the decorated barn and managed to get a great party off the ground. The music was lively and enjoyed by most and he even included a number of Afrikaans favourites for the older farmers and their wives to indulge in some *laangarm* and *sakkie sakkie*. A couple of visitors from Gabs, Barry Nolan and his wife Marion, regular entertainers at the capital's nightspots, lent a hand but proved too sophisticated for the Ghanzi crowd who promptly stopped dancing and sat down. Barry, fairly drunk by now, took it badly and had to be physically restrained. The booze truck did a roaring trade and by mid-evening there were many unrehearsed "cabaret" acts on the dance floor, much to the amusement of the throng of mainly Bushmen farmworkers who, having started the evening as onlookers, progressed to full, inebriated participation.

Star of the show was Kyle, who somehow managed to divest himself of his clothes and proceeded to stagger around the barn enticing and forcefully coaxing older Afrikaner ladies to dance. Some of these most conservative old dears had probably never seen their husbands naked, let alone a twenty-one-year-old Australian! Amazingly, everybody seemed to see the funny side and no offence was taken, possibly due to the effects of the *brandywyn*. At midnight the music stopped in respect to the Afrikaner tradition and religion, but by then there were very few left standing. People wandered off to the *bakkies*, Land Cruisers and a few bigger trucks and started the long drive home – it was at least ten miles to the farm gate! It had been quite a day. We didn't make any money, but we had given Ghanzi a day to remember.

The following morning I had to rouse the KGS staff and load some of the animals for delivery. Kyle, who by now was a fully employed staff member, could not be found. Bruce and I supervised filling the big Nissan truck and its trailer with wildebeest. As we finished at about 10 am, Kyle surfaced from wherever he'd slept, looking bad and probably feeling even worse. "Good morning!" I yelled. "Get this truck to Kuke Corner and try to be back tonight please." Without a murmur Kyle climbed behind the wheel. His favourite labourer, Pilitjies, also somewhat quieter than normal, climbed into the passenger seat and they drove out of the yard to start their 300-mile round trip to the Hainaveld ranch.

Over the previous season, as a volunteer, Kyle had made himself indispensable to KGS and got through an immense amount of work. His remarkable personality made him extremely popular with our farm clients, even if some of the local field staff strongly disapproved of his language and attitude. I held a meeting with the staff and explained that all Australians were the same and that Kyle swore just as much addressing me and probably would even if he were talking to the Queen! This seemed to instil some grudging acceptance and I offered Kyle a paid position for next year. He arrived back in Gabs after Christmas at home in New South Wales and we set about obtaining a work and residence permit for him. With not a little unorthodox lobbying in the right quarters, these essential documents were issued and he joined us as a full member of staff with the apt title of "wild animal manager". Before the season fully started he made himself more than at home in Gabs and was a very popular addition to the clientele at more than one of the town's watering holes. He stayed temporarily in the guest flat at the back of our garden and I gave him our oldest Land Cruiser to get around.

One night he really excelled himself by hitting a roundabout on the new bypass and sustaining two punctures on the same side of the Cruiser. He then swerved down the deep grass verge and came to a halt. In his unsteady state he was wondering how to get the vehicle moving again when a BDF Land Rover stopped and two of the soldiers walked down to offer assistance. Kyle for some reason misunderstood their intentions and flattened the leading soldier. The rest of the patrol then ran down and gave him a real hiding before throwing him in the Land Rover and taking him to the nearest police station. There he was put in a cell and proceeded to make a very noisy nuisance of himself. The police sergeant in charge noticed some blood on his face and promptly called the BDF requesting that they come back and take him away, explaining that he did not want to be accused of assaulting Kyle. After some time the BDF patrol duly arrived and took custody again. They somehow found out enough about him to work out that he stayed at my house and drove around to my address, before throwing him over the six-foot high gate into my garden and driving away.

This was 4 am on a Sunday morning. I came across a slumbering, bloodied body in the driveway and managed to get him to his room. At about 10 am he and I went to the police station to collect the Land Cruiser that the BDF had helpfully towed there. A lady police sergeant came across us as we were changing a wheel and approached with a stern face. "Sir, you must advise your son not to try to seduce the police officer who is arresting him!" I couldn't keep a straight face and didn't try to correct her. I followed her into the police station and enquired about the charges Kyle faced. "No charges," she laughed, "he taught us how to sing 'Waltzing Matilda.'"

TWENTY

BIGGER GAME

Giraffe were becoming a species in great demand by Botswana game ranchers. KGS had imported quite a few, usually from Namibia, but also from South Africa. They seemed to thrive under the extensive ranching conditions in Ghanzi and elsewhere. I decided to take a few key staff to witness giraffe capture in South Africa, where they used slightly more professional and less "gung ho" methods than the Namibians. I arranged a visit to Koos Bensch, a reputable capture operator who specialised in exporting wildlife all round the world and had a lot of experience with giraffe. Our small team with Kyle prominent as usual spent a weekend near Pretoria and learned some of the necessary skills.

Catching giraffe is exciting. It can also be a high-risk affair for both the operators and the giraffe. The animals are very tough, despite the doe-eyed looks and apparently gentle disposition. A large bull stands eighteen feet high and can weigh over a ton and half. They can and do kick with any foot, front or back. Even large predators like lions tend to leave them alone. They can also move very fast over long distances. All this makes them a challenging prospect. For these reasons and the need for very large and expensive transport equipment, game capturers, like lions, leave adult giraffe alone.

A further complicating matter is their physiological reaction to the capture drugs used in darts. It is necessary to give very high doses of opioid immobilising drugs, usually by a veterinarian darting from a helicopter. Once darted, the animal may appear normal for a few minutes, but then it tends to move in an extended gait, at first quite fast and co-ordinated. A few minutes more and the animal becomes less aware and crashes through bushes with its head held high, continuing to run, almost blindly. If it is allowed to slow down, fall, and become recumbent there is a high possibility that the drugs will be fatal. It is imperative that the animal is caught, restrained and given an antidote before this can happen. This involves a chase vehicle carrying at least six fit, strong men with a long rope. This vehicle must get in front of the animal and drop off the crew who try to trip the loping giraffe, something that needs skill, strength and coordination. As soon as it hits the ground someone holds the head down and the veterinarian must administer the antidote into the jugular vein without delay. Soon wide awake, the giraffe is held down by someone sitting on its head and neck, while a blindfold and cotton wool ear plugs are applied and a specially arranged rope harness is tied around the neck and between the forelegs. The animal can then be allowed to stand and guided with the ropes to a small recovery "chariot", loaded and taken back to the main transport vehicle. From shortly after darting until the giraffe is safely in the chariot, there is usually half an hour of frantic activity with chase vehicles and personnel suffering extreme wear and tear. For a plethora of reasons therefore, it is normal to target younger, half-grown animals, from about three years old.

We acquired the necessary capture chariot and then had a trailer that held four giraffe in two compartments manufactured in Windhoek. It was by far our most expensive item of kit, but hopefully would pay for itself before too long. We then started catching giraffe on Botswana ranches and distributing them amongst farmers. One or two ranchers had quite large herds of giraffe already and were eager to sell. They mostly wanted to sell males, but of course the buyers wanted mostly females for breeding purposes. We eventually came to an understanding with both parties that we would usually deliver pairs. After a few seasons we had distributed giraffe around many areas of Botswana and their numbers steadily increased on private land. We never captured from wild stock and all of the eventual hundreds of giraffe on ranches were bred from imported animals.

We had some very exciting times catching giraffe around the country. Transporting them could also prove very challenging on the rough roads and deep sand tracks that accessed many of the game ranches. If one fell down in the trailer it was an emergency. Because of their long anatomy, the huge animals struggled to regain their footing in a confined space and it was necessary to assist them in any way possible, often in the middle of the night. This was dangerous work, but luckily none of us was ever seriously hurt. We caught and delivered a large number with very few casualties, either animals or staff.

Gavin and Vicky's ranch, Kanana, a local name meaning paradise, became quite well known for its giraffe population. We used to capture perhaps twenty giraffe each year and distribute them to other game ranches, sometimes as far as the Limpopo Valley, 600 miles to the east. An Australian TV company approached Gavin and asked to film a giraffe capture operation. The crew duly turned up one year in May, the height of the capture season.

We had hired a helicopter and a very experienced pilot, Barney O'Hara from Zimbabwe, for the exercise. Kyle would dart and I would drive the chase vehicle. As is usually the case, the filming crew promised to keep out of the way, but then proceeded to interfere with just about everything we did. Camera crews, sound engineers, glamorous presenters and a director filled a second chase vehicle driven more sedately by Gavin. Both vehicles were in radio contact with Barney and we waited at a strategic crossroads for our instructions. Barney crackled that they had darted an animal and that it was in a group of twelve heading east. This was not good news because the ranch boundary fence was not far away in that direction. Under Barney's instructions we drove fairly slowly down a clear cutline keeping pace with the giraffe off to our right, but out of sight in thick bush. After a few minutes Barney became agitated and told us to speed up, turn right along the boundary fence and intercept the animals, one of which was clearly drugged. Barney's voice became more frantic, urging us to get a move on. I accelerated, with the rope crew hanging on for dear life and Gavin's filming truck was left far behind. On reaching the boundary fence and turning sharp right we saw a bull giraffe that had fallen into the fence and was flailing about entangled, fifty yards from us; we saw a group not far ahead disappearing into the neighbouring farm. I remember thinking the animal was far too big for our purposes and cussed Kyle for darting it. We braked alongside the stricken animal, Jonas and Nick, our top hands, grabbed the head and held it down, while the rest of us simultaneously tried to put on the hood and other capture paraphernalia and I quickly made ready to inject the antidote. We were all conscious of the dangerous flailing legs and the whole scene was a chaotic, dusty scrum as the film crew arrived and began to record the mayhem. All the time, the radio was squawking unheeded on the car's dashboard. The helicopter roared above us and I glanced up to see Kyle hanging out and gesticulating wildly. I raced for the radio and heard Barney screeching that we were wrestling with the wrong giraffe. The bull was not darted at all! Our target was a few hundred yards further south down the fence line!

I yelled for everyone to get back on board, left Jonas to remove the giraffe's hood and threw him some pliers to cut the fence wires and allow the bull to escape. We raced down the fence to where the darted animal was staggering along parallel to the wire and quickly pulled it down and administered the antidote. In a matter of minutes this smaller giraffe was ready to load and the chariot was positioned next to the fence. She walked smoothly up the ramp guided by a rope to the harness and hardly needed the rope behind her thighs to pull her in. Twenty minutes later we cross-loaded her into one compartment of the delivery truck and we were ready to look for another animal.

I was discussing the morning's exploits with the Aussie presenter and his director, trying to get an assurance that the confusion and mayhem surrounding the first animal would not feature in their programme, when Gavin appeared and quite understandably asked how and who was going to get his ten giraffe back from the neighbour's cattle ranch. I assured him we would do our best, but it would be wise to leave them until at least the next day. He seemed reassured, but was obviously still a little unhappy after supper around the campfire that evening. Barney, after a few beers, was making light of the situation and made the mistake of criticising the Kanana fence, quipping that it wasn't strong enough to hold giraffe. This was too much for Gavin, normally a placid giant, who grabbed Barney and threatened to do grievous damage unless he returned each and every escaped animal.

The following day we caught three more giraffe without a hitch to complete our delivery and the whole exercise was successfully filmed. We also took down a section of the fence allowing Barney to herd the escapees back into Kanana, a great relief all round.

Rhinoceros have a chequered history in Botswana. They were undoubtedly around during the late 1800s if the written accounts of hunters and explorers are true. Back then it seems that conditions were generally wetter allowing many species to roam more widely than today. Drying of the country gradually limited them to the north and hunting seemed to have finally accounted for them, with most authors claiming that they were extinct in Bechuanaland by 1900. It's possible that a few hung on in the vast tracts of remote bush or wandered in from neighbouring countries, but to all intents and purposes there were none until a few were reintroduced from South Africa to Chobe NP in the late 1960s. We also released some more in the 1970s when I was a biologist in the Wildlife Department. These were mostly in Moremi Game Reserve at Bodumatau, close to Third Bridge. None of these early reintroductions were successfully sustained. Interestingly, these were all white rhino, but a single black rhino was reliably reported west of Savuti in 1972.

Both white and black species were thought to be extinct for the second time by the mid-1980s. However, Eleanor, as Conservation Officer of the newly formed Kalahari Conservation Society, received reports that a rhino was "terrorising" cattle herders near Lephepe in Central District in 1985. An American biologist, Mark Murray, was despatched to check on the stories and came back with a confirmed sighting, in fact he had been chased up a tree! I suppose mostly because of its aggressive tendencies it was reported as a black rhino. This was exciting news! The powers that be decreed that it should be captured and moved to Chobe NP. Eleanor arranged for a team from Natal Parks Board to drive up to Gabs, as the only people with the equipment and expertise to handle this. When they arrived they were somewhat dismayed that the distance from Lephepe to Chobe was 500 miles, not the fifty they had been told. I accompanied them to Lephepe and we quickly found fresh spoor. Their leader, Ken Rochas, confirmed that the tracks were those of a black rhino and that it was the largest he had ever come across. He and I followed the tracks for an hour or so before coming across the animal, which turned out to be a large male white rhino – so much for the experts! We darted and loaded it without incident and the truck then set off for Chobe with Eleanor and I accompanying it in an escort vehicle. We released it in the Park the next morning, discovering it had knocked off its large front horn in the transport crate. We took this memento back to the KCS offices where Eleanor used it as a doorstop – different days indeed!

Years later it was decided that any rhinos that were found around the country should be relocated either to the newly created Khama Rhino Sanctuary near Serowe, or Moremi. Helicopter pilot, Barney O'Hara, and I spent several weeks pursuing and darting rhinos in the Chobe District and moving them with the assistance of the BDF. I don't think we caught the Lephepe rhino again, but we might have. We certainly caught several animals, both black and white, including some that had strayed across the Zimbabwe border that we could recognise from ear notches. During one capture I stupidly lowered myself into the crate next to the head of a black rhino in order to remove the ear plugs, which I couldn't reach from the top. I had already given the animal an antidote to the dart, but thought I would be fast enough, before it took effect. When I came to pull myself out I slipped and fell back, the crate was higher than I thought. The rhino was awake enough to notice me and swung his massive head into my corner of the crate. Luckily I hadn't yet removed his blindfold. It was a very dangerous situation and I had a moment of panic, but I suddenly found myself extracted by my collar at great speed. A BDF soldier on top of the crate had noticed my predicament and pulled me out like a cork from a bottle. His name was Poster and he became a leading light in rhino conservation. He was six-foot eight and very strong – I was very lucky.

Barney, a talented maverick, who could be difficult, was a superb helicopter pilot and a certified engineer. This came in handy when he needed to ignore warning lights on the dashboard or push the turbines just a little beyond the red lines on the temperature gauge, if we were taking off in extremely hot conditions. He always reset them before the aircraft went for mandatory checks and services. He could track rhino through the bush by following an animal's spoor, flying while hanging out of the open door.

He and I also darted quite a few lions from the DWNP JetRanger. For a while, despite all advice to the contrary, the DWNP insisted on relocating lions that were a problem in cattle areas. They were darted, loaded into crates and driven far into the bush, often into game reserves, where they were released. The inevitable outcome was that they were soon killed by resident lions or quickly made their way back to where they were captured. It was usually surprisingly easy to dart a lion from a helicopter. They generally ran away in a straight line and it was simple to get behind them and wait for a gap in the bush before quickly closing in and shooting. Just once or twice we got too close to a big male who spun around, jumped and tried to swat the helicopter, luckily unsuccessfully.

Once in Khutswe GR we tried the technique on a leopard that needed to be collared for a research project. Barney did his stuff and the big cat streaked through the bush a lot faster than a lion. Barney stuck with him and the leopard eventually climbed a lone tree in the middle of a small clearing. He made it right to the top and then looked sheepishly at our helicopter, perhaps realising that millions of years of evolution had not prepared him for this. I darted him and we backed off until he slid, half-asleep, down to the ground where we could land and fit the collar.

KGS continued growing and getting busier over the next few years and I spent most of my time, especially in the winter months, on game ranches across Botswana with our team. Kyle became an ever more indispensable colleague and I came to rely on him a great deal, especially when I had to be away with Barney or a number of research scientists who wanted animals fitted with telemetry equipment. These varied from elephants, rhino and hippo, through a wide range of antelopes and zebra, to lions and brown hyaenas. Kyle wanted to come along but we couldn't both be away at the same time.

On one occasion, during an FMD forced shutdown, he accompanied me with Mike Chase, an elephant researcher. We were driving in Linyanti in the dry season, when elephant concentrations there were at record levels. Kyle and I were on the back of Mike's Land Rover and driving through a moonscape of wrecked trees and shrubs with literally hundreds of elephants heading for the river. Very unexpectedly a cow some distance away shrieked and started to charge towards our vehicle. This was something Mike and I were used to and we were unfazed – at first – then it became obvious to me that she really meant it and, more unnerving, as she got closer several other elephants joined in the charge behind her. This was something new! I yelled at Mike to put his foot down and he did, but the Land Rover was not making much progress in the deep sand, hotly pursued by the angry posse of giants. He had just matched her speed when she was only a few yards behind the vehicle. I saw Kyle trying frantically to get headfirst through the tiny rear window into the cab alongside Mike. She could have reached us with her trunk, but this was curled protectively under her head, another sign that she really meant business! Thankfully the Land Rover had more stamina than the elephants and they soon lagged behind, but they had chased us at speed for almost half a mile, a very unusual occurrence. We were all very relieved and a little shocked – it had been very close! Kyle never asked to come along again.

As KGS became busier we began to be constrained by the availability of helicopters and capture pilots available to the private sector. There were none in Botswana and we seemed to be at the tail-end of the supply line from South Africa, where admittedly they were in big demand. They were often late arriving and we had the whole crew plus delivery trucks waiting for a couple of days kicking their heels. Sometimes they didn't show up at all. Apart from the annoying inconvenience it was very costly for us to sit around doing nothing except pay wages. I had been wondering for quite some time if we could afford our own helicopter, but more conservative influences like Eleanor and our accountant had always convinced me that the numbers didn't add up. Helicopters were extremely expensive to buy and to operate. The dangerous nature of game capture made insurance extremely costly and, finally, there were no maintenance facilities in Botswana, necessitating long, expensive ferry flights to South Africa on a frequent basis.

I had often spoken to Kyle about it, wondering if he would be interested in learning to fly. His response was non-committal, but he rarely showed anything close to enthusiasm about any proffered idea. I was reluctant to encourage him too much because it was a high-risk occupation and accidents, sometimes fatal, were all too frequent. I decided that although I was an experienced fixed-wing pilot, I was too old and too impetuous by nature to switch to helicopters, so for a year or so we carried on with increasingly unreliable service from South African operators.

In 2007 John Blythe Wood, a very experienced helicopter operator/pilot who we knew well, offered us a reasonably priced second-hand Robinson R-22. We bought it and this eased things a little, but we were still reliant on South African pilots. One cold night around the campfire, drinking rum and Coke, the subject came up again and Kyle said he would like to take helicopter lessons. It was agreed that KGS would pay for him to get his licence on the understanding that he would work for us for at least two years afterwards. So in January 2008 Kyle was in Johannesburg at flight school. Nobody expected him to cope with the academic ground schooling, but somehow he managed to pass his exams and within two months he had his Private Pilot's Licence. His flying was a revelation – he was a natural! Now came the long haul to accumulate 200 hours flying before he could qualify for his commercial licence and be allowed to work. This was always a challenge for young wannabe pilots and they struggled to log the required hours. Fortunately, being in remote bush locations allowed some "unofficial" flying courtesy of easygoing commercial pilots like John. Kyle took to capture work like the proverbial duck to water. Perhaps his experience of animal behaviour during years of capture work on the ground helped, but whatever, he very quickly became exceptionally good at driving animals into the boma. He even coped well with the notoriously difficult impala – one of our staples.

On a very cold June morning we were in Ghanzi catching assorted game on Jan Taljard's farm and Kyle was flying. Two policemen from Ghanzi arrived on the farm with a warning that Kyle should not fly any more under threat of prosecution because he didn't hold a commercial licence. This was a serious blow for us and we had to suspend operations. Luckily, we learned through John that a former colleague of his was unexpectedly available. He was an older guy with lots of experience dating back as far as the Rhodesian bush war. We managed to get him up to Ghanzi and he was flying in a couple of days. Kyle later found out that Barney O'Hara had reported him. He was none too pleased, having helped Barney for free the previous year with a big camp construction project in Zambia. Barney at the time was struggling in the private sector, trying to find work for his newly acquired Hughes 500 helicopter. Although he was a top pilot and the Hughes was a great machine, it was just far too expensive to operate for most game capture companies – you didn't need a Ferrari when a small pick-up truck would do the job. By the end of the following season Kyle had the necessary hours, passed the practical test with flying colours, and against all expectations even managed to pass the difficult theory exams to get his Commercial Pilot's Licence.

Having our own machine and pilot was a real game changer. Although the economics had seemed a gamble, the increase in work more than paid for the helicopter and KGS began to prosper. By the end of the 2010 season we had more trucks, our own mechanic and enough equipment to service two bomas.

Towards the end of 2010 KGS won a contract for a French organisation, CIRAD, who wanted to sample 200 buffalo for FMD and tuberculosis in northern Botswana, specifically the Chobe and the Okavango. The CIRAD representative was a Dr Ferran Jori who was attached to the Mammal Research Institute at Pretoria University. Ferran was responsible for hiring the field team and collecting the samples. I went to see him in Pretoria and explained what KGS could do. The job was an almost exact duplication of our buffalo sampling exercises in the 1970s, but this time we wouldn't be working for the government. Ferran wanted a bigger helicopter than our R-22, so I arranged to hire a Bell JetRanger through Peter Perlstein, a very experienced game pilot.

I called my old colleague Norbert Drager who had led the 1970s surveys and asked if he wanted to come along. Norbert was long retired in Grahamstown, but was very keen to come up as an observer for old times' sake. I also called an old college friend, Sandy Gill, in practice in England, who had been keen to visit for some time, explaining that this was an opportunity too good to miss. A few weeks later we were on the banks of the Chobe River in the National Park. We camped at the Elephants Without Borders compound in Kasane.

KGS was to catch the buffaloes individually and restrain them for sampling by Ferran and his team of young government veterinarians. We were instructed not to get involved in the actual sampling. Working on the clear Chobe floodplains was very easy and I darted about eighty animals for the sampling teams. KGS staff roped and secured the drugged buffaloes and then held them in the best position for Ferran's people to take blood from the jugular veins and a swab from their throats. It soon became obvious that the sampling teams were less than expert, but perhaps that should have been expected as apparently none of them, including Ferran, had been up close to a buffalo before. Ferran invoked "health and safety" regulations and refused to alight from his vehicle until the darted buffalo was completely trussed and helpless. At first we saw the funny side of things, but when Norbert pointed out to me that they were sterilising the throat samples, rendering them completely useless, through dipping the probangs (small sampling cups) in disinfectant, I couldn't help but point this out to Ferran. He immediately took umbrage and his attitude became quite aggressive. Basically, the message was "Mind your own business and don't interfere".

After moving to the Okavango for the rest of the samples, relationships became more strained. Ferran and his team of inexperienced vets seemed to lack any interest in doing the job properly. The "health and safety" attitude prevailed even among their drivers, who refused to drive their Land Cruisers across shallow rivers, despite watching KGS drivers do it regularly with identical vehicles. Even Sandy, a sixty-year-old, fresh out of the UK, rolled up his sleeves and did a fair share of the blood collections when younger vets had given up. I resorted to showing them how to take blood from the tail veins if they didn't relish going near the horns. In short it was a fiasco, but apart from Ferran, I think everyone enjoyed a couple of weeks in one of the world's most beautiful places. Inevitably, as Norbert had predicted, the eventual publication of the results showed that none of the buffalo had FMD virus – a complete farce! But KGS was handsomely paid, courtesy of yet another waste of international aid funds.

Almost next door to our base at Pangolin Farm in Notwane was the Mokolodi Nature Reserve. This was the brainchild of a prominent lawyer, Ian Kirby, who owned the land and lived in a mock castle overlooking an artificial lake in the Reserve. It was almost 10,000 acres in extent and included steep rocky hills and valleys with a section of flatter mixed woodland and grassland. Although the underlying motivation for the Reserve was no doubt the preservation of the owner's lifestyle, with the development of Gabs extending rapidly towards and around him, the area was a conservation success story and was fairly well patronised by Gabs folk and tourists. Because of its limited size and carrying capacity, without hunting there were always excess animals to be removed. This was extremely convenient for us and we tried to schedule a catching job there as close to the beginning of the season in March as we could. This allowed us to test new and repaired equipment, as well as dust the cobwebs off the staff before moving to more remote areas. We had a good working relationship with Ian's son Puso, who managed the Reserve for several years until he was sadly killed in a car accident. After that there was a series of managers of varying competence and we had good years and bad.

We always took off a mixed bag of plains game, mainly impala, wildebeest and zebra, but sometimes were asked to capture and sell kudu, giraffe and waterbuck in small numbers as well. Keen to diversify, Mokolodi operated a small reptile enclosure as part of their visitor and interpretation centre near the main entrance. There was also a cheetah rehabilitation program with a compound where the public could interact with the cats. A popular restaurant was a big attraction and they developed campsites, chalets and a conference centre. An active and imaginative advertising and promotion campaign ensured they were always fairly busy. Some of their initiatives were less successful though. They acquired a few tame elephants and visitors were able to walk with them in the bush. A number of Sri Lankan mahouts were brought in to work with the elephants and train some local people. Tragically, two mahouts were killed and the fallout from the incident wasn't managed particularly well. A male was destroyed as being the most likely culprit and the other elephants were transferred to an operation in the Okavango Delta.

Mokolodi was not big enough to house free-living elephants, but they were more successful with white rhinos. Their first rhinos settled well and bred successfully. When the rhino numbers grew, a few, mostly adult males, were darted and removed to other sanctuaries in the country in order to prevent them fighting and killing each other. Later the Reserve's management was allowed to sell a small number of rhino to approved game ranches as part of the national effort to re-establish the species in Botswana. Naturally, all costs and risks of these activities were for the buyer's account and the animals would be insured for the procedure and reintroduction period on the new ranch.

Bids were called for and Gavin applied on behalf of Kanana Ranch. Kanana was one of the approved rhino holding facilities and they already had half a dozen animals. Gavin was keen to obtain another breeding female and when Mokolodi advertised a seven-year-old for sale he outbid the competition and asked me to capture and move the animal for him

Our two-seater Robinson R-22 helicopter was not ideal for darting rhino, especially in the uneven, hilly and dense woodland of Mokolodi. We would need to make sure that a ground team could get to the darted animal as quickly as possible to deal with any potential emergencies and there were few suitable roads. Compounding the problem was that with myself and Kyle we were close to the maximum payload for the little helicopter, so we could not carry a great deal of fuel.

Flying first with a Mokolodi staff member to make sure we would recognise the correct animal, Kyle was less than enthusiastic about the project. He could only get short glimpses of the animal disappearing into the thick woodland as it tried to avoid the helicopter. However we positioned the crate in a likely spot and decided to give it a go. The rest of the day flashed by and we were not given the slightest chance of hitting the animal with a dart. When the light started to dim and it became unsafe we called it off and agreed to try again early the next day.

The following morning it took a while to locate the animal in Mokolodi's thick bush. When we did get a sighting it was nowhere near the crate. Since the rhino would have to be walked to the crate from where it went down we would have to get them closer together. Causing as little disturbance as possible we tried to monitor her movements until she was resting in the midday heat in a recognisable patch of bush. Luckily there was a rough track fairly close by and we were able to reposition the crate much closer.

In the mid-afternoon we took off and after some skilful flying by Kyle I managed to shoot a dart into the animal's thick-skinned rump. She was running through dense bush and good luck played its part. We kept her in sight for about five minutes and she began to slow down as the drug took effect, but when the drugs really kicked in she seemed oblivious to the machine's presence above her. She began to miss her footing occasionally and half tripped over a fallen log. Gradually she slowed down significantly and came to a stop with her head in a thick bush.

Kyle radioed the ground team, giving them her position and exhorting them to get there as fast as possible. Meanwhile we looked for a clearing as close to the rhino as possible where Kyle could land. We were lucky. About 250 yards away was a small gap in the bush that allowed him to put the helicopter down without touching the fragile and critical tail rotor on any vegetation. I jumped out immediately with my drug box and a blindfold and ran as fast as I could over the rough ground and through thick thorn bush until I got to the immobilised rhino. Before the ground crew arrived on foot I had been able to tie the blindfold around the rhino's head and stuff cotton wool into her ears. Hearing is not affected much by the drug we used, so ear plugs reduce stress considerably.

On their arrival the ground crew hacked at the bushes with pangas to give us more space around her and we applied ropes to her head and one back leg. The former is used to pull and steer and the rope on the leg is a brake. Eventually a second crew arrived and we secured her with five people pulling the head rope and three holding the leg brake in case it was needed. I injected a tiny dose of antidote into an ear vein and within two minutes she was awake sufficiently to be manipulated. A short, sharp shock from a cattle prod stimulated her to stand up properly and try to move. A few extras pushed on the animal's flanks as well, and there must have been ten or twelve people ready to move her to the crate, some 200 yards away. This was achieved surprisingly quickly and the brake hands needed help to stop her from by-passing the open door. A little "fine tuning" and she was up the short ramp and into the crate first time, a big relief. While Kyle supervised taking off the ropes and securing the rear door, I was able to reach down from the roof at the front end and remove the blindfold and ear plugs.

It took almost an hour of very careful driving to reach the main gate and then, with sandwiches and cold drinks on board and a quick check to see that she was comfortable and standing calmly we set off for Ghanzi. I was pulling the trailer with a 4x4 Isuzu diesel bakkie. Kyle accompanied me as co-driver and two of our field staff came along as well. Ghanzi is approximately 500 miles northwest of Gaborone and the road was fairly newly surfaced, having been a deep sand track until a few years previously. We left Mokolodi at about 5 pm and made steady, if unspectacular, progress via the diamond mining town of Jwaneng and on across the Kalahari Desert. There was very little traffic on the straight road and not much to see in the headlights; nowadays people are amazed when their "satnavs" instruct them to "turn left in 400 miles at the next junction". We took it very steadily, aiming to arrive in Ghanzi township around first light and then negotiate the final twenty-five miles of dirt roads with good visibility. We stopped frequently and climbed up onto the roof of the trailer to check that all was well with the rhino, but she seemed to be calm and "sleeping off" the drugs in a standing position. This was good because rhinos can damage their legs if they are folded under them for long periods.

Coming into Ghanzi at dawn is not an inspiring experience, though to us it was a welcome sight. We pulled into the town's one dusty fuel station as they opened for business at 6 am and filled up, thankful that they had some diesel, which wasn't always the case. I took over driving again from Kyle and we turned left, leaving the tar behind and headed west out of town on the corrugated dirt road towards the Namibian border. We were about three miles out and the sun had just breached the horizon behind us.

"Look Boss!" came the startled shout from the back seat accompanied by an urgent poking. I turned to see the trailer overtaking us on the right hand side! It had bounced off the ball and socket tow hitch and broken the safety chain on the rough surface. I had obviously been driving too fast for the conditions. I braked and we all watched in fascinated horror as the trailer careered across the road in front of us, hit a large calcrete rock on the near side of the road and toppled over into the bush.

As the dust cleared we could see that the crate was on its side with one of its axles torn off and the remaining one with wheels spinning uselessly. The top of the crate was facing away from us and I was desperate to see what state our charge was in. The top of the crate, now vertical, consisted of flimsy metal struts about six inches apart and wouldn't keep a determined rabbit in let alone an angry rhino. This was now the only obstacle to the rhino cow's escape, assuming she wasn't dead or badly injured. I told the others to keep quiet and out of sight while I crept around the trailer to assess the rhino. She stood looking through the struts at the bush beyond, but seemed remarkably unconcerned by having somersaulted and landed on her feet on what had been the side of the crate, but was now the floor. I crept back and discussed our options with the others. As long as she stayed in her cage we might be OK, but if she pushed the struts away and got out we had very serious problems – a wild rhino running down Ghanzi's main street would not be amusing, and having to shoot her would be tragic. I pondered what I might do with my limited drug supply. Injecting her might annoy her to the extent that she would break out through the flimsy barrier. If she remained standing quietly, that would be best. But how were we going to get back on the road?

Just then a local farmer arrived on the scene on his way into town. He was a neighbour of Gavin's and eager to help. He knew of a JCB digger in Ghanzi and went off to locate it. He also knew where we might obtain another axle and various bits of useful hardware. When he arrived back with his friend and the JCB there was quite a crowd of onlookers, some with helpful advice and some not. It took me all my time to stop them from going round to look at the rhino and provoking a charge that would have led to an escape.

Working as fast and as quietly as we could, we managed to bolt on the new axle and attach the two wheels without disturbing the rhino too much. But next we would have to pull the trailer over onto its four wheels, which meant that the rhino would have to move again as its "floor" changed once more. This we managed by attaching chains and pulling with the JCB very carefully, until the trailer dropped onto its wheels with a final thump. At least the rhino was now secured again and still didn't seem too much the worse for wear. Next was to straighten the "A-frame" towing hitch that was badly bent. We achieved a rough but functioning solution by hammering the steel chassis with the bucket of the JCB, a bit crude but effective.

Finally about 10 am we were re-coupled and on our way, slowly and carefully covering the last twenty miles to the farm gate, followed by a further ten, north into the ranch to the chosen release point. With my pole syringe I gave the rhino an injection of long-acting antibiotic to try to ensure no infection set in to its minor grazes and we opened the rear door of the trailer. She was reluctant to back out down the short loading ramp, normal behaviour for white rhino, but eventually we coaxed her down onto the sand and she trotted away into the bush, apparently none the worse for her traumatic experience.

TWENTY-ONE

FRUSTRATED DEVELOPMENT

Through the BWPA we tried very hard to promote this new kind of farming. Eleanor and I, along with Derek Moore, Ant Johnson and others campaigned ceaselessly to get official approval and support. We had proved that game ranching was good conservation; there were over fifty rhino and 200 giraffe in new areas, with several thousand zebra on ranches in areas where they had not existed for over 100 years. These were only the "flagship" species, but the boost to biodiversity and the increase in land dedicated to wildlife (over two million acres) were indisputable, or so we thought.

Gradually, KGS morphed into a busy, recognised company that grew as part of the expanding game ranching industry. I myself spent as much time running the day to day capture activities on farms as I possibly could, while Eleanor and our secretary, Florence Maribeng, ran the office in Gabs. It seemed that there was a steadily growing requirement for permits from either DWNP or the Vet Department. Nothing was made easy by the civil service, but it was worse because nobody in government had any experience of game farming and the administration's promulgation of regulations for the new activity were seriously delayed. Florence, backed up by Eleanor, spent an enormous amount of time just acquiring all the pieces of paper necessary for us to do our job. I too spent days and days travelling to minor district offices to get permits from Gabs endorsed. We also had to collect DWNP personnel from these offices to witness our operations. These people were usually the lowest ranked officers who hadn't the slightest interest in or knowledge of what we were doing. Often they didn't count the animals we caught, and sometimes didn't even know what they were. At the end of a day sitting in the shade of a tree consuming our refreshment and rations they would stamp a form and then we would drive them back to their offices, sometimes two hours away! It was all extremely frustrating and expensive for us and the farmers. Exporting was just as bad, with customs staff completely uninterested and unaware of either numbers or species of what was in our trailers. We had wildebeest mistaken for ostriches (even after a visual inspection)! We had antelope described not as mammals, birds or fish, but as "others" because that category attracted no duty and therefore needed less work. After all, surely even the most ignorant, uneducated official must know that impala and zebra are mammals? We laughed around the campfire and in the bar, but it was really a painful and frustrating time.

Eventually, spurred by our members' grievances we arranged for a delegation to meet with the Minister of Environment and Wildlife. This individual was the younger brother of the incumbent President Khama. Supremely arrogant, he had a reputation for taking all decisions, even minor ones, himself and had therefore emasculated the DWNP. Successive directors had resigned or were replaced because they were deemed completely ineffectual. The meeting proved a waste of time. Despite all the evidence placed before him, illustrating both the conservation and economic potential of game ranching, he priggishly declared "I haven't decided whether to support or crush your industry," and our delegation withdrew flabbergasted and very disappointed. The same man continually impeded the development of game ranching for years, even at one juncture refusing to recognise a judgement of the High Court on ownership of wildlife, claiming "I make the rules". Unfortunately, his relationship to the President made him untouchable and we reluctantly capitulated, managing to keep going only through the support of one or two junior officials who ventured dangerously close to subtle defiance.

One of the longstanding issues for BWPA was the acquisition of so-called valuable or "rare" species for multiplication on game ranches. These species were principally sable and roan antelope, but also tsessebe. Unfortunately these animals only occurred in the north of the country and that was an FMD area with restrictions of movement. Cattle from the same area were allowed out via a system of quarantines, although this was banned during active FMD outbreaks. The quarantine and export of roan antelope from Pandamatenga in 2001, described earlier, set a precedent and BWPA lobbied government to be allowed to repeat the exercise with Botswana game ranches as the ultimate destination. Permission was denied by the Director of Veterinary Services, but we considered that his reasons were not scientifically valid. A highly qualified, internationally recognised consultant was recruited by BWPA to conduct a risk analysis. Government was involved with BWPA in drawing up comprehensive terms of reference for the study and it took place in 2004. The conclusions of the risk analysis were indisputable: the movement of sable, roan and tsessebe could be easily managed, quite safely, through a well-documented quarantine system that was in use elsewhere, most notably in neighbouring countries. The report was circulated among various relevant government ministries; no negative comments were ever received, but despite vigorous lobbying over several years, the proposal was never acceded to. This very disheartening attitude of senior civil servants prevailed and was a serious impediment to the development of game ranching as a form of agriculture and conservation and particularly the recruitment of local citizen farmers.

In 2007 an opportunity arose to buy an interest in a Tuli Block farm. An old friend, Bill Halkon, whom I had known since we first arrived in Botswana, had been keen to buy a farm. Bill was from a Yorkshire farming family and had been involved in various aspects of agriculture and related civil engineering over the previous thirty-odd years. Botswana's biggest landowner, Derek Brink, owned several farms in Tuli Block, as well as elsewhere, and almost never sold a property. For some inexplicable reason he agreed to sell a farm in central Tuli Block to Bill, who asked Eleanor and me if we would be partners.

The farm was predominantly a cattle farm like most of Brink's empire. However, like most of Tuli Block it had resident wildlife, mainly impala, kudu and wildebeest, but with small numbers of other species like tsessebe, waterbuck and bushbuck that could be found in a fairly pristine area of riverine woodland along the three-mile stretch of the Limpopo forming our boundary with South Africa. A portion of perhaps 500 acres near the river had been cleared and attempts to irrigate the land to grow maize had been half-heartedly tried. A water pipe from a borehole near the river provided water in a central spine up the farm for the cattle. There were about 600 cattle on the property, about double the recommended stocking rate, and this situation had led over the years to pasture degradation and bush encroachment. Brink removed his cattle within a few weeks of our taking over and we set about converting the major portion of the farm into a game ranch. This involved taking down the internal paddock fences and upgrading and completing the perimeter fence to the standard required by law – ten feet high and twelve strands of wire.

Bill was the farmer, so he moved in with his wife, Jossie, and restored the farmhouse. Eleanor and I were mostly weekend visitors and treated the place as a welcome retreat from Gabs where the kids could enjoy some natural space. I became involved in developing the potential of the game ranch portion and we improved natural water points, opened new tracks and gradually created a fairly successful wildlife asset. After a year or two we introduced new species like giraffe, gemsbok, hartebeest and zebra. Through KGS I was able to acquire and deliver small numbers of these species economically as part loads of larger consignments to other farmers. Also through KGS we were able to catch and remove some of the impala and wildebeest to help to pay for the new arrivals.

The irrigation scheme, using water from the Limpopo was a great success and Bill soon had two centre-pivots delivering water to over 100 acres of lucerne for animal feed. We employed an Afrikaner manager, Oubaas Meyer, who mainly looked after the irrigation project and, together with Eleanor, organised the marketing of the lucerne, for which there had been only a seasonal demand, on a year-round basis. With some small subsidies from the game sales, the lucerne more than paid the bills and Sunnyside became a success story. We improved some of the outbuildings and storage and KGS increasingly exploited the farm's central location in Tuli Block as an operating base for our game capture and trading activities.

A number of game farmers had approached me to ask if KGS could harvest some of their excess animals and supply butchers with venison. We had occasionally cropped impala and wildebeest for Derek Brink and he marketed the meat through his own butchery, Senn Foods. To me this seemed like a logical progression of game ranching, after all, as the industry grew it would obviously produce more animals than could be sold alive, and all other forms of livestock farming, from beef to chickens, produced and sold meat, nobody just allowed their animals to die of old age. We therefore approached the authorities for permission to harvest game animals on registered ranches for meat. After the usual delays and debate the government eventually gave approval for the sale of game meat (venison) in approved butcheries. On registered farms we were allowed to cull animals and process the carcases to a "partially dressed" state, after which they had to be transported in refrigerated trucks to the butcheries where further dressing and sale could occur. A few farmers tried shooting animals themselves, mainly at night with spotlights, but they could not achieve an economic harvest. If they were near a sizeable market, like Francistown, one or two persevered and considered it worthwhile, but generally we had to explore a better commercial model. The biggest stumbling block was complying with veterinary regulations; animals were supposed to be inspected before slaughter and carcases had to be examined for parasites and other signs of overt disease.

Kyle had been involved in cropping feral animals in Australia, mainly horses and goats, and he suggested that we build a mobile abattoir that we could use in the bush. The design was simple enough and we constructed the basic units from steel with a couple of skilled friends doing most of the more demanding welding. The whole structure could be loaded on a flatbed trailer, transported and bolted together on site in a matter of a few hours by the same labourers that erected the capture bomas. The idea was to use the helicopter and boma to capture the animals and then, instead of loading them, divert them through the abattoir.

To adhere to the veterinary regulations we had to arrange with the nearest office for a team of meat inspectors to attend. All our staff had to undergo medical examinations and some basic training in meat hygiene. Luckily, because of my veterinary degree I was allowed to supervise the inspections, but a government official had to certify the carcases. By this time Kyle was an experienced game capture pilot, but he was also by far the most competent meat processor, or blockman, as they are known in the trade. He was going to be a very busy man. Finally, the big day arrived and we assembled the abattoir next to our crush at the business end of the capture boma on one of Derek Brink's ranches. Kyle flew off to locate a herd of impala and drive them towards the boma. Within twenty minutes he had herded about sixty animals into the first and largest of the boma compartments and the curtains had been closed. We then allowed the animals to settle down and I inspected them through binoculars to ensure they weren't suffering from any obvious disease condition. Next we then drove them forward into smaller compartments as in a normal capture. When about half of them were next to the crush most of our staff rushed off to wash quickly and change into white overalls and hard hats. Four men were responsible for driving the animals in groups of about a dozen into the crush and confining them in the narrow final chute that would double as a killing box. I stood on an elevated inspection ramp above the chute and shot each animal in the head with a .22 calibre rifle. A side door was then opened and the dead animals were taken out and bled on a sloping grid before being hoisted onto the abattoir proper. Here the various approved procedures took place and the government meat inspectors checked the livers and other organs before the partially dressed carcases were hung under shade netting to cool down. After several hours, often the following morning, they were cool enough to be loaded into the refrigerated trucks.

This new development gave KGS a modest financial boost and became a popular request from farmers. The problem was that Botswana was such a small market, even Senn Foods' nationwide distribution and the inclusion of venison into their salami and polony could not cope with the production of wildlife. One solution of course was export. But this was easier said than done. Precious little help was forthcoming from our own government, who merely said we should draft some protocols. The South African Department of Agriculture was much more helpful, giving us advice, and even sending a delegation to assess our operation. Their observers were impressed with our methods and performance, and after a few months of meetings and demonstrations they were prepared to issue us with import permits. On seeing these, their Botswana counterparts had little choice but to sanction our activities. Next was to secure a market. We eventually came to an agreement with Camdeboo Meat Processors in the Eastern Cape, a very large meat exporting company that had little trouble absorbing our production. We had little negotiating power, but they were fair in their pricing and we kept things very simple by paying the farmers nothing until we were paid by Camdeboo. We then simply divided the payment 50/50. It worked well and apart from an occasional minor grumble by the odd farmer, everyone was happy.

In our stride we could process 300 impala or 150 wildebeest in a day and that was profitable for us and the farmers. We gradually refined our methods so that we could load selected animals live and slaughter the rest. Often we would extract prime males for live sales. This would lower our overall slaughtered weight but the live sales prices more than made up for it. Of course the techniques brought the best returns when the demand for coloured animals started (see below), because we never had to release anything that Kyle brought to the boma. Everything was worth something. By the end of the second season our game-meat sales realised over a million pula and the live sales were booming. This was the start of a promising development in the industry and attracted a lot of attention. Unfortunately our "old friend" in the Ministry was unhappy and export of game meat was summarily banned – it was considered elitist.

Shortly before the ban we were culling blue wildebeest on James O'Reilly's ranch at Parr's Halt. Despite his name, James was culturally every inch an

Afrikaner and a bachelor. His mother lived on a neighbouring ranch and even though he was fifty years old she still ruled the roost. James bred beautiful, pedigree Brahman cattle that were much in demand, but he had game-fenced his ranch and also had good populations of several species. He liked to keep the wildebeest numbers down to prevent the transmission of *"snotsiekte"*, a virus deadly to cattle that the wildebeest carried.

It was late afternoon and we were all tired. That's when luck is pushed and mistakes happen. We had culled and processed about 150 wildebeest and there was just a handful left in the crush. I was shooting and Kyle, the flying finished, was supervising the men on the abattoir gantry. An unusually large bull was separated in the crush and I took aim with the .22 rifle at his head from about six feet away. He didn't flinch, so I tried again, with the same result. I called one of the men to bring "the big gun", a .308 rifle, from my car. I then leant as far down inside the crush as I could and, without thinking, fired at the bull's head from a couple of feet away. The brain shot killed him instantly, but the noise echoing from the steel sides of the crush painfully burst my eardrums and left me completely deaf. This lasted for a couple of days before my hearing partially returned. An audiologist in Johannesburg, a specialist in explosion damage, examined me a few weeks later, and pronounced my hearing permanently impaired by over fifty per cent, resulting in my having to wear hearing aids to this day. It was an expensive mistake and a salutary lesson in safety procedures.

Around this time a strange phenomenon started in South Africa among the game ranching fraternity. A demand was created for wildebeest that were actually a red colour, almost the same as red hartebeest. This colour variant originated among the wildebeest in the Limpopo Valley and these strange animals were occasionally found on Tuli Block farms. An enterprising game rancher on the South African side of the Limpopo, Barry York, had been breeding red wildebeest for a few years and it appeared as though the colour was due to a simple recessive gene. Put simply, this meant that a red male bred with a red female would mostly produce red offspring. It was a slow process, but Barry and one or two others had produced a viable number of the animals. When they put some of these on the market they immediately attracted high prices, far in excess of the 100 dollars that a normal wildebeest could command. Scarcity was a powerful attraction and Barry knew best how to exploit this. Within a couple of years red wildebeest were being marketed as "golden gnus" and their value sky-rocketed. By 2011 prices were in the region of 3,000 dollars at auction. Barry and some associates built a palatial facility near Modimolle north of Pretoria called Castle De Wildt and hosted elaborate weekend functions with game auctions as the main attraction.

Unsurprisingly KGS was inundated with enquiries and requests for these "golden gnus". These came from Tuli Block farmers wanting to export or South African game ranchers wanting to acquire the animals. A few farmers claimed they had one or, rarely, two or three. Sometimes they occurred on cattle farms that had not been licensed as game ranches and therefore could not legally trade in wild animals. Nonetheless we captured a small number from game farms and exported them to South Africa at great profit to the farmers, and at first KGS merely charged professional fees and expenses. A little later we would enter into an agreement with the farmers that we would bear all the costs of searching their farms with our helicopter and, if we were successful, export the animals at our expense and risk, later dividing the sale price between us. For this to work the farmers had to have implicit trust in our company and fortunately because of our track record and good personal relations this was never a problem. This windfall certainly benefited the company and made operations reliably profitable for the first time. We even discovered one of these much sought-after animals among our own wildebeest on Sunnyside.

The fad spread throughout the game industry in South Africa where there were over 10,000 registered game ranches. Other species became involved, from black impala and golden oryx, to copper springbok and many more. Specialist breeders started producing a range of species colour variants and the demand grew and grew. Of course it began to resemble, and then later took on all the characteristics of, a pyramid scheme with the inevitable results. But that was a few years hence. In the meantime Tuli Block wildebeest, as the origin of golden gnus, were at a premium. Already, certain breeders in South Africa were charging high prices for wildebeest that appeared normal but might be carrying the red gene and these animals were known as "splits". Such animals were priced more realistically and were within the budget of far more ranchers. Very soon we were able to market normal-looking wildebeest from farms that had produced a red variant for high prices to speculating farmers. These prices were two or three times higher than normal – 300 or 400 dollars – and this was good for KGS's business; far better than searching for the occasional, rare, overt red animal.

One never-to-be-forgotten sale was forty wildebeest to a farmer in the Eastern Cape, approximately 1,000 miles south of Tuli Block. Kyle and I delivered the precious shipment ourselves. It was July, deep winter, and we drove overnight in our old Isuzu truck with ill-fitting doors and no heater. We were wrapped in blankets in the cab and nearly froze, so the poor animals in the compartments must have had a tough night. Eventually, near Cradock, we offloaded them into a snow-covered paddock at about 10 am. The rancher had provided hay and game feeding pellets so they didn't have to dig for grazing, but we wondered how they would fare. Later we learned that they had all survived the traumatic change of environment and when they calved in December two red offspring were produced, to the delight of the farmer.

We also supplied another rancher in Limpopo Province with thirty-five female wildebeest from a farm in central Tuli Block. This was after the breeding season so most of them were pregnant. When they calved in December, five gave birth to red calves! This was sensational and the rancher was delighted. Of course the farmer who sold them did not know which of his many bulls might have sired the red calves, but when news got out his animals were in great demand, and to a lesser extent the same happened for all our Tuli Block clients. But even though a few lucky recipient farms got the odd red calf, most got nothing. Whatever, it was great business for KGS and we thrived until the Minister of Wildlife, the aforementioned T.K. Khama, abruptly banned the export of all wildlife from Botswana. His alleged reasoning, never publically explained, was to protect the country's genetic resources, but all he succeeded in doing was strangling a few enterprising game ranchers and crippling KGS with whom he was constantly in dispute over what he saw as our monopoly. We carried on servicing the domestic market for a couple of years, but with only 100 or so game farms, Botswana was slim pickings without an export market.

TWENTY-TWO

ELEPHANTS WITHOUT BORDERS

In the first years of the millennium I was still frequently employed to immobilise animals for various research projects around the country and this kept me busy and helped KGS to stay afloat. Every year since 2002 I had darted elephants for Elephants Without Borders, an NGO based in Kasane. EWB had started as a research project for Mike Chase, the grandson of Jack, my first contact in Botswana thirty years earlier. Mike had spent his life in the Botswana bush with Jack and his father John who was a professional hunter and guide. His mother Tina is the only woman to obtain a Botswana PH licence, so Mike's destiny was firmly lodged in Botswana's wildlife. He obtained a PhD from the University of Massachusetts for his study of Botswana's elephants and set up EWB to continue the work. Altogether we fitted over 200 elephants with radiotelemetry collars. Most of these were equipped with satellite functions as well as VHF radio transmitters. Many could be tracked in real time, but others were data-loggers that stored the GPS information until the collars were removed and interrogated in the lab. A colossal amount of data was obtained, mostly from Botswana, with a smaller number of collars deployed in Zambia, Namibia and southern Angola. A picture of elephant movements throughout the region was built up over the years showing seasonal movements of the breeding herds as well as the wandering bulls. Evidence of cross-border movements was plentiful and this, true to EWB's eponymous goal, was submitted to the various regional governments for planning protected areas.

Initially funding was limited and Mike relied mostly on an American donor, Player Crosby from Massachusetts, who tragically died in 2003 while piloting his plane. The work continued with some assistance from the US Fish and Wildlife Service and the San Diego Zoo, but EWB was constantly looking for new support beyond that from various local businesses, family and friends. Mike would occasionally call me to immobilise an elephant and fit a collar in an attempt to demonstrate what was involved in our work to a string of potential donors, mainly rich Americans that he had made contact with. We put collars on elephants and the VIPs would have their photographs taken while "assisting" us. I don't think this strategy yielded much, but at least they paid for that particular collar. I remember "performances" for one of the Walton brothers of Walmart, and the owner of Wrigley's gum, both billionaires, but with little forthcoming. Then Mike met Jody Allen, the sister of Paul Allen of Microsoft fame. She kindled an interest in her brother and they became major donors.

Paul Allen made a five-week trip around Southern Africa in 2013 and EWB were asked to show him their work. For his personal security the safari was shrouded in secrecy. I knew nothing; all I was told was to turn up in Maun with my dart gun and drugs on a particular morning. I flew in on Air Botswana to be met, not by our usual helicopter pilot but by a uniformed airman in charge of a seriously large machine. I remember it well because as I was walking across the apron towards the helicopter my phone rang and an employee told me that one of KGS's trucks had "fallen off the road" in Tuli Block. All I could do was tell the man to contact Kyle Smith before I boarded the helicopter and, still none the wiser, was flown into one of the Okavango's luxury lodges. On landing at Vumbura, I got out to be confronted by three serious-looking security men. One of them politely but firmly told me to put down my gun and drug box, then step back. Amused, I watched him approach and inspect the suspicious tools of my trade. He obviously couldn't figure out how the dart gun worked, so I explained and he let me carry on. He and his colleagues were apparently ex-navy seals, hired to look after Paul's safety.

In the background, also looking amused, was my old friend and helicopter pilot, Peter Perlstein, who had flown in with a more modest chopper from which we would dart the elephant. Peter, always cheerful, welcomed me and took me to the chalet I would be sharing with him. Vumbura was a large well-spaced, ultra-luxury lodge with a wing of about six chalets either side of an exceptionally well-appointed central lounge/bar and dining area. He explained that the whole camp had been taken over; Paul, Jody and her two kids, plus Paul's Italian girlfriend on one side and the hired hands, like us, the security detail, and a few others on the other wing. Peter introduced me to some of the others over a drink. There was another specialist helicopter crew from Cape Town who operated a fancy piece of kit called a heli-gimble that filmed the action from the air. Only two of these devices existed in the whole of Africa and they didn't come cheap. The crew were an Australian pilot and an English technician, both the best in the business. There was also a fourth helicopter that was used for "odd jobs" and mostly carried Doug Allan, a multi-Emmy Award winning film maker. He was there to record the safari privately for the Allen family. Clearly Paul didn't mess around! Everything went very smoothly and two collars were deployed without incident. We lived very, very well for a couple of days, with excellent food and drink, but the workers didn't get to mix with the principals in the evening; they stayed on the other side and even entertained themselves with a small band that had been flown in from the USA for a couple of nights – apparently Paul liked to jam with his guitar!

On my return to Maun airport I was walking across the apron alone after being dropped off by the Allens' helicopter. I was carrying my drug box and the same rifle-type dart gun. There was a medium-size jet at the refuelling point with its passenger door open. Near it was a guard of honour, about a dozen smartly turned out BDF soldiers with a sergeant major at the front facing them. As I drew near, with my gun over my shoulder, I called out *"Dumela Rra"*, the usual Setswana greeting. The sergeant major replied cheerfully and I carried on past the soldiers to the small terminal building. Then I saw the President of Botswana at the top of the jet's stairway! It was quite a contrast to the security "welcome" I'd received on my arrival at the Allens' camp.

The relationship between EWB and the Allens flourished for about five years. Funds were provided to build and operate a tented research centre in the middle of the Okavango. This was situated close to Abu Camp, the famous lodge started by Randall Moore with his tame elephants. Paul had already bought the lease for the concession area and upgraded the lodge as a top destination where African elephants could be ridden by guests. The tame herd inevitably produced babies and Mike was asked to take over its management, with the rehabilitation and release of animals as a prime goal. Things seemed to go well for a few years, but eventually there was some dispute with the Botswana Government and relations with Vulcan Inc, Paul Allen's business and philanthropic organisation, foundered. However, before the breakdown, the Allens funded the Great Elephant Census, devised and managed by Mike. This was a two-year aerial census program started in 2014 and covering the vast majority of the range states of African savannah elephants. It was a massive undertaking and involved very many organisations and individuals in lots of countries. I was only involved on the fringes, my skills as an observer are not the best and they had plenty of professional pilots to take on the job.

Ethiopia, a huge country in the horn of Africa with a dearth of information on its elephant population, was an important part of the census and it posed a number of questions, both logistic and scientific. Mike negotiated a collaboration with the Ethiopian authorities under which they requested that a number of elephants should be fitted with tracking collars during the census. He asked me to go with him and to assist with immobilising the animals and fitting the collars. Mike Holding from Afriscreen Films, an old friend and very experienced pilot, flew his Cessna 182 from Maun to Addis Ababa carrying lots of necessary equipment for us, including, illicitly, the drugs and dart guns which would have been impossible for me to import legitimately. I flew up with Mike from Johannesburg on Ethiopian Airlines. Kelly Landen was there to meet us with Sintayehu Djene, a researcher from Haramaya University. The next thing was to arrange for a suitable helicopter and pilot, not the easiest thing in the security-obsessed Ethiopian capital. There was no helicopter available locally, so Mike arranged clearances for a machine from Tropic Air in Kenya. This duly arrived, flown by a cheerful, bearded Kenyan called Mario Magonga. Mike Holding also arrived the following day after an epic flight from Botswana in his tiny Cessna. We now had a helicopter, spotter plane, drugs, darts, the right people and we were good to go.

Addis was fascinating; the contrast between this huge city at nearly 8,000 feet above sea level and our home in Botswana couldn't have been more stark. The hordes of people, congested traffic, air pollution and the omnipresent security forces were very foreign to us, but the people we met were friendly and warm. Everything about the country was different: the calendar – starting the year in August and seven years behind us; the time – midday was six o'clock; the Amharic alphabet and script; with a profound sense of the country's history, best illustrated by the skeleton of "Lucy", the oldest known hominid, in the National Museum.

The Ethiopians wanted to investigate the status of the Babile Elephant Sanctuary in the northeast of the country, close to Somalia. The sanctuary had been formed in 1970 on the instruction of Emperor Haile Selassie. It was reputed to contain a relic population of perhaps 400 elephants in two or three large herds. Its main problem was that it also contained almost half a million people in its 7,000 sq km. After a couple of days in Addis we flew to Dire Dawa, the nearest city to Babile, and made ourselves comfortable in a hotel while Mike and Kelly, with Sintayehu, completed all the necessary formalities for us to work in the sanctuary.

The next day we took off for Babile. Mike Holding flew Kelly and a couple of local officials in the Cessna, while Mike Chase, Sintayehu and I accompanied Mario in the helicopter. We flew through some green valleys and over some spectacular, dry mountains up to 10,000 feet before crossing a high, broken plateau and landing at a dusty airstrip next to a sizeable village. This was the sanctuary's administrative base. Before Mario had cut the engine we were surrounded by crowds of scruffy, very colourful youngsters, and then lots of adults, before some uniformed militia with automatic weapons arrived and cleared everyone back a safe distance. Sintayehu recognised one or two specific people who were there to meet us and we were all introduced. We were assured that there was a herd of 200 elephants in the vicinity and that at least two other herds of similar size had recently been reported in other parts of the sanctuary. We decided to fly immediately and deploy a collar in the nearby herd. Afterwards we would carry out a systematic census of the elephant population.

Mario, Mike and I soon found the large herd of elephants in a series of steep, forested, rocky gullies and were amazed that these huge animals were apparently able to move freely through this rough, uneven terrain, so different from Botswana. We had no idea of the comparative size of these elephants in relation to those in other parts of Africa, but it seemed most likely that they would be fairly small, like those in the Tuli area of Botswana. Mike said he would prefer to collar an adult male, so, after some pretty skilful flying by Mario, I was able to place a dart in the biggest bull we saw. By now the elephants were pretty disturbed and keeping tabs on the darted animal in the high trees wasn't easy, but after about ten minutes the bull stood under a tree, fanning his ears and shifting his weight on his feet trying to remain standing. Mario then had to find somewhere to land in the forest that was not too far from the elephant. He accomplished this with some difficulty and put us down in a small clearing about 300 yards from the bull. Mike and I gathered our equipment and made off through the forest. I ran ahead carrying only my medical kit to try to guarantee the elephant's safety.

I was amazed upon reaching the animal to find half a dozen young tribesmen watching him from about twenty yards away. The bull was by now lying on his side and snoring loudly through his trunk. I ran up and pulled his ear forward to shade the eye. Mike struggled up carrying the heavy collar and the lead counterweight that keeps the collar in the correct position. As soon as we laid out the collar it became obvious that it was far too short to fit around the beast's neck – he was a giant! There was nothing to be done except take some blood samples and a few measurements before reviving him and letting him rejoin the herd. We would have to pick smaller animals in future.

We divided the kit a bit more evenly for the return walk to the helicopter and Mike set off, leaving me to administer the antidote. By now there were at least a dozen onlookers, one with a small herd of goats! They were all enthralled and chatting excitedly, though none came very close. It occurred to me that these herdboys thought we had shot the elephant and they were excited at the prospect of a meat bonanza. Of course, none of them spoke any English and I certainly didn't know any of the local vernacular. I tried shouting and gesticulating that they should go away, but it did no good, they remained, laughing and watching intently. I showed them the syringe with the antidote and mimed injecting the elephant in a huge ear vein, then running away in the direction of the helicopter. No good – they just stayed where they were. At last I decided there was nothing for it but to inject the antidote for real and move away a safe distance trying to get them to join me. This also had no effect – until the great ear flapped back and the bull started to rock in an attempt to rise. Then my audience disappeared at speed between the trees and I picked up my things and made my way back up the path towards the helicopter.

Back at the airstrip, following our report, Sintayehu informed us that there was an extremely large bull in the sanctuary that had achieved notoriety a few years before by killing a veterinarian who had darted him. He was certain that this must have been the same animal. Whatever, we did manage to place two satellite tracking collars on elephants in the sanctuary. More interesting was our discovery, from the census, that the herd we had worked with was the only herd of elephants in the sanctuary. It was highly mobile, probably in response to disturbance by humans and was sighted by several communities, each of which thought it was a different herd.

Following this I had to return to Botswana to do a job for my friends Anna and Graham McCulloch who ran an NGO based near Seronga at the base of the Okavango panhandle. Mario and the helicopter returned to Kenya and the rest of the team continued with the elephant census throughout Ethiopia in the Cessna.

I was away about ten days putting collars on twenty elephants in the northern Okavango. On my return, Mario had been replaced by Jamie Roberts, his boss at Tropic Air. We flew down to the small market town of Jinka in the southwest. The flight gave an interesting perspective of the intense cultivation and dense population of central Ethiopia, in a very fertile and volcanically active valley. We stopped briefly at Arba Minch airport to refuel and were surprised to see a small but very active US military airbase servicing a fleet of Reaper drones that could keep tabs on most of the Middle East and the Gulf. The American airmen were friendly and not in the least secretive about their function. Other than the busy drones the airport didn't seem to have much traffic. We flew on to Jinka where we were based in a pleasant thatched lodge, with a leafy garden and open-air bar in the foothills while we explored the Omo Valley for elephants.

Jinka is a busy place with a grass or dirt airstrip (depending on the season) in the centre of town, almost surrounded by the busy market with its colourful stalls and produce. Peripherally were some brick buildings: banks, government offices etc. Mike's Cessna was the subject of a twenty-four-hour armed guard, probably necessary. The people of the region are a mix of several ancient tribes and the area has become known for anthropological tourism with European and American visitors ticking off as many of the different ethnic groups as they can in their limited time. In more remote areas, away from the big village these tribes live pretty much as they have for thousands of years. People like the Mursi and Karo are still primitive pastoralists, some of them living on a mixture of blood and milk like the more famous Masai of neighbouring Kenya. They all decorate their bodies with raised welts and scars or tattoos and many of the women have large plates inserted in their bottom lips. The men, mainly, also display grotesquely elongated ear lobes adorned with jewellery. The traditional gourds containing sour milk and blood had mostly been replaced by plastic containers – a sign of the times even here – and most of the men carried AK-47 automatic weapons, mainly as a status symbol, though we were assured that intertribal conflicts with cattle rustling, and sometimes the abduction of young women, were still common.

From our comfortable base in Jinka we flew in the helicopter down to the airstrip in town every morning, creating pandemonium amongst the hundreds of onlookers, especially children, who crowded around in noisy, excited throngs while we prepared the Cessna for the census. Clearing space for the take-off was a problem for the armed, outnumbered security men in blue fatigues, but eventually the Cessna and its survey crew would roar down the airstrip leaving a massive dust cloud in its wake and climb away in the direction of the South Sudanese border. In the chopper we would follow more leisurely to find a place to land, usually on top of one of the many hills that dotted the Omo Valley floor. Here we waited in the shade until the observers in the Cessna called on the radio to let us know they had seen an elephant herd.

The snaking, brown river was central to the wide valley, with spectacular views of mountains in the distance in South Sudan and Kenya. It was another marvellous illustration of the vast scale and grandeur of the African continent. Wide plains teemed with antelope that ignored the clatter of the helicopter as we sped above them and we saw occasional clumps of villages clinging closely to the river banks and its tributaries. We would home in on the GPS coordinates they gave us, find a suitable elephant and dart it. The Omo Valley still contained reasonable wildlife populations in 2014, with good numbers of elephant and various species of antelope. We saw huge herds of topi, but our vantage point in the helicopter gave us a big advantage over the odd tour group in a bus. It took a few days to deploy our quota of elephant collars and then we flew back to Addis, taking leave of our Ethiopian researchers, Jamie and his helicopter, and returned to Botswana. It was an unforgettable experience working in an immense and spectacular area with some of the most exotic inhabitants found anywhere on earth; I felt very privileged.

A year or so after we left, the third and largest of a series of dams on the Omo River came into operation. This has changed the ecology of the whole area for the wildlife and the people. The river no longer has a guaranteed flow in the dry season with devastating effects on the pastoralists and the few tribes that grow crops, an echo of the tragedy I had witnessed a few years earlier with Great Ruaha River in Tanzania. Anthropological tourism has increased, but although it brings in some much-needed revenue, this rarely filters down to the villages and local people in the valley. The way of life of these people, unchanged in thousands of years, is being altered forever. They will soon be gone. For some reason I feel it strongly and I'm bitter about what we are doing to these simple tribal communities, but in many ways it parallels the fate of our own Kalahari Bushmen that I've become inured to and hardly ever think of – it's very sad.

Botswana's neighbour receiving least attention is Angola. Maybe it's because we have no common border because the thin sliver of Namibia that was known as the Caprivi Strip separates the two countries, or maybe it's because it was Portuguese and therefore more "foreign" than the other neighbours. Almost no one from Botswana has ever visited Angola, although the Mbukushu community around Etsha in the upper Okavango Delta originates from there. Elephants of course do not recognise international borders and there has been movement between Botswana, across the Caprivi, and into southeastern Angola. There is little hard data, but it is thought that elephants mostly moved out of Angola into Botswana during the civil war in Angola that ended in 2002, but started to return as peace returned. EWB was keen to document any such movements and had already recorded signals from a few elephants collared in Botswana that had crossed the border into Angola as well as Namibia (Caprivi) and Zambia. Around 2010 we worked for short spells in Zambia and Namibia and fitted collars in both countries, but at that time had not yet received permission to work in Angola.

We had set up a field camp at a place called Bum Hill, an old military encampment with an airstrip, on the west bank of the Kwando River in Namibia. It was a pleasant spot and very convenient for our work in Namibia, but we had to fly over a corner of Angolan territory to work in Sioma Ngwezi NP in Zambia. We were taking old collars off elephants and needed to find them before the batteries died and they ceased transmitting.

Early one morning the two Mikes (Holding and Chase) were flying the Cessna spotter plane high above us. They were tracking the VHF signals from collared elephants. Kelly Landen and I were in Peter Perlstein's helicopter flying low-level across the Kwando River to Zambia. Mike Holding called on the radio to say they had picked up a strong signal from one of our elephants but it was in Angola. We looked around for a few minutes but saw nothing and continued on our track to Zambia. We managed to locate two elephants in Sioma Ngwezi and were able to dart them, retrieve the collars and let the animals go free again. On the way back in the afternoon we were over Angola and Mike called to say they had picked up the same signal again, very close. It was the collar on a female that we needed to remove and we circled low-level in the helicopter to try to find the herd. Kelly first noticed the elephants; they were in some thick woodland about a mile from the river heading deeper into Angola. We held a quick discussion with the two Mikes in the Cessna above and asked them if they could see any sign of human activity. A negative reply was the prod we needed to take a chance.

Peter landed the helicopter in a clearing on the river bank and we quickly removed the doors. I filled a dart with drugs and we were soon airborne again. We saw nobody and quickly located the herd with the female wearing a collar. Mike called to say they could still see nobody in the vicinity, so we swooped and darted the cow elephant and then circled for ten minutes until she went down. Peter chased the herd away and we landed as close to the cow as possible. We jumped out leaving the engine running and, with a slight thrill akin to kids illicitly stealing apples, we cut the collar off as quickly as we could, administered the antidote and ran back to the chopper. We were airborne as she got to her feet and with a sense of relief we landed again by the river to retrieve the doors.

We left Kelly in the helicopter with the engine running and the rotor idling. As Peter and I picked up the doors a number of armed soldiers stood up around us and our hearts fell. We stood with our arms raised and they approached to question us. Of course they spoke no English and we spoke no Portuguese. They also could not understand any of our poor attempts at native languages. There were six of them in scruffy, threadbare uniforms of a sort and we hoped they were regular Angolan forces and not a group of bandits or some irregular militia. Peter tried his inimitable bonhomie, laughing and pointing at the countryside and shouting "Namibia". The soldiers were unmoved, merely shaking their heads and saying "Angola". Behind us one of the men was shouting at a distressed Kelly and gesticulating with his hand in a cutthroat gesture, but he was pointing at the helicopter. He obviously thought she was the pilot and wanted her to cut the engine, but she didn't know how to. Peter, shouting "me pilot" and still laughing managed to get to the machine without being shot and stopped the engine. I looked up, saw the Cessna circling high above us, and hoped the two Mikes understood what was going on. Kelly, relieved that the man had not meant to cut her throat, was ordered out of the helicopter. I tried to explain things in a smattering of French with the odd word of Spanish, but to no avail. I showed them the huge collar and the darts, even, more reluctantly, the dart gun, but they didn't seem interested. Finally, the man in charge waved for us to follow and made off through the bush. We did as told and the others followed us. A few hundred yards on we joined a well-worn path and followed it. We were marched for about two miles through the bush in single file until we came to what was obviously their base camp.

The camp consisted of a small number of ramshackle huts with reed walls and scruffy thatched roofs. At first glance it would have been described as derelict. We were taken to a central hut where a sergeant sat in the doorway, talking on a fairly battered HF radio, hooked up to a car battery. The aerial was a long wire thrown over the roof. The sergeant seemed very friendly, but also spoke no English. The senior man from our patrol gave a report and then we were told to put all our personal effects on the floor. These were taken away and then we were sort of interrogated, but without the ability to communicate this wasn't very successful. There was some levity and we didn't feel very threatened, but one of the younger soldiers indicated that he would like a blonde wife, which made Kelly jump to my side and grab my arm in alarm. I said that Cristiano Ronaldo was *"number 1"* and a couple of the soldiers laughed and agreed, so they knew about the famous Portuguese soccer star who played for Manchester United. I indicated somehow that I was from Manchester and had watched Ronaldo play many times. That seemed to help to soften relations. After a while one of the soldier's wives brought us a can of fruit cocktail each and some canned ham. They also gave us some water to drink. Kelly was reluctant to eat and drink, but I persuaded her that it would help relations if we seemed grateful and we also didn't know how long we might be stuck there. She then ate a little but definitely wasn't going to drink the water. We were then taken to a large, fairly dilapidated hut, which was to be our accommodation. As a cell it had the sole advantage of having a door, so we could be locked inside.

Just inside the door was a small room with a small bed on one side. Round to the right was another larger room with a larger bed above which was a torn mosquito net. There was one small, dirty blanket. We gave Kelly the blanket and small room while Peter and I shared the larger bed. After dark we were locked in and it soon started to get cold. Kelly had trousers, but we were wearing shorts, so Peter took his flying jacket and put his legs through the sleeves to try to keep warm. I pulled down the remnants of the mosquito net and wrapped it around me. It was a very long, cold, uncomfortable night. In the morning we were allowed out into the camp area again and Peter and I tried once again to convince the sergeant that we were innocent, harmless scientists but he was obviously not about to let his important captives go. Peter was allowed to go back to the helicopter with three armed guards and bring it to the camp. One guard accompanied him in the helicopter, but kept his gun trained on him and wouldn't let him fly more than a few feet above the river.

On his return the sergeant wanted to fly to Luanda with him but Peter persuaded him that Angola was a huge country and it was much too far and out of range, and we only had limited fuel. Menongue, the district capital, seemed more reasonable, but this too was out of range. We continued to state our case as best we could to the sergeant and he repeatedly tried to contact his superiors at Menongue HQ by radio, but reception was intermittent and distorted. This went on for about two hours until we managed to persuade him that we had a telephone that he could use. He obviously didn't believe us and had never seen or heard of a satellite phone. He told one of his men to bring our belongings and we showed him the satphone. Peter demonstrated how it worked, by phoning Mike Chase at our Bum Hill camp. Mike assured us that he had contacted the District Governor who would arrange for our release. This was great news, but how would he contact our captors? The sergeant didn't know the telephone number of the officer in charge in Menongue, so we called Mike again and he supplied the number. Peter dialled, before handing the phone to the sergeant. His reaction was instant and very comical; he obviously recognised the officer's voice and leapt to his feet, standing at attention, shouting *"Sim Comandante!"* every few seconds. After a couple of minutes he returned the phone to us and indicated that we were free to go. We picked up our belongings and walked down to the nearby helicopter accompanied by a now very friendly bunch of soldiers, laughing and chattering. After handshakes and salutes all round we climbed aboard, Peter started up and we were on our way downriver to our Bum Hill camp and very relieved companions. Through it all Peter had remained as upbeat and cheerful as ever – the perfect companion for a spell in jail! A couple of years before he had even seen the funny side of things when a lion stole his pillow while he slept in our camp in the southern Kalahari during a scientific expedition for WITS University of South Africa.

Working with wild animals is seen as exciting, even thrilling, by many people. To a large extent I suppose this has been boosted by the exposure it has been given by television companies, especially channels such as *Nat Geo Wild* in recent years. Maybe it was always so; after all, my own ambitions were sparked by David Attenborough on black and white BBC in the 1950s. The main difference as I see it is that the early film-makers were genuinely providing what is now sometimes called "edutainment", focusing on information, whereas the bulk of popular natural history programs now create and exaggerate "drama" to an unrealistic level – *Ten Most Deadly Predators* or lions and hyaenas following the script of *Game of Thrones* are a far cry from the old *Zoo Quest*. Sharks, eagles and scorpions certainly trump mackerel, doves and beetles, regardless of their true life-histories. Is this part of the psyche that compels us to "save elephants" but ignore wildebeest?

Whatever the motivation, our work has always attracted interest from moviemakers and journalists. I was first involved in a television program in 1972 when we were testing buffaloes for FMD in Savuti. It was an American production for *Mutual of Omaha* and part of a series called *Wild Kingdom* starring Marlin Perkins. Since then there have been many film crews eager to record our activities with the more iconic species, especially elephants and lions. Sometimes it was for scientific reporting and sometimes purely for entertainment. The only thing that they all had in common was to promise that they would not get in the way or otherwise disrupt our work and then proceed to be a nuisance in as many ways as possible in pursuit of their images. Sometimes their requests would be minor impositions like being asked to wear the same clothes for several days running or, worse, to find the shirt/shorts you wore four days ago because they wanted to re-shoot a scene. Occasionally we would be scolded for standing in the wrong place and keeping the sun off their presenter or "star"; the fact that we were hanging on to a rope restraining a buffalo was no excuse! Some of the presenters wanted to be involved or appear so. This led to things like having my hands filmed performing some procedure and then the camera panning back to show the presenter standing where I had been, pretending my hands had been his. We often seemed to be repeating things like landing an aircraft "with less dust please" or re-positioning the helicopter to show the presenter sitting with the door off in the best light. Somehow we always got the job done eventually, whether our persecutors were Korean, American, Australian, French, German or British.

Of course the film crews were not responsible for all the mishaps that occurred. Wild animals, after all, are sometimes unpredictable and therefore uncooperative. But even us "experts" make mistakes and these are of course more embarrassing when the cameras are rolling. Some are easily rectified, but others can be expensive. On one occasion Bluey Carmichael leapt off the Land Rover, lay down behind a darted buffalo and to our astonishment pushed his arm, full length, into the animal's rectum. Luckily for him he pronounced it "not pregnant" before realising from our ribald amusement that it was a bull! During filming for one of my inspiring hero's excellent TV series, *Planet Earth*, I was asked to immobilise an elephant cow that, as closely as possible, resembled a previous elephant in order to continue the storyline. We were near the riverfront in Chobe NP and there were plenty of elephants to choose from. Peter and I searched for a while from the helicopter and eventually decided on an elephant in a group in Sedudu Valley, by the river. After calling EWB and the film crew and describing the spot we waited for the vehicles to show up.

Before long they arrived along the main road and we rendezvoused in the valley to plan the scene. Peter and I then took off and tried to get the small group of elephants moving towards the film crew. When we judged them to be in view of the cameras we swooped and I placed a dart in the rump of the target animal. We pulled away to let them calm down again and, on cue, about eight minutes later the elephant lay down on its side in a clearing, perfectly placed for filming. We watched as the film crew approached and dismounted, quickly setting up their cameras. Peter landed nearby and I jumped out and ran down to the scene. Kelly from EWB came up to me and grinning, asked sarcastically why the elephant had two trunks! Of course it was a young male and the effects of the drugs had caused its penis to relax and extend way outside the prepuce. It was an embarrassing moment – expensive too, as we had to start again and find a suitable female.

One BBC film-maker was very keen to get a shot from behind me showing the dart flying through the air and hitting the elephant's rump. We chose a bunch of bulls at a waterhole where they would be most relaxed. I approached the animals after telling Bill, the cameraman, which bull I would dart and instructing him to keep quiet and close behind me. My dart rifle used .22 blank charges to fire the darts. At about twenty yards I took careful aim and, with the camera trained, fired. The gunshot startled the elephants and they made off at speed in a cloud of dust. "I don't think I saw the dart hit," said Bill. "Neither did I," I replied, reaching into my pocket and producing it. I had forgotten to put it in the gun!

Prince Harry was a frequent unofficial, often secret, visitor to the Botswana bush. He and his older brother had first visited the Okavango as youngsters, and Harry had continued to do so, enjoying the freedom and fraternal company of like-minded young friends, unmolested by paparazzi. He often stayed with Mike Holding, in a tent in the garden overlooking the Thamalakane River. If Mike was busy with a filming project he would assist, even occasionally as a camera hand. We occasionally met when Mike was filming for EWB. Once he and I followed a darted elephant bull on foot through the bush for several kilometres, before I decided it wasn't affected by the dart and pursuing it further was pointless. He was carrying a heavy film camera and we were both pretty tired, though as a serving soldier he was a lot fitter than me. As we sat under a tree chatting and waiting to be picked up I noticed for the first time that he was barefoot!

Once, at Mike's filming camp on the Gomoti River, there was a shortage of accommodation and some of us had to overspill into a number of tiny "igloo" tents in a row. I woke one morning just as it started to get light and decided to walk to the campfire and make coffee. I must have disturbed Harry in the tent next to mine and he arrived at the campfire just as I had coaxed last night's embers into small flames. It was barely light, but against the dawn sky the trees were taking shape. I happened to glance towards the river, thirty yards away, and could just make out the shape of what looked like a leopard's head against the reeds. I pointed it out. To our amazement, a very large male leopard materialised and walked slowly towards us. At about ten yards Harry whispered, "What should we do?" "Nothing, just keep quiet and very still," I replied quietly. There wasn't really any choice anyway. The huge cat continued towards us and jumped on to a horizontal fig tree bough that skirted the fireplace on Harry's side about three feet above the ground. He then walked slowly past the young prince, within touching distance, and alighted behind us before continuing through the camp. He had completely ignored us! We were dumbfounded and thrilled beyond amazement. It remains one of the most memorable wildlife experiences of my life.

TWENTY-THREE

LIVING WITH ELEPHANTS

When I arrived in Africa as a young biologist in 1971 there was a severe drought affecting Tsavo NP in Kenya; the rains had repeatedly failed for several years. Animals were dying because no food was growing and the situation seemed catastrophic. Elephant and rhino were starving and as usual the very young and very old were bearing the brunt of it. A heated argument was taking place about the elephant population in the park because in their suffering they were devastating the vegetation. There was a stand-off between the "scientists" led mostly by Richard Laws who advocated reducing the local elephant population and the "naturalists" under warden David Sheldrick, who claimed that nature should take its course. I visited Tsavo briefly, witnessed the distressing scenes, and with youthful enthusiasm joined the Laws camp. Similar arguments have taken place unabated over elephant populations in East and Southern Africa for over fifty years. In Tsavo all those years ago the scientists lost out, at least six thousand elephants died of starvation and other species died too, including up to 3000 black rhino. Many observers were horrified, but most soon forgot. The perceived cruelty of the controlled shooting of a smaller number of elephants to ease the catastrophe was avoided. Sentiment and sympathy trumped logic and pragmatism; feelings beat facts.

Half a century later we are still nowhere near a consensus. Culling has been implemented in various situations and was arguably biologically successful in Kruger NP and in Zimbabwe. However, the myriad details of elephant ecology, particularly as they relate to biodiversity, are not fully agreed and anyway change with different populations in different circumstances. Long-term effects are also subject to other influences such as the rise or decline in poaching pressure, so it's impossible to get a really clear picture. The influence of western-based animal rights groups, projecting inaccurate propaganda, has also disproportionately swayed arguments. Nevertheless, in Botswana over the past fifty years there has undoubtedly been a massive increase in elephant numbers and the animals have spread out considerably, with effects that are very dramatic in some areas. There has never been any culling but there has been legal hunting for most of that time and, in the past few years, seemingly increased illegal killing (poaching) of elephants.

While I was busy with KGS and the more mundane aspects of wildlife management, things were changing in the world of charismatic African wildlife. Our elephant population seemed to have plateaued at about 130,000, but the decline in the Africa-wide population that was highlighted by the *Great Elephant Census*, and attributed to poaching for ivory, had created a new evangelism. Our then President, Ian Khama (His Excellency Lt. Gen. Dr. Ian Khama Seretse Khama) was proclaimed as the messiah, a role he revelled in. Overseas, "influencers" from a spectrum that included British royalty, showbiz celebrities, "cocktail conservationists" and animal rights activists jumped on the bandwagon backslapping and giving each other awards for spreading the gospel "*Save the Elephants*" that they knew dangerously little about. Of course countries further north, mostly with the connivance or active participation of their leaders, had allowed their elephant populations to plummet and were keen to trumpet the same message, after all, there were masses of dollars and lots of gossamer kudos in it.

The main disciples were the major tourist corporations who in Botswana and elsewhere had acquired the bulk of the attractive wilderness areas for ridiculously expensive lodges charging up to US$6000 per night. Some lodges had exclusive tenure over thousands of square miles of the best wildlife estate in the world. In Botswana very little of this land, the most fundamental human resource, was left available for the use of local people, whether for subsistence hunting, agriculture or affordable recreation. Another blow was the banning of hunting everywhere in Botswana except on registered game ranches, another exclusive preserve of rich people. In 2014, without any consultation and against the reported wishes of a majority of parliamentarians, President Khama suspended all hunting until further notice. Neighbouring countries in southern Africa were discomfited to say the least. Elephant and other species were thriving in the region compared to the corrupt shambles in East Africa and elsewhere on the continent. Conservation in its original guise of "wise use" was working fine. There was more wildlife in Namibia, Zimbabwe, and South Africa than there had been for a hundred years or more. Now they had had the rug pulled from under them by their erstwhile ally.

Breeding at or near the maximum biological potential, coupled with significant net immigration rates from neighbouring countries, the burgeoning elephant herds have spread over most of northern Botswana, especially where and when surface water was available. Most noticeably, this has occurred in the Okavango Delta where there are now ten times as many elephants as there were in the 1970s. During my fieldwork on buffalo elephants were scarce in the western half of the Delta. If we saw fresh elephant tracks west of the Boro River we remarked upon them, and an actual sighting of elephants – always bulls – was a red-letter day. As recent aerial censuses bear out, elephants are a constant presence throughout the Delta nowadays – and in significant numbers that are beginning to impact seriously on the habitat. Baobab trees were the first to suffer obvious depredation and other notable species, such as knobthorns, are now being affected. How these and other processes will ultimately change the Okavango remains to be seen, but in Chobe National Park there have been huge changes to the vegetation close to permanent water sources. In some areas, such as the Linyanti, dry season concentrations of elephants have exceeded anything recorded elsewhere on the planet, sometimes exceeding scientifically advocated levels by more than a factor of ten!

Botswana is experiencing more and more human/elephant conflict. While population numbers may or may not have stabilised, there is absolutely no doubt that Botswana's elephants have been spreading out in a big way, not only into neighbouring countries, but also within Botswana, most notably in the Okavango panhandle and the Chobe enclave, areas where human settlements have similarly expanded, but there are warning signs elsewhere. They began to be encountered in the northern part of the CKGR a few years ago, trashing the Kuke veterinary cordon fence that had been so infamous a few decades ago. Game ranches had been established in the Hainaveld, along the CKGR border, but their fences were equally ineffective barriers. Similarly, further west there were increasing forays into the Ghanzi cattle ranches. By the middle of the second decade of the twenty-first century there were regular incursions into the CKGR by large breeding herds and the more adventurous bulls became regular visitors to Khutse GR, even occasionally turning up close to human population centres in the southeast of the country.

This was not a desirable state of affairs; conflicting situations involving these giant beasts and mainly traditional farming communities escalated and increasing calls for compensation were raising the political ante. Mike Chase and I, with some friends, put collars on some of the most southerly bulls and their movements were tracked around the southern and eastern perimeter of the CKGR. We also put a small number on animals in the breeding herds in the northwestern corner of the Reserve, where we counted several hundred elephants.

Many years earlier a series of artificial water points had been drilled along the Passarge and other fossil valleys in the northern CKGR. These were to provide water for the wildebeest and other ungulates that inhabited the area and had been negatively affected decades ago by the construction of cordon fences that interrupted their natural dry-season movements in search of water. These "*fences of death*" were well documented and widely publicised at the time. The new water points also enhanced the tourist experience for the growing numbers of visitors who camped in the Reserve. The elephants who explored the CKGR during the wet season found that they could colonise the Reserve with the help of these artificial water resources. As our collared animals showed, they could then access the more southern areas with much more potential for conflict with human settlements. In a bizarre decision, the wildlife authorities, without scientific consultation, drilled more boreholes further south and equipped them for wildlife use instead of closing down the existing ones. This exacerbated the problem by enabling yet more elephants to venture further south.

To me, the situation indicated that the seemingly interminable debate about absolute elephant numbers was largely irrelevant and that accurate population estimates were an expensive mirage – a reasonable measure of the population trends and their seasonal distribution would be much more useful and more easily achieved. We knew beyond doubt that there were about a hundred thousand more elephants in Botswana than there had been forty years previously. What we needed most was an indication of where the elephants had spread to and what was their impact in those areas. This was very important where they came into conflict with human activities, but arguably equally important in designated wildlife areas where they were changing the natural habitats – potentially an ecological disaster.

In the early 1970s the first aerial censuses of wildlife in Botswana were aimed specifically at elephants. The first scientifically obtained elephant numbers came from a young German biologist, Malte Sommerlatte, who was based in Kasane and worked for the UN's FAO. We repeated and expanded on his censuses through the 1970s and 1980s. Later, other workers followed suit and there is a general picture of Botswana's elephant situation right up to the present. It is clear that numbers have increased fairly steadily over the past fifty years from about 40,000 to around 130,000, at least a three-fold increase, roughly the same as the simultaneous increase in the human population. The government of Botswana claims enormous credit for this increase but, despite the production and approval of a series of management plans, little has been done and the capability and efforts of the Department of Wildlife have been poor. There were significant changes under President Ian Khama as vastly increased resources were made available – although many professional conservationists disagreed with the philosophy and focus behind his policies, which were based overwhelmingly on military-style antipoaching, with little in the way of ecological management.

So, the main effects of the growth in Botswana's elephant population are the detrimental changes in biodiversity in large areas and increasing conflict between humans and elephants in others. There are still a few heretics that deny some aspects of the former, but the latter is indisputable and, if neglected, will only get worse. Some of the effects described have led to vocal outcries that "something must be done" – but what? Managing elephant populations is a herculean task. It should involve elements of monitoring, protection, control, dispersal, and, if it can be done properly and sustainably, utilisation. This is how wildlife management is conducted for any species and there is no scientific reason to make an exception of the elephant.

There are two fundamental drivers of this ecological and social calamity, both originating in western society: commercial tourism and the perverted perceptions of animal rights. The first is blindingly obvious and I've alluded to it above, but the second is more subtle and fertile ground for fanatics who are able to manipulate it to sway normally moderate and intelligent public opinion. The reintroduction of hunting in Botswana has met with a barrage of ferocious criticism from a wide spectrum of mainly foreign campaigners. The most prominent and vituperative commentary emanates again from the ranks of showbiz celebrities, a surprising source of ecological expertise. But it's emotive foundations become obvious when you consider that there are very large numbers of organisations dedicated to the preservation of cheetahs, whales, elephants, dolphins and primates – all animals towards which we share some emotional attachment – but very few, if any, dedicated to saving arachnids, molluscs, amphibians and rodents, even though many of these groups contain species that are far more seriously threatened than elephants and more valuable for a healthy environment.

Animal welfare, a worthy cause, is too often conflated with conservation. Animal rights issues and considerations of ethics are powerful but separate arguments and they cannot be directly applied to conservation matters. Objections to hunting are mainly based on moral or spiritual grounds and may be legitimate or hysterical. (I was once attacked by a Californian lady who was breeding "vegetarian lions.") They are rarely practical or based on fact. It is in the nature of most of us to empathise with victims, but the fate of any individual almost never has conservation significance. Almost all animal populations will sustain controlled hunting indefinitely and only changes in land tenure, status and occupancy are truly meaningful threats.

The hunting fraternity's doctrine is that well managed hunting does no harm to wildlife populations; wildlife is a renewable natural resource and with appropriate management will maintain itself, allowing some harvesting for various purposes. In fact, setting aside tracts of land of little use for anything else, as hunting blocks, is an effective way of expanding wildlife land and therefore a valuable conservation strategy. Unfortunately, hunters have acquired a bad name, often because of unacceptable behaviour in their own ranks through the ages, from British aristocratic colonialists to the Boer biltong enthusiasts of more recent times. But hunters vary, from the strictly ethical, through degrees of unscrupulousness to, in rare cases, downright depraved. Where recreational hunting is concerned it is up to the genuine participants and associations to maintain and demonstrate the highest ethical standards or their scientifically valid arguments will never be accepted.

Among the rural citizenry of Africa there is none of this bias; all animals are ignored, tolerated or utilised, unless they are a threat, in which case they are avoided or destroyed. A cheetah is not thought of more sentimentally than a rat. Poaching for ivory or rhino horn does not emanate from Africa; only meat and other beneficial commodities are of interest to rural people, until they have been corrupted and recruited by outside agencies. This utilitarian relationship between rural communities and wildlife can be managed and beneficially exploited if they are given stewardship of the resources. In the spirit of true conservation it will benefit both sides of the equation. A Zambian chief once told me that his people wanted to be meaningfully involved in decisions about conservation much more than they wanted the material rewards. Enlightened communities can be a powerful safeguard against foreign intrusion and commercial poaching. The middlemen in Africa, from local dealers to corrupt government officials, would then be out of business without the need for expensive and futile campaigns directed against them.

Effective conservation in the massive, still undeveloped, rural regions of Africa rests on land/territory/real estate/habitat – call it what you will. Dedicate sufficient space to wildlife and it will thrive. Planning for wildlife resources is simple in theory, it only becomes difficult without trust. Ownership can provide trust. Police and wardens become largely unnecessary where benefits are reaped locally. Some education may be necessary, but subsistence farmers will quickly learn that it's easier and more profitable to embrace wildlife husbandry if the benefits truly flow to them as individuals. Initiatives such as *Campfire* in Zimbabwe and others in Botswana and elsewhere have demonstrated some success, but have stalled because of stale national politics where central governments have not had the courage or vision to nurture the new approaches. Only in Namibia have similar community schemes proved more resilient, a model that is worth more attention.

Successful participation of communities in planning the management of the wilderness areas, requires real ownership. They must decide on land uses, with both photo-tourism and various forms of hunting no doubt featuring prominently. Consumptive and non-consumptive uses of wild resources have their benefits and these can be maximised for different landscapes and habitats. Luxury lodges cannot be solely for the profit of a few foreign companies, with a handful of menial jobs and insignificant monetary returns to the people. Likewise, vast areas of hunting terrain must be shared equitably between community management and high-end safari operations. Other consumptive uses should be encouraged from harvesting meat to thatching grass. No species should be considered exempt unless there is demonstrable evidence of its decline locally or, through ecological linkages, in other areas. There should be no role for sentiment in decision making, it only leads to skewed, inefficient and ultimately harmful management. Sustained education and social change in the rural villages and communities are needed. Recent experience has shown that merely handing colossal amounts of money to naïve communities is not the answer. Villagers cannot be expected to manage luxury lodges and other projects without guidance. This must come from trained outsiders, honest brokers, who are employed by the communities to look after the interests of the local people in dealing with sophisticated entrepreneurs. Sensitive dealing with the grass-roots traditional institutions operating within the communities is also necessary.

Botswana is fortunate in still having enormous areas largely uninhabited by people; unsurprisingly this is where the vast majority of its amazing wildlife bounty exists. The historical record of wildlife conservation for which Botswana receives continuous, patronising praise is actually one of laissez-faire in which most wildlife, especially in the north, has survived relatively unmolested and people have for the most part pursued their livelihoods in other parts of the country. There are and have been exceptions such as the erection of veterinary cordon fences, limited hunting, insignificant poaching and pockets of agriculture, but these have mostly had little effects on wildlife populations and almost none on elephants. Elephants have thrived and have sometimes been provided with assistance to maintain their growth and expansion. Food has not been a limiting factor as long as water has existed naturally or artificially alongside it. Herds of elephants require prodigious quantities of drinking water and in a dry country like Botswana permanent supplies are only available naturally in the rivers of the northwest. Seasonally the situation varies from year to year; in wet years there are plentiful supplies from rainfall in ephemeral pans that are common in many areas and may last through to the next season's rain; in dry years these are less plentiful and vast areas may remain waterless for several months. This variation naturally "rotates" the feeding patterns of the herds and gives habitats time to recover. Similarly the water available in pans draws elephants away from riverine woodlands, allowing them some respite. Provision of artificial water points through drilling boreholes has allowed many elephants to obtain dry season water unnaturally and this has had the effect of allowing the animals to expand their range, with the survival of more calves and an increase in the population. The resulting local modification to major vegetation communities such as mopane is usually insignificant, but in more vulnerable habitats, such as riverine woodland, it has serious, undesirable consequences. Manipulation of natural resources always has consequences, there are no end-points in ecology, nature goes on.

Monitoring elephant population trends and distribution should be a continuous function of management; information feedback is crucial to success. Over the vast and expanding range of elephants in Botswana only aerial censuses can provide enough information. By their very nature aerial censuses are crude and inaccurate, but by repeating them at regular intervals good data on the trends of the elephant population can be obtained. These intervals should be as short as possible, ideally twice a year, once every wet and dry season. EWB have conducted the best censuses recently in Botswana showing that the elephant population appears to have stabilised at around 130,000 animals, but this needs constant updating by comparable methods. Unfortunately, despite the acquisition of several aircraft at great capital expense and the formation of an in-house "air-wing", DWNP have not completed a census for almost a decade.

Antipoaching efforts were minimal for many years; there was no need for an intensive and expensive antipoaching program while there was little evidence of any significant illegal hunting. The elephant population was growing at an exponential rate, there were few signs of carcases or other signs of illegal activities and outside the parks and reserves the vast majority of the elephant range fell into safari hunting concessions where the presence and legitimate activities of safari companies provided sufficient deterrent to organised poaching. The ban on safaris and other legal hunting in 2014 changed all that and the intensified efforts of DWNP and other government agencies, not least the military, was not a successful deterrent. Neither, it would seem, was the allocation of large areas for exclusive photographic safari use since several recently recognised "hot spots" of elephant poaching fall within these areas.

Botswana doesn't have a reputation for "big ivory". The spectacular tuskers of East Africa or Kruger NP have never occurred in the Botswana/Zambezi population, despite the presence of the biggest and heaviest animals recorded on the continent. Typically a mature Botswana bull elephant has short, thick tusks. Observers who bemoan elephant conservation in the country, claiming that large, trophy bulls have been shot out are mistaken. Only a handful of hundred-pounders have been shot since 1970 – whenever it happened it was quite an event and everyone knew about it! When records and censuses were started in the early 1970s biologists and hunters were of the opinion that Botswana had a predominantly young, highly fecund elephant population and all the demographics and hunting records since then have tended to confirm this. Records of tusk weights from hunted bull elephants over a twenty-year period prior to the hunting moratorium in 2014 indicate an average trophy weight of between 50 and 60 pounds every year. This remained constant even though the hunting quota varied between 30 and 300 elephants per annum.

In terms of population management, hunting a quota of trophy bulls can only be a part of a control strategy. It is a valid utilisation of the resource, but at practical levels in an elephant population as large as Botswana's it cannot affect population numbers and can only have local effects on distribution. Some ecologists believe that the elephant population in Botswana needs to be massively reduced in order to slow down and hopefully reverse further damage to the natural environment and begin to restore biodiversity; one or two actually advocate culling at hitherto unseen industrial scales. While the ecological theory may be sound, the feasibility of such a policy is impossible. All that can be done is targeted interventions at strategic locations. These should be focal areas of conflict with human communities and identified ecologically sensitive areas. With careful planning and management they could involve limited culling of family groups, safari hunting, non-lethal deterrents and perhaps even some live removal. The vast majority of financial and material benefits must accrue to identified local communities and be monitored for effectiveness, something that has not always happened before.

The debate will go on, but environmental and community benefits can be realised with proactive management, and if the animal rights fanatics are ignored, the utilisation and conservation of an enormously valuable natural resource can proceed for the benefit and to the credit of the country. It has become increasingly urgent that we address this situation and devise successful strategies to minimise conflict between people and elephants. Human property is being destroyed and damaged on an increasing scale and people are being killed. The present government of President Masisi, with a more pragmatic approach, is beginning to address the problem realistically. Hard decisions need to be taken, but despite overwhelming factual evidence, the debate rages. Entrenched positions will not change until there are positive signs of alleviation and this could take decades of appropriate field management, community engagement and political determination. Through it all there will be serious opposition, with powerful media support, from those well-meaning, but dangerously prejudiced and badly informed sections of our society. As Ian Parker states in his book *Oh Quagga* – "fact is all too easily forgotten amongst the prejudices of belief".

EPILOGUE

BOTSWANA 2021

In 2015, looking to the future, Eleanor and I decided to build a house in Kasane. The idea was to be close to the northern, neighbouring countries with wilderness and wildlife that we could explore as we got more free time. We obtained a plot of land on the edge of Kazungula village, about five miles from Kasane and close to the borders with Zimbabwe and Zambia. The land overlooks the Chobe River, with the Zambezi visible in the distance. In fact it's possible to see four countries from the property with Namibia just across the river – unusual, if not unique. The main entrance to Chobe NP is about seven miles to the west, so the house is ideally placed for our purposes. Almost daily herds of elephants and frequent buffalo visitors add to its attractions. One evening on returning home we disturbed five lions lying at our gate! Luckily, for once I hadn't activated the gate motor before rounding the corner into the driveway. If we'd chased them into the plot I don't know how we would have got them out.

One of the factors determining our move was the sale of our farm, Sunnyside. Bill, who did most of the work, decided he wanted to move on and received a good offer. Our options were to take over the work and match the financial offer or go along with the sale. With much regret, we decided on the latter option and sadly the farm went to new owners who at least had the capital to develop it further as a successful dual-purpose enterprise.

Building a house is not for the fainthearted, especially in Africa. Our chosen construction company, Wharic (but sadly no longer involving Whatley or Richards), was based over 600 miles away in Gabs. They left most of the work to locally employed, poorly or untrained artisans and the inevitable happened. With very little supervision, the labour force built most of the house three or four times before it was deemed habitable. Even then there was a dearth of level surfaces, straight lines and functional plumbing. The inevitable litigation cost nearly as much as the house, took longer than building, and neither party achieved satisfaction. The outcome was much DIY and expensive repairs but ultimately a comfortable home.

Eventually, towards the end of 2015, we were able to move up to Kasane from Gabs. Our house in the desirable centre of Gabs was quickly sold and Kyle bought the remnants of KGS at a knock-down price, so I was to all intents retired. I still had my dart guns and a Land Cruiser, so I was able to assist clients like EWB and other researchers such as Wildcru from Oxford University, who were collaring lions throughout the north of the country.

A word of warning to retiring veterinarians… it is an impossibility if the community you choose has no veterinarian. Your professional oath and your conscience mean that demands are never-ending. Even in far-flung rural Africa, where professional standards and liability are arguably more lax, it's a time-consuming and sometimes challenging way of life. The nearest private practitioner to Kasane with acceptable facilities was at least six hours' drive away, so you can guess what happens to emergencies like road accidents or wounds from wild animals for example. From there it's a small, if unwilling, step to general practice. I help out where I can, but I cannot provide adequate standards of treatment in a shed or on kitchen tables. Government veterinarians are scarce and anyway usually not experienced or equipped to handle clinical work. It's an insoluble problem with domestic animals, but perhaps more so, in Kasane, with wild animals.

I am frequently called on to help by the Wildlife Department or members of the community for anything from warthogs injured by vehicles to elephants maimed by wire snares and just about anything in-between. The red tape makes it much worse; I cannot intervene unless authorised in each case by the Wildlife Department. In theory there is a veterinarian posted to the Wildlife Department in Chobe, but the post is often vacant and the occasional young incumbents seem less than enthusiastic. At times it can be difficult to get permission to do anything, especially afterhours or at weekends and usually the situation is urgent. Of course there is no system for me to be paid or to be reimbursed for drugs and other consumables such as darts. The outcome is that I pay for everything and frequently act without permission. For a while EWB "legitimised" my interventions and covered some of my costs, but since they lost their research permits following an unfortunate dispute with the new administration this has not been possible.

A ludicrous example a couple of years ago involved a snared buffalo. I was called at 6 am on a Saturday by an expat who was an Honorary Game Warden. He reported that a buffalo bull was caught in a cable snare next to the road about half a mile from my house. I called Mike Chase of EWB and he said they would cover the costs of darting. We tried to contact the local Wildlife Officer, but were unable to reach her. I drove to the scene and found the animal with a steel cable around its neck, securely tied to a stout tree, with about ten yards of free play. The bull was very wild and tried to charge the vehicle, but came to a cartwheeling stop at the end of his cable. It was a dangerous and acute situation and to add to the problems the road was blocked because it was just within his reach. I darted him and removed the snare, ascertained that his wounds were only superficial and administered an antidote. We watched as he came round, got to his feet and took off into the bush. The job was finished before 7 am.

Later that day the Minister of Wildlife, T.K. Khama (my old "friend" from KGS days) called EWB and gave Mike Chase a severe dressing down for allowing me to act without his authority. The local Wildlife Officer, on learning later what we had done, had complained to her Director and he had contacted the Minister. Khama said that under no circumstances were any animals allowed to be darted or destroyed without his personal say so. I should have been flabbergasted but, knowing the man, I was merely saddened. Anywhere else, with another authority, we would have been thanked for relieving an animal's suffering and removing a dangerous threat to the local community.

Recently I was called to try to rescue an elephant cow that was lying in a shallow pan in front of one of the local tourist lodges, about sixty miles west of Kasane. The pan was 100 yards wide but less than a foot deep, fed by a borehole operated by the lodge. Apparently the cow had been involved in a dispute with a bigger elephant and slipped after being charged. Twelve hours later she was still lying on her side unable to get up in the slippery mud. I arrived with a friend, Tony Griest, who had arranged for his JCB digger to come from a nearby village. While we were waiting I decided we should tie tow straps to the ankles of the elephant, ready for the JCB. I didn't want to use immobilising drugs because I wasn't sure how long the JCB would take to arrive. Telling Tony and our two staff to be very careful not to be hit by the animal's trunk, I proceeded to tie a strap to the lower back ankle. It was quite difficult working in the shallow, muddy water with a very treacherous base. The next thing I knew was looking up into the bright sky with two very concerned labourers and Tony looking down and asking if I was OK. They helped me up and I seemed to have escaped with only bruises. One of the men exclaimed, "Ah Boss, but you can fly!" I had been kicked on my right shoulder and landed on my back several feet away. The JCB arrived soon after and we managed to extricate the cow and leave her on the dry bank but sadly she died a short while later without regaining her feet. There had been no way to ascertain her condition before we got her out, so maybe she had suffered internal injuries in the fight the night before.

Another more recent elephant incident occurred when I received a telephone call from the Director of Wildlife in Gabs. He asked if I could go immediately into the Park and rendezvous with the former President Ian Khama on the riverfront. A young bull elephant was standing on a dry floodplain about 200 yards from the road. The former President, some family and bodyguards were watching from the road. We'd known each other for many years, but we didn't always see things the same way. He explained that he had seen the young elephant in the same place the day before and that it couldn't walk properly. He had reported it to the local Wildlife Office, but nothing had been done. Now, twenty-four hours later, he was annoyed and had called the Director in Gabs. I said I would do what I could.

I watched carefully as the bull limped painfully with a very swollen lower left front leg. I couldn't see a wire, but I thought it was almost certainly caused by a snare. Eleanor was with me and she knew Ian Khama better than me so she explained what I would do while I prepared a dart. We then drove in my car across the rough floodplain to within fifty yards of the elephant at which point it tried to make off, but was severely hampered. I approached on foot and darted him. He only moved a few yards before standing still and then falling down. I quickly examined the leg and found a steel cable embedded just above the ankle, perhaps four inches deep. The wound was severe, but fairly fresh, maybe four days old. I cleaned the surface pus and dirt with my hands and with the help of one of Khama's nephews and Jonathan Gibson, his host at the nearby Chobe Game Lodge, we managed to externalise part of the cable with a tyre lever. Cutting it was another matter; we tried heavy-duty bolt cutters and a hacksaw but with little success. Eventually, by unravelling a few strands at a time we cut them using the nephew's Leatherman tool. It took quite a while, but the animal remained immobilised. After almost an hour's work we removed the cable noose and I was able to give the antidote to revive him. Within five minutes he struggled to his feet and made off across the floodplain, walking much better without the steel bracelet – a successful outcome, but that's not always the case with these cruel indiscriminate traps. Back at the road we were cleaning up when the Wildlife Department's young vet drove up having finally been located. We didn't wait to hear what the ex-President had to say to him.

Kasane and Kazungula are overrun by warthogs – they are everywhere. Pigs in general are intelligent and adaptive and can exploit niches such as suburban gardens, industrial yards and downtown informal markets. Warthogs are common in the bush where they mainly feed by grazing and rooting. In urban environments they do this on road verges and in gardens, but they also enthusiastically feed on rubbish provided by humans. The dumps at the back of houses, shops and supermarkets are prime food sources. In the course of these activities they often either step on or force their snouts into tin cans and plastic rings of all kinds that they cannot remove and which cause damage or prevent them feeding. They are also frequently hit by vehicles and sustain injuries. These animals, which mainly delight tourists, are either ignored by the local population or persecuted for causing damage to property or dogs that chase them. In November they give birth to litters of cute piglets, which cause further delight and nuisance in equal amounts and provide bounty to local packs of dogs that hunt them. Introduce into this situation a fair number of humane and sympathetic individuals and the result is an inundation of calls to remove plastic or wires, fix broken legs etc. The costs of darting these pigs is considerable and often futile. Apart from the removal of snares or plastic bottles, they usually cannot be treated successfully and often have to be destroyed.

Elsewhere, in other towns – those without tourists – such as the mining centre of Orapa, the pigs are declared vermin and they have occasional exercises to reduce their numbers. These are justified on sanitary grounds and the culling of large numbers of warthogs provides meat for local consumption. Here in Kasane the apathy of the council together with the sensitivities of many expats means that the problem, together with that of stray dogs, another blight on the village, remains intractable. As a veterinarian it's expected that you will provide time and expensive resources in dealing with these problems, showing compassion and sympathy that may be relevant to the individual animal, but which does nothing to alleviate the situation at large. The explosive growth of the village results in ever more incidents of human/wildlife interactions and demands promulgation of a policy to deal with the situation. But official action happens only when an unfortunate villager is killed by an elephant or buffalo, maybe once or twice a year, and wildlife in town becomes a transient headline.

Bushbuck are beautiful antelopes with a similar problem with a different slant. The local subspecies, the Chobe bushbuck, is particularly attractive, decorated with spots and broken stripes on a rich red coat. They are quite rare these days mainly because the enormous increase in elephants locally has destroyed the thick riverine bush that is their required habitat. There are none at all left locally in the Chobe NP, but pockets of suitable habitat remain in some of the fenced properties along the river in Kasane and Kazungula and a few bushbuck find refuge here. These include hotels, the golf course and a few large houses. An initiative sponsored by EWB was to capture as many animals as possible and remove them to a temporary safe haven on the riverfront owned by Chobe Farms, where there is sufficient suitable habitat to allow them to flourish. We darted and moved as many as possible and numbers now appear to be increasing, though their long-term future is still uncertain.

*

As I write the world is in the grip of the Covid-19 pandemic, Kasane's hotels are empty, so too are the exclusive, luxury lodges in Botswana's wild concession areas. The local community, so dependent on the tourist trade, is suffering. Many local tour guides have gone back to their home villages and reverted to subsistence farming. Luckily we are having a good rainy season so there will be enough food, but cash is hard to come by and the town is eerily quiet, with an 8 pm curfew. News of vaccines overseas is heartening, but no one knows when these might be available in rural Africa. For us our "lockdown" is not particularly onerous. We have been able to enjoy travelling and camping in beautiful wilderness areas that once again, like the 1970s, truly live up to the name – days without seeing any tourists; undisturbed wild animal populations; nothing but animal sounds around the campfire at night and lots of time to reflect on the times and adventures described earlier in this book.